Tempered – not quenched

Tempered – not quenched

MARTIN UPHAM

Lawrence and Wishart Limited
LONDON

Lawrence and Wishart Limited
99a Wallis Road
London E9 5LN

First published 1997
Copyright © Martin Upham 1997

British Library Cataloguing in Publication data.
A catalogue record for this book is available from the British Library.

Cover design: Andrew Corbett
Copy-edited, designed and typeset by
The Running Head Limited, London and Cambridge.
Printed and bound in Great Britain by
Redwood Books, Trowbridge.

Contents

Who built Thebes with its seven gates?
In all the books it says kings.
Did kings drag up those rocks from the quarry?
And Babylon, overthrown time after time,
Who built it up again as often?

From *A Worker Reads, and Asks These Questions*, by Bertolt Brecht

Foreword by Keith Brookman,
General Secretary, the ISTC

Many of you will be aware of that great work by Sir Arthur Pugh, *Men of Steel – By One of Them*, which was the story of early trade unionism in the iron and steel industry which led ultimately to the formation of the ISTC (then BISAKTA) in 1917. After that date the history of the of the iron and steel industry and the history of the ISTC become one and the same.

Sir Arthur continued that story up to 1951, and in the penultimate paragraph of that lengthy book he posed the question, 'Who will write the story of the next fifty years, if it be written?'

For the next forty-five years that question remained unanswered. However, conscious as I was of our impending eightieth anniversary, I could think of no more appropriate form of celebration than commissioning this book, and I am grateful for the support of the Executive Council in agreeing to my suggestion.

There have been periods in our history when it may have looked doubtful to some that we would be able to survive until our eightieth year. Nationalisation, denationalisation, renationalisation and finally privatisation of the major parts of our industry, coupled with massive restructuring and painful closures: we have seen them all and we are still here to tell the tale. Smaller, but stronger. Tempered, not quenched – hence the choice of title.

Men of Steel had the subtitle *By One of Them*, and I think that it also applies to the author of this book, Dr Martin Upham. Martin worked for the ISTC in our research department during the turbulent years from 1975 to 1988. He compiled the alternative plans to retain steelmaking at a number of plants in this period, inspired *Steelworkers' Banner*, our first tabloid, was the principal author of *New Deal for Steel*, and was national co-ordinator of the union's trailblazing political fund ballot campaign in 1985.

Of course the views expressed in the book are Martin's own, with information painstakingly gleaned from our archives and from his personal experiences. But I am sure that you will agree that his knowledge of the ISTC has enabled him to look beyond the printed page and tell the story of this union and the people who served it. A thread running throughout his work is that my predecessors, to a man, were committed to the union and the industry and were tireless in working to improve the conditions of the membership. We are indeed indebted to those who have gone before us and it is important that they should not be forgotten.

This is the story of a union and its members that have experienced many changes in what has always been, and still is, a cyclical industry. Tremendous difficulties have been encountered, but have always been overcome. Indeed, as I write, it is likely that our future path will not be an easy one.

As General Secretary, I would commend this book to our activists, members and all others who care for and wish to learn more about our union. The Iron and Steel Trades Confederation has made a positive contribution to the British way of life. We are proud of our heritage and optimistic about our future.

The ISTC is eighty not out. This is to me not a bad score by any standard. I hope you agree.

Introduction

This book picks up the story of Britain's steelworkers from where it was left by Sir Arthur Pugh in his monumental record *Men of Steel*. It begins in 1951, with the Labour government of Clement Attlee in its last years of office signalling some relaxation, after years of austerity, by holding the Festival of Britain. It ends in 1997, on the eve of the election of yet another Labour government, which plans a 'Millennium Experience' to surpass the Festival. Steel has continued to be a key industrial material throughout the years between, but the Britain which relies on it has changed overwhelmingly.

The pages which follow reflect these gathering changes. In 1950 the steelworkers' union was formidable in size and influence, and enormous authority attached to its leader, who represented members at the commanding heights of the British economy. In Chapter 1 the British Iron, Steel and Kindred Trades Association is profiled, and the story is told of how it weathered the rapid transition of nearly all private firms into the new state-owned Iron and Steel Corporation of Great Britain. Within two years rapid political change had resulted in the return of most of those firms to the private sector, and the Organisation had to deal with that as well. During both experiences, its priorities were overwhelmingly industrial, not political, as it strove to maintain the fabric of collective bargaining that was slowly bringing improvements in the membership's standard of living. Chapters 2 and 3 describe the interregnum of private ownership from 1953 to 1966, dog days for the steel industry, when misplaced investment decisions contributed to an under-capitalised industry losing ground to re-equipped rivals. BISAKTA remained a powerful disciplined force, and those years brought great social advances in pay, pensions and holidays to its members, who for the most part enjoyed peaceful relations with their employers.

How this comfortable picture began to change is recounted in Chapters 4 and 5. The towering development is the formation in 1967 of the British Steel Corporation (BSC), the second attempt by the state to run the industry during the period covered by this book. The early years of BSC saw the achievement of many long-cherished bargaining objectives while the Corporation still saw itself as an organisation with social obligations. But the satisfaction BISAKTA felt over this was offset by two challenges. The first was successfully beaten off when the union established its right to be the principal representative organisation for staff in the steel industry. The second was less easily dealt with.

For many the whole purpose of state ownership was to facilitate the creation of a modern steel industry. But with the publication of the 'Ten-Year Strategy' in 1973, a new phase opened. Across Britain, area after area with long and proud associations with steel faced a challenge to its economic viability and even its very existence. Modernisation was coming, but a high price was to be demanded. Chapters 6, 7, 8 and 9 recount the years when the bills came in. The Iron and Steel Trades Confederation (the ISTC, as it was now more commonly known) had to handle the social consequences not only of the closure – with unnecessary haste – of older plant, but also of the shutting of relatively new plant which in no circumstances could be considered obsolete. The long agony of steel, which began in the mid-1970s, lasted for more than a decade and a half.

While suffering this torment, Britain's steelworkers were abandoned by their government. They were left to face subsidised rivals while their own financial support was rapidly withdrawn. Their domestic markets shrivelled, neglected by successive governments which signalled their indifference to the country's manufacturing base and to the impact of imported products. As a result the shrinkage of the steel industry, which was perhaps inevitable, was far more painful than it need have been. Did any other British union have to face a twin assault on the scale of that met by the ISTC in January 1980? The combination of an insulting pay offer and huge redundancy announcements could be met only one way. Few strikes are recorded in these pages, but when the members of the ISTC finally went on national strike at that time they acted in accordance with their own traditions: the country has never witnessed solidarity on such a scale since. After the strike much of the energy of the ISTC went into managing decline: if jobs could not, finally, be saved then the sting of redundancy had to be eased financially. In the early 1980s that, sadly, took as much time as bargaining over pay.

Chapters 10, 11 and 12 cover the transition to the world of today. By the later 1980s steelworkers were experiencing a substantial boom for the first time in years, and this handed government the opportunity to restore private ownership to steel – the fourth such change the union had had to deal with. Once British Steel plc had emerged from the former BSC, the social significance of this political change became apparent, with assaults on work practices, the pattern of bargaining and social benefits. But this book ends on a hopeful note, recording the recent changes which have turned the ISTC into one of the most professional outfits among Britain's trade unions.

The structure adopted has been to divide the account according to the terms of office of the union's leaders whose personality, outlook and record are described in the appropriate place. But this is not meant to be the story of leaders alone. The members of any trade union *are* the union, and nowhere is this more true than in the ISTC where – to take the obvious example – lay representation is more extensive than in many comparable bodies. This book aims to lay down a reliable and accurate account of the years 1951–97 to which union members – and others – can refer should they need to. Its use of the written record naturally reflects the work of full-time officers and union leaders; there has been no intention to exclude the tens of thousands of volunteers – who to many members are their regular point of contact with the union – from this history.

Steel and its trade union have survived. Other industries and unions have been less fortunate. There has been enormous pain, but there have been triumphs as well: in industrial democracy, in serious superannuation for manual workers, in the fight for independent working-class representation and, latterly, in professional presentation, the ISTC has often led the way. As one who for thirteen years lived some of the history recounted by this book, I feel privileged to have been asked to write it. *Tempered – Not Quenched*, a phrase from the vocabulary of steel, is written in tribute to those who have sustained not only one of the country's most successful industries, but one of its most effective unions as well.

Martin Upham, May 1997

1

Out of the post-war straitjacket
Lincoln Evans (1950–3)

'The influence the Confederation exercises in this industry today is
due to the highly responsible and intelligent way in which it has
always conducted its affairs.'

From a distance of fifty-five years it is difficult to conjure up the Britain of the
post-war era. Steel had been worked flat out during the war and steel exports
were required to buy foreign exchange in the peace. When production difficulties arose in the later 1940s and early 1950s they were problems of shortages and not of over-supply. Thus the tinplate industry came in for
considerable criticism in 1951 for being unable to supply the canning industry
with all its needs. In fact it wished to do so, yet it also had to recover export
markets lost over the previous decade. By a further paradox, many mills in
South Wales, the home of tinplate, were still idle as late as 1951 due to manpower shortages, and foreign labour was brought in. Statutory controls for the
industry as a whole were not lifted until as late as 5 May 1953, when the
industry was in the middle of its second post-war switch of ownership.

At the end of 1950 the British Iron, Steel and Kindred Trades Association (BISAKTA) recorded 112,687 members organised in 634 branches. Its
position as the premier union in iron and steel was unchallenged.[1] Sir Lincoln Evans,[2] the Organisation's General Secretary, occupied a position of
great eminence at the TUC. He had been a member of the post-war Iron and
Steel Board between 1946 and 1948[3] and the following year joined the prestigious Economic Planning Board, remaining a member until his retirement
as General Secretary in 1953.

Evans took some satisfaction from fact that industry was now in the
hands of a new generation of managers with minds 'not coloured by the old
hostilities' and who accepted trade unionism. At the same time he was

4

unusually apt to speculate openly as to whether union minds had changed as much as they ought to have done. Living standards could not, he insisted to colleagues, be higher than productivity could sustain. Demarcation disputes continued in a world which had rendered them irrelevant by getting rid of unemployment and want. They were an obstacle to that higher productivity which would make higher living standards possible.[4]

The report of the union's Central Office to its Executive in February 1951 tended to reflect industry's growing confidence in economic recovery, boasting of 'all-time record' output in excess of sixteen million tons of steel ingots and castings, and an increase of 40 per cent over the average for the years 1935–9. The problems of Britain's post-war steel industry related not to demand and sales (home and overseas sales were alike dubbed 'overwhelming' in the report) but to supply. There were constraints on output both from insufficient supplies of iron ore and from shortages of operatives.[5] The report records, without a trace of irony, the long after-shadow of wartime controls, noting that 'the industry decided not to pass on' increased costs of ten shillings per ton of finished steel production to the consumer.[6]

With raw materials scarce, competition between user industries was inevitable. In 1952 Evans lent his voice to those who were calling for increased supplies to iron foundries to be curtailed. Steel, he argued, was a much more efficient material than iron, and should not be held back from higher output by shortages of supply. In this, he was at one with the British Iron and Steel Federation (BISF, the principal voice of the owners). This was not just rhetoric. In 1947, when Britain was short of steel and investment by the producers had raised capacity, BISAKTA had made an agreement to introduce continuous working in the industry. Members in Rotherham and Consett had dissented and declined to operate the agreement, but the Organisation threw its full authority behind it by threatening no less than 1395 members with expulsion. After they acquiesced the agreement was implemented nationally and a surge of output followed. BISAKTA was criticised on the left for such actions, but saw its duty as being to the national interest (it had been among those criticising the employers for their earlier failure to invest) and to an agreement reached by its accredited representatives, including those of the dissenting employees.[7]

What kind of organisation did Evans head? Its regional membership profile reflected the established pattern of the industry, one as old as the Industrial Revolution itself.[8] The largest Division was No. 3, covering South Yorkshire and the East Midlands, which had 21,062 members. Close behind were the 20,490-strong No. 6 Division, which contained the major steel and tinplate plants of West Glamorgan, and No. 2 Division, whose 19,259 members worked adjacent to the Tees, elsewhere in the north-east, or in Workington. Scotland (No. 1 Division) had 13,232 members; the Midlands, East and West (No. 4 Division), had 10,608, and Monmouthshire and East Wales (No. 5 Division)[9] had 13,237. A Division encompassing North Wales and the north-west region of England as far north as Barrow (No. 7 Division) had 11,682 members.[10] In the south, another segment of the membership, the London Areas, grouped 3117 members, mostly occupied in the Kindred Trades evoked by the BISAKTA title. This section of the membership made copper, brass, zinc and bronze products, often by processes akin to those employed (on a larger scale) in iron and steel making. At the beginning of the 1950s the London Area still had ex-steelworker members who had moved south between the wars.

The 'supreme governing and administrative authority'[11] of BISAKTA was the Executive Council, a twenty-one-strong body of lay members which held quarterly meetings in the boardroom at Swinton House, King's Cross, the London location of Central Office. Executive Council members, who were expected to remain in employment, represented sections of the membership identified either by their employment in a particular iron and steel-making process or by trade, a structure reflecting the amalgamations which had followed the creation of the Organisation in 1917.[12] The sections were:

Section (a) Blastfurnace (including coke-producing plant)

Section (b) Street Smelters (covering all types of steel production)

Section (c) Steel Rolling Mills (covering any class of rolling mill, with forges in addition)

Section (d) Tinplate and Welsh Sheet Trade (a section which operated regardless of the department an employee was in)

Section (e) Malleable Iron and Non-ferrous Metals (a non-occupation-based section covering all employees in these trades)

Section (f) Steel Sheet Trade (intended for all steel sheet employees not embraced by section (d))

Section (g) Tube Trade

Section (h) Nut, Bolt, Rivet, Nail and Light Iron and Steel

Section (i) Steam, Hydraulic, Electric Service, Engineering and Maintenance (a section which included the membership's ubiquitous crane drivers and also those trade, craft or maintenance men who were members of BISAKTA)

Section (j) Clerical, Administrative, Technical and Supervisory (the most recently created section, which embraced all white-collar staff)

Section (k) General Labour (for all unskilled workers other than shift workers).

For the purpose of counting votes in Executive elections, these sections were cross-cut geographically into three electoral areas. Area 1 comprised Divisions 1 and 2; area 2 comprised Divisions 3, 4 and 7; and area 3 comprised Divisions 5 and 6. It was complex, but it produced a lay body which contained a diverse cross-section of work experience and regional representation. This was the body that for much of this period bore the principal responsibility for the affairs of BISAKTA. In the pages which follow there are frequent references to Executive decisions; often the Executive was quite simply the only body which could decide. At no other level, to take the obvious example, could strike action be authorised. There are also references in the following pages to the actions and careers of a sequence of strong union leaders, but they too on occasions had to defer to the Executive, the body to which they owed their original appointment.

The structure of BISAKTA was unusual in other respects as well. There was no regular conference, though the Rule Book provided for them as the need arose, and they were occasionally held in the quarter-century before an annual delegate conference was inaugurated. But each Division had an annual Branch Officers' Conference (BOC), and these were large affairs with representation from all branches by lay officers in the appropriate Divisions. The identity of each Division was reinforced by the presence of a divisional office (in 1951 these were located in Glasgow, Middlesbrough, Rotherham, Birmingham, Newport, Swansea and Manchester;[13] the London Area was administered from Central Office) from which one to three full-time organisers worked under the direction of a Divisional Officer.

The empowering of a lay executive was no accident. For influence in BISAKTA lay with the officials – and especially the secretaries – of the Association's branches. Each of these was plant-based and would cover an occupation or a group of occupations reflecting the sections outlined above. The branches were autonomous and jealously guarded their right to negotiate with management over staffing, pay and conditions. Branch officers (perhaps the secretary but often the works representative) would also take up individual grievances. Where a dispute could not be resolved, the branch secretary was directed by the Rule Book to contact the Divisional Officer. He or another official would then meet an employers' representative bilaterally, and if he could not then settle the matter, he would refer it to Central Office.

In practice, the favoured route for dispute resolution was to establish a Neutral Committee containing two representatives of either side. This remained a lay affair, and its neutrality rested on the provision that none of the representatives worked at the firm of the dispute.[14] There was provision for a national conference of employers and union officers if the Neutral

Committee (which was empowered to call witnesses) could not reach a solution. In the 'heavy steel trade' (covering melting and rolling) the reference point where a Neutral failed to agree was a National Joint Sub-committee and, if this failed, arbitration. In practice, however, the overwhelming majority of cases were resolved at local level. If occasionally there was an individual rather than a class action the usual device was an 'ad hoc' committee, similar in form. Negotiations about general or national questions – pay and conditions above all – were conducted by a Central Joint Committee with representatives from the main employers' organisation (the Iron And Steel Trades Employers' Association, ISTEA) and representatives of appropriate branches.

Outside the heavy steel membership stretched a panoply of conciliation or negotiation boards. The Sheet Trade Board (STB) covered that industry in England and Wales; the Midland Iron and Steel Wages Board covered employers and workpeople at mills and forges in the Midlands; Scotland was covered by the Board of Conciliation for the Regulation of Wages in the Pig Iron Trade of Scotland and the Scottish Iron Trade Conciliation and Arbitration Board. The name of each conveyed its broadly similar function, but they also featured in common the principle that the sole representative of workpeople in their area was BISAKTA. The single exception at this date was the Welsh Tinplate Trade Joint Industrial Council, which dealt with all matters relating to the pay and conditions of tinplate workers in South Wales. This was a multi-union body, principally because the Transport and General Workers' Union had a significant membership in the sector.

By a paradox, the BOCs themselves became a vehicle for those who believed that there should be a BISAKTA annual conference. The 1952 London Areas BOC called for a national conference of the Union to be convened annually 'to enable the rank and file members of the union to discuss matters of common interest'. The Executive responded by permitting a joint conference of the area with No. 4 Division in 1953, but when it met the Branch Officers reiterated the London Area's demand. In 1955 the No. 3 Division BOC also called for a national conference 'in order that national policy can be formulated';[15] in 1956 it shifted its ground, this time motivating the call by the need to be in line with all other national organisations, and to establish 'more democratic control' and a 'deeper interest in the affairs of the Society'.[16] After this the issue tended to be submerged for a time, and did not resurface until 1959 at the No. 1 BOC.[17]

In the 1950s and 1960s these attempts met with little success, and it is worth asking why. In fact the arguments were less clear cut than many believed, for there was a case for resisting the shift to a national conference on democratic grounds. The May 1953 issue of *Man and Metal* observed that nearly one thousand members had participated in that year's BOCs, making a ratio of one per 120 members, far greater than in two (unnamed) large unions with annual conferences.[18] Participation at that rate was hardly likely to be achieved by an annual conference. Moreover the change, if it involved an annual *delegate* conference, would have implications for other parts of the BISAKTA constitution. The Executive Council, vested with policy-making powers, must find its position under threat from such a body, while BISAKTA's full-time officers, currently the servants of the Executive, would inevitably gravitate into the orbit of the proposed conference. In view of the fact that a conference was later established, it must be concluded that the membership of 1950 had not been convinced of the need for change.

For the union was proud of its level of organisation, fastidious about communications, committed (in the fashion of the time) to sustaining a high level of membership services and fiercely loyal to the Labour Party and its leadership. *Man and Metal*, the monthly BISAKTA journal founded in 1923, was heavyweight, like the union itself. Twenty densely packed pages went out every month; the articles, often long and detailed, witness to the level of education among steelworkers, many of whom had had to provide it for themselves. Adjacent to these articles were frequent adverts for the products of steel firms, testimony to the breadth of the journal's readership, which extended beyond the membership. Each month in the early 1950s featured articles by the metallurgist A. Jackson on 'Steelmaking for Steelmakers' – no mean tribute to the pride the melters' union took in its skills. Nor was it all industry: this same period also witnessed 'Design Affects Everyone', a series from the pen of Noel Carrington, as well as film reviews by Paul Holt, the *Daily Herald* film critic. *Man and Metal* was also conscientious about its reporting role. Regular monthly features included 'News of the ICFTU', a serialisation of key TUC policy documents and 'Current Educational Topics', the column of the redoubtable Ernest Green, who had that year retired as the General Secretary of the Workers' Educational Association (WEA).

Green's high profile was no accident. His appointment after World War I as General Secretary of the WEA had been a catalyst for the Workers' Educational Trade Union Committee (WETUC), which BISAKTA had founded in 1920.[19] The BISAKTA education programme of the 1950s was run in conjunction with WETUC. An impressively extensive range of courses was on offer with locations country-wide.

A considerable portion of BISAKTA's budget was given over to obtaining compensation for members injured in accidents at work. In an age much less safety-conscious than our own and when plant still bore the signs of wartime neglect, accidents were all too common. When they occurred, only skilled legal representation could force some employers to face up to their financial responsibilities. BISAKTA's links with the legal profession had always been unusually close. The Swinton House Central Office also housed a solicitors' firm, Russell Jones and Walker (commonly known as 'the legal services'), which had been co-founded by a BISAKTA legal officer of the inter-war years and the son of James Walker, a prominent BISAKTA officer and Labour MP of the same period.[20]

An example of the legal services' activity came in February 1953, when they won a landmark case at the Court of Appeal. Fighting a compensation claim on behalf of a member's widow, they contested as inadequate compensation awarded at the Swansea Assize. At the Court of Appeal they successfully argued that the value of the member's house should not, as was then the practice, be deducted from the award. The Court of Appeal upheld the principle, ruling that no deduction at all should be made.[21]

Another facet of BISAKTA's services was assistance in the recovery of ailing members. Since 1947 the membership had had the immense good fortune to possess the magnificent Larkhill Convalescent Home at Conway, North Wales, the outcome of a generous donation from the United Steelworkers of America following World War II. Injured or sick members medically certified as likely to benefit from convalescence were accommodated free at Larkhill, where they were put under the care of matron Hilda Jones, whose great-uncle had caused the home to be built ninety years before.

But the core service of BISAKTA was its representation of members in negotiations. Though very dominant in iron and steel, BISAKTA never represented more than 70 per cent of employees in the industry, a factor which complicated representation throughout the period covered by this book: the socialist aspiration of an industrial union had never been achieved. Steelworkers also engaged with a variety of employer or joint bodies, but at their head was the dominant employers' association, ISTEA, founded in 1922. Throughout the inter-war, wartime and post-war periods BISAKTA had tenaciously clung to national negotiations with ISTEA and with other employer or joint bodies as the best way of advancing the general living standards of steelworkers. Local negotiations there had always been, but landmark improvements like the 1919 National Eight Hours Agreement (the Newcastle Agreement) had been achieved at national level.[22] Thirty years later, the same could be said when steelworkers won one week's holiday with pay. Would this legacy of national bargaining survive with massive changes in the industry's ownership in prospect?

Changing environment

For in prospect they were, with a Labour administration in office committed to public ownership of iron and steel. Legislation had been at the back of the parliamentary queue, but in 1949 it was finally laid before the House. That December Evans published a dispassionate outline of the government's proposals for state ownership, The Iron and Steel Bill, where he sounded an absolutely confident note that the negotiating machinery 'which has done so well in the past' would not be altered by Labour's putative Iron and Steel Corporation. This view was endorsed even by severe Labour critics of the old private firms,[23] and was indeed the only point on which they and Conservative opponents of nationalisation agreed.[24] Indeed, it is remarkable how much of the Conservative case rested on the allegedly rising living standards of steelworkers, to which its protagonists attributed the industry's relative industrial peace. In fact, though labour costs rose by 60 per cent in the six years from 1946 to 1952, this increase was outstripped by transport and new plant costs to steel companies – though it did exceed the rise in the price of coking coal.[25] Wages, an important component of which was piece rates which gave higher rewards for greater output, were indeed rising, but so were the prices of goods in the steelworker's household budget.

While the 1949 devaluation brought significant gains in competitiveness to UK steel products, there was (as always for steel) a counter-productive impact in terms of higher imported raw material costs. But by 1950 BISAKTA had given three years of national backing to continuous working in the cause of boosting production, and this economic expansion had brought with it an ugly sister, inflation, which was causing a deterioration in living standards. As Evans pointed out in his 1951 New Year message, the current sliding scales had been designed to operate where all variables were dictated by the market; in the Britain of 1951 prices were government controlled, while raw material costs could fluctuate violently. He speculated on whether some other method of wage regulation might have to be found when prices reached their 'normal' level.[26] By the middle of the year he had begun to strike an ambivalent note, praising Labour for doing more to hold down prices than any previous government, yet acknowledging that the members' interests required an arrest of the continuing fall in purchasing power. He coupled his verdict that wage claims were legitimate with a warning that they should also be responsible; but the change in tone was unmistakable. Workers were getting some benefit from an automatic cost-of-living adjustment, but this did not apply to the whole wage packet. During 1951 this was recognised by an increase of 8.5 per cent in the cost-of-living adjustment.[27]

The February 1950 election returned Labour to office but with a majority of only five; a second contest in October 1951 restored the Conservatives to power and the atmosphere began to change. BISAKTA had a broad sympathy for the industrial objectives of the companies, particularly while they continued to be constrained by raw material shortages. Yet by the middle of 1952 a note of frustration had crept in, with Lincoln Evans complaining that co-operation was rendered more difficult by the habitual secrecy of the employers. Greater disclosure, he argued, would lead to a more informed approach to wage claims.[28] In this Evans was akin to his counterparts in the United States, as a study despatched there by Sir Stafford Cripps had found.[29] But 1952 in fact confounded fears of the impact of Conservative government and tended to lend support to those who believed industry might go its own way. In 1950, BISAKTA had judged the moment ripe to revive its claim for a forty-two-hour week. Though this was not immediately achieved, national negotiations now yielded a reduction to forty-four hours as well as an extra week's paid holiday, bringing the number of days' holiday per year (with bank holidays) to eighteen. Improvements of this order were unlikely to be won on all fronts simultaneously. Evans was prominent throughout the week in proceedings at the 1952 (Margate) Trades Union Congress, and his speech in the debate on wage restraint clearly contributed to the General Council's success in gaining endorsement of this controversial passage in its Report. Evans's argument – familiar to *Man and Metal* readers – was that high nominal increases in pay were pointless and self-defeating: the value of money fell, and many were put out of work by rising costs. 'We all pay each other's wage increases,' he declared at the end of a speech described by the press as one of the best ever delivered to the TUC.

BISAKTA was prominent not only in the TUC but also in the Labour Party: the membership overwhelmingly backed the Party and 90 per cent paid the political levy. In policy debates the union leadership took a view broadly sympathetic to the Labour establishment,[30] despite the fact that Evans, unusually among BISAKTA General Secretaries, never served on the National Executive Committee (NEC). The dramatic departure of Aneurin Bevan, John Freeman and Harold Wilson from the government in April 1951, in protest against the Gaitskell budget, was given short shrift by *Man and Metal*, which ridiculed the idea that 'the imposition of a charge on teeth and spectacles is a matter of principle sufficiently important to justify the resignations'. In the shape of Assistant General Secretary Harry Douglass, a member of Labour's NEC from 1948 to 1953, the union had a forceful advocate of this view.

It was the era of the Cold War, and *Man and Metal* mounted a relentless critique of 'Iron Curtain' countries and the plight of trade unionists there.[31] Nor was it slow to denounce unofficial strikes in other industries, warning that communists might gain a foothold in Britain thereby. There was rising concern among steelworkers about increases in the cost of living, but on the eve of Labour's 1951 election defeat *Man and Metal* was in no doubt that a Labour government was more likely to serve union interests than a Conservative one. The journal's recommendation to members was curiously muted: it counselled unionists thinking of switching their votes that they might be jumping out of the frying pan into the fire. In fact Labour's national vote actually increased, and the union may have been excessively concerned that there might be an anti-government backlash among the membership.

With Labour out of office, BISAKTA held out the possibility of a short-lived right-wing government in view of the small size of the Conservative majority – a common view at the time – but its main concern was over the likely future behaviour of the new Opposition: there must, warned *Man and Metal*, 'be no sign of internal dissension'. It was to be disappointed: Labour was on the brink of its most shattering internal conflicts of modern times. One year later the journal was in despair when the 1952 (Morecambe) Labour Conference unseated Herbert Morrison from the NEC. The following year Evans was part of a group which canvassed abortively for Morrison to be returned to the NEC *ex officio* as Treasurer.

There was a practical side to this political advocacy. BISAKTA had two sponsored Members of Parliament throughout the 1950s. Jack Jones[32] and Dai Mort[33] were stalwart trade union MPs through the early period of this narrative. The union was one of the first to recognise the importance of professional services in parliament, voting in 1950 to give a £100-a-year retainer to cover the expenses of its MPs.[34]

The TUC – with Evans prominent in its counsels – responded in measured fashion to the return of the Conservatives to office. This was a shade too statesmanlike for some, but Evans robustly defended its view. Of the unions' links with Labour he commented 'supporting a Party is an entirely different thing from becoming merely an instrument of its policy', concluding that it was the political independence of the British unions which gave them their international prestige.

Nationalisation, denationalisation and after

Evans's years at the helm of BISAKTA were dominated by reactions to two events: the nationalisation (in January 1951) and the denationalisation

13

(piecemeal from 1953 onwards) of the iron and steel industry. It is surprising to discover that the subject did not figure more largely on the agenda of the BISAKTA Executive during 1951, a marked contrast to the furious controversy which the proposal provoked in the nation at large.[35] Evans himself had favoured a less ambitious nationalisation plan than that actually adopted by Labour.[36] But his December 1949 pamphlet, 'The Iron and Steel Bill', carefully and neutrally laid out the main provisions with the explicit intention of explaining the extent of change to come. The pamphlet is almost free from comment on the merits of the bill, though a clue to Evans's private thoughts may lie in his remark that it did not address many questions which might be answered only by experience. This reticence occasioned a small amount of restiveness: the Executive received calls from two branches,[37] one concerned over 'apathy' about the imminent shift in ownership and the other alleging obstruction by the BISF, but felt unable in either case to take any action. This was relatively little rank-and-file comment when such a major change was pending. For this nationalisation, unlike its 1967 successor, was tremendously far-reaching, extending to every firm with an output of 50,000 tons of iron or 20,000 tons of semi-finished steel: ninety-seven companies were covered by the schedule, and that excludes their subsidiaries.

Evans himself remained cautious, anticipating that the companies would have a great deal of autonomy and that the new Iron and Steel Corporation of Great Britain (ISC) would not interfere in day-to-day affairs. This, he hoped, would avoid rigidities which had proved a handicap in other nationalised industries.[38] There seems to have been relatively little involvement of BISAKTA in the actual framing of the legislation, although Jack Jones, the Organisation's sponsored MP for Rotherham, was Parliamentary Secretary at the Ministry of Supply which was carrying the bill through. Evans, a former member of the Iron and Steel Board, refused George Strauss's invitation to join the Iron and Steel Corporation, arguing that he was more useful to the industry in his union post.[39]

But no sooner had the ISC taken over responsibility for the industry than the political context changed. In opposition the Conservatives had resisted nationalisation with a fierceness not always apparent when they challenged other Labour measures; there could be little doubt, however, that they would move rapidly to repeal the Iron and Steel Act. The BISAKTA Executive again faced questions, this time from five branches, as to how it would handle what was surely to come. In December 1951, after a lengthy discussion, it resolved that continued public ownership was in the best interests of the nation; that public ownership was the proper and most effective means of public control; that repeal would keep the industry in 'the cockpit of politics';

and that if it occurred nonetheless the union would support the Labour Party in a continued commitment to renationalisation.[40] In view of the later chequered political history of the industry, the third point seems particularly well chosen; it was also a much more definite statement than any of those which had accompanied the original nationalisation itself. The following year, however, when the Executive received a demand from the No. 1 Division Branch Officers' Conference (BOC) to 'take all possible steps to block' the Conservative administration's denationalisation plans, it chose only to take note of the resolution.[41] Subsequently the EC declined a suggestion from the Atlas branch in Sheffield to form an alliance against denationalisation with others in the nationalised industries. (Though it was not apparent at the time, steel and road haulage were to be the outer perimeter of the Conservatives' denationalisation objectives.) Not everyone was ranged either for or against ownership, however: Lanarkshire No. 1 branch suggested the purchase of a small number of shares in each of the companies earmarked for return to the private sector. This farsighted proposal was regretfully deemed by Evans to be not permissible under the rules, 'whatever the advantages'.

In September 1952, the Executive considered the White Paper on denationalisation and heard advice from Evans that it might consider tabling amendments to safeguard the interests of the membership. It took the view that this would be premature and awaited publication of the bill, which occurred on 6 November. In fact the bill followed the White Paper in envisaging an Iron and Steel Board (hereafter the Board) to supervise the industry and promote efficient supply under competitive conditions – but also an Iron and Steel Holdings and Realisation Agency (ISHRA), which would sell off the assets of the nationalised companies, though with no timetable: a slow pace was clearly envisaged. This was less drastic than some had feared, but it did follow hard on the original nationalisation.

The November 1952 Quarterly Executive followed the Second Reading debate in the Commons. Jack Jones, now in opposition and naturally attracting attention because of his triple qualifications as former steel melter, onetime BISAKTA official, and junior minister responsible for nationalising the industry, had forcefully advocated the Labour case that the new Board should have compulsory powers. He wanted to see it able to compel firms to amalgamate. Evans had interpreted other of Jones's remarks in the debate as a personal attack on himself and also as an unwarranted disclosure of the confidential deliberations of the Executive. The MP's disclaimer of any intention to refer to Evans was accepted, but he was implicitly rebuked when the Executive deplored any public reference to its private discussions.[42]

The EC convened in a special meeting on January 16 1953 to give detailed consideration to the Iron and Steel Bill. Evans, who had received a knight-hood in the New Year's Honours List,[43] reported on the likely impact on the union's membership, the subject of recent meetings between the TUC and the Ministry of Supply. At other meetings between the TUC General Council, Labour's NEC and the Parliamentary Labour Party (the PLP, which had jointly formed an Iron and Steel Sub-committee to monitor the bill's content and progress), amendments to the bill had been drafted, and these all received Executive approval. The labour movement seemed unanimous in opposing the Conservatives' intentions in principle while attempting constructively to amend them. The Executive discussed appointments to the new Board but decided to defer making policy on the matter.

Thirteen days after the Executive met, Duncan Sandys, Minister of Supply with overall responsibility for the bill, clearly indicated that he envisaged the inclusion of a trade union element in the Board (though it was only to be one of many). The significance of this for BISAKTA quickly became apparent and caused two more Special Meetings of the Executive, on 16 April and 1 May. It had returned to the question of Supervisory Board appointments because Sir Lincoln Evans had learned that these would include one which would be full-time, and he himself had been sounded out for office. It was not as if there was no precedent for BISAKTA involvement at a high industrial level. He himself had served on the (pre-nationalisation) Iron and Steel Board between 1946 and 1948. The Executive discussed the difficult question of its future relationship with the Board, and finally recognised that, as an accomplished fact, it could not be boycotted. There was always the possibility that if BISAKTA declined to be represented another organisation might be invited to fill its place, and this consideration must have influenced the outcome. A discussion then followed on whether Evans should join the Board in a part-time or a full-time capacity. His preference was for the former, which would have allowed him to remain General Secretary, but the feeling was against him; at the second meeting the Executive resolved that he should accept a full-time appointment 'in order to ensure that the interests of the workpeople should find expression'.[44]

The news proved controversial, however, when debated among the membership. Evans's action was for the most part supported. There was implied criticism at the No. 2 Division BOC, which deplored the Iron and Steel Act and urged on the EC 'more effective measures in future to inform the electorate that this is the decided policy of our Organisation';[45] but three other BOCs backed the decision to join the Board. A Special Executive of 12 June was dominated by an article in the Bevanite weekly *Tribune*, written by the paper's editor Michael Foot,[46] which fiercely criticised the Evans appointment. Foot had charged that in accepting the vice-chairmanship of the Board, Evans had dishonestly betrayed the labour movement for monetary gain,[47] and that in so doing he had gone against the overwhelming wishes of the BISAKTA membership. Unsurprisingly, Evans was authorised to take legal action against what was clearly a defamatory attack. The Executive issued a supportive statement insisting that his appointment had been made with its full knowledge and backing, and viewing 'with disgust' attacks from 'quarters who [*sic*] have no responsibility to our membership'.

In the union's own journal, *Man and Metal*, Evans was more forthright still. This, he charged, was all part of the cold war which the Tribune Group had been conducting. The new Board had nothing to do with de-nationalisation – that was a matter for the ISHRA – only with the way the industry was to be run in the future. Abstention from Board participation would, he declared, have been 'a complete abdication of the right trade unionists have always demanded to have a say in the direction and control of industry'.[48] His position was in fact entirely consistent with the view he had taken since before the Conservatives had returned to office: unions could not function if political preferences took priority over industrial obligations. A union's job was to secure the employment of its members under the best possible conditions.

Changes of attitude towards denationalisation were also in evidence in the wider trade union movement, where BISAKTA was of course a major player. The following year, in Douglas, Isle of Man, a fairly emphatic resolution of the 1952 Trades Union Congress was replaced by a more concrete approach which implied that the ownership of each industry should be considered on its merits, with no automatic presumption that public ownership offered the best solution to its problems.[49] Even before this, the June 1953 meeting of the TUC's Economic Committee had overwhelmingly passed a resolution upholding Evans's view of the right relationship of unions to the Board, though it had received letters critical of the appointments.[50] The 1953 Congress saw the debate revisited one last time, but there was never likely to be an altered verdict. Evans powerfully defended his actions, and a resolution which 'strongly deprecated' them was heavily defeated.[51] Jack Owen of the Blastfurnacemen joined him on the Board as a part-time member.

Though the political controversy died after this, the legal action was firmly pursued. But the wheels of British justice grind exceeding slow and only in Autumn 1954, with a hearing finally imminent, did *Tribune* capitulate. In an apology read out in the Queen's Bench Division of the High Court[52] *Tribune* declared it had never meant to make a charge of dishonesty and regretted the inconvenience it had caused to Evans. As to the policy issue, *Tribune* maintained that it had intended to argue that denationalisation, and not the appointment, was against union policy. It accepted, however, that its argument had been misconstrued, and so offered to publish a series of facts[53] which upheld Evans's stand. In consequence the defendants made an 'unqualified withdrawal' of the allegations and offered a further apology. Evans – now into the second year of his Board membership – could scarcely have wished for a more complete victory, and he pressed no claim for damages.

From a perspective of forty years it is difficult to do justice to this controversy, which certainly clouded Evans's last months as General Secretary. To his critics, still smarting from the Conservatives' success in so rapidly reversing a key legislative change of the Attlee government, accepting such an appointment constituted an endorsement of denationalisation – a charge he parried by pointing out, with truth, that the Board would not be responsible for any asset disposal. He also argued that this was an opportunity for influencing steel industry policy: had there been no such appointments, he suggested, there would still have been complaints from the left.

Yet the EC itself – overwhelmingly sympathetic to Evans – was unclear on this point. During his time of office they rarely crossed him, yet on the incompatibility of Board membership and full-time office they were implacable. Finally the dispute has to be viewed within the politics of the time. Evans, like a number of other senior TUC leaders, was engaged in a fierce controversy with national and international communism, a distinctive feature of which, in their view, was the subordination of trade unionism to the state. The boundaries between this battlefield and the ongoing conflict within the Labour Party with Aneurin Bevan and his associates (the closest of whom, of course, was Michael Foot) easily became blurred. Some of those closest to Evans[54] saw the intensity of the vituperation he suffered, and the accusations of treachery, as a signal that his critics' chief motivation was to achieve a society where the state was supreme in all spheres. That such accusations should be flung at Michael Foot and others suggests that the accusers were insufficiently discriminating in their allegations of communist sympathies.

In line with EC wishes, Evans retired from union office on taking up his Board appointment. He left in August 1953, to an accolade from *Man and Metal* that he would still continue to serve the industry to which he had devoted his life. His valedictory article appeared there three months later. It contained an expression of his philosophy as succinct as any he had offered during his seven years at the top:

18

The influence the Confederation exercises in the industry today is due to the highly responsible and intelligent way in which it has always conducted its affairs. It has always striven to create a healthy climate of industrial relations. It has invariably stressed the importance of technical efficiency and encouraged new methods in the belief that where those things exist it is far easier to obtain higher standards and better conditions than would be possible if they did not. As a Union, from the very early days, its policies, procedures and methods have been based on that assumption, and experience has fully shown how right it is.[55]

Main trends 1951–3

By May 1953, the impact of steady economic growth on the steel industry had been such that government controls over distribution of iron and steel products were relinquished. Of course the denationalisation of the industry began to take effect in that year, but the issue went deeper than ownership: Britain's iron and steel industry would henceforth function in a much more liberalised national economy. Labour's Harold Wilson had, as President of the Board of Trade, lit a 'bonfire of controls' to withdraw from excessive government intervention. Ironically, however, it was the successor Conservative government which captured the public imagination with the rhetoric of free enterprise and personal wealth enhancement which was to bring it thirteen years of office from 1951. Like it or not, Britain's steelworkers would be dealing with private enterprise for the foreseeable future: events from 1951 to 1953 showed that they would meet this challenge with industrial rather than political considerations uppermost in their minds.

But if the nation moved towards greater competition on the national scale, it was unconvinced about international competition. The Schuman Plan of 1950 and the moves which led to the establishment of the European Coal and Steel Community (ECSC) met with great scepticism in Britain, where both political parties were inclined to stay aloof. BISAKTA was not critical of the ECSC's original decision to abstain from the High Authority in May 1950, since this would have entailed putting key British industries 'under the problematical jurisdiction of a supra-national authority'; but it was careful to keep its options open thereafter. In this the Organisation was unusual, not only among British unions[56] but among employers and politicians as well.[57] When in 1952 an invitation arrived from the British government to nominate an assessor to a permanent delegation to liaise with the High Authority, BISAKTA responded with the nomination of Harry Douglass, then Assistant General Secretary. A delegation of Executive members was sent to study the Community in 1955.[58] Two years later the first reaction of BISAKTA to the prospect of a Common Market was cautious. A Free Trade Area was attractive, once 'proper safeguards are worked out'.[59] Meanwhile the ECSC was under way, and the Organisation looked with satisfaction in 1957 upon 'a growing relationship between the two main coal and steel producing areas of Western Europe'. But the union was not immune from basking in the afterglow of empire and rather complacently observed that the problem of free trade area membership would be 'to put the peasant on his feet'.[60] Within a decade BISAKTA's would become one of the most urgent voices advocating that Britain should seize its opportunity in Europe.

Notes

1 Its nearest rival, the National Union of Blastfurnacemen, Ore Miners, Coke Workers and Allied Trades (henceforth NUB), had about 25,000 members in 1952. J. Owen, *Ironmen* (1953), 40. The NUB organised coke and iron workers in England and Wales but BISAKTA represented them in Scotland.

2 Sir Lincoln Evans, CBE (1889–1970), was General Secretary from 1946 to 1953. He had joined the Steel Smelters at the age of sixteen and became secretary of the King's Dock branch in 1919. He was appointed Organiser in No. 6 Division in 1932. In 1935 the Executive Council considered the appointment of two Assistant General Secretaries in view of the approaching retirement of Sir Arthur Pugh, but deliberately gave six months' seniority to John Brown, then Divisional Officer in No. 1 Division. Evans therefore became Assistant General Secretary at the start of 1936 and General Secretary ten years later. He was made CBE in 1948 and received a knighthood five years later.

3 Where he sat with Ambrose Callighan of the NUB until Callighan's retirement in 1948.

4 *Man and Metal* (January 1951). The back cover of this issue carried a government advert urging greater productivity.

5 *Reports* (1951), 28. Raw material supplies were on the minds of BISAKTA's Clerical Supervisory Workers' Conference and its No. 1 Area Committee later the same year: both bodies passed resolutions expressing fears about the threat which such shortages posed to employment.

6 *Ibid.*, 31.

7 The story is told in A. Pugh (publishing anonymously), *Men of Steel, By One of Them* (1951), 581–2.

8 For an apt comment on the 'crab-like' movement of the industry away from the original location of the coke-using iron industry, see D. Heal, *The Steel Industry in Post-war Britain* (1974), 198.

9 No. 5 Divisional Officer Ernie Hickery had been in post since 1946 after six years as Organiser in No. 3 Division. He was to receive an OBE in the 1957 Queen's Birthday Honours.

10 Its Divisional Officer since 1950 had been A. Griffiths, who had been an Organiser since 1941. He too would receive an OBE in the 1957 Birthday Honours.

11 Defined as such in the BISAKTA Rule Book.

12 Confederation had in effect produced two organisations, BISAKTA and the Iron and Steel Trades Confederation (the ISTC), the one intended to be the functioning union and the other a confederal body permitting the founding organisations to express themselves as units. The terms were employed almost interchangeably by participants during much of the period covered by this book. The name was reviewed in 1974 and so ISTC is used from 1975 onwards.

13 The No. 7 office moved from Manchester to Knutsford in 1971.

14 For the first period covered by this book this meant that another firm affiliated to the Iron and Steel Trades Employers' Association (ISTEA), which combined most BISF members, would supply the employers' representatives; BISAKTA would supply experienced representatives from another plant. Firms not belonging to ISTEA had a similar agreement with the union.

15 *Reports* (1955), 121. The resolution was rejected.

16 *Reports* (1956), 121.

17 *Reports* (1959), 135.

18 It is difficult to gauge opinion among the membership from the pages of *Man and Metal*: letters tended to divide evenly for and against the idea.

19 For BISAKTA's pioneering work in the development of trade union educational programmes in this period see Pugh, *op. cit.*, 289ff. and *passim*.

20 John (son of James) Walker continued to advise BISAKTA into the 1970s. For the appointment of Arthur Russell Jones, who retired in 1955, see Pugh, *op. cit.*, 362. Though an independent firm, Russell Jones and Walker was universally known to BISAKTA members as the 'legal services'. Since the practice continues it has been adopted in this book.

21 *Man and Metal* (March 1953).

22 In this instance the employers were the Steel Ingot Makers, who amalgamated with others to join ISTEA three years later.

23 Steel's negotiating machinery had 'worked well', according to Wilfred Fienburgh and Richard Evely of the Labour Research Department (*Steel is Power: The Case for Nationalisation*, 1948, 37). They withheld their blessing from other aspects of steel's industrial relations, however: wage calculation was 'incredibly involved' and trade union organisation 'diffuse'.

24 See Aubrey Jones, *If STEEL Is Nationalised* (1950), 11ff.

25 The figures were: labour 160, transport 175, coking coal 152, new plant 168 (1946 = 100). The figure for the price of metal goods exported was 168, suggesting improved profits. D. Burn, *The Steel Industry 1939–1959: a study in competition and planning* (1961), 266.

26 *Man and Metal* (January 1951).

27 Burn, *op. cit.*, 340.

28 *Man and Metal* (July 1952).

29 One British employer was startled to read a CIO placard which read 'the greatest crime a company can commit against the employees is failure to make a profit'. (Cited in P. Hennessy, *Never Again*, 1992, 377). But the experiences of American steelworkers had been quite different from those of their British counterparts. By the middle of the 1950s, steel wages in the US were four times as great as those in the United Kingdom.

30 In his classic *Trade Unions and the Labour Party since 1960* (1960), Martin Harrison included BISAKTA in a group of unions not known to have voted against the NEC since the war.

31 See for example the June 1951 issue, which carried no less than three hostile items on the Soviet Bloc as well as a denunciatory leader.

32 J.H. Jones (1894–1962) was a melter at Lancashire Steel's Irlam Works for thirty-two years, a local councillor for fourteen years and a branch secretary and later EC member. He was educated at elementary school and at University College Bangor. He was MP for Bolton (1945–50) and for Rotherham (1950–62); while MP for Rotheram he continued to work as a welfare officer at Irlan. He became Parliamentary Private Secretary to Lord Pakenham in 1947, and in October of that year Parliamentary Secretary to the Ministry of Supply, where he remained until March 1950. There he shouldered important responsibilities for piloting the Iron and Steel Bill through the House of Commons. He was noted for his outspokenness.

33 D.L. Mort (1888–1963), a former crane driver from Briton Ferry, held many local BISAKTA offices (including fourteen years as a branch secretary), rose to be an EC member twice in the 1920s, and was a former member of the Neath Borough Council. He was MP for Eccles from 1929 to 1931 and for Swansea East from 1940 to his death. For a time during the Attlee government he was Parliamentary Private Secretary to Sir William (later Lord) Jowitt.

34 The level was cut when parliamentary allowances were introduced in 1954.

35 Prime Minister Clement Attlee himself later commented that 'of all our nationalisation proposals, only iron and steel aroused much feeling, perhaps because the hopes of profit were greater here than elsewhere' (quoted in Hennessy, *op. cit.*, 202).

36 He later claimed that only his absence from the country deprived him of the chance to persuade Ernest Bevin to back Herbert Morrison's compromise plan when the cabinet reached its crucial decision in 1947 (B. Donoghue and G.W. Jones, *Herbert Morrison: Portrait of a Politician*, 1973, 402–3n). It has also been suggested that there were some differences between him and Harry Douglass, who was to succeed him in 1953 (on this point see K.O. Morgan, *Labour in Power 1945–51*, 1984).

37 Frodingham No. 2 and Phoenix Staff No. 1 (*Reports*, 1951), 118.

38 *Man and Metal*, January 1951. In this Evans anticipated the views of many later commentators. He seems at all times to have envisaged an almost autonomous existence for the companies within the ISC.

39 See G. Ross, *The Nationalisation of Steel* (1965), 129.

40 *Reports* (1951), 216.

41 *Reports* (1952), 113. A resolution from the No. 3 Division BOC also called for 'immediate repudiation of this unnecessary and harmful measure'; No. 6 Division BOC wished to see 'the strongest possible action' by the trade union movement in resistance. Press reports of Rotherham members considering a strike to prevent denationalisation drew an anxious Sir Arthur Pugh out of retirement into the pages of *Man and Metal*. Pugh was concerned not only about militancy but about the early exchanges in the Commons over steel which accurately prefigured its continued politicisation at the hands of both parties. 'Is the game of "pull devil, pull baker" to be continued ad infinitum?' he asked (*Man and Metal*, January 1952).

42 *Reports* (1952), 211–12.

43 The event was formally acclaimed in the Executive minutes, though one member, J. Shea, rather spoiled the show by dissenting 'in principle': *Reports* (1953), 28.

44 *Reports* (1953), 110.

45 *Reports* (1953), 118. The EC rejected the implication that it had failed to keep the electorate informed.

46 'The Amazing Case of Lincoln Evans' (29 May 1953). Evans defended himself in *Tribune* the following week, 5 June.

47 The post attracted a £5000 salary.

48 'Trade Unions and the Steel Board', *Man and Metal*, June 1953. On this occasion Evans, who often wrote anonymously and sometimes under his own name, wrote under the by-line 'the General Secretary'.

49 TUC, *Interim Report on Public Ownership* (1953).

50 *Man and Metal* (July 1953).

51 It does seem to be going too far to conclude that the appointment meant that the union's enthusiasm for nationalisation had 'waned' (D. McEachern, *A Class Against Itself: Power in the Nationalisation of the British Steel Industry*, 1980, 103). Evans had never been an 'enthusiast' in the first place.

52 Sir Lincoln Evans (Plaintiff) and Tribune Publications Ltd, Michael Foot and Merritt and Hatcher Ltd (Defendants), 1953. E. No. 1969 (11 October 1954).

53 These were: that Evans had been recommended by the EC to accept the post; that he had informed it that he would only accept with its approval; that two BOCs had heavily voted for a union member to join the Board while another had agreed without a vote; that EC minutes showing a wish to associate with the Board were in circulation twelve months previous to the announcement; that Labour front benchers had endorsed the full-time Board appointment of union officials in the Commons on 13 May 1953; that the 1953 TUC had endorsed Evans's action; and that only twenty-four out of 662 branches had passed resolutions critical of the action.

54 Sir Arthur Pugh for example. See *Man and Metal* (August 1953).

55 Sir Lincoln Evans, 'Adieu', *Man and Metal* (November 1953). Evans remained full-time Deputy Chairman of the Iron and Steel Board until 1960, serving as a part-time member after that date. He had joined the General Advisory Council of the BBC a year before stepping down as General Secretary and continued in this post in retirement. He died on 3 August 1970.

56 When Herbert Morrison first heard of the Schuman Plan he is reputed to have said 'It's no good, we cannot do it, the Durham miners won't wear it' (Donoghue and Jones, *op. cit.*, 481).

57 See Burn, *op. cit.*, 464–73 for British attitudes to the early development of the ECSC.

58 *Reports* (1955), 131.

59 'Notes and Comments', *Man and Metal* (February 1957).

60 'Notes and Comments', *Man and Metal* (June 1957).

2

Back in the private sector
Harry Douglass (1953–9)

'The best wages agreements in the world are of little use to
the unemployed.'

New leadership

Harry Douglass succeeded Sir Lincoln Evans as General Secretary in August
1953[1] after serving as Organiser, Divisional Officer and Assistant General
Secretary. He was easily to maintain Evans's position as one of the 'Big Five'
who dominated the leadership of the TUC. This burly Teessider became
well known for his pro-Establishment views and was a committed partisan in
Labour's intense policy debates during the 1950s, firmly espousing German
rearmament and smiting the Bevanites hip and thigh; internationally he
rebutted communism and advocated the mission and role of the International Confederation of Free Trade Unions (ICFTU).[2]

But it was as an industrial figure that he became best known. In some ways
he resembled the American union leaders of his generation. He was un-
embarrassed about advocating efficiency ('the best wages agreements in the
world are of little use to the unemployed'), since unproductive firms would
be the first to go to the wall. Nor did this imply just a positive reception for
employer proposals: unions should in his view be prepared to take the initiative in productivity schemes. This was already characteristic of BISAKTA's
record and became even more pronounced with Douglass in the leading role.
Indeed, steel's prosperity at this time owed as much to the union as to
management. High wages and high profits could and did coincide, and Douglass preferred to negotiate with a profitable firm where advances could be
gained rather than (as was sometimes the case) with an unprofitable firm. He

was fond of quoting what he described as 'the one basic fact', that a country or industry could not consume what it did not earn.

This stance was sometimes criticised for compliance towards the employer and a lack of militancy. In fact Douglass was completely pragmatic. His goal was a high standard of living for BISAKTA membership. He defended the strike weapon in principle, but again and again expressed his fears that misuse of it in the form of unofficial stoppages was blunting its effectiveness. He also had a specific fear that unofficial strikes were allowing the communists to gain a foothold that might otherwise be unattainable.[3] Of course the absence of strikes in steel was principally due to the effectiveness of the dispute procedure, but the personal outlook of the General Secretary was surely a factor in shielding the industry from strikes in 1957, the worst year for stoppages since 1926. It was no surprise when in 1962 Douglass gained the chairmanship of the British Productivity Council (BPC), which promoted industrial efficiency throughout those years.[4] His stance was not universally popular, and when he received criticism in the labour movement's press (which was often) he reacted to it with waspish attacks.

Douglass was also a well-known figure internationally: indeed, the Organisation may well have been at its most prestigious in global terms during his tenure of office. He was President of the International Metalworkers' Federation (IMF) in 1960–1, and for many years before 1961 was Co-President (with Dwight McDonald of the USWA) of the IMF Steel Department. He took these responsibilities seriously. The affairs of international trade unionism were widely publicised to BISAKTA membership during his years of office, and he was an able and pugnacious propagandist against communism.

In August 1953, Douglass was succeeded as Assistant General Secretary by David ('Dai'), Davies who had only recently achieved national prominence. Davies had only been appointed as an Organiser in 1950 (though he had at that point already served two years as a member of the Executive).[5] His abilities were widely recognised and this rapid advance was unsurprising. Rising to the second position in BISAKTA so quickly caused Davies to serve a long apprenticeship, but he used it to develop a national political profile and a reputation in international trade unionism, so much so that in 1961 he succeeded Douglass as Co-President of the IMF Steel Department. BISAKTA's reputation also brought recognition to two lay officials. Executive member D.J. ('Dai') Thomas was awarded the Men's Gold Badge at the 1958 Trades Union Congress.[6] Another member, Alf Braddock, was to receive this accolade in 1964.[7]

Dealing with private industry

Surveying the period between the beginning of denationalisation in 1953 and the renationalisation of 1967 – a period which more or less corresponds to Douglass's term of office – one authority identifies three main features: growth was based on existing firms; many firms in the industry were technically conservative; and there was a diffident attitude towards Europe.[8] Without doubt the broad economic context was expansionary. Output rose steadily, though subject to what became a familiar four- or five-year cycle. In the five years from 1952 to 1957 production expanded by an average of about one million tons annually. The 17.61 million tons of output for 1953 (50 per cent above the 1945 figure) showed what the industry was capable of once shortages of raw materials had been overcome. The disappearance of the constraints of the last fifteen years meant the progressive withdrawal of state influence and not only of state ownership: by the end of 1954 the only steel product still under statutory control was tinplate, where rising demand had kept in production a number of handmills marked down for scrapping. Even so, record outputs were not enough to prevent short supplies of sheet and tinplate for British industry; imports had to be tolerated (175,000 tons in the case of sheet) since the alternative – curtailing exports – was unthinkable in a Britain that was still hungry for foreign exchange.

Output per man year rose by 21 per cent in the six years from 1948 to 1954, a statistic which impressed *Man and Metal* but looks less secure in retrospect. The Board's (1954) Special Report on Development envisaged fairly major expansion of output to meet a rapid growth in general industrial investment. Nor would rising output just be the result of driving plant (and people) harder: new melting capacity coming on stream at Lackenby and Shotton alone meant an additional one million tons of capacity. 1955 brought agreement to build the Brinsworth strip mill and make a major investment at Workington. And sights were continuously being raised. In meetings during 1954 with Scottish unionists (including John Lang, No. 1 Divisional Officer) the Board's chairman and vice-chairman heard of (and were persuaded by) the case for heavy-end investment in Scotland (where Colville's as yet remained in the public sector). That September brought the announcement of new blastfurnace plant at Motherwell, with concomitant enhancements of Glasgow Dock's capacity to handle coking coal. Sensing that the wind was in their sails, Lang and the others soon began publicly to press the case for adaptation of the Ravenscraig mills for strip output, in their view a natural move which would help attract a larger share of the car industry to Scotland. The Board was of course responsible for seeing that the industry could supply domestic needs,[9] and at last this goal was in sight. Where redundancies still occurred it was in the context of an industry which was re-equipping itself, and they did not lead to persistent unemployment.[10] As Douglass commented, denationalisation might have its faults, but a lack of capital wasn't one of them.[11]

For BISAKTA the early years of denationalisation were indeed relatively untroubled. There were many reasons for this. The life of the Corporation had been brief; unlike in the second period of public ownership (1967–88), there had been little opportunity to make social gains. In some ways the most remarkable feature was that so little had changed by 1953, despite the public ownership.[12] Then there was the modulated nature of the process itself. Sale of the industry proceeded rather slowly at first – it was government policy to get the best price rather than rush – though it later accelerated. At the time Douglass succeeded Evans only two companies had been sold by public issue of their shares and five by negotiation, their combined share of UK capacity being over 17 per cent.[13] Within twelve months, however, sixteen undertakings had gone, carrying 146 subsidiaries representing about half the Corporation's activities which had been nationalised. In fact, total denationalisation was never achieved, and this contributed to keeping the ownership dispute bubbling. In Vaizey's words, 'Over the whole period of 1953 to 1964 . . . the industry's finances were dominated by the problem of selling the shares of the companies in the City.'[14]

But as the industry gradually returned to the private sector what were the prospects for steelworkers' living standards? There was certainly some discontent. The sliding scale reflected inflationary movements in the cost of living, so nominally incomes were rising, but Douglass felt no confidence that a wage increase would bring a higher standard of living, given the tendency of accelerating inflation to erode real wages.[15] He was frustrated when employers complaining of high costs were unwilling to draw their workforce into discussions about solutions. Many firms could contain higher labour costs since they were a relatively small proportion of total costs, and this was still more true of the bigger plants. In practice, labour costs in the years 1953 to 1959 advanced faster than other significant costs such as that of plant, a sharp contrast to the immediate post-war period.[16] Melters' earnings advanced considerably in the 1950s, but the impact of this was offset by the relatively wide differential between the first hand and those lower down the scale.

By 1954 Douglass was speculating that there were limits to the extent to which increasingly centralised negotiations would bring solutions to all industrial relations problems. However, the resolutions of that year's HST (heavy steel trade) Area Conference[17] pointed towards difficulties which almost demanded national solutions. Area 1 registered its dissatisfaction with the holiday agreement over the fact that leave could be split or staggered or both, and because one month's notice left recipients insufficient time to book accommodation. Area 2 wanted to extend the full cost-of-living bonus to eighteen- to twenty-one-year-olds. Area 3 urged on the Executive a claim for a forty-two-hour week for those on continuous working, while Area 4 went further and pressed for a forty-hour week without loss of earnings. These were straws in the wind; the leadership had to draw up pay claims which reflected both the members' mood and the interests of the industry. But they clearly indicated that aspirations were rising.

There were two topics which would clearly have a national solution or none at all: safety at work and pensions. The organisation was broadly satisfied with the accident prevention record of UK employers. Legislation in place was regarded as probably the best in the world, and its standards were thought to be exceeded by many employers.[18] The first issue of *Safety*, a BISF accident-prevention magazine, showed that the accident frequency rate at Appleby-Frodingham had fallen from 3.27 per hundred employees in 1947 to 1.11 in 1956. Yet even in 1957 one out of every sixteen steel workers suffered some kind of accident. The BISF view, as expressed in *Safety*, was that human rather than mechanical factors caused most crane accidents.

As for pensions, it was possible to make some progress towards adequate pension benefits on a company basis, but there was inescapably a need for a national standard. In 1956 the BOCs of Nos. 4 and 5 Divisions called for a pension scheme (if possible non-contributory), introduction of which, they felt, was 'overdue'. The Executive concurred and the following year felt able to give a lead to the gathering feeling in the Divisions. It tabled a resolution – endorsed by all the 1957 BOCs – which called for an industrial pension scheme, entitlement to which would not be jeopardised by the need to transfer from works to works for reasons of advancement or redundancy.[19] That same year No. 6 BOC specifically addressed the proliferation of individual company schemes and urged the Executive not to accept the employers' refusal to establish a national scheme as final. In 1959 No. 1 BOC returned to this theme, demanding a 'superannuation pension scheme throughout the steel industry', a demand the No. 5 Division echoed with its call for a 'pension on retirement for all steelworkers'. Some indication of the pressure that was building up may be gathered from Douglass's decision to report to the August 1959 Executive all firms which had introduced a pension scheme during the previous quarter or indicated their intention to do so.[20] And the pressure was beginning to tell: by February 1960 additional pension schemes had been introduced at firms employing 30,000 members, bringing the total number thus covered to 91,000, some 85 per cent of them in production branches. Those still excluded worked, for the most part, in small companies.[21]

But with so much of the total remuneration package locally negotiated it was the negotiations machinery which remained the key to employer-employee relations. The integrity of the machinery of negotiations runs like a thick vein through most of this history. BISAKTA had fought hard to establish its pyramidal structure, which forced the disputants on both sides to sit down with each other: on the union side this meant that lay people directly elected from the workplace were present at every stage. After this a neutral committee could be convened, and it was the union's boast that there had only been extremely rare instances during the previous thirty years when it had been necessary to go further. Observing the wider scene from this secure base, Douglass deplored an increasing tendency to have recourse to strikes, suggesting that 'communism and strikes have become synonymous terms', though he was careful to acknowledge that discontent was really about unsatisfied wage demands.[22] In summer 1954 he was to be confronted by a serious dispute within his own industry.

At this time coke-oven workers were not consoled for their relatively low earnings by the expectation that they would one day be on a melters' rate: they were, after all, working in some of the most unpleasant conditions in the industry. At Margam, frustrated coke workers had walked out over a pay claim even before going to a Neutral Committee, in defiance of advice from the Joint Branches Committee to use the negotiating machinery. This Joint Committee in fact had two Executive members upon it, and at a special meeting of 29 July the whole Executive took a tough line, dubbing the stoppage 'an unwarranted breach of the negotiating procedure'.[23] It clearly regarded the conciliation machinery as an alternative to the suffering consequent on industrial disputes,[24] a view vindicated when it learned in August that the Neutral Committee had upheld the branch's claim.[25] The dispute attracted considerable publicity, much of it unflattering to the Executive, which was written down as a remote and unresponsive body. Douglass skilfully dealt with the attacks in the union's own journal, and emphasised that the men had returned to work with their claim not advanced at all.[26]

But the Margam dispute was unrepresentative of BISAKTA's activity during this period. Where industrial relations were disturbed the actors tended to be engineering workers with a quite different pay package. In a multi-union industry the actions of a relatively small group could paralyse a major works.[27] The implications of a national dispute were even more grave.

In 1956 the craft unions in steel sought a new agreement from ISTEA without binding arbitration, and a substantial increase in wages. That April, rejecting an increase which was no larger than that offered to production workers, the craftsmen imposed a national ban on overtime which rapidly disrupted production. This was followed by sporadic strikes in some areas, and not until 7 August was normal working resumed. The conflict had been prolonged by failure to use the industry's procedural agreement (which lapsed early on); but it was also a pivotal dispute which helped define the parameters of process and skilled trade unionism in the industry.

The heart of the craftsmen's case was frustration over a pay offer which did not give them a sufficient differential over production workers, and it was this which drew BISAKTA into an active role. Regardless of the settlement, the impact of the dispute on production workers' earnings was very great and feelings ran high. They were not helped by comments attributed to the chairman of the Craftsmens' Committee which disparaged process workers' skills. Members in plants hit by the action who were working normally – as they endeavoured to do in conformity with instructions from Central Office – were accused by craft union members of betraying trade union principles. A Court of Inquiry into the dispute had been appointed under the chairmanship of Sir John Stewart. Stung by the criticism of other unions, the Executive, meeting in special session on 10 July, decided to attend and give evidence to the Court.

Douglass's statement to the Court[28] twelve weeks into the dispute was an eloquent and classic defence of the industry-specific skills of the steelworker. He lamented the way that BISAKTA members' skills were being denigrated: for the first time this was happening at the hands of another union. Yet the industry-specific skills of a process worker were acquired over a much longer period than a craft apprenticeship. He went on vigorously to defend BISAKTA's promotion system, its procedures and its commitment to the steel industry.[29]

Four years after this, the Amalgamated Union of Building Trade Workers (AUBTW) laid claim to the work of lining the basic Bessemer converters at the Abbey Works. Here was a classic recognition dispute with the claims of craft and industrial unionism laid side by side. Efforts by BISAKTA to secure an agreed settlement under the auspices of the TUC, or through arbitration, were resisted by the building workers, who eventually tried to press their claim through strike action. The dispute spilled over into the Ebbw Vale plant of Richard Thomas & Baldwin (RTB). After extensive publicity in 1962 the AUBTW finally agreed to arbitration under the chairmanship of Professor Daniel Jack, who in November fully upheld BISAKTA's claim to the

31

work. In March 1957 BISAKTA's resolve had again been tested. The Executive met for two days in special session to discuss a new national engineering dispute which had brought some works, notably Irlam, to a standstill. This time some BISAKTA members employed as maintenance men had joined the strike, a clear sign that during a dispute local rather than national loyalties could be paramount. Nevertheless, the Executive insisted that it could not in any way authorise them to participate.

Finally, at the end of the decade, came another dispute in South Wales which seemed to stretch beyond issues of pay and conditions to touch relationships between union leaders and their rank and file. A special Executive meeting on 9 March 1959 upheld the action of the General Secretary in deposing the officials of the Avon staff branch and of the Port Talbot, Margam and Abbey Joint Committees and exonerating Divisional Officer Alf Vincent whom, it was alleged, the former had 'vilified' in statements to the press. The dispute began with the dismissal of a member of the Avon staff branch, and was taken through several stages of procedure before management finally agreed to refer it to arbitration. The response of the branch and Joint Committee was an immediate strike. Telegrams from the EC to the branch and the Committee arrived instructing them to go back into procedure, but these instructions were only reported to the membership four days later, to be followed almost immediately by a return to work.

The officials concerned conceded that the dispute had been unconstitutional in that it involved defiance of the Executive and the Divisional Officer; for its part the Executive acted in the belief that 'such behaviour was not only calculated to impede the good relationship at present existing between the Employers and the Organisation, but could, if unchecked, lead to a situation where agreements which have proved advantageous to our members would be seriously interfered with'. The situation was reviewed by the Executive at the May quarterly meeting, but it reaffirmed its decision despite local protests that the punishment imposed was unnecessarily harsh.[30] A lot of unfavourable publicity resulted, however, with accusations of 'dictatorship' being levelled both at Douglass and the Executive for deposing the five local officials.[31]

Elections, steel and renationalisation

Eyewitnesses recall that the bitterness of Labour's factional disputes in the 1950s exceeded those even of the 1980s. After his defeat in elections for the Party Treasurership in 1954, an enraged Aneurin Bevan turned on leading union figures who – like Douglass – had withheld their support from him. Stung by the ferocity of this attack Douglass struck back, denouncing 'the luxury of following the path of easy popularity' and suggesting that the Party would 'seriously have to consider whether it can continue to allow his [i.e. Bevan's] activities to go by default'.[32] In this battle between right and left, steel nationalisation was a key socialist commitment.

But a general election was pending. With the big vote imminent, a holding resolution of No. 1 BOC reaffirmed the Division's support for its Executive in resisting denationalisation 'despite the bait thrown out by the employers to workers to buy shares in the denationalised steel companies'.[33] At BISAKTA schools it had been evident for some time that many members anticipated Labour's return to office and the renationalisation of steel. The Conservatives had in fact survived for four years with a small majority, picking up by-election seats to improve their position. Douglass had been a harsh critic of Labour's internal affairs, but had no hesitation in recommending to members that backing Labour meant backing trade union principles.[34] Despite this solidarity, the outcome was depressing: the Conservatives surged to what remains their most impressive share of the poll since 1945, taking 345 seats in the process.

Once the election had gone and Labour had suffered its severe defeat, Douglass returned to his theme: 'if, in the future, the Labour Party is to regain the confidence of a majority of the electorate, the power of those elements responsible for openly dividing the Movement must be severely restricted'.[35]

But for the active membership, the issue of steel nationalisation had not died with Labour's defeat. The following year No. 2 Division BOC called again for it, a view only 'noted' by the Executive; but the appetite had increased, for No. 4 Division now believed that public ownership should be spread across 'a high proportion of [the British economy's] manufacturing and distributing processes'. In 1957 No. 2 Division called on the EC to pledge itself in favour of renationalisation 'in order that the next Labour Government may be clear as to our wishes when they return to office'.[36]

In fact renationalisation was getting further away, not nearer, and with important consequences for industrial relations. Following the denationalisation of the Steel Company of Wales (SCOW), spun off as a separate company from RTB in March 1957, its bosses withdrew from ISTEA, a move with serious implications for the constitution of the Heavy Steel Trade Area Committees. The November 1957 Executive authorised the union's leaders to convey their 'extreme concern' about the withdrawal of SCOW to ISTEA and if necessary to BISF.[37]

The sale of £40m-worth of shares in SCOW had reduced the state's holding in the iron and steel industry to one-sixth that of the defunct

Corporation.[38] Central Office's attitude was conditioned by concern for the industry's prospects: steel was under attack for being unable to bring on stream sufficient capacity to match domestic demand. What if this lack of capacity reflected an investment strike by private sources fearing renationalisation by a future Labour government?[39] The active membership, however, had the bit between its teeth. In 1958 No. 1 Division BOC called on the Executive to reaffirm its position on nationalisation, and No. 2 again called on the Confederation to declare its policy so that the public could learn of its policy agreement with the Labour Party. No. 3 Division went further and referred to the 'anti-nationalisation' speeches of the steel 'bosses', suggesting that a trade union gathering be convened by BISAKTA to rally support for the contrary view and assist Labour.[40]

When the 1959 BOCs met, No. 1 Division had not shifted from its view. It called again for a policy statement to 'set all doubt at rest' as to BISAKTA view and to repudiate the views of the 'steel barons'. The Executive reacted sharply: there could be 'no justification for any doubt remaining about the Organisation's policy regarding the renationalisation of the Iron and Steel Industry'.[41]

The sale of SCOW not only threatened the establishment of national standards but also focused fear of redundancy, something rare in recent experience. A special Executive meeting of 30 January 1958 heard that Barrow, Scotland and South-West Wales were the most seriously affected areas. Union leaders were authorised to meet SCOW on the matter and additionally to make approaches to RTB (a meeting was held on 14 May). At a meeting with SCOW on 27 February it emerged that 2000 new jobs would be created as a result of the completion of the Abbey Works (the company's principal plant), news which drew the sting of job losses to some extent.

There had been a conflict between No. 5 and No. 6 Division concerning the attendance of delegates from the latter at the Heavy Steel Trade No. 4 Area Committee following the withdrawal of SCOW from ISTEA. The EC resolved the dispute by amalgamating the Division No. 5 delegates with those from Divisions 4 and 7 to form a No. 4 Area Committee, as had been the practice before the formation of the No. 5 Area Committee. In the case of SCOW the EC heard on 22 May 1959 that a special committee, resembling a Heavy Steel Area Committee but handling matters only at the company, had been proposed to the company, but by the end of the year no positive reply was forthcoming.[42]

In other respects BISAKTA relations with employers were good. During the 1950s the amount of advertising in *Man and Metal* by BISF member companies tended to grow.[43] With recession thought to be damaging the re-election chances of the Conservative Party in 1959 there was speculation that steel interests might be planning to run anti-nationalisation campaigns, though the BISF's *Man and Metal* ads did not have this character. Douglass admired the cohesion of the BISF under the 'redoubtable' Sir Andrew Duncan, whom he credited with fusing the disparate steel interests into one unified structure. After Duncan passed from the scene in 1958 Douglass was less sure, citing the 'spasmodic and uncoordinated introduction of pension schemes' as evidence of division among the steel firms. Now with the defection of SCOW there was division in national negotiations as well.[44]

In April 1959 the Chancellor of the Exchequer introduced a budget characterised by cuts in income and purchase tax. These were inevitable counter-recessionary steps in the era of pump-priming, but they also had the effect of boosting Conservative popularity. Labour's proposal to renationalise steel was published the same month,[45] and *Man and Metal* clearly directed readers towards a Labour vote, recalling that the give-away budget of 1955 had been followed by emergency austerity measures, which history seemed to be repeating itself. But Labour crashed even more spectacularly than in 1955, leaving the government to command the Commons with a 100-seat majority. For BISAKTA this had two immediate consequences. Steel nationalisation seemed to recede into the distance, and for many Labour thinkers became part of the ideological baggage the Party had to shed if it was ever to recover power. Internally, fire was turned against the left as the scene was set for Gaitskell's great conference confrontations of 1959–61. In the immediate aftermath of the 1959 defeat, *Man and Metal* reflected the general melancholy, bitterly regretting that the 'political cohesion' of the unions had been shattered by MPs, and noting the electoral reverses suffered by Michael Foot and Ian Mikardo, two prominent figures on the left.[46]

Recession returns

In 1956 it seemed that however much steel output might expand, domestic demand would stay ahead of it. In the national press this was fairly freely interpreted as the outcome of decisions made by a conservative industry. At this date BISAKTA itself made no public criticisms of the investment plans of the employers, though in Parliament the first doubts were starting to be audible.[47] That autumn brought the Suez crisis, which for BISAKTA represented above all a threat of disruption of production. An industry struggling to meet burgeoning home demand (and responsible by 1956, with engineering, for 50 per cent of the value of exports) was naturally frantic at the prospect of oil rationing when this fuel powered 40 per cent of ingot output.[48]

In 1957 a difference of opinion was aired between the Board and the BISF, each of which had recently reported on prospects and plans for steel.

In the BISF view the Board had over-estimated likely demand for steel and tinplate in 1962; but at that time the Board was already looking for additional modern strip capacity to come on stream to meet this expected demand, and it – not the Federation – was the most influential interest group.

The Tinplate Delegate Conference in 1957 registered its concern at the impending closure of a large number of handmills, calling for all necessary steps to achieve employment for members at cold reduction plants.[49] Some 690 men faced redundancy from Pontardawe and Gorseinon:[50] it was a test of BISAKTA's attitude towards modernisation, complicated by the fact that huge demand for the product had kept the handmills in operation for years beyond expectations. A 1958 report saw little future for the mills beyond the end of the following year, and the union sadly acquiesced, arguing only that production should be maintained where closure would devastate the local community. Its general stance was that most energy should be concentrated on prodding the government towards promoting industrial diversity.

But tinplate's sectoral woes were now absorbed in general recession. 1958 brought the lowest output since 1954, a fall of no less than 2.13 million tons of crude steel which reduced Britain's performance to 19.57 million tons; though there was a recovery in 1959, that year's output of 20.19 million tons was still below the 1957 figure. The impact on present hopes and future expectations was severe. By autumn 1958 the downturn in trade was sufficient to cause doubts to be raised over the Board's forecast of twenty-nine million tons of demand by 1962. And yet on 18 November the fateful decision to sanction the Board's recommendation for two strip mills was announced in the Commons by the Minister of Power, Lord Mills. The authorisation envisaged a half-million-ton initial capacity for sheet and tinplate at the Newport site of Richard Thomas & Baldwin, and a similar expansion of capacity for sheet and light plate by Colville's Ltd at Ravenscraig.[51] The bizarre timing of the strip-mills announcement could be presented as far-sightedness. At the time minds were dominated by the much more immediate experience of recession. Britain entered 1959 with its capacity utilisation of steel and iron at 76 per cent or worse. BISAKTA attributed the slowdown to a government credit squeeze, the impact of which was proving difficult to reverse: restrictive measures pushed unemployment up by a quarter of a million in 1958, and steel unemployment rose fivefold.[52] The union was also unenthusiastic about the industry's response, though BISF – under pressure from nationalisers who motivated their plans for steel on its commanding position in the UK economy – was starting to argue that far from being in control, it was an industry which depended on the demand generated by others.

Notes

1 Harry Douglass (1902–78) – who had become a member of the British Steel Smelters' Association at the age of thirteen – was appointed Assistant General Secretary in August 1945. He was a melter and member of Eston Grange No. 1 branch. He rose to be a member of the Executive and was appointed Organiser for the reconstituted No. 7 Division in 1935, achieving Divisional Officer status in the same Division in 1941. As General Secretary he was immediately elected to the TUC General Council and joined its Finance and General Purposes Committee and its Economic Committee, of which he later became chairman. In his retirement year (1966) he became chairman of the TUC. He was also a member of the Department of Scientific and Industrial Research Council and (in 1962) a member of the National Economic Development Council. He was knighted in the 1964 New Year's Honours List and received a life peerage in 1967, taking the title Lord Douglass of Cleveland. In 1954 he was elected President of the International Metalworkers' Federation.

2 See for example 'Notes and Comments', *Man and Metal* (October 1954), which trenchantly defends a recent TUC decision not to hold joint ICFTU/WFTU talks.

3 'The vampires of disruption work hard and trade unionists slumber when they should be attending branch meetings'. *Man and Metal* (January 1956).

4 Using, *inter alia*, the pages of *Man and Metal*.

5 From the start Davies had made his mark as a thinker about industrial prospects. He was the moving spirit behind the Sheet Operatives' Discussion Society at his native works of Richard Thomas & Baldwin (RTB) in Ebbw Vale. He was also a qualified music teacher.

6 Thomas (1894–1971) had joined BISAKTA on entering the steel industry in 1924. He was for many years secretary of Margam 2 and rose to be President of the Executive Council (EC) in 1943. When he retired at the end of 1960, Thomas had been elected to that body on a record nine consecutive occasions. He was noted for his local voluntary work and was awarded an MBE in 1961.

7 A.H. ('Alf') Braddock was a branch secretary for thirty-three years. When he was first made secretary of Cargo Fleet No. 2 in 1927 there were two branches and 175 members in his own branch. Branch membership had quadrupled two years later. He was elected to the Executive in 1942, becoming President of the EC in 1948, and at the time of his award had been a member of the Teesside Joint Committee since 1927. He became President for the second time in 1965.

8 J. Vaizey, *The History of British Steel* (1974), 166.

9 Apart from tinplate the only exception to this rosy picture was heavy plate, where there was an excess (thought to be temporary) of demand over supply. The shortages brought a great deal of unfavourable publicity to the employers, but Douglass was sympathetic, commenting that it would be 'unfortunate had the industry allowed itself to be stampeded into laying down additional plate mills to meet a transient need . . .', *Man and Metal* (February 1954). Here was a union leader who would not lobby for new investment regardless of the circumstances.

10 The troubled tinplate sector bore the brunt early in 1953, when no less than 5000 tinplate workers were made redundant. Of these 1250 were transferred to other tinplate mills, and 1850 found other work. By November of that year only 138 were registered unemployed, while tinplate mills due to open were expected to take 550 workers on (House of Commons, 3 December 1953). For many older workers the impact of redundancy was softened by grants from the Tinplate Labour Fund, established in 1946 and funded by an employers' donation of 1d per box of tinplates produced. In November 1954 the value of the fund exceeded £500,000.

11 *Man and Metal* (January 1955). This was a view diametrically opposed to that of nationalisation advocates, whose hopes were rising in this election year (see below).

12 At the Midland Iron and Steel Wages Board, the Board chairman confidently forecast that it would not be affected in any way by nationalisation; at denationalisation the Operatives' Secretary (Sir Lincoln Evans) contrasted the political dispute over ownership with the fact that Board relations had not been affected 'in the slightest degree' (E. Taylor, *The Better Temper*, 1976, 32).

13 House of Commons, 22 February, 23 November 1954.

14 Vaizey, *op. cit.*, 156.

15 A £ which would buy 20s in October 1951 had an internal purchasing power of only 18s 5d in May 1955 and 17s 7d in January 1956, when the new Retail Price Index was launched. (House of Commons, 20 June 1955, 22 March 1956.)

16 See Burn, *op. cit.*, 592ff.

17 BISAKTA's members in the heavy steel trade (coke and iron making, melting and primary rolling) convened annually to discuss elements in the pay award.

18 'Notes and Comments', *Man and Metal* (December 1957).

19 *Reports* (1957), 121.

20 *Reports* (1959), 190. The number of firms without schemes was noted with concern, and continuous review decided upon.

21 *Reports* (1960), 28–9. Douglass was instructed to approach the BISF again over recalcitrant employers.

22 *Man and Metal* (January 1954).

23 *Reports* (1954).

24 *Reports* (1956), 122.

25 Dissatisfaction still persisted over the date from which the increased earnings were due to apply.

26 *Man and Metal* (August 1954).

27 A major AEU stoppage in early 1964 was an example of how little the Organisation could do when its members were unable to work because of an external dispute. It ended only on 1 February after 400,000 tons of output had been lost, and at a cost of £1,500,000 in lost wages. So frequent had this experience become that there was a standard reference point, in the shape of a 1961 Executive ruling, for occasions when advice was sought by members as to how they should act when members of another organisation were on strike at their works. For an example of the decision being prayed in aid, see 'SCOW-AUBTW Dispute – Margam and Port Talbot Supervisory Branch' (*Reports*, 1967, 140).

28 Reproduced in *Man and Metal* for August 1956.

29 The Report of the Court of Inquiry admonished both parties to the dispute, the employers for not energetically seeking a new agreement and the craft unions for not using local machinery once the national agreement had lapsed. *Report of the Court of Inquiry appointed by the Minister of Labour and National Service to Inquire into the Dispute between the Iron and Steel Trades Employers' Association and the National Joint Trade Unions' Craftsmen's Iron and Steel Committee* (Cmnd. 9843, August 1956).

30 It was finally lifted in August 1962.

31 Douglass noted that the deposed Joint Committee Chairman stood as a communist candidate in the 1959 municipal elections.

32 *Man and Metal* (October 1954).

33 *Reports* (1955), 120.

34 *Man and Metal* (May 1955). Much of his critique of the 1951–5 government related not to steel policy but to the scrapping of controls, accompanying which had been a sharp acceleration in the cost of living fuelled by inflationary tax cuts.

35 *Man and Metal* (June 1955). A key Labour response to the defeat, the Wilson Report on Party Organisation, was viewed as irrelevant and (in a scarcely veiled jibe at Harold Wilson) 'a tool for personal advancement'.

36 This too was only noted, however (*Reports*, 1957, 123).

37 *Reports* (1957), 232. Correspondence followed, none of it of any comfort.

38 House of Commons, 28 March 1957.

39 This fear is aired in 'Notes and Comments' (the editorial column of *Man and Metal*) for August 1957.

40 It was resolved that no action be taken. A further resolution from the Division suggested that BISAKTA convene a conference of relevant union executives to draw up a plan for the publicly owned industry 'in such a manner as will clearly indicate to the workers what we mean by Public as against Private Enterprise' (*Reports*, June 1958, 133).

41 *Reports* (1959), 136. This BOC also called for compensation to be given at the share value at the time of nationalisation, an opinion the EC only noted, regarding this as a matter for the future Labour Government. In October 1957 *Man and Metal* had published without comment a BISF analysis which purported to demonstrate there was a wide dispersal of steel-share ownership, with small shareholders to the fore.

42 *Reports* (1959), 254. The proposal was in effect to put the No. 6 DO in the same position as the General Secretary at the head of the heavy steel trade, and below him a miniature version of the national structure. October 1964 – the same month which saw the return to office of a Labour government committed to nationalise steel – saw the expiry of three months' notice given by SCOW of withdrawal from the STB and the Galvanising and Conciliation Board.

43 The character of these ads was not purely industrial: there were profiles of senior employees as well. Nor was it just BISF members: SCOW placed its Chairman's statement on the annual report several times in the late 1950s.

44 See Douglass's (misleadingly titled) article 'Steel Nationalisation', *Man and Metal* (December 1958).

45 *Steel and the Nation – Labour's Plan* argued that the industry was inadequately supervised and controlled in the interests of the country. However, it made no critique of the strip-mills decision of 1958 (see below).

46 'Notes and Comments' (October 1959).

47 See for example the exchange of 26 January 1956 between Austen Albu (Labour) and Peter Thorneycroft, President of the Board of Trade.

48 There was temporary use of the despised fuel creosote pitch to make up the short-fall.

49 *Reports* (1957), 194.

50 Though tinplate employment fell by 2400 in the first nine months of 1957, only half of those affected failed to find work, an indication of the general buoyancy of the labour market at this time (House of Commons, 31 October 1957, 12 February 1958).

51 This decision is the most condemned investment in UK steel history. Remarkably, it was made at a time when the government was not yet in a position to estimate the cost of Spencer's Newport project (soon to be known as Llanwern); it contained a blank cheque in respect of construction costs at both locations; and it envisaged an over-capacity of Scottish sheet which it was 'hoped' would attract user industries to Scotland. The trade unionists of the time deserve more credit than they have had, however. The STUC (with BISAKTA influential in its councils), while grateful for the announcement, emphatically combatted the notion that the presence of strip capacity would of itself do the job, and called for additional intervention to tackle Scottish unemployment, then twice the English level.

52 2672 in January 1958; 12,808 in January 1959 (House of Commons, 4 March 1959).

3

From slump to boom

Harry Douglass (1960–6)

'Let no one mistake tolerance and co-operation for weakness.'

Facing the 1960s

The huge Conservative triumph at the 1959 polls might conceivably have led to a drive to divest the state of the remainder of its holdings in steel. Instead, the Conservatives used Richard Thomas & Baldwin (RTB, the state's largest remaining stake in steel) and generous aid to Colville's as a means of gaining new capacity. When the Iron and Steel (Financial Provisions) Bill to authorise these capital loans was laid before parliament in February 1960, the irony was not lost on some Tory backbenchers. The union could, however, derive considerable satisfaction from 'the extent to which the principle of State assistance to industry is now accepted by a Conservative Government'.[1]

But Tory backbenchers were to taste a little more blood yet with the cut-price sale of the Llanelly (*sic*) Steel Co. to Duport in July 1960. Douglass's frustration over the way ownership and not performance in steel came to the fore was increasingly public.[2] But then came the battle for Whiteheads. This Newport works, formerly associated with RTB, was separated from it at denationalisation. In 1963 Stewarts and Lloyds bid for it, but their bid was trumped by RTB, now the biggest remaining state steel asset. RTB's success caused consternation on the Tory right and raised doubts about the government's continued commitment to state sales.

The union had approached the 1960s with some optimism, relieved that the industry had now completely emerged from recession, anticipating demand of 24 million tons and sure that there was a capacity of 25.5 million tons.[3] Output in 1960 vaulted over the highest annual level so far (1957) to

41

reach 24.7 million tonnes[4] of crude steel. Production had risen in just one year by more than 4 million tonnes, and home demand by over 3 million tonnes. Two new giant plants were being built in Scotland and Wales: the Queen opened the new Llanwern Works in October 1962. There was technical advance too: in 1958, continuous casting became possible at Barrow Steel, after six years of experimentation, while four years later the first of the electric arc furnaces, which were to make Templeborough the biggest such plant in the world, was opened.

Then, just as suddenly as it had stabilised, steel production wobbled. By the end of 1961 2.25 million tonnes of output had been lost and production was below 1956 levels. The grim impact of this on men and profits led unions and industrialists to make common cause. Industrial leaders lamented that they could not rely on steady economic growth when making their plans, that several turns of the economic cycle would occur during the life of a plan to build a major plant – and of course several were in progress at this point. Douglass backed them vigorously through the BISAKTA media. Credit restrictions (the Macmillan government's favourite fine-tuning instrument) and tax rises, with their deflationary impact, were the despair of those – employers or union officers – who wanted to plan ahead. Steel suffered twice over, as purchasers bought steel when credit was cheap, and destocked when interest rates were high.

It fell to Douglass to present the General Council's report on the dismal economic outlook to the 1961 Trades Union Congress. He used it to excoriate Chancellor of the Exchequer Selwyn Lloyd for his indifference to the unions and to negotiation machinery and for his promotion of a pay pause, while spelling out the terms on which the union movement might be prepared to co-operate with him in future. He also took the opportunity to contrast the economic progress made by the Common Market countries with the slow growth of output at home.[5] Only in the following year, when Macmillan cashiered half his cabinet and installed an expansionary Chancellor in the ample shape of Reginald Maudling,[6] did the macro-economic circumstances start to change.

This new phase of 'go' took time to take effect. Douglass looked back on 1962 as 'calamitous', especially for the heavy end, and with good reason. *Metal Bulletin*, that authoritative monitor of developments in the industry, identified twenty works which closed between 1957 and 1963, half of them with iron-making plant. Only in August 1963 did output rise above the levels of early 1961. What a contrast, observed the General Secretary, with the steady expansion in France and Germany, where the state took a significant role both through extensive direct ownership and through planning! At the

1963 Trades Union Congress he developed this theme further, defending the General Council's decision to participate in the newly launched tripartite NEDO Council ('Neddy') against critics who saw it as collaborationism, and urging that planning was the only possible alternative to unemployment. The unions, he declared, 'must fight [for] their conception of planning whatever government is in power'. As time passed, Douglass grew ever more enthusiastic about 'Neddy' and what it represented. He saw it as the best hope of avoiding 'stop-go'; it was 'as a result of trade union and independent opinion, to sweep the nonsense of a free-for-all into the dustbin of history'.[7]

By 1964 the steel industry was clearly recovering. 1964 and 1965 were both years of record output, and when the cycle eventually turned down the dip was much shallower than that of 1961–3. Between December of that year and February 1964 the BISF felt able to revise its output forecast of 24.5 million tonnes upward by a further one million tonnes. The powerhouse behind this recovery was booming domestic demand, and it was an upswing which was almost to keep the Conservatives in office after October's general election. But before the New Year was many months old the first signals of what was to be a full-scale crisis in the country's balance of payments were starting to appear. In the case of steel there was great cause for concern in the burgeoning sale of imported steel at prices way below those asked on the home market of the exporting countries – dumping in other words. In June 1964 the BISF took the unprecedented step of filing a formal application for anti-dumping duties with the Board of Trade. This led to no immediate action, and it was only with the arrival of Labour in office in October that a 15 per cent surcharge on a wide variety of goods, including iron and steel products, was introduced.

Reshaping the Organisation

As the 1960s began, the generation which had guided BISAKTA since the World War II was ready for retirement. In February 1961 John Lang ended fifteen years as No. 1 Divisional Officer, to be succeeded by John Irvine.[8] In November it was the turn (after seventeen years!) of No. 3 Division's W.E. ('Bill') Stead.[9] In May 1963 they were followed by A.E. ('Alf') Vincent, No. 6 Divisional Officer,[10] and ten months later by Jack Senior, who had the same rank in No. 2 Division.[11] In June 1964 came the turn of No. 4 Divisional Officer Joe Profitt,[12] who was shortly followed by Arthur Griffiths, the Divisional Officer of No. 7 division.[13]

The composition of the membership to be represented by the new full-time officers was also changing. Membership at Fords, for example, lapsed in 1964.[14] In the industry as a whole, administrative, technical and clerical staff as a percentage of metal manufacturing employees rose from 13.7 per cent to 18.9 per cent in the ten years to 1958. The existence of some 104,000 people who might potentially be BISAKTA recruits was exercising many minds. The public perception of BISAKTA tended to be of an organisation of process workers, and numerically they still dominated. Yet BISAKTA had organised separate staff branches since the rupture with the National Union of Clerks (NUC) in 1937.[15] Twenty years on, the focus for BISAKTA staff aspirations was the Clerical, Laboratory and Supervisory Staff Conference, which in 1958 called for 'restrictive clauses' in the staff agreement to be removed to allow all staff grades to be brought into the Organisation wherever it was the major negotiating body.[16] The following year it revisited the issue, forecasting correctly that the advent of automation would swell the numbers of staff employees and urging 'a more persuasive means to organise such people within our Association, thereby avoiding what could become a serious undermining of the structure of the Confederation'.[17] In 1960 the Conference shifted the angle of attack, urging greater attention by branch officials and by divisional organisers to the problem of recruitment.[18] It also broadened its interests, seeking a thirty-five-hour week for staff, a uniform system of salary scales, hours, holidays and conditions for clerical grades and, crucially, national negotiations.[19]

Douglass reported to the February 1964 EC that he had had discussions with the General Secretary of the Clerical and Administrative Workers' Union (CAWU) regarding the membership it had established in some sectors of the steel industry. CAWU had made proposals to the Organisation which the latter had found unacceptable. Having rejected them, the Executive considered the possibility of appointing a special organiser to deal with staff but rejected this too, unconvinced that it would result in 'a satisfactory solution'. Its alternative approach was to lodge a claim for an extra week's holiday for supervisory or clerical staff, and to approach the ISTEA director on the problems of staff organisation 'in the light of existing evidence'.[20]

This did not deter the Staff Conference. That year it called for the establishment of staff area committees, with representation to a national committee, aimed at synchronising salary claims and establishing national standard working conditions. This the EC dismissed as impractical, but it accepted another, calling for Clause 2 of the national agreement to be 'deleted or amended', the aim being to secure 100 per cent membership of BISAKTA. It met ISTEA on this issue on 16 July 1964 and again on 21 October, in a meeting delayed by the general election. After further meetings the union still had not achieved any shift in the position of the employers. An unyielding letter received during the February 1965 EC proved the last straw, the Executive concluding that no purpose would be served by more discussion and opting instead to refer the matter of renegotiation of agreements to the imminent Staff Conference.

When this conference met in May it demanded that the employers be given three months' notice of termination of the Machinery of Negotiation Agreements applying to Section (j) (see Chapter 1), and the Executive concurred. In November it was informed that the agreements had been terminated in view of the lack of employer interest in revision. It retained control over events, however, by only noting a resolution from the influential Cleveland staff branch calling for a London Conference of Section (j) representatives to be convened before any new meetings with the employers were held. There matters rested until they exploded in a new form after steel renationalisation.

In 1963 a request was received from the Clyde Area Joint Committee to publish redundancy agreements in *Man and Metal*. Douglass's response, ratified by the Executive, reveals the way that unions of this era continued to work. It was, he insisted, the policy of the union to make this information available, but at branch meetings and not through the journal. The minutes record the Executive's view that publication, which might quite possibly increase readership, 'could well diminish the attendance at branch meetings'.[21] Nevertheless, a major step towards improving communications was taken in January 1964, when *Man and Metal* was launched in a new quarto format on art paper.

In other ways as well BISAKTA sought to improve the level of services it offered the membership. Deduction of contributions at source (the 'check-off') offered considerably greater security of income to the Organisation and the possibility of much greater confidence in planning. In November 1966 ISTEA agreed in principle not to influence its members for or against the check-off, leaving local management and unions free to agree on its application.

Even before this, representation was at a continually high level. The union's legal services dealt with thousands of cases each year. They won a spectacular case in December 1962 at the Durham Assize on behalf of G.E. Sidey, a Consett slinger. Sidey's claim for compensation for an industrial injury had been greeted with extensive libels from the company, which had forced him into two years' litigation.[22] Yet for all the rejoicing over resolving a case like this, the union felt deeply the contrary tug of the consequences of accidents. It was rightly proud of the record of the legal services in recovering compensation from employers after accidents – £19,000 for a young South Wales member left paralysed in the spring of 1965 broke all records – yet it continually acknowledged and urged that the solution was safe working and not monetary payments, which could never put things right.

Those whom convalescence could help still had access to Larkhill, where BISAKTA had gratefully raised a memorial to commemorate Philip Murray, late USWA President, the donor of $10,000 ten years before. In 1958 Lancashire Steel Manufacturing Co. of Irlam had furnished a splendid addition to the complex in the form of a Summer House. Yet the original structure was more than a century old and showing its age, and extensive damage by the elements in 1962 brought home this fact unavoidably. Despite being pronounced in sound condition by the Ministry of Works, Larkhill had in fact been built directly on shale rock, and it was these foundations which were now relentlessly slipping away. Two surveys confronted the union with the unpalatable truth that the place was beyond repair. And so in May 1963, the Executive examined plans prepared by H. Hubbard Ford and authorised the beginning of a new building.[23]

Educational topics continued to feature prominently in *Man and Metal*, with news of WEA affairs; signs of a lack of interest among BISAKTA members were deplored. But real developments in the Organisation's education programme would have to await a change of national leadership. Some of the membership, however, were still thinking about constitutional change. In 1964 both the No. 1 and No. 7 BOCs renewed their pleas for an annual national conference, though in the former case there was an attempt to pre-empt criticism by conceding that such gatherings should not impair the autonomy of the Executive. That same year No. 6 Division BOC called for all in the steel and tinplate industries to be organised by BISAKTA and for the EC to pursue the matter 'with every vigour'. The view that industrial unionism would be desirable was widely held, and not only in the union: that June the TUC convened an Iron and Steel Conference to discuss possible improvements in relationships among the unions: BISAKTA, the British Roll Turners and the National Union of Blastfurnacemen (NUB) were to attend. There was no immediate outcome.

Pay and conditions

The question of a national redundancy scheme had been raised with the BISF in the 1950s, at which time the employers took their traditional view that it was a matter for each individual firm. But the urgency with which such a demand was pressed would clearly depend on the economic circumstances. Pressure from the rank and file was felt again in 1963, as fears of unemployment mounted during the back end of a severe recession which had brought substantial membership losses.[24] Efforts the same year to pressurise Midland

Wages Board and Sheet Trade Board employers to concede a national redundancy scheme proved unavailing, though a chink of light emerged when heavy steel trade employers asked for further time to consider the idea. And indeed there was still some doubt about the urgency with which steelworkers themselves viewed the claim. The Executive was quite prepared to press it, but told branches that it had a lower priority than winning better holidays.[25] The need for a national redundancy scheme was acknowledged in Labour Party policy, and legislation – the Redundancy Payments Act – was introduced by the new government in 1965. This at least put a floor under some of the arrangements in steel, where problems continued even at this late date when men were not fully redundant but working at reduced capacity, a particular problem in Scotland and the north-east.

Other parameters of industrial relations were also changing. The Industrial Training Act, 1964, inaugurated a new era in workplace skills. Charles Williams, Chairman of Parkgate Iron & Steel Co. and also of the BISF Training Committee, was appointed Chairman of a new Iron and Steel Industry Training Board (ISITB). BISF employers were well in advance of their counterparts in other industries, having sustained a Training Committee since 1948. BISAKTA joined them in hoping that the new board would build on the voluntary machinery established over the last sixteen years. When it first met in July 1964 the ISITB numbered Dai Davies and the No. 5 Divisional Officer, Ernie Hickery,[26] among its members. They also had the services of Lincoln Evans, still deputy chairman of the Iron and Steel Board, as an assessor. Within a year the ISITB had taken over responsibility for training in 180 companies in 630 establishments with 325,000 employees, its activities to be funded by a £7 per capita levy payable in two instalments from April 1965.[27] Operative and apprentice training were thought to be the areas of greatest need, and that was where activities began.[28] The Board faced serious problems. The steel industry embraced a large number of jobs, and a real challenge was posed by the fact that so little was demanded of junior operatives who might with luck and in time graduate to the most responsible positions (melter, roller), where immense skills were traditionally needed. It would in the future not be enough to expect knowledge to be picked up en route through the promotion lines, and so the ISITB would have to devise the means to impart a broad-based training early in working life.

But progress in pay is the ultimate test of a union's ability to deliver a higher standard of living. For BISAKTA the key pay agreement in these years was the Melters' Brown Book, a source of perennial frustration. With grievances mounting, the union finally gave ISTEA one month's notice of termination of this set of agreements on 11 March 1965. Faced with an absolute refusal by the employers to consider new arrangements, the Executive opted to process one case in each of the HST divisions through the procedure. On 16 and 17 September the two sides met again and were able to resolve grievances at Round Oak, Cargo Fleet and Redbourne (though not at Hawarden Bridge or in the Lanarkshire Works); on the substantive issue of the Brown Book itself, however, they remained apart, and ISTEA was served notice that the union side felt it had no alternative to pursuing local negotiations where the earnings of the melters warranted revision. The employers, for their part, indicated that they were still attempting to compile an acceptable national agreement. At branch level frustration soon bubbled over. In Scotland the melters took industrial action after negotiations stalled. The Executive, however, stayed with its principled view that the Brown Book remained in being until replaced, and declined to give the stoppage official backing.

With this dispute on the boil the union was also frustrated at the refusal of ISTEA to agree to a Heavy Steel working party to consider an increase in wages and a service pay award to craftsmen's mates. In May 1965 it was decided to approach the Minister of Labour, Roy Gunter, to see if he could persuade the employers. This option had previously been unavailable; once public ownership was restored in 1967 ministers would regularly become players in the industrial relations drama.

It is very noticeable from the resolutions passed in 1965 by Area Conferences in particular – and also from those passed by the staff – that ambitions to improve pay and working conditions had broadened considerably. This reflected in part the more favourable political atmosphere after October 1964, and in part expectations that public ownership would soon be restored; it also suggested much greater confidence that employment and membership[29] were now booming, in stark contrast to the recession of only three years earlier. Old ideas were becoming a new orthodoxy: the May 1965 Staff Conference called for branches to submit claims for equal pay for equal work within a centrally and divisionally determined timetable.

But the time was also ripe to shorten working hours. A landmark was reached on 24 November 1965, when ISTEA agreed to bring in the forty-hour week effective from 4 July 1965. After some hiccups it was introduced on time, together with premium payments of 20 per cent for 6 p.m. to 6 a.m. shifts, Mondays to Fridays, for production shift workers (to whom the forty-hour week was not, for the moment, applied). The forty-hour week for craftsmen's mates, craftsmen's labourers, and other workers employed on maintenance conditions was achieved on 7 October. At the same meeting a 5 per cent rate increase was agreed for single shift production workers who benefited neither from the forty-hour week nor from the Premium Payments Agreement.

Midland Wages Board employers at first declined to concede the forty-hour week that year, but finally agreed to introduce it effective from 5 July. This too was coupled with premium payments for production workers on the 6 p.m. to 6 a.m. shift, Mondays to Fridays.[30] The forty-hour week arrived for men on forty-two hours under Sheet Trade Board conditions, effective from 4 July, though with a narrower application than was the case in the other two bargaining units.[31]

The negative side of the Labour experience appeared after the Party had gained a second term of office. The country speedily entered an economic crisis which brought in its wake a pay freeze and then a prices and incomes policy. In 1966 the EC was aware of serious pressure for an annual increase in rates at the BOCs. Only after a long discussion in August was it decided to support the government's proposals for a prices and incomes standstill which lasted until the beginning of 1967. But misgivings were widespread. Douglass was always in the mainstream of TUC opinion – indeed he was one of its principal influences – and he had been one of those who bluntly voiced doubts about the emergency measures of July 1966: they included a wage freeze, which he regarded as impractical.

Political stance

In the dramatic debates which shook the Labour Party after its 1959 defeat, BISAKTA was unequivocal. It said little in public when Gaitskell moved later that year to delete Clause 4 of the Party's constitution: since it usually gave him such strong support this was perhaps a sign of some inner unease. But the vote of the 1960 (Scarborough) conference for unilateral nuclear disarmament was 'out of all proportion to the real feeling in the movement'; and Gaitskell's defiance (which led ultimately to a reversal at the 1961 party conference), received full backing. Douglass admired Gaitskell, whom he saw as a 'virile' leader. However, Gaitskell's last campaign was built on a passionate rejection of Macmillan's proposal to apply for EEC membership, and on this the cautious Douglass had by then reached conclusions which were to guide the Organisation over the next three decades.

After a period of wishful thinking about the European Free Trade Area (EFTA), BISAKTA wasted little time on sentimental expectations that it could ever be on level terms with an increasingly powerful and cohesive Common Market. By the middle of 1961 the Organisation's weight was cast decisively in favour of entry.[32] In 1962 Douglass had to present a balanced case to the Trades Union Congress, where opposition in principle was gathering. He bought time by winning endorsement of the General Council view that a final verdict could not be reached until the terms for Britain's entry were known, but did not conceal from delegates his belief that the EEC was not the cheap-labour rival they believed. The point was that steelworkers – like the miners – simply knew more about the EEC. The General Secretary himself had been a close observer of the ECSC for a decade. And by 1963 the industrial trends were unmistakable. UK steel output had risen 28 per cent in the previous ten years: the corresponding figures for Western Germany, France and Italy were 80 per cent, 76 per cent and 187 per cent. No BISAKTA leader was likely to turn against an economic network which had so powerfully shown itself able to throw up consistent economic perform- ance which converted into higher demand for steel.

A political era came to an untimely end in 1962–3 with the deaths of Jack Jones and Dai Mort. Throughout Labour's turbulent policy debates of the 1950s they had played a part as MPs for Rotherham and Swansea East. Mort had notified his intention to retire at the next election, while Jones met his end in a car crash on 31 October 1962. Great disappointment was felt among the Rotherham branches when the constituency party selected Brian O'Malley of the Musicians' Union as its candidate to replace Jones, and the Phoenix Joint Committee went so far as to propose disaffiliation. The EC, while sharing the resentment of its local branches, counselled that disaffilia- tion would be unwise.[33] Mort died on New Year's Day 1963 after nearly a year of ill-health. The union was no luckier in his Swansea East constituency, where an EC member had been nominated to succeed Mort in a less hurried selection but still failed to carry the day. The local BISAKTA branches were as aggrieved as their Yorkshire comrades.

Three months later pragmatism had set in, with the Margam No. 3 branch suggesting that the new Aberavon MP be adopted as a sponsored candidate and the Swansea Joint Committee proposing that temporary arrangements be made with other sitting Labour MPs until such time as members of the Parlia- mentary Panel were returned to Parliament themselves. That these worries were not confined to areas with a tradition of sponsored representation was signalled when the No. 4 and London Area BOCs called on the Executive to ensure that BISAKTA was represented in the next parliament. Only in 1964 was some relief gained with the news that Donald Coleman[34] of the Abbey Technical Branch had been selected as prospective parliamentary candidate for Neath. Coleman was one of the successful intake of new Labour MPs when the Party returned to office in October, after thirteen years.

Douglass had once harboured severe doubts about Harold Wilson, but he gave Labour emphatic backing in the 1966 election, though *Man and Metal* acknowledged that there were worries in the trade union movement, notably about the 'early warning' provisions in the Prices and Incomes Bill passing through parliament that year. But he was never likely to subordinate union interests to any political party, and he was to level trenchant criticisms of the pay freeze that was to follow so soon on the Prime Minister's second electoral triumph.

Renationalisation of steel

The extent to which the political initiative was shifting to the Labour side was apparent when, in February 1963, Labour entered one of its first debates with Harold Wilson as leader and gave a convincing display of unity behind both Clause 4 and the commitment to renationalise steel. The atmosphere had changed. Whereas in the 1950s it had seemed to be Labour that was backward-looking with its nationalisation proposals, Wilson was now adroitly coupling public ownership with the concept of modernisation. With a general election on the horizon and Labour still committed to restoring public ownership, this issue gained new urgency for BISAKTA. The Executive successfully put a resolution supporting the proposal to restore public ownership before all the 1964 BOCs. There seems still to have been some unease about the Organisation's attitude, and it was in response to requests from the branches at SCOW that it convened a Special Meeting on 1 October. Against the background of a virulent anti-nationalisation electioneering campaign mounted by the employers, BISAKTA now issued a statement.[35]

The statement recalled that thirty years had passed since BISAKTA had first called for public ownership of iron and steel, but reflected that 'agitation based on bygone history' would be futile if lessons had not been learned from it. The thesis of the statement rested on more recent developments, however: whereas the recession of the 1930s had afflicted all countries equally, the impact on Britain of the recession of 1962 had been disproportionate. The statement charged that on the continent, margins were narrower and living standards higher than in the UK, where indeed many steelworkers had suffered unemployment. Despite the fact that 'official strikes have been unknown and unofficial strikes few and far between', despite strenuous efforts to obtain the highest outputs and an unquestioning acceptance of twenty-four-hour and weekend working, EEC countries had raised their production by 94 per cent in 1951–63, a period which had seen British output rise by only 44 per cent. Singling out Germany's much-improved performance, the statement complained: 'whilst Germany now consolidates her claims, we flounder in a sea of uncertainty'.[36]

But the argument now took a surprising turn. The rate of expansion, it was claimed, was determined by the amount of capital and labour available: labour had been wasted by unemployment, while 'there had been too much dependence on Government capital'. This comment could be read as a free-market statement, but was probably intended to castigate the weak investment record of most of the newly denationalised firms after 1953. Lamenting the waste of steelworkers' skills and the failure to provide them with security for their old age, the statement concluded: 'the question is whether a *nationalized* [*sic*] steel industry could have done worse if it tried'.[37]

It was a pity the statement did not have a greater impact. BISAKTA's was an unusual, authoritative and distinctive voice. Instead the British public was starting to hear half-baked arguments about over-manning which, with the certainty of water dripping on a stone, were eventually to lead to the catastrophes of the 1980s. In its 'Special Report on Development' for 1964, the Board estimated that UK steel production would hit 27 million tonnes in 1970 on the assumption of a 3 per cent growth rate. Forecasts like these were to become the core of the argument over steel's future for the next twenty years, but of course Britain was on the eve of a period of disappointing growth which was to undermine faith in planning. The board's report envisaged that by 1970 some five million tonnes of capacity would be obsolete, foreseeing a new challenge for employers and unionists alike. But the part of its text which drew headlines in the right-wing press was the implication that over-manning was rife in the industry.[38] In fact output had risen by 31 per cent since 1955 with a constant workforce. Indeed the gross total of almost 300,000 employed in steel disguised a drop of 20,000 in the number of process workers.

In October 1964 Labour was narrowly returned to office with a four-seat majority. BISAKTA welcomed the new government's determination to introduce renationalisation at an early date, though at this point it expected nothing but obstruction from the Opposition parties, which were unexpectedly powerful. Douglass led a TUC delegation to be briefed by Fred Lee, Minister of Power, on 11 December 1964 and was clearly impressed with the pragmatism of his approach.[39] To a Special Meeting of 3 February 1965 Douglass reported that arrangements had been made for a further meeting, this time informal, with the Minister of Power to exchange views on steel nationalisation. The Executive went on to discuss the general principles which ought to be embodied in the Nationalisation Act, but held back from publishing its conclusions.[40] In May it took no view on the 1965 White Paper either. This coyness has drawn substantial criticism, with BISAKTA and the TUC being castigated for having no ideas about the shape of the industry at this particular time.[41] Their public silence was interpreted as a lack of enthusiasm for the project: there were even allegations in the *Sun* (then a Labour paper) that Douglass was lukewarm about nationalisation.[42] Certainly the union leadership had made common cause with the employers over many industrial issues in the long years since denationalisation began, though the statement of autumn 1964 showed that there was a willingness to criticise the performance of the major firms. But the reticence had deeper roots. Douglass (and in this he was supported by his Executive) had an aversion to too close a mixture of trade unionism and politics. This, to him, was the cardinal defect of communism. The job of a union was to react to political initiatives if it had to, but otherwise to have an industrial agenda. The union had no wish to run the proposed nationalised steel industry, but only to prevent such a major change from damaging the interests of those working in the industry. An over-elaborated union position would lead to the Organisation assuming management responsibilities. In the next decade this problem would arise again when future plant configuration moved to centre stage.

The weaknesses of this position were twofold. First, on the principle that nature abhors a vacuum, Labour would seek advice elsewhere if it did not come from the largest union; secondly, a nationalisation of the 1960s was bound to be different in kind from an exercise of the post-war era such as the formation of the Iron and Steel Corporation of Great Britain: new ideas were in the air which had been unimagined in the 1940s.

How the Labour MPs Desmond Donnelly and Woodrow Wyatt held up steel nationalisation, without ever deflecting prime minister Harold Wilson from his ultimate goal once he had a majority, has been ably told.[43] In fact Labour was not to be in a position to renationalise until the March 1966 general election had delivered it a comfortable majority over all other parties and a large cushion against backbench revolt. That done, however, the government moved rapidly, and if BISAKTA was to have an influence it would have to move rapidly too.

The 1966 BOCs in No. 2 and No. 3 Divisions strongly backed the move to restore steel to the public sector, with the former gaining Executive agreement on the need to publicise the case for it. On 14 June, ahead of a new meeting with the Minister of Power, Douglass successfully submitted a paper of comments on nationalisation to a Special Executive for approval. At the regular August meeting the Executive rejected a suggestion that it should form a consultative committee, in the belief that such contacts would have to be channelled through the TUC.[44] But in fact the TUC was already under some pressure from the National Craftsmen's Co-ordinating Committee (NCCC) to persuade it in the direction of at least an element of workers' control, and a change of minister (for Fred Lee had been replaced by the rather more forceful Richard Marsh) meant that the government might well be more receptive to such a proposal. However, there was concern in November when Douglass's exclusion from the Organising Committee to prepare nationalisation was reported. Douglass was by now on the very eve of retirement, but EC members complained of 'the Minister's apparent failure in making the appointments to pay regard to the special position of the Confederation', and decided to seek an early meeting with him.[45] In the end Sidney Harris joined the organising committee of what was soon to become the British Steel Corporation (BSC) – the only shop floor worker who has done so.[46]

The end of the Douglass era

Harry Douglass had been knighted in the New Year's Honours List for 1964. In autumn 1966, shortly before his retirement as General Secretary, he succeeded to the chairmanship of the TUC, a position he continued to hold after his retirement, serving out his full term. In 1967 he was elevated to the House of Lords with a life peerage, taking the title Baron Douglass of Cleveland. Curiously, the Executive minutes for 1966 carry no formal notification of his retirement on the last day of the year. It was to last twelve years.

Waiting not in the wings but increasingly centre stage was the most experienced deputy the Organisation had ever had. Neither friends nor enemies questioned his abilities as a speaker or administrator, and he had proved fearless in exposing any internal wrongdoing. Nor was he just a parochial figure. If Douglass had been a mover and shaker at the TUC, the same could almost be said of Davies at the Labour Party. His many years of continuous service as a member of its National Executive Committee culminated in the chairmanship of Party Conference for the year 1962–3. In this capacity it fell to him to preside over the 1963 (Scarborough) conference, which was widely expected to be the last before the general election. He was also entrusted with delivery of a eulogy to Hugh Gaitskell, who had died the previous January. When the BISAKTA Executive later acclaimed his performance in the chair it was reflecting universal opinion.[47]

This prominence was not only political but international. He presided over the Fifth International Steelworkers' Conference of the IMF in Luxembourg in June–July 1965 and two months earlier had been nominated by the Executive for the position of honorary secretary of IMF's British Section. In September the Executive also authorised him to accept an invitation from the Minister of Labour to join the National Dock Labour Board as a part-time member.[48] The following February he was, unsurprisingly, the only nominee to succeed Douglass as General Secretary and was appointed to that post as of 1 January 1967.[49] The Executive now had to look ahead to the appointment of a new Assistant General Secretary. Jim Diamond was appointed to the post from a shortlist of four that February, and acted in that capacity from August.[50]

Harry Douglass had been the longest-serving General Secretary since Arthur Pugh. Appointed General Secretary in the year denationalisation began, he retired with the industry about to open a new chapter of public ownership. On the debit side, the union may be open to criticism for failing to foresee the neglect of the industry in the long years of private ownership.[51] Was it blinded by Sir Lincoln Evans's position on the Iron and Steel Board, a body Douglass himself joined in a part-time capacity in 1960? There certainly was a tendency to echo the views of the Board and to defend the industry as a whole from the criticism it received when supply was still falling short of demand as late as 1956.[52] With Labour in office again after 1964, Douglass could seem curiously detached from the issue of ownership, for example when he defended the Board's pricing policy as one which balanced profit and efficiency against the social need for employees to stay in work. Yet some of the criticism he has attracted amounts almost to a suggestion that he did not seek to have any influence over the shape of the new BSC:[53] in fact he was far from indifferent, but he had a strict view of where the division of labour lay between unions and companies and was determined not to trespass.

Yet there was a case for the defence of steel's performance, in that the industry as a whole actually exceeded output targets set for the middle 1950s at the start of the decade. As for the employers themselves, in 1957 'Notes and Comments' praised them as far-sighted for their planned expansion of the ore-carrying fleet to seventy-four vessels by 1962. This perfectly illustrates the mood of the time, when the principal problem anticipated was a fight to secure enough supplies to maintain sufficient output. The possibility that demand might fall short of capacity was anticipated by few, and the prospect of UK total ingot capacity reaching 28 million tons by 1962 almost occasioned euphoria.

And after the return of Labour to office in the 1966 election – an event which removed all doubts about steel nationalisation – *Man and Metal* was guarded about BISF's announcement that it would undertake a structural study of the UK industry. This initiative (which was to become the Benson Report) came 'rather belatedly', as the journal observed.[54] It was indeed a deathbed repentance.

Notes

1 'Notes and Comments', *Man and Metal* (March 1960).
2 For a clear exposition of his view that the avoidance of redundancy and the welfare of workers was paramount, see 'Notes and Comments', *Man and Metal* (August 1960).
3 'Notes and Comments', *Man and Metal* (February 1960). Capacity utilisation rose from 75 to 95 per cent during 1959. Among product sectors only sheet gave rise to some concern, with the result that Colville's and RTB agreed to expand sheet capacity at the two new strip complexes then under construction at Llanwern and Ravenscraig.
4 From this date output is given in metric rather than imperial measure.
5 Though in many ways an orthodox advocate of the EEC, Douglass was in some respects unusual in pointing out that hourly wage costs in the ECSC were higher than in the UK. This observation confirmed his view that company profitability brought employee benefits.
6 A man who was 'skilful and courageous' in the eyes of Douglass.
7 'Notes and Comments', *Man and Metal* (January 1964).
8 Lang (1896–1961) was appointed an Organiser in 1942 and became Divisional Officer four years later. During his fifteen years in post he became Chairman of the STUC (in 1950) and was that body's Treasurer for many years; he was also Chairman of the Labour Party's Scottish Council and a member of the Scottish Board for Industry. He played a prominent public role in clinching the Ravenscraig project. He was awarded the OBE in 1951. Tragically Lang died on 3 June 1961 after only three months' retirement.
9 W.E. Stead (1896–1973) joined the Steel Smelters in 1911, became Secretary of Acklam 1 in 1926, and an Organiser in 1936. In 1944 he was appointed Divisional Officer No. 3 Division. When an inquisitive journalist asked him the secret of Sheffield's good industrial relations he replied, 'we always believe in catching our flies with honey, not vinegar'. He was succeeded by Emlyn Roberts.
10 Vincent (1898–1996) had been in the sheet mills at Pontymister before World War I and returned there, still aged only twenty-three, to become a melter after the hostilities. He was made Organiser, No. 2 Division in 1937, moved to No. 5 Division in 1943 and succeeded Douglass as No. 7 Divisional Officer in 1945. In 1950 he moved to No. 6 Division on the retirement of Jack Johns. In this post he was Chairman of the Workmen's Side of the Welsh Tinplate and Sheet Trade JIC and secretary of the Workmen's Side of the South Wales Siemens Steel Board. Colonel Bevan, leader of the Siemens Trade Employers, described Vincent as 'the most fearless man I have ever met'.
11 Jack Senior hailed from the Parkgate Works and was Works Rep. for the Rotherham No. 1 branch. He was appointed an Organiser in No. 2 Division in April 1940 and succeeded Tommy Meehan as Officer in that Division eleven years later. He was awarded an MBE in 1956 and became Vice-chairman of the Northern Regional Board for Industry. In retirement Senior pursued his interests in local government,

joining the Middlesborough Borough Council in 1971 and also serving on the Cleveland County Council. At the age of seventy-five Senior was presented with a Certificate of Merit for Outstanding Voluntary Service by Labour's NEC.

12 Profitt worked at the Britannia Works of Dorman Long & Co. where he was secretary of two different branches. He was appointed organiser in 1942. He succeeded Bob Clarke as Divisional Officer in No. 4 Division in 1953 and became vice-chairman of the Midland Iron and Steel Wages Board. During his period in post he had to handle the decline and disappearance of the Midland malleable iron trade, but also witnessed the rise of the steel and tube industry in Corby.

13 Griffiths spent twenty-three years as a full-time officer, having entered the industry at the age of fourteen, and rose through the Sheet Trade Board to the EC in 1938. In 1941 he was appointed an Organiser in No. 7 Division and became Divisional Officer in 1950. He was awarded the OBE in 1957.

14 See *Reports* (1964).

15 The story is told in Pugh, *op. cit.*, 526–7.

16 *Reports* (1958), 207. The issue was raised in the context of possible renationalisation, but EC members were of the opinion that the matter could not wait until then.

17 *Reports* (1959), 206. The EC noted the resolution, protesting that everything possible was already being done to organise staff.

18 *Reports* (1960), 206–7.

19 A further resolution called for a parallel national agreement to that existing for heavy steel employees. The EC considered these matters were best dealt with locally.

20 *Reports* (1964), 40–1.

21 *Reports* (March 1963), 50.

22 Sidey received £250 damages and an unqualified apology for a letter that had been written with malice. *Man and Metal* (March 1963).

23 The new Larkhill opened in March 1967 (see below).

24 See for example the 1963 Area No. 4 Heavy Steel Conference, which called for the Central Negotiating Committee (CNC) and the Executive to continue to press for a national scheme, and that year's staff conference, which resolved that action should be taken *at national level* (their italics) to ensure that union members be given preference over non-union members in redundancy arrangements.

25 The STB also rejected this claim in 1964.

26 E.H. Hickery (1904–83), entered the steel industry in 1918 and took a one-year scholarship at Swansea University in 1935 on the way to graduating four years later in History, Geography and Economics. He became organiser in No. 3 Division in 1940 and Divisional Officer, No. 5 Division in 1946, and served briefly as National Staff Officer in 1968–9. He was awarded the OBE in 1957.

27 The costs of training rapidly rose: in the year 1966–7 the per capita levy was £18 per employee.

28 Davies became Vice-chairman after his appointment as General Secretary, and was joined as a member by his AGS, Jim Diamond. In 1970 the ISITB was reconstituted

with three members from the Organisation, and the third place was allocated to the newly appointed National Staff Officer, H.A. 'Sandy' Feather.

29 Membership in May 1965 was 130,291, the highest ever recorded. Employment in the iron and steel industry for the week ending 8 May 1965 was 316,090.

30 At the Midland Wages Board, the most contentious issue was the payment of shift premium payments to shift production workers to maintain their differentials. Agreement was finally reached around the principle that these payments be introduced at no extra cost to the employers (Taylor, *op. cit.*, 33).

31 *Reports* (1965), 208–9. Douglass immediately followed up this key advance with a claim to ISTEA for forty-hours worked over a five-day week of eight hours a day, Monday to Friday, with time and a half for Saturday working.

32 The first really unqualified statement to this effect is to be found in 'Notes and Comments' for June 1961. Two months later Douglass himself used the same vehicle to be typically forceful: brushing aside talk of Commonwealth betrayals and complaints of associating with those defeated in the war, he insisted that the coming decision would show whether public affairs were dominated by confidence or fear.

33 *Reports* (March 1963), 14.

34 Donald Coleman (1925–89) was a staff member and metallurgist at the Abbey Works of SCOW. He represented Neath from 1964 until his death. Coleman was PPS to the Minister of State for Wales from 1967 to 1970 and junior whip throughout the 1974–9 Labour government.

35 *Reports* (1964), 258–60.

36 The union's presentation sharply differs from the perceived wisdom. By 1964 there was virtual unanimity that the steel industry was in pretty bad shape, but the analysis of causes by historians includes that of Pryke, *Public Enterprise in Practice* (1981), that 'productivity was low in Britain because plant was over-manned and because the utilisation of equipment was poor' while Dudley and Richardson (*op. cit.*) glibly speak of 'trade unions resistant to technological change'. None of the authors seems aware of the October 1964 statement by BISAKTA – which perhaps explains their failure to address the arguments advanced in it.

37 The possibility of nationalisation if Labour won was, of course a local electoral issue as well. The Hawarden Bridge Joint Committee was angered by 'expensive propaganda' from John Summers, the employer, on behalf of its local Conservative candidate and issued a ringing endorsement of the Labour MP Eirene White and nationalisation. This statement, issued on 3 September 1964, features especially the lack of national sick pay, redundancy or pension schemes.

38 Typical was the *Daily Sketch*: '"Too many workers," says Steel Board'.

39 'They are extremely flexible. They did not ask us there just to tell us what they intend to do but to ask for our ideas.' Quoted in K. Ovenden, *The Politics of Steel* (1978), 89.

40 *Reports* (March 1965).

41 Most forcefully expressed by Ovenden, *op. cit.*, 89ff.

42 *Reports* (June 1965), 132.

43 Ovenden, *op. cit.* (1978), 47–74.

44 *Reports* (September 1966), 203. One rare instance of some thought being given to the shape, rather than the fact, of public ownership is provided by the Staff Conference which, in 1966, called for 'trade union staff workers' to be represented 'on any Boards that control sections of the Industry'. The resolution was noted by the Executive. *Reports* (1966), 225.

45 See next chapter.

46 Sid Harris (Temple 2 Branch), a former Mayor of Rotherham, had served on the Executive for eighteen years, and on the CNC of the HST for nearly thirty years. The organising committee set the tone of the new corporation. The first two appointments were of Lord Melchett, chairman, and Ron Smith, the former General Secretary of the Union of Post Office Workers, who was made board member with special responsibility for advising on the development of personnel, industrial relations and social policy.

47 *Reports* (1963), 235. Davies's performance in the chair at what could have been a difficult Labour conference was praised by *The Scotsman*, which commented on his 'great skill and tact, helped by his own pleasant personality, a ready wit, and a delightful Welsh accent'.

48 His salary for this post was paid into union funds. *Reports* (1967), 12.

49 He was knighted in the New Year's Honours of 1973.

50 Jim Diamond (1924–80) was Assistant General Secretary of BISAKTA from 1967 to 1973, when he took early retirement due to ill-health. He had joined BISAKTA in 1946, been group leader on Coatbridge Town Council and became Organiser of No. 1 Division in 1960. In July 1967, even before taking up his duties as AGS, he joined the ISITB, and that October, Labour's National Executive. After his retirement he served on the Main Board of BSC.

51 In June 1955 *Man and Metal* had commented: 'there appears to be no reason for steelworkers to view the activities of the Board with anything but confidence'.

52 See for example 'Notes and Comments', *Man and Metal* (October 1956).

53 See for example Ovenden, *op. cit.*, 133.

54 'Notes and Comments', *Man and Metal* (June 1966).

4

The heyday of nationalisation
Dai Davies (1967–70)

'We are a Union of the Steel Industry and our members have no
interest outside steel.'

Dai Davies took over the helm of BISAKTA as 1967 began. In many ways he
came to office better prepared than any of his predecessors, having served on
the Executive and – during a long apprenticeship as Assistant General Secretary – held diverse positions in the labour movement.[1] His political profile
before taking office was unusually high.[2] In politics Davies took broadly the
same stance as his predecessor, though he had more opportunities to air his
views. He also represented continuity in that he, like Douglass, favoured
Britain's entry into the EEC. This was not a utopian vision, but rather a gritty
recognition that not much progress was likely to be made outside. Davies was
already a well-known figure before getting the top job, and his arrival coin-
cided with the biggest structural shift in the ownership of steel since World
War II.

Other personnel changes around this time included the retirement of No.
3 Divisional Officer Emlyn Roberts in March 1967,[3] and his replacement by
Alex Hogg.[4] In Scotland, where BISAKTA was at a peak of its influence over
the labour movement, the long-established John Irvine[5] was President of the
STUC for 1967–8, and his Divisional Organiser Arthur Bell chairman of the
Scottish Council of the Labour Party.[6] In South Wales it was all change when
both Ernie Hickery and Jim Williams[7] retired late in 1969. Their successors
were John Foley[8] and Stan Biddiscombe.[9] In No. 4 Division, Jack Gavin[10]
succeeded Alan Potter.[11] The last of this generation to depart was No. 7 Divisional Officer Tommy Watson,[12] in April 1971.

It was a time of other changes too. In 1971 No. 7 Division moved out of Manchester to a new and more transport-friendly location in Knutsford, while No. 2 Divisional Office shifted from its Albert Road premises to Marton Road the following year. *Man and Metal*, another public face of the Organisation, also took on a new appearance. It adopted a new cover and increased use of pictures from 1965, and four years later moved to a full-colour cover.

Nationalisation

The 1967 nationalisation of iron and steel covered fewer firms than that of 1951, but they were much larger: the fourteen firms brought into the new British Steel Corporation (BSC) each had an annual liquid steel output in excess of 475,000 tonnes. Though drawing the line at this level of output left a considerable number of firms in the private sector, the formation of BSC led ineluctably to dissolution of the BISF.[13] And BSC differed from other public bodies created in the post-war era in that it had the responsibility under statute for recommending its own organisation.[14]

What had been the union input into planning the shape of this new public sector body? In 1931 unions had proposed that the existing structure of firms should be dissolved, a suggestion endorsed by the TUC and made by diverse other organisations over the years. In fact this now occurred, though to what extent it was due to union views being pressed is uncertain; even the Benson Report, sometimes dubbed a deathbed conversion proposing rationalisation under private ownership, also implied restructuring. Eventually, indeed, the Iron and Steel Act 1969 dissolved the private companies and transferred their assets to BSC.

The meeting between Minister of Power Richard Marsh and a BISAKTA delegation took place on 14 December 1966, with the union side under Davies's leadership. The unionists' anger that the organising committee lacked practical experience had been partly assuaged with the appointment of Sid Harris (see above) and Ron Smith, but they also insisted that they expected to be consulted before any major decisions on the future structure of the Corporation were reached. This was evidently regarded as a satisfactory outcome, for agreement on the need for 'close liaison' was reported to the EC.[15] In 1967 all BOCs passed an EC resolution welcoming the Iron and Steel Act and the arrangements for close consultation.[16]

On 25 July 1967 the EC met to hear a detailed report from Davies on the preparations for nationalisation, covering grouping of companies, workers' participation, consultation and trade union recognition.[17] The TUC Steel Industry Consultative Committee was now in being and had frequent meetings with BSC on these and other matters (see below). The EC agreed that Davies be nominated to the Iron and Steel Advisory Committee then being established by the Minister of Power,[18] and that the names of appropriate members be forwarded to the TUC for consideration as appointees to BSC's new area boards.[19] EC members had been contacted individually by Davies concerning an NUB proposal that there should be a six-strong joint sub-committee formed by the two unions to deal with matters of common interest arising from nationalisation. Since all these members returned favourable replies, the EC as a whole agreed to the suggestion and appointed the President, General Secretary and Assistant General Secretary as members.[20]

But this idea was now absorbed within a larger one: all the nationally recognised unions at BSC were invited by the TUC to compose a national committee which would be available for collective consultation. This body, the Trade Union Congress Steel Industry Consultative Committee (TUCSICC, formed in April 1967), speedily became the means whereby the unions collectively also negotiated non-wage improvements in the remuneration package of BSC employees. TUCSICC, which was staffed by the TUC,[21] was throughout its lifetime chaired by the BISAKTA General Secretary of the day, and BISAKTA, being the largest organisation in the industry, always had the largest delegation. BISAKTA was vigilant in ensuring that TUCSICC did not involve itself in pay negotiations, for such a development would have cut at the heart of its representational system.

TUCSICC was due to be informed in March 1968 about the names of workers' representatives on the Group Area Boards, but by that date the delay in naming names and the method of appointment were already giving cause for concern.[22] When the twelve appointments were made they included the names of Ward Griffiths and Cyril Whur, both Executive Council members, each of whom was obliged to resign his position as a result.[23] The full list included Jack Sturman and Sid Waring (Midland group); Jim Slater (Northern & Tubes group); Eddie Griffiths and Cyril Whur (Scottish and Northwest group); and Ward Griffiths (South Wales group). It was a huge breakthrough for worker representation, certainly suggesting that the new BSC would be a different type of public corporation.[24] This first batch of employee directors took up their posts in April 1968. It seemed to vindicate *Man and Metal*'s bold expectations of the previous year that BSC would be 'not merely a turning point in the development of public ownership – it also promises to be a brave experiment in industrial relations'.[25]

While there was considerable resistance to the scheme from management, there was also disquiet on the union side. This took two forms, with some critics arguing that the employee directors were representing management views to the unions, and others (like No. 1 Division BOC) calling for a system of elections for workers' representatives on Boards. The Executive's response to the second group was to open the door to nominations from the branches when future vacancies should occur; it was not, of course, in a position to compel BSC to accept these nominations, as subsequent events were to prove. An early fruit of this shift of policy came two years later, when the branches in the appropriate BSC groups were allowed to make nominations directly to the TUC.[26] By then No. 3 Division BOC was effectively calling for an extension of the scheme, wanting the Executive to insist on 'workers' representation and joint consultation at all levels'.

The first group of critics had identified an important flaw in the scheme. BSC's approach to removing conflicts of interest had been to insist that employee directors stand down from their union positions. However, those trade unionists who took the view that employee directors embodied a form of collaboration interpreted this as a suspicious sign, and the authors of the scheme later acknowledged that this stipulation was a mistake.[27] By 1969 the employee directors themselves were persuaded that they should be allowed to hold non-negotiating union positions, but as yet they were unable to convince the Steel Committee.

Even after the 1970 changes to the scheme, the EC was careful to keep lines of communication to the employee directors within the agreed margins, refusing a request from one of their number, Donald Sutherland, to attend the No. 1 BOC on the grounds that this was an 'essentially private' event.[28] New nominations were requested by BSC in 1972, and this time passed through the TUCSICC secretary. The ten new directors, appointed in 1973 to product divisions, were allowed to continue in union office and participate in consultative meetings. They included Jim Slater and Cyril Whur (General Steels), Jim McLaren (Strip Mills) and Alan White and Ken Clark (Special Steels), the last two of whom were Executive Members.[29] At this time employee representation also reached the highest levels with the appointment to the Main Board of Ward Griffiths, who was joined by Jim Diamond on his retirement as Assistant General Secretary.

The new bargaining agenda

As economic conditions deteriorated in 1966 and 1967, membership fell sharply[30] and fears of unemployment and insecurity again mounted. For the individual member the first approach of recession usually took the form of declining earnings, so at meetings with ISTEA in December 1966 and February 1967 the opportunity was taken to canvass a claim for a guaranteed wage. The ISTEA did agree to give 'urgent consideration' to the union view and to conduct an 'intensive study' of ways of increasing security of employment. However, it insisted that its deliberations would be coupled with 'a review of wages systems, manning and flexibility in the use of labour arising from the use of such techniques as work study, job evaluation, etc.'.[31]

The Melters' Sliding Scale had for decades been at the heart of collective bargaining in the industry. But it was a relic of the previous epoch in an era of ever more centralised negotiations, and the employers were increasingly determined to be rid of it. In February 1967, as the decks were cleared for a new era of public sector bargaining, the Executive endorsed the recommendation of its National Negotiating Committee to accept abolition. But the best guide to the development of opinion on pay among the members continued to be the heavy steel trade Area Conferences. These met annually and passed a large number of resolutions relating to wage improvements and conditions. Over time these resolutions might be endorsed by the Executive and become BISAKTA policy; but in any one year they would nearly all be 'noted' or deemed 'impracticable'. Their value to the historian lies not in their immediate policy impact, but in the evidence they offer of the genesis of ideas later to be taken up by the whole organisation.

In fact, BISAKTA had now entered an era in which non-pay elements almost vied with wages for importance in the total remuneration package. At a meeting on 1 May 1967, Midland Wages Board employers agreed in principle (by a 'declaration of intent') to the introduction of a forty-hour week for shift-workers, effective as soon as possible after 1 July. Pursuant to the precedent of two years earlier, however, they insisted that this be brought in at no additional cost; indeed, they went further and demanded a host of changes in working practices. This provoked a crisis at a Standing Committee meeting on 20 July, at which where the two sides could not agree. The outcome was agreement that the forty-hour week should be brought in on a company-by-company basis, a process which took no less than three years![32] The forty-hour week was won in 1967 at the Sheet Trade Board and Galvanising Conciliation Board by a similar accommodation, but much more quickly. Progress was much easier when you were dealing with one employer.[33]

But the real lift to non-pay elements was achieved at BSC, where public ownership of itself created an atmosphere in which so many long-standing objectives could be realised. Indeed the value of public ownership to steel-workers at BSC is beyond dispute. National agreements at BSC were to be made in the next few years covering improved holidays; employment and income security (1969); superannuation for staff (1969) and for manual grades (1973). BSC also incorporated its social values in other ways, for example by the establishment in 1969 of the Joint Accident Prevention Advisory Committee (JAPAC), of which Davies was twice chairman. These agreements were negotiated by TUCSICC under BISAKTA leadership.

Such improvements in the quality of working life were not simply handed over by the employers. Management was determined to achieve more efficient driving of plant. In 1968 BISAKTA received a document from BSC offering proposals for raising productivity, modernising the wage structure and improving employment conditions; after clarification, it was referred to the Heavy Steel Central Negotiating Committee (CNC). The following year BSC's ideas had hardened into the 'Green Book' productivity proposals. The CNC rejected BSC suggestions for the heavy steel trade in principle on 26 August 1969, but its decision provoked protests from the membership. The Executive responded by allowing the CNC to press for an improvement in the BSC terms, but not to push matters so far as a breakdown. Finally, on 27 November, the CNC acquiesced in the BSC proposals.

The structure of bargaining

February 1967 brought the demise of one of BISAKTA's oldest bargaining units, the Siemens Steel Trade. Closure of RTB's Gowerton Works on 30 April left the Albion and Llanelli Works as the only two still producing and covered by the Trade. ISTEA agreed to extend its umbrella to cover them, and this necessitated an adjustment in the constitution of the HST. The problem was resolved by recreating the No. 5 Area Committee, which had gone out of existence in the 1950s when SCOW had withdrawn from ISTEA (see above). The new No. 5 Area would consist of the works in Nos. 5 and 6 Divisions, while a revised No. 4 Area would comprise those in Divisions Nos. 4 and 7.

Since World War II, ISTEA had presided over the progressive centralisation of pay negotiations. When new demands were tabled by the union side, the question was always how far all member firms would be prepared to agree.[34] Now, with the formation of BSC, the ultimate amalgamation had taken place, and the political atmosphere of the late 1960s – unlike that of the early 1950s – was not encouraging for those who hoped for a chance to reverse it. Moreover, it had been clear almost from the outset that BSC was willing to see important enhancements in the employment package, and in areas which had often proved sticking points in the past. The new Corporation had its own priorities and would not reflect the approach of the surviving private steel companies even though some (GKN for example) seemed to have a foot in both camps.[35]

On 6 March 1968 ISTEA was dissolved, handing all its public sector responsibilities to the BSC the next day. This was a relatively painless transition, since all existing agreements, established customs and practices continued wherever they had been contracted by any part of ISTEA and BISAKTA. BSC opened its involvement with responsibility for the iron and steelmaking activities of scheduled ISTEA companies, including the machinery of negotiation agreements; agreements covering wages, salaries and conditions of employment; and agreements on deduction of contributions at source and trade union membership.[36] Further rationalisation of the public/private sector boundary occurred when five BSC works withdrew from the Midland Wages Board early in 1970.[37] There was little enthusiasm for this move on the Executive, but it felt unable to prevent them taking this step.

Some[38] of the companies now outside the BSC formed a new employers' body, the Independent Steel Employers' Association (ISEA), following the dissolution of ISTEA. In a move parallel to that in the public sector, ISEA took over responsibility for all ISTEA agreements with BISAKTA which applied on 6 March 1968, both in respect of the machinery of negotiations and in respect of wages and conditions of employment. The chairman of the Formation Committee, G.E.D. Halahan, proposed that all such agreements should continue, just as before, until either side wished to instigate negotiated change, and BISAKTA concurred.[39] Soon afterwards the two bodies decided to continue the review of a forty-hour week for production shift workers. In a landmark step they agreed to adopt the standard neutral committee and national joint sub-committee structure for the resolution of disputes,[40] and to establish a union negotiating committee to match the coverage of the employers.[41] ISEA was careful to insist, however, that it would not commit itself in advance to agreements made at BSC. This proviso was entered at the time of talks about security of employment, but it anticipated a gulf of perception between public and private sector employers which was to widen with time. In November 1968 the new structures yielded a satisfactory outcome, with the award of a substantial increase in minimum normal weekly earnings to lower-paid private sector workers.[42] A guaranteed week for the private sector was finally achieved on 8 December 1970. At that date the employers conceded a claim for a five-day guaranteed week at 80 per cent of average earnings.

Pay bargaining and the government

Few had realised it in the early 1960s, but Britain had entered a period where government policy would have an incremental impact on the country's celebrated 'voluntarist' wage-bargaining system. BISAKTA, like most unions, had been restive under the Lloyd pay pause, but within twelve months of taking office Labour had also begun to urge pay restraint. After the 1966 general election, pressure intensified. In his last months of office Douglass had issued rumbling warnings about the likely results of a pay freeze (see above). Faced with the 1967 prices and incomes standstill (period of severe restraint), the TUC was torn between its wish to help Labour and the rising expectations of its members. At the special conference of Executive Councils convened by the TUC on 2 March 1967, BISAKTA backed the TUC's policy to support restraint. Almost certainly this was the majority view of the membership: the only overt sign of rank-and-file discontent with the policy came during the HST Area No. 3 Conference, which passed a resolution arguing that the wage freeze was in reality a wage cut and did not address the problem of redistribution. Yet government drift in the direction of incomes policy continued. BISAKTA wished at all costs to avoid it, but despaired of votes at Congress such as that in 1968 which rejected the voluntary machinery devised by the TUC itself: BISAKTA felt that co-operation and loyalty to TUC decisions was the key. Rejecting those decisions would make a statutory pay policy certain.

But the 1964–70 Labour administration did not only wish to shape the wage round: it also sought to reform industrial relations themselves. Barbara Castle's 1969 proposals – popularly known as 'In Place of Strife' – were greeted with alarm across a wide range of trade-union opinion. BISAKTA members shared this view. The organisation had long insisted that only voluntary methods should be used in industrial relations, and it had a horror of the compulsory element in the Castle proposals: penal clauses were unnecessary, impracticable and objectionable. The Executive accepted a resolution from the No. 1 Division BOC which called on unions to use 'every means at their disposal' to secure the withdrawal of the 'penal clauses' in the Castle proposals. BISAKTA delegates loyally supported the TUC document 'Industrial Relations: Programme for Action' at the TUC special conference of June 1969.

BISAKTA itself remained a tightly disciplined and loyal organisation. The Executive was as willing vis-à-vis BSC as it had been in the past to curb any unruliness. A 1969 stoppage at the Abbey and Margam Works brought reprimands to the branch officials whose 'unconstitutional' actions were thought to have contributed to this stoppage, though in this instance they fell short of the most severe sanctions, apparently because the officials were thought to have a case in their complaints about the procedure for choosing members of the negotiating committee.[43] Less fortunate were the officials of Corby No. 6 Branch. In June 1969 they were deposed from office for supporting unofficial strike action, a step which had 'brought the Organisation into discredit'.

Relations with other unions

Until 1967 TUC Group No. 7 (Iron and Steel and Minor Metal Trades) commanded two seats on the General Council, but that year they were reduced to one, a move which stimulated 'considerable' concern on the EC.[44] Davies of course experienced no difficulty in filling Douglass's place at that year's Congress,[45] so the immediate casualty was the National Union of Blastfurnacemen. But the Organisation's concern was well-founded: there were natural limits to the growth of steel's industrial unions, while the gross TUC membership was in exponential growth. The huge influx of public service and white-collar membership must numerically swamp the traditionally powerful production and manufacturing unions unless they could find some means of retaining their influence. In the short term BISAKTA's influence and prestige at the TUC remained immense – as events were shortly to demonstrate – but in the medium term a new role might have to be found.

One approach might be to rationalise the complex structure of steel-industry trade unionism. The dual ISTC/BISAKTA structure of 1917 had been shaped to facilitate the entry of other unions into one organisation when they felt ready for the step: there is no doubt that BISAKTA's founding fathers envisaged one industrial union in the spirit of their times. Over the decades these hopes had faded. Not all parties to the 1916 discussions had joined up to the final project; the rupture with the National Union of Clerks (NUC) had seemed for a time to bar the way to white-collar growth; changing definitions of the steel industry brought general unionism increasingly into the bargaining units dominated by BISAKTA. These factors were not new, but in 1967 the British Steel Corporation was.

Even before BSC was established, the complexities of consulting so many organisations and identifying a union 'view' were apparent. Once the Corporation as a single employer faced the practical difficulties of meeting such a large number of organisations, these complexities became glaring. In the spring of 1968 BSC's national negotiators faced three different kinds of trade-union organisation. There were the industrial unions like BISAKTA and the NUB, whose lifeblood for the most part was iron and steel, and who now found the majority of their membership (overwhelmingly so in the case of the NUB) was in the public sector. There were the Transport and General Workers' Union (TGWU) and the National Union of General and Municipal Workers (NUGMW), large organisations whose members tended to be employed at the finishing end of the production process or in ancillary groups: their steel members comprised a very small proportion of their overall total, and this total was at this date more concentrated in the private than in the public sector. Finally there were the craft unions.

The existence of the National Craftsmen's Co-ordinating Committee (NCCC)[46] has suggested to some writers a greater unity among skilled workers' representatives than was in fact the case. In fact, no less than thirteen autonomous organisations were members of NCCC in spring 1968. In no case was their steel membership (which was overwhelmingly at BSC) more than a small proportion of their overall membership. BISAKTA's relations with craftsmen could be prickly, and reflected contrasting views of the value of 'skilled' and 'semi-skilled' labour. From time to time initiatives would be floated for the rationalisation of relations: thus in spring 1974 NCCC convener John (later Sir John) Boyd wrote proposing talks to establish a National Joint Industrial Council for the steel industry. An Executive sub-committee met NCCC representatives, and in February 1975 the idea was accepted in principle. However, after a special executive had considered the implications for the Organisation's constitution, no further action was taken.

There was a fourth category of unions: those which had membership at BSC but did not enjoy national recognition at the time of nationalisation. At this date there were two of these: the Clerical and Administrative Workers' Union (CAWU) and the Association of Scientific, Technical and Managerial Staffs (ASTMS).

Again and again in these pages we shall see the absolute commitment to the steel industry felt by BISAKTA and the NUB and how it opened up conflict with other union organisations. But the raw material for conflict went wider. Most production workers in membership of BISAKTA possessed skills which were highly prized within the industry but were not easily tradable outside, where they were generally described as 'semi-skilled'.[47] By contrast, the skill status of most craftsmen was independent of the industry in which they worked. The existence of different organisations representing different grades of employee tended to consolidate the cleavages between them. And these differences could also be expressed through different philosophies of representation. The lay tradition in BISAKTA was very powerful at Executive, branch and negotiating committee level, and full-time officers were appointed by the lay Executive. In most craft unions, however, full-time officers, who were elected, were the only participants in negotiations.

Steelworkers could and did come together in a common interest, as when TUCSICC was formed to represent them in public-sector non-wage negotiations. But when it came to matters of pay BISAKTA (and for that matter the NUB) was implacable: there could be no question of surrendering a separate bargaining identity, for the interests of those to be represented were just too divergent. When, some years later,[48] BISAKTA and NUB representatives met TUC representatives to discuss structures and development in the light of the TUC's position after the Donovan Report, there was no major change.

Staff organisation and the Pearson Inquiry

The May 1967 EC returned to the vexed question of the entry of white-collar unions into steel. Reports of conflict with CAWU, the Association of Supervisory Staffs, Executives and Technicians (ASSET) and other organisations had been a regular feature of its meetings in recent years: these unions' actions were motivated (in the BISAKTA view) by the wish for a foothold as the industry entered into nationalisation.[49] The 1967 staff conference did not mince its words, singling out the 'intrusion' of ASSET (later ASTMS) in particular with grave concern and calling on the EC to 'subdue' it. The EC was of the opinion that it was already fulfilling the requirements of the resolution. It merely noted further resolutions calling for every effort to be made to gain recognition from the employers for established staff branches, and for a review of administrative and negotiating structures in the light of nationalisation.

Of course nationalisation did not end the problem: a new complaint about poaching at Port Talbot was forwarded to the ASSET head office in February 1968. Intensive discussions took place in the TUC organising committee, in TUCSICC and with BSC personnel director Ron Smith, and they culminated in an historic decision of the BSC board[50] which affirmed that recognition decisions were its own prerogative and that its policy was to rationalise 'trade union interests'. The Board determined that for all iron and steel activities except for those covered by the engineering and other industry agreements:

- ASTMS and CAWU claims for national recognition should be rejected, but local recognition would continue where local agreements (established before 10 July 1967) were in place.
- The six nationally recognised unions[51] would be offered local recognition throughout BSC where branches or the framework of branches existed, or as soon as they could be established, including locations where ASTMS and CAWU were already recognised.
- The six would be given 'every reasonable facility for recruitment' and employees should be encouraged to join whichever of the six was appropriate for them.
- The negotiating functions of the staff associations would cease forthwith and those of consultation and communication would end as soon as arrangements had been made for their transfer to the 'six'.[52]

This was an emphatic victory, greeted with satisfaction by the BISAKTA Executive; but it was aware of strike threats issued by ASTMS and CAWU against BSC, and in May took out an insurance policy by resolving to direct members to co-operate in keeping the industry working should these things come to pass. Continued conflict and rivalry over staff organisation confounded BISAKTA's hopes. In the summer of 1968 Ernie Hickery, Divisional Officer No. 5 Division, was brought temporarily to Central Office to direct efforts to recruit staff grades, but by November the Executive had resolved to appoint a National Officer to direct staff matters; it had already determined on staff organisers in the divisions.[53] The following year H.A. ('Sandy') Feather,[54] the first appointee of modern times to come from outside the full-time staff, succeeded Hickery as National Staff Officer, and the appointment of divisionally based staff organisers came soon afterwards.

Pressure on the leadership continued to build. That year's staff conference registered considerable impatience over the difficulty of recruiting staff in sufficient numbers, implicitly criticising Davies for not achieving results within the time available, and calling for 'force' to be used to compel recognition of BISAKTA staff branches.[55] However, Davies had secured a considerable victory in getting BSC (no doubt following its own inclinations in any case) effectively to endorse the TUC position. The organisation was in the strong position of defending the status quo.

But a new element now entered the situation when Barbara Castle, newly appointed First Secretary of State at the Department of Employment and Productivity (DEP), resolved to establish a Court of Inquiry to inquire into the dispute. This was not welcome news, for what need was there for an inquiry when satisfactory arrangements were already in place? There was a strong suspicion – openly voiced by Davies – that political pressure on the First Secretary had forced her hand. The initiative seemed more ominous still as it became apparent that neither the chairman of the inquiry, Lord Pearson, nor its other members had any knowledge or experience of conditions in the steel industry.

On 18 July, Davies, courteous as ever, attended the inquiry at Pearson's request and made a statement with the full backing of the Executive. He was polite but implacable: at the very start he made it clear that his organisation was opposed to the court and was not committed to co-operate with any recommendations it made. There followed a masterful survey of BISAKTA history, its commitment to industrial unionism and its philosophy of industrial relations – not 'as one of two sides ranged against each other in a state of permanent hostility, but as part of a joint enterprise which reconciles its problems against a background of common interest'. Davies reviewed the generally harmonious record of relations with the steel industry's employers and attributed it to the negotiation and conciliation machinery which existed in essentially the same form in every sector thereof.[56] Central to the success of this machinery – though Davies did not make the link explicit – was the un-wavering commitment to agreements. Recalling a phrase of Lincoln Evans, Davies declared that 'We believe that signing an agreement is like signing a cheque – it must be honoured.'

He then turned to the point directly in dispute. The attempt to portray the Organisation as a purely manual union, without competence in representing staff, was dismissed as 'utter nonsense'. With deadly effect he recalled the failure of CAWU's predecessor, the NUC, to organise steel industry staff between the wars and how, for thirty years, BISAKTA had done the job dir-ectly: with more than 11,000 members it outnumbered any other single union in non-manual grades by four to one. This was the positive side, but he could land blows as well, as he demonstrated when he detailed aspects of the CAWU and ASTMS recruitment drives.[57] BISAKTA, by contrast, was a union in and of the steel industry, so committed to it that it co-operated with change whenever it was in the industry's interest, even when that meant painful experiences.

Finally Davies rebutted the charge that the dispute was a membership squabble. Public ownership had led directly to the creation of TUCSICC, the first formal body representing the industry's unions on a common basis; as for BISAKTA, it had previously and voluntarily given up membership to others in the interests of creating an orderly trade union structure. The same objectives dictated keeping the white-collar unions out. Thus far he had been magisterial, but there had to be an iron hand in the velvet glove, and his conclusions made it clear that his organisation regarded the situation as one of 'extreme gravity'. There must have been a hush with his closing words: '. . . we are prepared to take whatever action may be necessary in our interests at the outcome of the Court's deliberations.'

The Organisation's position could scarcely have been more clearly put, but Pearson would not have been appointed if the government only sought endorsement of the actions of BSC and TUCSICC. His recommendations embodied a call for BSC to reverse its decision and grant the two complaining unions national recognition. The principle the court appeared to elevate above all others, in respect of union membership, was absolute freedom of choice; in the concrete circumstances of heavy industry, however, this would lead to fragmentation and impotence. Almost unbelievably, the court had failed to give weight to the long history of BISAKTA/CAWU relations; it was hardly surprising that its appeal to the larger organisation to 'act with their traditional responsibility and forbearance' met with hollow laughter. Peace, as *Man and Metal* observed, 'is of doubtful value if it has to be purchased at *any* price'. What was sauce for the goose was sauce for the gander: if strikes aimed at gaining recognition were not condemned, then they could hardly be condemned if mounted in defence of steel's negotiating machinery.

Once Pearson had reported, events moved rapidly. His recommendations were rejected by TUCSICC, and Davies began to emphasise the possibility of industrial action to protect the Organisation's interests. A special Executive meeting of 9 October 1968 quashed press speculation that it did not support him in his stance, taking the extraordinary step of making clear that both his public and his private utterances had their full support.[58] Evidence of a new harder line came when in November the EC resolved to inform BSC that continued non-recognition of its Appleby-Frodingham staff branch would lead to a withdrawal of labour. In No. 7 Division both the Irlam and Brymbo Joint Branch Committees were pressing for action.

In the same month TUCSICC, led by Davies, met officials of the DEP and informed them of the Executive's unanimous rejection of the Pearson findings. This was followed by a meeting with Ron Smith, who announced that he planned to recommend to the BSC board local recognition for CAWU and ASTMS on equal terms with TUCSICC members.[59] TUCSICC swiftly countered that if this became Board policy its unions would tell their members to take instructions only from members of TUCSICC unions and to handle only that work approved by members of those unions; they requested an urgent meeting with the Board. Their pressure bore fruit in the shape of a meeting with Lord Melchett on 17 December, but in the absence of a commitment not to proceed with ASTMS/CAWU recognition, TUCSICC scheduled a meeting to reaffirm its position. But the common front with BSC was clearly breaking up: there was a danger that this might become a dispute with the employer. In sombre mood, Davies shared with the membership his conclusion that the Corporation had caved in to pressure from Barbara Castle.[60]

After a delay to accommodate internal consultations by the NCCC, the meeting was convened on 13 January 1969. It unanimously resolved to instruct all members now employed at BSC and formerly covered by ISTEA (including former SCOW employees) not to handle work from members of non-TUCSICC unions or to take orders from them. Acting under powers given by the EC on 3 January, Davies issued an instruction to BISAKTA public sector branches along those lines.

Press coverage of developments tended to present the TUC decision as weak leadership. Meanwhile, concern about the way the BISAKTA case had been distorted in the press led Davies to break with past practice and engage a public relations firm. On 21 January 1969 readers of the *Sun*, *The Times*, and the *Guardian* woke up to a statement from the Organisation which re-iterated the main points of the argument and made the intention to strike – 'against all its peaceful traditions, and for the first time since the General Strike in 1926' – unmistakable.[61]

Mrs Castle now played one of her last cards and sought TUC assistance in resolving the dispute. On 22 January the TUC General Council accepted a recommendation from its Finance and General Purposes Committee (F & GP) that the TUCSICC unions suspend their threatened industrial action pending a TUC inquiry into steel staff unionisation. The BISAKTA executive, however, in special session on 24 January, saw no reason to lift the planned action, though it did accede to a request to meet the F & GP that afternoon.

In a tense atmosphere Davies returned to the Executive at 6.30 that night bearing the message that the F & GP would enter into discussions with all unions to produce a solution, and that neither the Pearson findings nor a previous recommendation of the Organisation Sub-committee of the TUC would bind it. This did not move the Executive, but they remained in session and now received George Woodcock and Victor Feather, the top two men at the TUC. Woodcock reiterated the earlier offer, undertook that discussions with the F & GP would start on 27 January and promised that body would stay in continuous session until it could make a recommendation back to the General Council. Only now was the instruction lifted.

It proved a shrewd move. The F & GP's ultimate recommendations upheld BISAKTA's position, and on 7 February 1969 they were endorsed without opposition[62] by the General Council with the words that the TUC-SICC unions were 'collectively the most representative group on the union side'. A separate matter, the recognition claim of the Steel Industry Management Association (SIMA – see below), was summarily dismissed, while ASTMS and CAWU should, in the General Council's view, be limited to whatever recognition they had achieved by 10 July 1967. In labour movement terms it was a total victory, and TUCSICC so informed Lord Melchett on 17 February.

Having looked to the TUC to resolve the dispute, Mrs Castle, it was thought, could scarcely ignore its recommendations. But what of the employers? BSC, firm with TUCSICC and BISAKTA in defending its 1967 decision, was now wobbling disastrously. Its proposals for staff recognition fell far short of the General Council's unanimous recommendations, and in February the Executive rejected them outright.[63] In May it reluctantly concluded that 'if the Association was to protect its legitimate interests, the use of industrial action could not be ruled out'.[64] But branches would be discouraged from going it alone with any necessary action being planned from the centre.

With the new National Staff Officer in post and staff organisers now in place in several divisions,[65] the Organisation felt able to launch a national staff recruitment campaign. It was certainly needed in view of the emergence of SIMA as a dangerous rival for middle management membership and one which was regarded by BISAKTA members as a non-union body. There were many complaints of BISAKTA staff members being discriminated against in promotions. The 1969 staff conference called for the regularisation of staff members' position within BISAKTA, including the establishment of a national negotiating structure at BSC and exploration of the possibility of parallel machinery at group level and within the private sector.

At BSC progress had been made in formulating a National Recognition and Procedure Agreement. The BISAKTA EC agreed a TUCSICC draft in August 1969. Recruitment proceeded and the number of branches rose by thirty-one in the second half of 1969, mostly through a staff influx.[66] In February 1970 the National Staff Officer recorded that there were more than 4000 staff members in No. 2 Division alone; by the end of the year No. 3 Division had also passed this total. He submitted proposals for the establishment of a national negotiating committee for staff members to the May EC, which in turn referred them to a sub-committee. This sub-committee's recommendations were endorsed by the August EC, which promulgated a national negotiating committee for staff members for the first time.[67]

But on the ground animosities persisted, now compounded by local clashes among the TUCSICC unions themselves. During 1970 work proceeded within the TUCSICC on the standardisation of conditions of employment and a rationalised staff structure. As late as 1972 the conflict with non-TUC-SICC unions was still causing local stoppages.[68]

The February 1969 TUC statement had firmly dismissed the claim of SIMA to be considered a union for bargaining purposes, but the 1968 BSC Board decision on staff recognition also promulgated a position on middle management. BSC made explicit its belief that a single Corporation-wide organisation would be the most effective solution, but insisted that such an organisation should have 'substantial and widespread support' prior to recognition. In 1968 it therefore rejected bids for recognition both from TUCSICC and from CAWU and ASTMS insofar as they claimed to represent managers. The following year, however, it recommended SIMA as the appropriate union for steel industry middle management, a decision which outraged BISAKTA's staff conference.[69] By now the dispute about recognition was already moving into a different phase with the Conference also passing calls for the National Staff Officer to prioritise the establishment of a new staff negotiating structure. The drama was passing away and a long war of attrition was beginning.

Notes

1 Sir David Henry Davies (1909–) entered the iron and steel industry at the age of fourteen and joined BISAKTA in 1929. His industrial background was in the steel sheet trade, as secretary of Ebbw Vale sheet mills No. 2 branch, secretary of the Ebbw Vale Joint Committee, Operatives' Representatives on the Sheet Trade Board and a member of the Board's Joint Standing Committee. He was elected to the Executive Council in 1948 and become Assistant General Secretary in 1953 after three years as an organiser in No. 5 Division. He chaired the Joint Advisory Committee on Safety and Health in the Iron and Steel Industry from 1965 and became Secretary of the British Section of the IMF in 1960. His training responsibilities had been extensive, and after ten years' service on the Iron and Steel Operatives Course Advisory Committee he joined the new Iron and Steel Industry Training Board in 1964, becoming vice-chairman three years later. He became vice-chairman of the National Dock Labour Board in 1966 and joined the General Council of the TUC the following year.

2 Davies had served on the Ebbw Vale UDC from 1945 to 1950, and on Labour's National Executive Committee from 1954, becoming vice-chairman in 1962 and chairman in 1963 (see previous chapter). He became Treasurer of the Labour Party in 1965, but resigned the post when he became General Secretary.

3 Emlyn Roberts (1902–67) entered the steel industry at the age of sixteen, was an Executive member from 1936 to 1945, was appointed an Organiser in 1945 and in 1961 became Divisional Officer, No. 3 division. Tragically, Roberts died only six months into his retirement.

4 Alex Hogg (1908–) had been appointed Divisional Organiser, No. 3 Division, in 1955.

5 John Irvine (1906–) retired in January 1969 and was succeeded by Arthur Bell.

6 Arthur Bell (1915–88) was appointed a Divisional Organiser in 1957. To cap the Division's success that year, the Fraternal Delegate to the STUC in 1967 (when Irvine began his term of office) was Lord Douglass.

7 Jim Williams (1904–83) entered the steel industry at Morriston in 1921 and rose to be secretary of the Morriston No. 1 Branch. He became Divisional Organiser, No. 5 Division, in 1946, transferring to No. 6 Division after six months and there making his name managing the huge transition in steel and tinplate which the area experienced after World War II, when no less than fifty works closed. He was appointed Divisional Officer, No. 6 Division, in 1963.

8 John Foley (1930–) ended a long career with the Organisation on 1 May 1992. After a period on the EC he was appointed Divisional Organiser in No. 7 and later (in 1966) No. 5 Division, where he became Divisional Officer in September 1974. He was made Divisional Officer of the amalgamated Nos. 5 and 6 Divisions from July 1981.

9 Stan Biddiscombe (1920–) was appointed Divisional Organiser, No. 4 Division, in 1957 and transferred to No. 6 Division three years later.

10 Jack Gavin (1915–) was appointed Divisional Organiser, No. 4 Division, in 1964. In 1976 he served for a time as acting Assistant General Secretary during the illness of Bill Sirs.

11 Alan Potter (1921–) was appointed Divisional Organiser, No. 2 Division, in 1953; he transferred to No. 6 Division ten years later for a brief period before moving to No. 4 Division, where he was appointed Divisional Officer in 1964.

12 Tommy Watson (1909–84) first held union office as secretary of Redbourne No. 1 Branch and became Divisional Organiser, No. 7 Division, in 1950. He was appointed Divisional Officer, No. 7 Division, in 1964. To the guests at a retirement party Watson announced that he was returning to his native Lincolnshire because the poaching was much easier there.

13 It was disbanded in October 1967, passing on its services as appropriate either to the BSC or to the new British Iron and Steel Producers' Association (BISPA).

14 Vaizey, *op. cit.*, 180.

15 *Reports* (1967), 33. The views of branches were also reported to the Executive. They included concerns about the future shape of national negotiating machinery, and the appointment of 'opponents of steel nationalisation' to the putative corporation or to its organising committee. The most abrasive of these, Niall Macdiarmid, remained on the Board until 1970.

16 *Reports* (1967), 152–3. The text of the resolution read: 'That this Conference welcomes the passing by Parliament of the Iron and Steel Bill bringing into public ownership the major part of the iron and steel industry. It strongly approves the provisions made in the Bill for worker-participation in the Organisation and operation of the industry and the Minister of Power's undertaking to keep in close touch with the Association on all aspects of steel nationalisation.' No. 1 Division went further and denounced the appointment of Macdiarmid as deputy chairman of the organising committee following his 'vicious' attack on nationalisation, concluding with a call for workers' control. No. 3 Division called on the EC to insist on 'workers' representation and joint consultation at all levels'. The EC thought it had already dealt appropriately with the Macdiarmid issue, but accepted the second resolution since this corresponded to its own policy.

17 Presiding over (but shortly to leave) the EC was Joe McKay, recently appointed Labour Relations Officer at the Lancashire Steel Manufacturing Company, Irlam. McKay was to die that September.

18 The Committee included five union representatives.

19 Twelve names were agreed at the August 1967 EC, three for each company group. The names of nine middle managers were submitted in November in response to a further BSC request. Altogether the TUC had ninety names, which it boiled down to thirty-four for submission to BSC.

20 *Reports* (1967), 208. The following February the Executive agreed to an NUB proposal to enlarge the committee in order to broaden its scope, and it held a series of meetings during the year.

21 Denis Delay was to be its sole secretary for the whole of its twenty-one years.

22 The EC heard complaints from the Hawarden Bridge Joint Committee in February 1968. Further fears were aired in May, leading Davies to explain the procedure whereby nominations were passed from the union to TUCSICC and thence to BSC.

23 *Reports*, May 1968. An accord between the principal unions and BSC of July 1967 directed that employee directors could serve on the boards responsible for their own works but would have to relinquish their union positions on appointment. J. Bank and K. Jones, *Worker Directors Speak* (1977), 13.

24 The *Report on Organisation 1967* (Cmnd. 3362, August 1967), had defined three objectives for the Corporation, two relating to market performance and the third stipulating 'ensuring the efficient and socially responsible utilisation of human resources'. This, the commitment of Richard Marsh, and the presence at senior levels in the Corporation of figures committed to workers' participation, ensured the emergence of a worker director scheme.

25 'Notes and Comments', *Man and Metal* (February 1967).

26 The EC were polled individually by Davies in a circular of 12 December 1969. The February 1970 meeting agreed to forward ten names under this procedure. The appointment of one of these, Jack Leonard, led to his resignation from the Executive that May, and he was joined as an employee director by another Executive (and Parliamentary Panel) member, Donald Sutherland. A gap in the nominations was filled when, in August 1970, eight names were submitted from the Strip Mills Division. A middle management member, Geoff Davies of Llanwern, was selected that autumn.

27 Bank and Jones, *op. cit.*, 13.

28 *Reports* (1971), 113; the decision was reaffirmed the following year (*Reports*, 1972, 116).

29 At the end of 1974 they were joined in the strip mills division by Joe Lewis and David Williams.

30 At the end of 1966 the recorded figure dipped below 120,000.

31 *Reports* (1967), 43.

32 Taylor, *op. cit.*, 33.

33 In practice, implementation within the heavy steel trade was on a works-by-works basis, as indicated in a schedule attached to the agreement.

34 In one of its last acts, ISTEA proposed that the existing disputes procedure would suffice to handle complaints arising under legislation pending to extend the Race

Relations Act. The Executive was quite prepared to make an agreement, but doubted whether existing procedures would prove adequate. There was a strong feeling that any conciliation board in the procedure would need to include a representative from 'the racial group from which the complaint is brought' (*Reports*, 1967, 304).

35 For more than two years BSC was organised into Areas which reflected the config-uration of inherited works, a state of affairs which allowed company loyalties to survive. Only after this were Product Divisions introduced.

36 At its February 1968 meeting the Executive determined to ask the public sector Sheet Trade Board, the Galvanising Conciliation Board and the Midland Wages Board companies to follow suit by nominating BSC representatives. The former Steel Company of Wales (SCOW), which under private ownership had withdrawn from ISTEA (see above) remained outside the new framework for some time, pro-voking tensions at the Abbey Works where there was dissatisfaction with the Heavy Steel and Finishing Mills Negotiating Committees, which met separately. Only in November 1969 did BISAKTA win consent to consolidate the company (and therefore the Port Talbot Works) within the general BSC agreements (*Reports*, 1969, 136, 285). The BSC offer, accepted with pleasure, was subject to STB approval and initially sought to except any ongoing negotiations at Port Talbot from national settlements arising from current manpower and productivity agreements.

37 See below.

38 As manufacturers virtually all private companies were united as the British Inde-pendent Steel producers' Association (BISPA), but not every BISPA member wished to be committed to industry-wide deals, which was what ISEA member-ship implied.

39 *Reports* (1968), 164.

40 BISAKTA anticipated that there might be a shortage of neutrals from private sector works, and obtained an agreement that it might exceptionally bring in neu-trals from the public sector.

41 Davies was authorised to set up such a committee by decision of the August 1968 EC, and its constitution was determined in November (*Reports*, 1968, 213, 307).

42 They received a rise of £1 0s 1d on normal weekly earnings of £12 1s 5d (exclusive of shift premiums and overtime). MWB minimum earnings rose by £1 at the same time, but were already 5s 0d in advance of ISEA level. Comparable advances were also negotiated in the minimum earnings of HST, STB and GCB employees at about this time.

43 *Reports* (1968), 285.

44 *Reports* (1967), 163.

45 He secured 7,487,000 votes against his nearest rival, the Sheet Metal Workers' Les Buck.

46 Founded in 1950 on an initiative of the Amalgamated Engineering Union to con-solidate the representation of skilled workers to the steel employers.

47 There were of course tradesmen in BISAKTA as well, and they had their own section, Section (i), for Executive elections. However, many of these craftsmen were in the new (post-1967) private sector, for example at Round Oak Steel Works.

48 The initial consultation took place on 29 January 1970. It led to the inauguration of a joint sub-committee, but little else.

49 It was reported that the EC approved of steps already taken to counter the activities of rival unions. Certainly a number of cases had already been taken through the TUC disputes procedure.

50 Taken on 15 May: see *Man and Metal* (June 1968) and *Reports* (1968), 150.

51 ISTC, NUB, TGWU, NUGMW, the Amalgamated Union of Building Workers (AUBTW) and the NCCC (which for these purposes counted as one union).

52 For the text of the Board's decision, see *Reports* (1968), 150. In practice the problem was very far from solved. In the autumn of 1968, for example, there was a crisis at the Corby Works when full-time officers were unable to secure the disbandment of a 250-strong Tube Works Foremen's Association and could not obtain staff recruitment facilities (*Reports*, 1968, 300).

53 There were five staff members among the ten applicants for an organiser's post in August (*Reports*, 1968, 223). The first specifically designated staff organisers were appointed in February 1969.

54 H.A. Feather (1937–) was appointed National Staff Officer in March 1969, and later served on the Steel Committee and the ISITB. As a member of the Parliamentary Panel he twice stood as a sponsored candidate for the Corby constituency. He resigned his post in April 1994.

55 For the text of these resolutions see *Reports*, 1968, 234. Both resolutions were noted.

56 Of course the exception was the multi-union Welsh Tinplate Trade Joint Industrial Council, and Davies did not disguise this from the Court.

57 Reading this statement one can almost hear the gasps in the court as Davies described how non-CAWU members were offered their net basic pay if they stopped work in support of that union's recognition claim.

58 *Reports* (1968), 282.

59 There seems to have been some hint that ASTMS and CAWU had threatened strikes in the car industry: certainly Davies believed that this was a factor in the BSC decision.

60 *Man and Metal* (January 1969), 1. His reticence about her had slipped. By this date she seemed 'to know so little about industrial relations'.

61 'The Steel Dispute: Why Put the Clock Back 50 Years?'

62 Davies, as chairman of the Steel Committee, did not vote.

63 The industrial action instruction meanwhile remained suspended (*Reports*, 1969, 39). Members at Clydesdale took unofficial action in support of the recognition of two staff branches early in 1969.

64 *Reports* (1969), 136.

65 The number of these was eventually raised to six.

66 These figures should be treated with care, as many pre-1969 staff members were not separately organised in branches.

67 It had three sections: (a) for supervisory staff, (b) for technical and laboratory staff, and (c) for clerical and non-supervisory staff. Each Division would be allowed to elect one representative from any section before the annual Staff Conference; at the conference a further eight representatives would be elected, subject to the requirement that no section would have fewer than four representatives.

68 As for example at Lackenby, where a stoppage (retrospectively made official) occurred after three foremen on the concast plant refused to take instructions from SIMA shift managers. The matter was resolved bilaterally by Davies and Finniston: recognition was conceded in return for a union commitment not to pressurise SIMA members there to join (*Reports*, 1972, 187, 191). Subsequently the local recognition and procedure agreement was challenged by SIMA, which at the National Industrial Relations Court accused both BISAKTA and BSC of committing an unfair industrial practice. The NIRC advised SIMA to withdraw the charge (*Reports*, 1974, 469–70).

69 Among a number of resolutions on the subject was one calling for industrial action. The EC did not back this and was generally cautious in threatening strikes to obtain representation rights for managers, but in August it did authorise the Spencer Middle Management Branch to enter strike notices if, after seven days had elapsed, its long-standing claim for recognition had not been conceded. The threat proved an effective one, for recognition was granted before the next quarterly EC meeting.

5

Expansion at last?
Dai Davies (1970–5)

'. . . the need to develop a modern and competitive steel industry'

Introduction

BISAKTA's membership peaked at 133,749 in November 1970, boosted by the influx of almost 30,000 staff members; the number of branches had risen to 814. Earlier the same year steel output returned to the record levels of 1965. However, the unexpected return of the Conservatives in the June 1970 general election had challenged many assumptions, and the union was now to enter the most turbulent period of British industrial relations since the 1920s. The spectre of denationalisation proved evanescent, but industrial relations legislation provided a major headache. On top of this the membership had to suffer the worst recession in the industry since before World War II.

A change of government

By 1970 Labour had been in office for six years, and seemed well advanced towards Harold Wilson's avowed goal of becoming Britain's natural governing party. For steelworkers the impact of Labour had been enormous, dominated by the establishment of the British Steel Corporation with all its attendant blessings and not a few curses. As for politics, relations had not been altogether happy: BISAKTA had clashed with Barbara Castle, Wilson's closest lieutenant, on the three major issues of staff organisation, steel pricing policy and 'In Place of Strife'. General economic conditions were improving, but living standards had felt the impact of Chancellor Roy Jenkins's deflationary measures since 1968. The pages of *Man and Metal*, usually so loyal to Labour, register a sense of unease at the drift of government policy. On the Party's NEC Diamond – who succeeded Davies in

October 1967 – had followed in his predecessor's footsteps by reliably backing the leadership.

But in the summer of 1970 there seemed little reason to expect political
change. That February the Conservatives had used a censure motion to
allege that nationalisation had 'retarded the progress of the industry and
reduced the service to the public'; but when pressed their spokesman, Sir
Keith Joseph, had felt unable to commit himself either for or against a sale. In
reality, much of the Conservative critique related to problems which BSC
had inherited, and this undermined their case. BISAKTA was far from
uncritical of the Corporation – and especially of its vacillations over the staff
organisation affair – but the general view was that public ownership had
brought much-needed stability and a shelter for the steelworker from the
economic cycle. It was tempting to feel that the Conservatives were unready
for office and therefore unlikely to obtain it.

The Executive Council had a formidable bank of evidence to put before
the membership in June 1970 when it urged a Labour vote. Output, and with
it earnings, had risen and the industry was at last being modernised. Where
there was a social cost, retraining, earnings-related benefits and redundancy
payments were cushioning the blow. Stability and prosperity in the industry
to which they owed their living should lead steelworkers to cast a Labour
vote.[1]

In fact Labour's complacent campaign failed to stir the electorate, and
Edward Heath's Conservatives confounded poll readings to gain seventy-
seven seats and a comfortable overall majority. BISAKTA could not hide its
disappointment, but hard-headedly acknowledged that the Conservatives
would claim to have a mandate for every item in their manifesto. The union
also made plain its determination to challenge vigorously government measures which would 'adversely' affect the membership, a category which
included pay, capital investment in steel, income and employment security
and collective bargaining rights.[2]

Kill the bill!

What was to become the Industrial Relations Act 1971 first surfaced as the
Conservative Green Paper 'Fair Deal at Work'. BISAKTA's first reaction was
to condemn its approach as over-theoretical and likely to lead to a burden-
some legislative framework. When the bill appeared, Davies insisted that the
unions were united against it, though he suggested that there might be more
public support forthcoming if the unions devoted some time to explaining
what they were for as well as what they were against! But BISAKTA loyally
supported the campaign that the TUC was now gathering to resist the bill,

and on 21 February Londoners were treated to the unusual sight of the historic 'Iron and Steel Trades Confederation' banner held aloft as part of the monster official protest, estimated at up to 250,000 strong.

BISAKTA also backed the seven recommendations put by the General Council to the TUC special conference at Croydon, and a guiding resolution put before the 1971 BOCs by the EC was carried by all of them.[3] In May the EC agreed to implement the Croydon decisions by instructing all members serving on industrial tribunals to resign on the day the bill received Royal Assent.[4] Difficulties were encountered, however, over the next step in TUC resistance, which required affiliated unions to withdraw themselves from the new Register of Trade Unions. BISAKTA had received advice from the legal services that its present rules precluded it from taking this step. In November 1971 a Rules Revision Committee was established to draw up amendments which would make deregistration possible.[5]

On 20 March 1972 BISAKTA received a certificate from the Registrar registering it as a trade union under the 1971 Act, a notification which confronted it with the issue of deregistration. The Rules Revision Committee presented its conclusions to the EC on 28 March. But the EC, acting under solicitor's advice, felt the need to protect union funds after deregistration. The legal services anticipated an immediate loss of £140,000 in tax relief (greater than the anticipated annual surplus of £128,000), and so the proposed rule changes were drafted to leave the way open for deregistration while protecting the trust funds from actions for damages. There needed to be specific provision to ensure that powers to take industrial action under rule rested only with the EC and the General Secretary. But a new sub-clause 20 (a) was also put out to ballot covering the possibility that contributions might have temporarily to be raised as a result of deregistration.[6]

Ballot returns were in by 9 May – but to the consternation of the EC they showed a vote of 30,769: 19,592 in favour of the rule alterations, which fell short of the two-thirds majority required by Rule 47. In the EC's view this meant that rule alterations could not be made to allow deregistration; it would therefore not implement the Act 'in any way which would run counter to the views of the Trade Union Movement'.[7] Davies was instructed to convey the decision to the TUC and indicate that any advice from it would be welcome.

As must have been anticipated, the news did not please the TUC. Davies and EC representatives were called before the General Council on 17 July to account for the failure to deregister, and the next day Swinton House was notified that BISAKTA had been suspended from the TUC for remaining registered under the 1971 Act. This summary action was a great wound to the pride of a union which so valued its long association with the TUC; the failure of the TUC itself to offer constructive advice as to how to get out of the dilemma was so much salt rubbed in. Bitterly the union ruminated that the need for responsible voices to be heard at the TUC was as great as ever.[8] One of them had now been silenced.

For all that, suspension from the TUC would be lifted only when the Organisation deregistered. Faced with what it viewed as 'an emergency situation', the EC concluded a week later that BISAKTA's best interests lay with immediate action to deregister. Davies was now instructed to request the Chief Registrar to remove BISAKTA from the Register and to inform the TUC that he had done so. It was further resolved to obtain the members' approval as soon as possible, but this time without the inclusion of rule changes which would bring about an increase in contributions.[9]

In August the matter was again put out to ballot. A covering note explained that accepting suspension from the TUC would 'jeopardise and endanger the work of the Association', scarcely an exaggeration in view of the experiences of the last three years in the staff field alone. Some indication of the distaste felt by the leadership for the situation it now found itself in may be gauged from the assertion that 'in the present serious position' members would agree to any loss being borne by the general fund; the only alterations to rule now being tabled were those legally necessary to protect the union under the new Act. A vote in favour, it continued, would not bring about an increase in contributions.[10] The need for a positive result was paramount. Branches polled throughout the month, the last day for returns being the 22nd. Turnout exceeded that in the first ballot by 4805, an increase of nearly 10 per cent, but the extra votes were scarcely needed because the membership had voted for deregistration by a majority in excess of 7:1.[11] Suspension was cancelled forthwith. BISAKTA was now back within the family of the TUC, but the whole episode had been an unpleasant shock.

Ten-Year Strategy

The reason why steel nationalisation commanded support beyond socialist circles was because it seemed to so many to be the only means of achieving a domestic steel industry on the scale and of the modernity required. The drive to build this industry dominated the first decade of the Corporation's life, just as the social consequences of shedding unwanted works dominated the second. As early as 1970, No. 1 Division BOC called for a new iron-ore terminal and a 'modern steel complex' in Scotland.

In fact the late 1960s had brought a happy conjuncture of economic boom and the first spring of modernisation. In 1969 Scunthorpe Division broke all records with an output of 3.3 million tons of steel: the Appleby melting shop alone was responsible for more than one million tons. The Templeborough melting shop sustained an output of 1.5 million tons while Park Gate turned out over 600,000 tons of finished steel. Meanwhile a £76m scheme was authorised to enhance Spencer (Llanwern) and Ravenscraig and lift their output to 2.2 million tons and 3.5 million tons respectively.

Eventually the industry was to have its modernisation, but it was also to have a great deal of pain. Some plants did not even survive the first, heritage, phase at BSC. As early as 1968, the closure of the Open Hearth steelmaking department at Parkgate had attracted substantial criticism, including strictures from Executive member Jack Clark which were echoed at national level by full-time officers. One of TUCSICC's early initiatives was to approach BSC for the establishment of a policy to deal with closures: a move which showed that the former accepted that changes would occur but sought to channel them through defined procedures. By August 1968 Davies was able to report progress towards an agreement which would specify advance notice of closure and full consultation. Meanwhile TUCSICC had drawn up a list of objectives for a redundancy agreement.

So far nationalisation had proved a mixed blessing. Huge advances had been made in approaching long-standing bargaining goals and further success was in prospect. There had also been considerable success in socialising the new Corporation through the introduction of the employee-director scheme and in other ways. However, the possibility of adverse political intervention had been brought painfully home by the staff recognition dispute, and BSC found from the outset that its freedom to achieve the prices it felt its products warranted was severely curtailed. Because steel was the raw material of so much of manufacturing, the temptation for governments to take counter-inflationary steps at its expense was irresistible. BISAKTA was a sturdy ally of the Corporation against artificial depression of its profits by successive ministers of both parties. Why should an increasingly efficient industry make losses to subsidise inefficiencies elsewhere? it asked as Mrs Castle, and her DEP and other ministerial successors, intervened again and again to slow down or cancel steel price increases.

How serious was the threat to the public ownership of steel during the Heath administration?[12] At the end of 1970 the Conservatives were speaking the kind of free-market language which was to become familiar ten years later. BISAKTA backed Lord Melchett in the battle he was reported to be having to retain the size, structure and ownership of BSC, but there was open talk from ministers of hiving off special steels, constructional steels and chemicals from the Corporation he headed. The Executive was sufficiently concerned to table a resolution affirming its support for continued national-isation and opposition to hiving-off at the 1971 BOCs.[13] TUCSICC wrote to the government protesting at rumours of partial privatisation which had appeared in the press. Davies, practical as ever, linked the possibility of de-nationalisation to the even greater danger that the modernisation pro-gramme itself might be in jeopardy: it was 1971 and the grand plan everyone was waiting for had still not appeared. By March monthly steel output had slumped to its lowest level for eight years. With steel prices restrained, clo-sures accelerating and investment apparently deferred, the comparison of Heath to an old-style ironmaster did not seem far-fetched.

Davies briefed Michael Foot, now Opposition spokesman on steel, in advance of a Commons debate on 18 March 1971 provoked by a rash of BSC redundancy announcements. Attempts were made by BISAKTA-sponsored MPs Eddie Griffiths and, especially, Donald Coleman to lay the blame on the government for the plant that was being shut down: there had to be urgent implementation of the modernisation plans. By now the unions had been notified of BSC's intention to cut out 2600 employees by September at Openshaw, Corby, Gorseinon and Roundwood, with the Kaldo plant at Park-gate to follow in 1972/3. On the heels of this came the grim news that BSC now sought to eliminate 7255 jobs at a further ten plants, including Irlam where losses were to exceed 4000. The whole town was woken up by a vig-orous anti-closure campaign – a harbinger if ever there was one – including a huge march on 21 May. A conflict over the role the union should play broke out between Davies and the No. 7 Divisional Officer, Bill Sirs.[14]

The closures had a considerable employment impact in the spring and summer of 1971, though staff aged sixty-two or over who took early retire-ment at this time benefited from the recently concluded national agreement. Steelworkers' fears were accumulating, and were compounded by the way that general unemployment had soared and seemed to be concentrated in the parts of the country where they lived. The EC sought a meeting with Lord Melchett, and the Organisation publicly demanded that closures at least be deferred until there was some prospect that they would not just add to cur-rent distress.

One year later the epoch-making Ten-Year Strategy was finally pub-lished. It was a product of the determined economic expansionism which characterised the Heath administration from the winter of 1971–2. The unhappy Sir John Davies had been succeeded at Trade and Industry by Peter Walker, who pressed ahead with gusto. The widely held impression that the strategy was authorised without sufficient testing may be erroneous, but its output-led approach fitted well with the government's new stance.[15] Dai

Davies met BSC chairman Sir Monty Finniston on 30 June and was informed of a BSC strategic evaluation exercise to probe the options in the report of the Joint Steering Group. The Corporation promised to consult the unions before submitting final proposals for government approval. Davies added his own plea to the Executive that it should agree on future development plans, 'otherwise the Confederation's influence would be greatly restricted'.[16]

For 1972 the EC tabled two resolutions at each BOC. The first expressed anxiety at the high level of imports, 'particularly from Japan', when there was much spare capacity, and called for action against discriminatory trading practices. The second indicated profound concern at manpower cuts at BSC, called for the postponement of redundancies until local employment opportunities were available and called on the government not to restrict BSC's development plans, which anticipated output of 41–2 million tonnes by 1980.[17] This concern in particular had now become a focus for all critics of the government. The delay in announcing the final investment plan had in fact been caused by doubts about demand forecasts, but in Commons debates[18] doubts over the sincerity of the government's commitment to an annual capacity in excess of 40 million tons were the principal stick with which it was beaten.

Finally, on 8 May 1972, the Ten-Year Strategy appeared, proposing five major integrated steelmaking sites, with a possible sixth at Scotland which was to be equipped with new direct reduction technology. Union opinion was hostile. The government had indeed scaled down BSC plans and was thinking in terms of 28–36 million tons by 1980. Since 1970's tonnage was 27.7 million this was hardly cause for cheer. First impressions were that this was 'a shallow exercise in doctrinaire politics' and would perpetuate the under-performance which had allowed Britain to slip so far behind the steelmaking nations it had once led. BISAKTA's influence on Labour thinking was great, and Griffiths and Coleman were to the fore in urging the government to think big when the Opposition moved a censure motion on 23 May.

But this was only one facet of the matter. For while the future industry would be smaller than had been hoped, there would still be extensive closures and job losses that would affect every region of the country. It came as a shock to learn that no less than 24,936 BSC employees had been shed during 1971, and an even greater one to discover that 80 per cent of these were production workers.[19] A key aspect of the strategy was the phasing out of open-hearth steelmaking by 1980: this must mean an even greater loss of process jobs. BISAKTA stood by its commitment to modernisation – the union press acknowledged that open-hearth technology would soon be as out of date as

1 Blast furnaces, Stewarts and Lloyds, Corby, July 1955

2 BSC Shotton, July 1974

3 and 4 How it used to be

5 Steel sheetworkers, 1966

6 Fettling a steel furnace

7 Jack Leonard, BSC
   Worker Director

8 Les Bambury, London
   Area Organiser

9 Bert Dismore, London
   Area Organiser

10 Alan White, BSC Main Board Director

11 A steelworker in parliament: Bill
    Homewood MP, April 1982

12   Maureen Todd at the ADC

13   ISTC delegates at the Women's TUC, 10 March 1978

14 'Lord, Lord, where art thou?':
Ken Sessford, Consett
Executive Member, at the TUC,
1980

15 AGS Jim Diamond in buoyant mood at Swinton
House

16 TUC Gold Badge recipient Jack Clark accepts the award from TUC President David
Basnett, September 1978

17   Conference highlights: Dai Davies addresses the Special BISAKTA Conference, April 1973

18   Conference highlights: The Prince of Wales meets the Union, June 1979

19 Industry Secretary Eric Varley meets Bilston representatives, Labour Party Conference, 4 October 1978

20 Jim Callaghan rallies the unions in opposition, ISTC Executive, July 1979

21 Tony Benn backs Bilston's fight, October 1978

puddling furnaces – but it was not going to acquiesce in the change unless the breathing space before closure was used to provide employment opportunities. Government time-wasting had squandered the opportunity to modernise during a period of expansion; this kind of shift while there was a recession would compound the misery.

The full implications of the Ten-Year Strategy were spelled out by Walker in a statement of 25 January 1973 to the House of Commons. 'It is only by modernisation,' he declared, with reference to the position a decade thence, that 'we can secure the 180,000 jobs then remaining at BSC.' What a pregnant 'then' that was! For to arrive at 180,000 it was necessary to subtract first the 27,000 jobs already lost, then to add a further 20,000 announced losses and finally to top up with 30,000 extra reductions by the end of the decade. The possibility that even all this might still not secure the remaining 180,000 jobs occurred to very few. In the debate which followed Walker's statement it was Griffiths who voiced BISAKTA's principal concern when he asked what would be done to attract alternative industries to areas threatened with closures. He was told that communities which were substantially affected would have the appropriate government departments at their command to help with diversification 'years before the closure'.

Now that the government had finally shown its hand, difficulties began to appear on the Opposition side. Individual MPs wished very naturally to protect their constituency interests, but this was not and would not be the position of BISAKTA. It had always had a pro-modernisation stance, and would not easily switch to backing a plan to keep obsolete plant in being in order to avoid closures. Only now were the implications of this becoming widely appreciated, for modernisation was no longer a demand but a reality.[20] So serious were the implications of the Ten-Year Strategy that BISAKTA resolved upon the unusual step of summoning a conference of the Association in London on 18 April 1973. To guide discussion a draft resolution was put before delegates, its main arguments capturing the Organisation's outlook at this critical moment:

- the need to develop a modern and competitive steel industry;
- deep concern at 'the grave effect on employment of the prospective plant closures';
- doubt that the proposed expansion of output to 33–5 million tonnes by the late 1970s and to 36–8 million tonnes by the first half of the 1980s would be sufficient to meet the demand the government's envisaged economic growth would generate, or to take advantage of the opportunities offered by EEC accession;

- a call for BSC to be allowed 'to extend its activities into other appropriate production areas' and enter into joint ventures with other enterprises;
- the need to require BSC 'to create job opportunities among its own employees by entering stockholding, transport and handling and using its own workforce for presently contracted-out work';
- the need for each closure proposal to be examined by a bipartite committee with a remit to cover the economic and social consequences of closure, and for closure to occur only where searching examination had revealed there was no alternative;
- where closure was inevitable it should not take place 'until satisfactory job opportunities' had been made available in the locality for all those who would be made redundant;
- and the need for special attention to be drawn to the government's 'major responsibility' wherever redundancy occurred.[21]

This seminal resolution anticipated the arguments of the next decade. It was not easy to write. The experience of closure was not new, as the process of plant scrapping and renewal was part of the life cycle of the steel industry. But closure on this scale was unprecedented and posed serious problems for regions which had never experienced genuinely full employment. Characteristically, the resolution reaffirmed BISAKTA's long-standing commitment to modernisation. The 108 delegates backed it overwhelmingly[22] after a day-long debate.

Afterwards the resolution was circulated to interested parties. The Industry Minister, Tom Boardman, replied that the government accepted its joint responsibility with BSC for tackling the social consequences of modernisation, indicating that the former's proposed measures were in the White Paper. He also undertook to give sympathetic consideration to BSC proposals for changes to its scope of activity if they were designed to promote employment and complementary to its main functions.[23]

By 1974 discussions within BISAKTA at to the future shape of British Steel had moved on. At the BOCs the Scots were showing signs of uncertainty over Hunterston,[24] but were the first to raise the issue of the extension of mini-mills as a resurgence of the private sector; their call for the whole of the industry to be acquired for the public sector was 'approved in principle' by the EC. A doubt as to the orientation of leadership policy emerged when the same division demanded that the EC specify what forms of action it had in mind to resist closures.[25]

Time was passing. Less than three months after Labour returned to office on 1 March 1974, the incoming Industry Secretary, Anthony Wedgwood

Benn, authorised a review of the proposed closures. This review, led by Lord Beswick, inevitably focused on the social consequences of industrial modernisation. His interim (February 1975) report[26] responded to the fears of the steel areas by, effectively, postponing the evil day. Closures which had seemed imminent would now fall due from late 1978, with the exception of Ebbw Vale where BSC proposals for the closure of iron and steelmaking were accepted by the government. It was a further breathing space, but would it be used to create sufficient alternative employment? As to the scale and configuration of BSC, Beswick proposed no radical change except that the government should permit it to accelerate its investment programme so as to reach a capacity of 37 million tonnes in the early 1980s. His findings were greeted with relief, but it was to become all too clear that he had bought only time.

Development of union services

On 30 March 1967 the new Larkhill convalescent home had been opened by Dai Davies in the presence of the two previous General Secretaries, representatives of private industry and local dignitaries. The new structure drew praise from architects.[27] It incorporated sixteen double bedrooms, eight single bedrooms and a basement (made possible by the slope of the site) which served as a games area. There was no doubt that the Executive's decision to locate the new building on the site of the old was vindicated, for the home's visitors and residents continued to enjoy the former views of Conway Castle and Llandudno to the east and the Snowdon range to the west. Over the next quarter of a century thousands of convalescing members were to see it.

An historic recommendation of the Education Sub-committee to the August 1970 Executive required Central Office to present proposals for setting up a structure for trade union education within BISAKTA.[28] Jim Diamond was given responsibility for leading an inquiry into enhanced educational provision, and this led to the first BISAKTA residential course on industrial relations being held for one week at Ruskin College, Oxford, in July 1971.[29] The following year brought a more systematic approach to education in the divisions, with each of them hosting four-day training courses. The summer school now expanded to accommodate fifty steelworkers, and the familiar syllabus of address by the General Secretary, history of the union, briefings on Central Office procedures, branch administration and negotiation techniques, and speeches by MPs began to emerge. In 1973 the problem of numbers was handled by providing a spring and an autumn course, each with twenty-five students. But the union also continued to support and encourage attendance at summer schools now held under the auspices of the WEA, which had formerly been provided by WETUC.[30] In

August 1974 EC congratulated Diamond's successor (Assistant General Secretary Roy Evans – see next chapter), who had taken over responsibility for the programme, for the production in draft of a Branch Officers' Manual.[31] In April 1975 the first Advanced National School convened at York University, with places open only to those who had attended previous divisional or national (short) schools.

Effective from 1 January 1974, the Executive Council substituted the name 'Iron and Steel Trades Confederation' for BISAKTA. The former Confederation now took the unused name 'Combined Association of Metalworkers' (CAM), but henceforward existed only for formal purposes.[32] The way was now clear for formality to correspond to reality. In practice the Organisation was increasingly known as the Iron and Steel Trades Confederation or by its acronym ISTC: Davies, for example, had consistently opted for this label throughout his evidence to Pearson even though *Man and Metal* was at that very time running recruitment ads asking BSC staff to join BISAKTA. With confusion removed the new name quickly became well known, though some argued a price was to be paid in that it imperfectly reflected the entire range of membership by losing any reference to the 'Kindred Trades' which comprised most of the London Area membership and were present in some of the Divisions.

As time passed, the possibility of a national conference was again in the air. This hardy annual had been revived by No. 2 Division at the 1971 BOC, but interest was seriously reawakened by the 1973 conference and seems to have been unstoppable thereafter. That year the No. 1 Division BOC sought such a gathering to plan a campaign backing BISAKTA's criticisms of the development strategy, and a policy-making conference; No. 2 Division sought a conference to address 'the social consequences arising from rapid technological advances'; No. 4 sought such a conference to meet 'the requirements of national economy and changes in the steel industry'; and No. 7 called for a national conference of branch officers annually nine weeks after the BOCs. Of these, the No. 7 call was put before the Rules Revision Committee[33] but not out to ballot. That opinion was hardening is evident from the re-presentation of the demand in 1974 by the BOCs of Divisions Nos. 1, 2 and 4 and the London Area, and (for the first time) No. 5 Division. The following year all but No. 2 Division reiterated their demands, and they were joined by Division No. 7.

White-collar membership again

In May 1971 the Executive heard that agreement on proposals to form the basis of a national award had been reached between TUCSICC and BSC. At the National Staff Committee, however, there was serious resistance to the draft, and TUCSICC representatives returned to negotiations to secure an improvement. The agreement was not finally notified by the EC until November and was signed by TUCSICC shortly after. This disagreement had illustrated a gap in procedures, which was resolved by conferring on the National Staff Committee the status of a national negotiating committee.[34] To eradicate local problems in implementing the award for 1972, a joint BSC/ISTC National Joint Co-ordinating Committee was established in February.[35] That year it was also agreed in principle to establish a similar committee for private sector staff.[36] Indeed, 1972 turned out to be a strong year for the staff organisation, which gained almost 1000 new members in the first half of the year, largely owing to the spread of the union into laboratories outside the traditional steelmaking centres. The new Co-ordinating Committee met several times and ratified local agreements for bringing in at least part of the national agreement on salary structures and conditions of employment: most day staff were now on a thirty-five-hour week and equal pay for women would be achieved 'within the next 18 months'.[37] The Staff Conference, always willing to pass resolutions, was extending its range to embrace a large number of non-wage benefits: in 1972 it voted for retirement at sixty for staff grades. When the government-backed Pay Board and BSC Boards agreed to full implementation of the 1973 agreement, the way was open to local negotiations which would for the first time put the majority of all staff on common conditions of employment.

Across in the private sector, finalisation of a 'National Recognition and Procedure Agreement' was imminent,[38] and now the possibility of establishing a National Joint Consultative Committee was raised with the ISEA. The employers for their part pleaded, with some justice, that some of their member companies were often only marginally involved in steel production, and BISAKTA was prepared to live with their wish to have a period of experience of the new national agreement before taking further steps.[39]

While BISAKTA had entered the 1970s with substantial staff membership, there were considerably fewer grounds for optimism over management recruitment. The union had now entered on a prolonged and bruising battle with SIMA for the allegiance of these grades, a battle which was to last for more than a decade. In this conflict the union often encountered a major obstacle in the shape of local labour officers (later personnel managers), whose lack of enthusiasm for a union presence among close colleagues sometimes undermined progress made at national level. BISAKTA policy had been laid down in its Circular 19/70. The EC had to fend off complaints from its own middle management branches about the slowness of movement, but endorsed Davies's wise view that a national agreement would not be achieved until BISAKTA could prove it had the membership to support the claim.[40] The following year there were contacts between the two organisations, and the EC guardedly concluded that unnecessary conflicts which might jeopardise relations should be avoided. Despite its wishes, however, a local clash was now to reveal anew the gulf between the two sides.

During December 1972 BISAKTA was at odds with BSC over recognition and negotiating rights at the (Scunthorpe) Anchor Project. When some members were instructed to implement hot trials at the medium section mill they refused, in line with union policy. They were suspended by management and a total stoppage ensued, for which the Scunthorpe membership received full Executive backing. The stoppage was suspended, on a BISAKTA initiative, on 2 January 1973, when BSC agreed to national talks within a twenty-eight-day period, during which there would be no hot trials at the BOS plant but they would be permitted in the mills. A settlement proved elusive, however, despite meetings during January. At its February meeting the EC was forced to renew its ban on trials at the BOS plant.

The dispute dragged on through the spring, with the BISAKTA leadership under heavy criticism from its own branches and from individuals. Frustrated at the unwillingness of BSC to meet its demands (and its reiteration of a desire to see a BISAKTA/SIMA accommodation), the EC authorised Davies to write to Finniston to warn him that it could no longer be relied upon to limit the dispute as it had done hitherto. On 7 May the EC decided to grant a request from 140 Scunthorpe BOS plant members for unemployment benefit, and on 18 May, at his own request, Lord Melchett visited the EC to discuss the dispute.

Melchett put a formula to the EC: suspension of SIMA recognition in the Anchor, BOS and Concast plants; 'immediate, rapid and meaningful discussions' on SIMA/ISTC amalgamation under an independent (and jointly agreed) chair; in the event of failure of the talks there would be reversion to the *status quo ante* and BSC would consider the scope of national recognition of both unions; all three parties would intend not only to resolve the Anchor dispute but also to address its underlying causes with a view to preventing a recurrence. Later that day the EC conveyed its agreement to Melchett's formula. The following day he visited SIMA to put the same points to them.

Joint meetings were held on 10, 17 and 23 July 1973 under the distinguished chairmanship of Industrial Relations Professor Hugh Clegg. Drafts were exchanged and each side agreed to refer them back to its ruling body.[41] By the autumn, however, hopes had collapsed. In November Davies reported to the EC that the committee (including, by implication, Clegg himself) had concluded that no purpose would be served by further negotiations, since SIMA was prolonging them without any serious intention of entering into a transfer of engagements. This was not to be the last middle management clash at Scunthorpe.

BISAKTA requested Monty Finniston, who had succeeded Lord Melchett as chairman following the latter's sudden death in May, to implement point three of the Melchett formula, and Davies received EC backing for adopting a more aggressive recruitment policy.[42] Finniston felt that the matter must be referred to his Board; after further exchanges BSC proposed a new national joint industrial council which would include SIMA. Having taken his organisation to the brink of a strike over a similar issue in the staff sector, Davies was not likely to agree. The Executive was under pressure from branches to seek a national recognition agreement and establish a national management staff committee, and in May 1974 it called for the reconvening of the Clegg Committee in a final attempt to resolve the matter, failing which it would reconvene in a special meeting.

Progress was at last made in June 1974, when national recognition was gained for ISTC middle managers. This, in the view of Executive President Hanbury Williams (a staff man), posed the issue of establishing some kind of national machinery for those grades; but this step, on the advice of Davies, was deferred.[43] Notwithstanding this caution, morale rose on the breaking of the stalemate. Recruitment efforts were enhanced, and many supervisory grades were transferred to newly established middle management branches.[44] SIMA braced itself for a recruitment onslaught, and by May Feather was announcing that he hoped soon be able to report a 'substantial' increase in membership.[45] Middle management first met BSC in national negotiations on 7 November 1974.[46] Some of the flavour of the time may be gauged from the March 1975 quarterly report of London Area organiser Les Bambury, who recorded that 'a small branch of members of middle management employed at the Brimsdown works of Delta Enfield Cables' had been formed. So interest had spread not only to the private sector but to non-ferrous metals.

Pay and politics

Public sector employees found increases in their earnings tended to be below the rate of inflation from the time the Conservatives returned to office in June 1970. The U-turn of 1971, which had set the context for expansion at BSC, had also marked a shift towards pay restraint, and steelworkers found their wage aspirations blocked as the Employment Department introduced limits on increases with statutory effect. With inflation accelerating and government pressure on the public sector to minimise pay increases rising, the EC came under considerable pressure from the HST Area Committees to win a substantial award. Area No. 2, for example, called for an all-round rise of 35 per cent.[47] And at times major public sector advances could be secured, as when the rise in the minimum day rate at BSC rose by 10.5 per cent. If the private sector had been at any advantage this was soon lost when a pay freeze was legislated in the autumn of 1972. Many companies at this date still retained a cost-of-living sliding scale which they had fought to retain – almost certainly at a cost of higher general increases. They now stood to lose the benefits of the scale, even though it had been legitimately negotiated long before.

But BISAKTA did not find itself driven – like the electricity supply workers in 1970, the post office workers in 1971 and the miners in 1972 – into industrial action. In 1972–4 the country experienced a massive series of national stoppages, but BISAKTA always balanced its desire to be part of the movement against the Conservatives against its powerful sense of responsibility to steel. When the 1973 TUC Special Congress called a day of national protest for fair policies on prices, pensions and pay on 1 May, the EC took the view that there were already adequate opportunities for protest and called on its members not to stop work.

With Edward Heath in Downing Street there was little doubt that a new application to join the EEC would be presented at an early date. BISAKTA entered the 1970s more convinced than ever that membership of the Common Market was essential for Britain, but in this it represented – for the time being – a minority view in the Labour Party. BISAKTA began increasingly to feel frustration at the way a difference over principle was disguised as a debate over terms (though this of course was to be the way Labour finally found some unity over the issue). The Organisation's delegation attended the 1971 Labour Special Conference mandated to back the NEC statement but to vote in favour of entry should the statement fall.[48] In later years the Executive always resisted calls, notably from No. 1 Division, to reconsider its traditional stance.[49] From 1973 BISAKTA had direct representation on the European Coal and Steel Consultative Committee (ECSC), and it had every intention of using this foothold to the full to protect the interests of the British steelworker. Indeed, the Organisation's early positive attitude was now reaping dividends, for Davies in June 1973 became the first ever British President of the ECSC, a key liaison post to hold during the country's first year of membership. Decisions such as that of the 1973 TUC to boycott EEC committees did not affect what BISAKTA did as an individual union, but the Organisation could only shake its head at the folly of leaving a clear continental field to the employers' associations.

Nor was it simply a matter of union prestige. For 1973 had also seen the introduction of the Iron and Steel Employees' Readaptation Scheme (ISERBS), which provided steelworkers (and miners) with non-repayable financial aid which over time was to flow into make-up of wages following redeployment, funding retraining, or early retirement. These costs were partly covered by the EEC,[50] but the commitment depended on matching funding by the UK government. The significance of this was to become apparent twenty years later when ISERBS was abolished, but in the medium term ISERBS benefits figured hugely as social compensation in steel areas all too soon to be devastated by massive closures. Equity was achieved for BISAKTA steel members at firms making products not covered by the Treaty of Paris when Davies negotiated, on their behalf, an agreement to match the provisions of ISERBS. This was the Employment and Income Security Agreement (EISA).

In 1974 gathering discontents with the Conservatives over pay, employment law, public sector cuts and unemployment precipitated two general elections, the first of which returned Labour to office and the second of which briefly produced for it an overall majority in the House of Commons. *Man and Metal*, which tended to set the tone of the Organisation's approach, was much more muted in its support for Labour. BISAKTA was not impressed with the lack of constructive thinking about steel on the Labour side, and the increased salience of the EEC as a policy issue tended to divide the Organisation from many in the Party. And both at the TUC and in the Labour Party, the union was increasingly disturbed at the drift to the left. In the February contest the two sponsored MPs were easily returned, and Parliamentary Panel member Dennis Turner was only 4000 votes behind the Conservative in Halesowen and Stourbridge.

But the new militancy of the Labour Party was about to claim the scalp of one of the two BISAKTA MPs. During 1973 Eddie Griffiths had been embattled with his constituency party in Sheffield Brightside. He had been accused of failing to keep his promise to live in the area, of associating too closely with Conservative MPs and of being unrepresentative of local Party opinion. Though he remained the Labour candidate for the February 1974 general election he failed to regain the constituency party's nomination for that year's second election. His appeal to the Party's National Executive was turned down on 11 September and he decided to stand as an Independent Labour candidate. But the official Labour candidate comfortably saw off his challenge and this marked the end of Griffiths's political career. At the end of the year he seemed to lay blame on the Organisation for his failure, though without much evidence.[51] Elsewhere Donald Coleman was comfortably returned at Neath, and Dennis Turner was desperately unlucky to stop just 851 votes short at Halesowen; Paul Flynn, another panel member, achieved a creditable result in Denbigh. Despite these auguries, the net result was to reduce ISTC parliamentary representation again to one; but BISAKTA hoped to benefit from having in office a Labour government committed to a consensual social contract.

The private sector

Nationalisation had left a private sector of about 110 companies employing some 95,000 people and producing about two million ingot tons at 160 works. Its output consisted mainly of special steels whose high value belied this ton-nage, for it accounted for one-third of annual industrial turnover in iron and steel. In this period there was, in the words of David Heal, a 'ragged frontier' between public and private sectors, which actually passed through such plants as Shepcote Lane. It would also be true to say that it was a shifting frontier as works like Brymbo, briefly nationalised, passed in 1969 back into the private sector. The challenge for BISAKTA was to sustain comparable progress on terms and conditions for the membership left outside BSC, and if possible to increase its size.

Many of the private firms took up membership of the Iron and Steel Employers' Association (ISEA), while others were covered by the Midland Wages Board. At nationalisation, the withdrawal of five companies forced the Board to recast its constitution on non-territorial lines, and by 1972 ten operatives were being nominated from the General Board section and four from Cold Rolling. Difficulties erupted from time to time over the extent to which management could be involved in persuading recalcitrant members to join the union.[52] These could feed into conventional disputes, such as the failure to agree a BISAKTA claim for £3 per forty-hour week in December 1971, at the end of a two-year agreement. The dispute had to be referred to arbitration (which under the MWB constitution was by the president of the Board), but the spirit of the arrangements is best illustrated by the imme-diate acceptance of his award, even though it fell considerably short of union hopes.[53]

At first, BISPA was very much what was left after nationalisation. The largest producers had gone, and there were many rollers and re-rollers which depended on the new BSC for their supplies. Under the 1967 Act ministers continued to have a responsibility for this private sector, but for many years the responsibility was not activated. It was galvanised not by the state but by the arrival in the 1970s of new foreign owners willing to invest in electric-arc-based steelmaking: Sheerness Steel in 1972, Manchester Steel in 1973, and

Alpha Steel. BISAKTA organised a private sector CNC to co-ordinate its approach. Companies in ISEA were prepared to negotiate general improvements, and after some years a pattern emerged whereby private sector pay increases could compare well, but attempts to obtain improvements in non-wage elements to match those being obtained at BSC were like drawing teeth.

In 1972, BISAKTA obtained an agreement at the new Sheerness steel-works conferring sole organising rights upon it, a step which drew protests from John Boyd, the General Secretary of the Amalgamated Untion of Engineering Workers (AUEW) and the NCCC convenor.[54] The works was accommodated more generously in the structure of the HST Private Sector in 1973, when each of the divisions in Area No. 5 was allocated one representative on the CNC and two on the Standing Committee. However, 1974 brought a seven-week craftsmen's strike which arose essentially from a dispute between AUEW and BISAKTA. All the craft unions backed their members in a bid for recognition; BISAKTA members remained in employment for all but the last few days of the stoppage. It was referred to a TUC Disputes Committee, from which the Confederation sought a ruling under Bridlington Principles 7 and 8. The result was a triumph for BISAKTA, with maintenance ancillary workers coming into membership in November.[55] They joined other works in the private sector where craft and maintenance grades were BISAKTA members, such as Round Oak or Brierley Hill.

Inauguration of Sheerness was one of the last major achievements of H.C. ('Bert') Dismore, who retired in November 1972 after twenty-five years as London Area organiser.[56] His successor, Les Bambury, had been the London Area Executive member for the last eight years. Outside steel, the 1970s threw up some possibilities of membership growth. In the spring of 1971 Davies met the leadership of the Laminated and Coil Spring Workers' Union (LCSWU) to explore the possibility of a merger, but assimilation was found by the end of the year to be irreconcilable with Rule 27.[57] A further attempt to merge was made in the following year, but it too foundered, on the impracticability of BISAKTA's offering the smaller organisation autonomy within its rules.[58]

The succession

The 1973 New Year's Honours List brought a knighthood to Dai Davies, as earlier ones had to his two predecessors. Though it was a cause of personal and BISAKTA pride, the accolade also underlined that an era was drawing to a close, for Sir Dai was due to retire the following year. Awareness of this was heightened when in May 1973 Jim Diamond, who had recently lost his wife, informed the Executive of his intention to seek early retirement on grounds of ill-health, confronting it with the need rapidly to find a suitably qualified successor. It resolved this problem by requesting Davies to stay on for one year beyond normal retirement age and deciding to appoint two Assistant General Secretaries forthwith so that they could work up experience in post.[59] After applicants had been examined by the TUC a shortlist of eight was interviewed by the EC; the fifty-five year old William ('Bill') Sirs, Divisional Officer of No. 7 Division, and the forty-three year old R.L. (Roy) Evans, Organiser of No. 6 Division, were appointed. Sirs's seniority seemed to be acknowledged with his immediate nomination to the NEC of the Labour Party.[60] Evans was given responsibility for the expanding education programme. Nominations were opened under Rule 6 for a new General Secretary at the November 1974 EC, Davies being due to retire on 1 December the following year. At their meeting on 19 February 1975 the EC accepted a recommendation of its Organisation and Staffing Sub-committee that Sirs be appointed against two other nominees: Evans, and Roger Williams of the Statistical Department. Soon after this Sirs was nominated to the TUC General Council for 1975.

Sir Dai Davies had led the ISTC from nationalisation to the point where steel's longed-for modernisation was about to arrive. As the ISTC's only leader to date to deal with BSC he must be given credit for gaining maximum advantages for the membership from the opportunities available to them. Huge advances had been made in terms and conditions, and it seemed that the insecurity of past years had been consigned to the historical dustbin. Davies's skills as a negotiator and speaker had been called on extensively to defend the union's position in the new public sector, and he had succeeded in fighting off the challenge from the non-steel staff unions. The employment conditions of members in the public sector, and to a large extent also in the private sector, had been revolutionised in these years. Pensions were a glittering example. All BSC manual grades now belonged to a superannuation scheme which, for those who enjoyed a working life of reasonable length, would give them financial comfort in old age.[61] And on the eve of Davies's retirement the staff scheme was upgraded to factor in full inflation-proofing, a frozen 'modification factor' (which reflected contributions to state pensions) and a more liberal interpretation of average pensionable salary. Elsewhere, while there might not be greater security at work, there was substantially greater compensation when it was lacking, and the working week was shorter and set to be cut yet more.

The Pearson episode had underlined BISAKTA's position in the TUC: if no longer one of the Big Five, the Organisation had brilliantly mobilised the entire movement against what might have been a mortal threat. Yet this position had undoubtedly been eroded by events surrounding the Industrial Relations Act, when the eventual shift of policy had been undignified and had given an impression, however unjustified, of lukewarm opposition to Conservative legislation. Moreover, all was not well at BSC: massive change hung in the air and there was something of a vacuum in policy terms at BISAKTA. The stance of welcoming and co-operating in modernisation had stood the Organisation in good stead for nearly half a century. Now at last actual modernisation was near. Would a new leadership be able to harness it to advantage?

Notes

1 The June 1970 *Man and Metal* carried a remarkable double page montage of cuttings reporting record outputs at plants across the country, overprinted with the slogan 'We Made It Under Labour'.

2 'A "New" Government', *Man and Metal* (July 1970).

3 The resolution affirmed a long-standing view that good industrial relations and observance of agreements did not depend on 'legal enforcement'. The Bill would, it argued, adversely affect relations in steel by inhibiting the effectiveness of union officials and thereby 'have serious repercussions' on efficiency. The intrusion of the law into traditionally voluntary areas of union organisation and collective bargaining was condemned (*Reports*, 1971, 141).

4 *Reports* (1971), 151. One nominee, G. Cook of Corby No. 4 branch, was not renominated to Industrial Tribunals by the Organisation in 1974, specifically due to 'his failure to conform to TUC policy in relation to the Industrial Relations Act' (*Reports*, 1974, 578).

5 Meanwhile branches were instructed to stay out of agency agreements (*Reports*, 1972, 58).

6 The strange wording of this clause stated in effect that any increases in contributions consequential upon deregistration would be rescinded when the circumstances no longer applied ('Revision of Rules', 1972).

7 *Reports* (1972), 117.

8 *Man and Metal* (August 1972).

9 *Reports* (1972), 189.

10 To avoid any possible remaining uncertainty the boxes for the cross on the ballot paper were marked 'FOR the action of the Executive Council in taking immediate steps to deregister' and 'FOR the proposed alterations of Rules set out within and required to enable the Association to deregister'.

11 The votes were: for immediate steps to deregister – 48,456 to 6710; for the proposed alteration of rules – 48,050 to 6700 (*Reports*, 1972, 263). The 1975 rules revision ballot restored the previous position of BISAKTA within the law.

12 Heath had committed himself to denationalisation in 1965 during the passage of the legislation which established BSC, but he did not return to the idea, and

suppressed a report of the nationalised industries policy committee which advocated the restoration of private ownership. J. Campbell, *Edward Heath* (1994), 235.

13 The resolution called for the government explicitly to renounce major changes of ownership of steel in order to dispel uncertainty, and warned that any attempt to return profitable parts of BSC to the private sector would be opposed by 'all the strength and determination' at command. It was approved by all BOCs, though No. 1 Division carried an amendment (rejected by the EC) which opposed all change and rejected private interests buying shares in BSC. *Reports* (1971), 141. Among the Scottish membership, concern was sharply focused on the prospect of a new complex at Hunterston which it was thought would ensure viability. In 1971 No. 1 Division BOC passed two resolutions urging more action on the Executive.

14 Area No. 4 called in 1971 for Irlam to be kept as an operating unit of BSC, a demand which in the view of the EC was already being met by its continuing concern for all members affected by closures. *Reports* (1971), 151.

15 The Prime Minister himself would not agree to Walker's expansion proposals before the BSC Board had been interrogated by the full Cabinet. Campbell, *Edward Heath* (1994), 485.

16 *Reports* (1972), 220.

17 Each BOC passed the resolutions but No. 1 Division went further, reaffirming its Hunterston demand but linking it to the EEC which it called – unsuccessfully – on the EC to oppose. *Reports* (1972), 154.

18 For example that on 16 December 1971, in which many speakers used examples from *Man and Metal* to buttress their arguments.

19 Craft grades had increased by over 2000.

20 It is impossible to read the Commons debates without wincing at the glibness with which some MPs on the Labour side talked about 'superimposing' on the plan an extra five or seven million tons of 'ingot capacity'.

21 The resolution, which pledged the full resources of BISAKTA in support of these demands, was passed at a special EC meeting on 30 March 1973. *Reports* (1973), 115.

22 One voted against and there were four abstentions.

23 Within the divisions concern tended to focus on fear of redundancy, with the exception – as ever – of Scotland, where BSC was urged into stockholding. The Scots had, of course, secured one of their objectives with the inclusion of Hunterston in the strategy, though time would show that the commitment was not irrevocable.

24 Calling, for example, for the Scottish output target to be raised from 4.5 to 8 million tonnes, but also for the building of a petrochemical complex. *Reports* (1974), 468.

25 *Reports* (1974), 469.

26 Beswick's second report, published later the same year, dealt with Scotland in much the same fashion.

27 *Illustrated Carpenter* commented that the building 'achieved an almost perfect

marriage with the landscape', and praised its 'strong sense of security and serenity' (quoted in *Man and Metal*, March 1967, 99). Larkhill was to receive the Group A commendation in the 1968 Civic Trust awards.

28 *Reports* (1970), 236.

29 The twenty-two-session course was a huge success and set a precedent in being attended by prestigious speakers including Vic Feather and the two BISAKTA MPs.

30 In October 1971 BSC ceased to make a charge for deducting union contributions at source, in exchange for which BISAKTA agreed to put aside the savings for funding the education and training of permanent officers and any special training thought desirable for BISAKTA officials. *Reports* (1971), 267.

31 *Reports* (1974), 541.

32 *Reports* (1973), 311–12. The transfer was ratified by the CAM on 20 February 1974.

33 *Reports* (1973), 158.

34 BSC welcomed this proposal, which was enjoined on the EC by a large number of South Wales branches in the last quarter of 1971. In effect the step shifted staff members into the same circumstances as industrial grades, with common conditions and general increases negotiated nationally while individual salary structures, jobs and manning were subject to local negotiation (*Reports*, 1971, 304–5). In 1973, however, the EC rejected a request to allow members of the committee to attend the National Staff Conference in that capacity and not as branch delegates (*Reports*, 1972, 57). The following year the EC resisted pressure from the same branches to authorise the National Staff Negotiating Committee to meet BSC directly to negotiate all staff salaries and conditions of service outside TUCSICC (*Reports*, 1973, 145).

35 *Reports* (1972), 46.

36 At the instigation of the Spencer LD Foremen's branch (*Reports*, 1972, 166). Within the private sector extensive membership had been established, and in most establishments there were local procedure agreements. Feather met the ISEA early in 1973 but found it resistant to the notion of common conditions of employment and salary levels, and indeed to the prospect of national bargaining. Nevertheless, drafts of a staff recognition and procedure agreement were exchanged that summer. With agreement in sight approaches were made to the MWB, in most of whose works local recognition rights had been obtained for staff.

37 *Reports* (1972), 231.

38 It was signed at the end of 1973. While similar in a number of respects to the public sector agreement, that for the ISEA differed crucially in that it gave sole recognition rights to BISAKTA.

39 *Reports* (1973), 302.

40 *Reports* (1971), 32. In February complaints of SIMA activity were reported from Scunthorpe, Parkgate and Consett.

41 BISAKTA had to acquiesce in a rather leisurely SIMA timetable: its General

Secretary had reported that he was unable to convene the SIMA National Council before 23 September, an apparently unavoidable delay which seemed to conflict with undertakings given to the late Lord Melchett.

42 *Reports* (1973), 260.

43 The November 1974 EC, acting on a request from the influential Spencer managerial staff branch, asked Central Office to examine the membership distribution with a view to putting a plan for electing a negotiating committee before its next meeting. From the same quarter, the EC itself began to come under pressure to have middle management representation.

44 There was some over-enthusiasm. In November 1974 the EC noted that the Teesside MM Branch sought sole recognition at the new Redcar complex even though it only had one member there. It was told that the Organisation intended to honour the terms of the new agreement.

45 *Reports* (1974), 528. Many of the resolutions to that year's Staff Conference, calling for tougher action against SIMA, were overtaken by the winning of recognition; but signs of appreciation of the new situation were evident in the broadening vista of resolution subjects, such as superannuation and dates for the opening of negotiations.

46 The Confederation side consisted of an ad hoc negotiating committee in the absence of a formal representative structure. In February 1975 the EC accepted proposals for the formation of a Middle Management National Negotiating Committee comprising one representative of each division plus Central Office representatives.

47 *Reports* (1971), 151.

48 *Reports* (1971), 175.

49 As for example when it resisted putting the issue out to ballot or a conference. *Reports* (1973), 157.

50 The EEC derived this money in part from an ECSC levy paid by all steel producers within its territory.

51 *Reports* (1974), 567. The standard account of this general election concludes: 'the affair served as a text for charges about the growing left-wing dominance in the Labour Party, but it centered as much on personal as on political grounds' (D. Butler and D. Kavanagh, *The British General Election of October 1974*, 1975, 208–9.

52 In 1972 the employers were given a sharp warning by Davies, the Operatives' Secretary, that they depended on BISAKTA to provide a membership for the Board. This seems to have been effective, because soon afterwards two-thirds of them were operating the check-off.

53 He ruled for a £1.50 increase plus cost of living. See Taylor, *op. cit.*, 34.

54 *Reports* (1972), 166.

55 *Reports* (1974), 598. Analogous problems were brewing at Patent Shaft, where, in the view of Divisional Office, local AUEW officials were following their own policy regardless of instructions from their national officers. The issue had arisen

when a number of ISTC members had defected to the Engineers' union and a great deal of difficulty was encountered in persuading them to return.

56 Dismore (1908–76) had worked at the Enfield rolling mills and E & E Kaye before his appointment in 1947. During his quarter of a century as Area Organiser he organised the rolling mill attached for a time to Ford of Dagenham.

57 *Reports* (1971), 131, 284. The EC thought the answer lay in the LCSWU first winding up its affairs.

58 This had been the wish of the LCSWU at its 1971 annual meeting, which had been attended by Divisional Organiser Joe Pickles. The final form of the proposal was that LCSWU should be temporarily affiliatied but retain its autonomy (*Reports*, 1972, 144).

59 *Reports* (1973), 131–2. Davies actually retired in May 1975.

60 *Reports* (1973), 191. The effective date of appointment of each was 10 September.

61 All existing works schemes were superseded by the new scheme in which the BSC commitment would be 5/3rds that of the members. There were additional credits in order to phase in older workers, and inflation-proofing in the years before retirement.

6

The price of change
Bill Sirs (1975–9)

'No plant is safe under this management.'

Introduction

Bill Sirs[1] was to prove an unusual General Secretary. He came to office vested with more democratic hopes than any of his predecessors. He was to be the only ISTC[2] leader to bring out his members on a national strike. He achieved greater fame among the public than any who preceded him. Yet this same man also faced accusations of autocratic rule, and belied charges of militancy by becoming a staunch supporter of the Labour Party leadership in the toughest phase of its battle with the left. Sirs made his presence felt early and attended his first full EC with the rank of General Secretary side by side with Davies: his was a baptism of fire.

BSC: the first crisis

For years, job losses had been considered in the context of modernisation, a juxtaposition underlined by the publication of two Beswick Reports in February and August 1975. Yet this same year brought a slump in home demand which speedily hustled BSC into crisis: between 1973 and 1975 2.5 million tonnes of home consumption (measured in crude steel equivalent) were lost.

The Steel Committee,[3] where Sirs had succeeded Davies as Chairman, met BSC on 5 May 1975 to learn the details of a plan for 22,000 redundancies, already featured in the press. BSC, pleading recessionary pressures, proposed to load low-cost plants at the expense of others which faced a longer-term threat and now might close far sooner. To facilitate this step BSC wished to suspend the Guaranteed Week Agreement (GWA), a measure which the

106

Steel Committee rejected along with other aspects of the plan: what was the agreement there for if not for use when times were hard? The unions enlisted the help of Tony Benn, Secretary of State for Trade and Industry since Labour's return to power the previous year. Benn was incensed at Finniston's failure to give him advance warning of the cuts and had issued a public reprimand to the BSC Chairman. He indicated his backing for the unions' resistance to job losses on such a scale, and on 8 May attended a meeting with the ISTC Executive. Benn believed that a short-term recession should not be used to expedite long-term closure plans; that steelworkers' morale was a 'priceless asset'; that premature closure at Irlam and Skinningrove had contributed to shortages of supply during the two previous years; and that attempts were being made to exclude government from the nationalised industries' affairs. He called on Executive members to back his call for a tripartite meeting to discuss steel's present problems.

After his departure the EC agreed its own plan for submission to the Steel Committee. It included opposition to GWA suspension; support for Benn's tripartite initiative if bipartite talks failed; acceptance of voluntary redundancies after consultation, and where over-manning existed; work-sharing 'in order to get a fair spread of employment across all Works'; elimination of all unnecessary overtime; rejection of the immediate closure and redundancy programme; and reaffirmation of the principles contained in the 1973 National Conference resolution.[4]

A serious confrontation built up, every step attracting extensive press coverage. On 19 May the Steel Committee again met BSC and, after prolonged talks, concluded a 'Current Trading Agreement' which it was hoped would 'go a long way to meeting the employment cost reductions' sought earlier. They agreed to eliminate all unnecessary overtime, and to keep overtime working and the use of contractors under local and national review on the basis of the BSC policy of a high productivity and high earnings industry'; they agreed that absenteeism (then 14 per cent) 'needed to be reduced by positive joint action'; and on other measures: rigorous control of recruitment, except for school leavers; maintenance of the GWA;[5] voluntary redundancy with accrued pension entitlement where it was mutually agreed that over-manning existed and after full local consultation with appropriate individual unions; a detailed schedule of plant loading for the plants subject to the Beswick Review.[6] While many questions remained open, this was a substantial achievement for the unions. In the years to come the agreement was cited by the usual critics as one of many worthless undertakings – but they had fought off a substantial closure and redundancy threat.[7]

Yet the recession in the industry continued.[8] In June BSC ended weekend working, a very unpopular move which terminated premium shifts and bit deeply into earnings; discontent was multiplied where managers insisted that work-measured incentive schemes (WMIS) must be self-financed before any lead-in (i.e. enabling) payments to such schemes could be made. At Port Talbot such actions had already precipitated a strike. Sirs was temporarily able to contain the discontent with his proposal of an EC/BSC meeting following a scheduled HST negotiation, but when the EC met BSC Director of Industrial Relations, Gordon Sambrook, on 23 June, it was without success: the Port Talbot stoppage was made official.[9]

Following further discussions with BSC, a Special EC agreed revisions to the 19 May agreement on the current trading position. BSC continued to press the unions, pleading that it was losing £5m weekly and moving into debt to pay current costs, but it met stiff resistance to its proposal for 20,000 redundancies. The new agreement specified 'further urgent discussions' on weekend working, but offered flexible working 'subject to local agreement'. BSC's prerogatives on plant loading were reaffirmed, and decisions on waiving the GWA were referred to local discussion; but the provisions governing redundancy by age or short service were on a national schedule.[10]

Under the terms of the two agreements there was some alleviation of the trading position at BSC; by November some £67m in savings had been realised. But the Corporation's position was fluid and the direction of current trade adverse: it was expecting losses of £340m for the current year, with a similar outlook for 1976–7. To the Steel Committee unions it now announced that permitted borrowing would not cover employment and development costs and that it would have to save £200m on employment costs. The unions were challenged to come up with proposals on how to achieve savings, in the absence of which the Corporation would take 'serious action' on 1 January 1976. This new threat was extremely grave. The Executive regarded savings of this order as hopelessly impracticable, and recalled with some bitterness the planning errors of recent years which had left BSC with insufficient iron-making capacity. It did look at the possibility of cancelling the GWA, but finally opted for seeking, through the Steel Committee, a detailed works-by-works breakdown of the losses being racked up before taking further action.

Sirs led the Steel Committee in further talks with BSC on 11 December. The unions proposed to BSC that it should maximise non-employment cost savings 'and provide evidence that this was being done'; that it should consider selling assets and in particular those overseas and those not required for job creation; that it should require a greater equality of sacrifice between lower-paid workers and higher management and between different categories of worker. In return the Steel Committee and NCCC would ensure that the two agreements would be carried out 'in their entirety' at the Corporation.

In fact there was an issue of faith at stake. BSC was not convinced that the unions' offer would generate savings on the scale it was seeking. It announced suspension of the GWA for employees with less than five years' service from 11 January 1976 and for others from 8 February; preferential allocation of production loads to non-premium-bearing shifts; the opening of redundancy terms to staff and industrial grades; enforced redundancies where existing manning levels could no longer be afforded; and the loading of high-cost works and departments only after low-cost operations had been fully utilised. This, in the unions' view, represented a potential redundancy situation on the scale of 40,000 workers when taken together with the premature closure of older plants under the Ten-Year Strategy.[11]

With their backs to the wall the unions played the ultimate card. On 19 December, the day after submitting a report to a special meeting of his Executive, Sirs led the Steel Committee at a meeting with the Prime Minister. The purpose of the meeting was to lay complaints against BSC for its unilateral announcement of 11 December, and to request the PM's intervention to secure its withdrawal. In his reply Wilson was sympathetic, but stated his conviction that savings would have to be made; he also pointed to the serious state of industrial relations in the industry, selecting the blastfurnace dispute at Llanwern (see below) as an example. The government would not intervene; but he did advise an early meeting with Eric Varley, who had succeeded Benn as Industry Secretary in June.

This duly took place on 22 December. To Sirs's outline of the gravity of the situation, Varley replied that the government was committed to full implementation of the Beswick Report: effectively this meant that no premature closures should occur. He referred to a recent government decision to make £70m available for stockpiling (effectively allowing output to be maintained in the temporary absence of immediate sales), and held out the possibility of more in the following year. He acknowledged the importance attached by workpeople to the GWA; while he could not instruct the BSC to lift suspension, he was prepared to discuss the matter with management, and recommended the unions again to do the same.[12]

Subsequent discussions with BSC's Chairman, Chief Executive and Managing Director of Personnel covered not only the cost-education proposals but also the Port Talbot stoppage, bringing in the local management at one point.[13] At a further meeting with Varley on 19 January 1976, the Steel Committee secured his support for ensuring that a new bilateral meeting scheduled for three days later would be held. Again the unions pressed him for government assistance in helping BSC make its savings. BSC and the unions met on 22 January and stayed in talks for more than twenty-four hours. The final outcome was the famous '23 January 1976 Agreement',[14] which was to cast its shadow over the years to come. Under its terms, the two sides agreed that a 'high wage, high productivity' industry should be their goal; that 'inbuilt' over-manning would go within two years; that 'low-cost' plants and low premium shifts would be favoured; that flexible working would begin at BSC; and that earnings revisions would be considered in the light of government anti-inflation policy (see below). BSC lifted the threat to the GWA.

The 1975–6 drama had been publicly played out, the first of many such which would occur in the years ahead. It had also reinforced in the popular mind the idea of a bloated British Steel Corporation, swollen with over-manning. In later years, management complained that the agreement of 23 January had not been honoured, though in fact the next three years brought a drop of 24,000 in the workforce[15] for a marginal rise in output while absenteeism fell. And yet, though the ISTC did not know it at the time, BSC was already in possession of international manpower figures which showed that its labour costs were the lowest in Western Europe.

Pay and the government

Under the Conservative government, the EC had endorsed the 'special case' of the miners, effectively acquiescing in the efforts of the NUM to restore colliery workers to the top of the earnings league. But the consequences of this continued under Labour once the Social Contract became a 'voluntary', but in practice universally observed, policy. The Area No. 1 Heavy Steel Trades Conference moved out of the usual context of specific proposals into generalised criticism, observing 'with concern' the decline of production workers' earnings relative to those of craftsmen and ancillary grades; it also declared that the union could not be 'bound by the so-called Social Contract' which had failed to achieve Labour's promised redistribution of wealth.[16]

As the summer of 1975 wore on, the prospect of a government-enforced incomes policy cast a shadow before it, and became a reality on 11 July.[17] All outstanding claims were examined to see if they would be compromised by the government's proposed legislation. That year's HST talks operated under two constraints: not only was there incomes policy, but also the agreement carried a codicil offering the ISTC co-operation 'to assist the Corporation to justify the . . . claim' (to the government) by raising the savings target under the 19 May agreement from £100m to £110m.[18] It was also felt necessary to defer the claim for a minimum wage paid to all males and females aged eighteen years and over. The heavy steel settlement, made barely two weeks before the July guillotine fell on settlements above £6, was worth 14 per cent, with a 2 per cent cost-of-living adjustment per month on top: with inflation reaching an annualised rate of 26.9 per cent that August, this was needed.[19] But a major difficulty for the ISTC arose over the introduction of WMIS. Only in December was final clarification received from the Employment Secretary that the only payments above the £6 which could flow under WMIS would be for schemes implemented before 11 July, the date when the incomes policy became operable.

With the approach of Phase II of the incomes policy in 1976 there were isolated signs of discontent, but only No. 1 Division was opposed to continued restraint in principle.[20] The 1976 pay round progressed in fairly straightforward fashion.[21] By and large increases were sought and achieved up to the ceiling of £2.50–£4.00 imposed by Phase II, but grievances due for resolution were starting to accumulate: in November the EC resolved that the 1976–7 agreement should date from 1 January 1977, and that it would not accept any ban on the restructuring of wages and conditions of BSC staff and process workers after August 1977.[22]

Would there be a Phase III of incomes policy? During 1977 opinion hardened at the ISTC. On 30 March, Sirs wrote to Len Murray at the TUC, suggesting that while a new phase of pay policy was desirable it should incorporate flexibility, so that productivity and incentive schemes could be negotiated for production workers.[23] By the summer of 1977, calls for the restoration of free collective bargaining were being received from across the Organisation, including Areas 1 and 4 of the Heavy Steel Trades; other areas and Staff Conference delegates, while not going so far, were pressing claims which would certainly be incompatible with extension of the Phase II regime. In June the ISTC's Annual Delegate Conference called for a greater degree of flexibility in pay policy, a position the EC was happy to endorse. The ISTC's 1977 Congress motion was submitted before that year's compact between the TUC and the government which provided for a maximum increase of 10 per cent: it rejected 'any further lowering of living standards' and called for the restoration of differentials and eradication of wage anomalies at the local level, genuine productivity deals, and consolidation of previous supplements into basic rates. The Organisation's traditional position was, however, protected by appending to this critical stance a call for bargaining objectives to acknowledge 'the overriding priorities of the national economy and voluntary acceptance of the social contract'.[24]

Sirs was by now under considerable pressure arising from the accumulated grievances of the past two years. He wrote to BSC suggesting that all

WMIS agreements frozen during the period of the pay policy be now implemented, and he followed up the demand with a request to the Department of Employment. BSC continued to maintain that all payments under such schemes had to be self-financing, a stance which blocked the widespread wish for lead-in payments to be made. Talks with BSC led to two possibilities emerging: one would allow for schemes which would go live at once, with lead-in payments paid retrospectively; the other meant straightforward productivity deals, with both sides sharing the savings. With some light at the end of the tunnel at last, talks proceeded, facilitated by correspondence with Employment Secretary Albert Booth, which at last seemed to open up some space for manoeuvre.

But the substantive problem remained. The HST public sector claim for 1978 was for a 10 per cent increase, consolidation onto basic rates of the 5 per cent paid under Phase II and double time for the May Day 1978 Bank Holiday. The employers' offer, worth 6 per cent on gross earnings, had been rejected and Sirs now persuaded Varley to become involved. Whether through his assistance or by other means, substantial improvements were now made in BSC's offers both to staff and to the HST, though consolidation was not achieved. Nonetheless, it took three months to make the agreement and it was bought with a vast number of commitments by the Organisation on absenteeism, new plant commissioning, productivity and reduced operating costs. BSC was also clearly still attempting to hammer all the unions into one wage-bargaining unit; and the utmost vigilance had to be exercised to ensure that WMIS discussions were not brought within the ambit of the pay talks.[25] Oddly enough, that year's settlements for 10 per cent were made with relative ease at the Sheet Trade Board and even ISEA (see below).[26]

The autumn of 1978 brought the events which caused Labour's pay policy to implode when it sought to restrain pay rises to 5 per cent. Sirs now found himself in a critical position. When the General Council received a document drawn up by its Economic Committee and the Government on collective bargaining, costs and prices, he stood opposed. He argued that the document went against policy determined at the 1978 Congress, and that certain aspects of the guidelines seemed to confine those engaged in self-financing productivity deals to a ceiling on their returns of one-third.[27] Steelworkers had cut labour costs' share of spending at BSC from 34.4 per cent to 29.9 per cent during the three years of incomes policy, and their pay could not be accommodated within the Chancellor's proposed pay guidelines of 5 per cent. At BSC the stage was set for yet another drawn-out national pay negotiation. Failure to consolidate the 5 per cent Phase II supplement still rankled, and negotiations spanned the winter months. In March the ISTC was on the brink of arbitration,[28] and resolved not to support any further productivity deals or WMIS schemes until the claim was settled.[29] Only on 2 April was agreement reached for an 8 per cent increase, improved conditions and establishment of a joint working party to consider consolidation of supplementary payments, the minimum adult wage, a formula for current earnings for holiday payments, supplementary payments for employees absent through sickness and anomalies in re-adaptation benefit and the remuneration of middle management grades. Arbitration had been avoided, but such a difficult pay round could only be an omen.[30] It was to be the last held under Labour rule.

In the private sector, the activities of the staff membership could be overshadowed by those of their public sector colleagues, though at the Staff Conference from the mid-1970s time was given over to their affairs, and indeed to those of private-sector middle management as well. In summer 1976 the Private Sector National Staff Committee met the employers for the first time at national level. Pay bargaining had, at the employers' insistence, been reserved for local negotiations; but the union side presented a claim to make union membership a condition of employment at all ISEA companies. Also discussed were the possibility of an employment and income security agreement to parallel that in the public sector; redundancy pay; and the implications of readaptation aid.

Many employers did not want their staff organised – a tangible difference between public and private-sector attitudes. In 1978, severe difficulties were encountered at Sheerness Steel over the recruitment of staff and supervisory grades, even though the Union had obtained a favourable ruling from ACAS. Finally the most senior officials were sent to the plant to meet management, armed with a grant of authority to the General Secretary to call an official strike should such action be necessary.[31] After leading two meetings with management, Roy Evans reported that full negotiating and organising rights for clerical and administrative staff had been conceded and there was to be a limited procedural agreement for supervisory staff in line with ACAS recommendations.[32] This conflict contrasted sharply with the good shop floor relations which existed in Sheerness at the time.

Heavy steel negotiations in the private sector were another matter. Some success was gained in matching the movement of pay in the public sector: in 1978, for example, 10 per cent, the maximum possible under Phase III of the incomes policy, was achieved. The Sirs years saw a sustained effort to extend the bargaining remit at ISEA talks to in nationwide sick pay and superannuation schemes, and this met with some success. But when it came to membership itself, ISEA would not conclude an agreement to match the enabling pact between BSC and the ISTC. Private employers were to be quick to scent the wind after Labour lost office in May 1979. Sensing intransigence in the talks, ISEA/HST requested an overtime ban, while ISEA declared that if there were to be arbitration it would resist government intervention. Sirs was left with powers to reply by imposing a complete overtime ban as necessary, but in October 1979 the ISEA presented national ISTC officers with a document which proposed to end national pay negotiations: it was referred to the private sector CNC of the heavy steel trades.[33]

Reshaping BSC

After their first (1974) meeting at a joint conference at Heathrow, the ISTC and BSC agreed to establish four working parties to consider aspects of their relationship and report back. Working party No. 1 was to recommend the basis on which staff conditions would be extended to certain manual grades; No. 2 was to recommend organisational and procedural methods for achieving closer involvement at all levels of plant, with particular emphasis on job satisfaction, team working and flexibility; No. 3 was to recommend procedures to speed settlement of disputes at works, works group, plant or national level; No. 4 was to recommend appropriate pay structures, taking into account 'the relationship between datal and incentive payments allied to productivity, guaranteed week provisions and income security'.[34] The reports of the working parties reached the EC in June 1975. No. 2's was accepted, as was No. 3's after some modifications of detail. But No. 4's, with its recommendation for graded wage structures and job evaluation throughout the industry, needed, in the EC's view, 'deep and long consideration'. ISTC members of the No. 1 working party thought their remit too narrow, and received backing for their proposal to investigate single status at ICI and the Dutch steel firm of Hoogovens.[35] When the Heathrow working party on HST conditions reported, the EC felt unable to accept its proposals without agreement at the other three working parties whose remits touched on single status.

Late in 1976 Sir Charles Villiers was appointed BSC Chairman, and quickly made his mark with a series of proposals for a partnership with the unions. On 3 December, a conference of the ISTC, NUB and BSC was held at Heathrow, where BSC tabled proposals for a Steel Contract, at the heart of which was rationalisation of the union structure.[36] In its original form the contract required agreement to proceed by 23 January 1977, but the EC rapidly formed the view that the contract was essentially a management attempt to hustle them into a National Joint Committee – a single bargaining unit – by a specified date, and rejected it for that reason; it also instructed Sirs to write to the NUB inviting them to talk to BSC about the other proposals in the contract.[37] On 6 April the EC agreed to a NUB suggestion that a joint working party of the two unions be established. Proposals were formulated for works councils, divisional councils and a Steel Council. The Steel Committee met BSC on the matter in September at Windermere, and there the employers accepted in principle the appointment of a Main Board, of which one-third would be nominated by the trade unions. Since BSC concurred that the majority of these would be ISTC/NUB members, the EC authorised Sirs to proceed with a working party to inquire into the details.[38] The working party recommended the establishment of a Biennial Steel Conference of nationally recognised unions.

Back in June 1976 new names had been forwarded to BSC to replace employee directors Slater and Sutherland, who were due to retire under the BSC scheme. But the vista was widening, and the EC now approved a statement of evidence on the issue of extending democracy within the public sector.[39] Publication of the Bullock Report, which recommended equal representation of union and management on the Boards of private companies, precipitated a discussion between BSC and the Steel Committee on how to compose the 'y' factor of people outside the industry on the BSC Board. An ISTC amendment tabled at Labour's 1977 conference rejected a blanket approach, calling for participation to extend flexibly from the shop floor to the main board, to allow for the specifics of each industry and to be firmly based on union machinery.[40]

In 1978 matters had advanced sufficiently for Varley to offer a BSC Main Board with six union members. This was 'noted' by the EC: they wanted seven, with the extra seat coming to the ISTC. In August they agreed three names[41] designed to offer ability, together with representation of England, Scotland and Wales and of manual and staff grades: Alan White (Temple 1), Jim MacLaren (Ravenscraig 2), and Don Caddick (Hawarden management). Doubts about co-ordination were addressed by inviting them to attend the Executive as observers during its Thursday and Friday sessions and requesting that they make a report.[42] A Steel Committee working party proposed facilitating Main Board nominations with multi-union liaison machinery: a National Steel Trade Union Advisory Conference and Divisional Steel Trade Union Advisory Committees. But the conference was rejected out of hand by the EC, which was already opposed in principle to a two-tier system.

BSC agreed to an ISTC request that briefing seminars be held in the divisions on the subject of its proposed Steel Contract, and these took place early in 1979. That July a one-day national Steel Conference was held at Redcar, where delegates heard the BSC view of the state of the steel market outlined. BSC wished to hold a second conference six months later, but there was a general feeling within the union that this and other vehicles of the Steel Contract were being used to achieve corporate objectives, but not its own long-term target of single status for manual and staff grades. This frustration was expressed in August 1979, when the Executive threatened withdrawal from consultative processes unless there was early progress towards the cherished goal.[43]

On invitation from BSC, Sirs had joined its Planning Committee, a move which implied at least some joint responsibility for determining the future direction of the industry.[44] As early as February 1979, however, he was voicing his concern that the committee was not functioning correctly, as it had not been involved in the early stages of the Development Plan;[45] but in August he was authorised to undertake a study of the industry with a view to preparing an alternative strategy to that of BSC.[46]

The components of such a strategy were regularly debated at the Annual Delegate Conference (ADC), which in 1979 urged pressure on purchasers to buy British steel, and called for a joint union and management venture to be established to inquire into diversification, perhaps through BSC (Industry), the Corporation's job-creation arm. However, the EC stopped short of accepting a Conference call for a halt to any further closures.[47] This was in reality the old reluctance to develop a policy for the steel industry for fear of picking winners. In fact the Organisation had been moving towards a different approach for some time. Thus, the short-time working of the mid-1970s had increased the attractiveness to the membership of import controls. The 1975 Staff Conference called for the government to bring in such controls, and the EC 'approved in principle'. In 1976 the No. 1 Division BOC condemned the use of private stockholders by BSC.[48] Awareness of the role played by stockists in raising import penetration of the UK home market for steel was rising fast,[49] and the two issues fused at the 1978 ADC, which, with EC blessing, called for nationalisation of the stockholding sector. The old agenda had been blown away by the weak competitive performance of BSC and the ISTC was now *de facto* developing a policy of its own.

The Steel Committee and union relations

The crisis leading up to the January 23 agreement had not endeared the Steel Committee to many union members. Complaints poured in from many branches and from the National Staff Committee: the Steel Committee had exceeded its consultative status; there was poor consultation and communication with lay members; discontent was bubbling over unnecessary delays in dealing with proposed changes in national agreements. Most critics preferred the ISTC to represent the membership on its own; failing that, the Committee should be enlarged to include lay members.

At a special EC of 22 March 1976 the Steel Committee's defenders carried the day, referring to the lengthy and impressive sequence of breakthrough agreements on pensions, holidays and the GWA, though a proposal to place the ISTC President (a lay person) on the Committee was popular and backed by Sirs. The General Secretary observed that it was the executives of constituent unions which had established the Steel Committee, and that BSC had a statutory obligation to meet all recognised unions. On the practical side he had improved communications, which had certainly been strained during the recent crisis, and innovated by summoning Divisional Officers to London as appropriate – which he would do again as necessary. He undertook to represent Executive views on an enlarged membership and on the circulation of minutes to the Committee.[50]

Meetings between TUC General Secretary Len Murray and the Steel Committee originated proposals to double the Committee's size and to establish a National Iron and Steel Industry Consultative Committee with forty-two members, including the present Steel Committee. The Executive agreed to doubling the size of the Steel Committee provided that the ISTC had six seats, but referred the other proposal to a joint working party which it had recently established with the NUB.[51] By summer 1977 proposals had emerged which would reconstitute the Steel Committee with nine seats for the ISTC/NUB, two apiece for the TGWU and GMWU and four for the NCCC. The extra ISTC places would be filled by the National Staff Officer, the President and the Vice-president, with a place being held in abeyance for a middle management representative, pending the result of the SIMA merger ballot (see below).[52]

Meanwhile another possible avenue for union co-operation was opened. The ISTC had taken seriously an earlier BSC proposal for a National Joint Industrial Council (NJIC). A statistical analysis had been undertaken to establish accurately the proportions of union representation across BSC, and in June 1975 Sirs submitted it to the EC. But he advised them that Confederation influence had first to be consolidated and even extended before the plunge was taken, and recommended that this be their priority. The Executive response was to defer discussions on an NJIC for the time being;[53] two years later[54] BSC concluded an enabling agreement to facilitate local union membership agreements with the ISTC. But in 1975 Sirs did not conceal his doubts from the membership. Would an NJIC have the commitment to the industry and the authority that the Confederation had? Would craft unions in membership relinquish their loyalty to district committees? Would other unions have full-time officers dedicated to the steel industry alone?

The NUB was an exception to Sirs's strictures, but recurring inter-union problems with it had led to a meeting of the two executives on 15 July 1975. One month later they agreed to establish a joint working party to examine the Port Talbot dispute.[55] It proved a false dawn – one of many in these years – for the blowing in of the new No. 3 blastfurnace at Llanwern, scheduled for the following year, was to be massively delayed by a huge dispute over rates. Relations between the two unions passed continually between hot and cold.[56]

In outlook and membership the NUB were closest kin to the ISTC, but the bigger organisation was now to be further embroiled with an organisation which was not a TUC affiliate at all. The inaugural meeting of the full ISTC national Middle Management (MM) Committee was convened in summer 1975: it drew up a comprehensive claim to establish a national middle management salary structure for the public sector, along with conditions of employment.[57] But MM members faced renewed problems at Scunthorpe, and awareness of slow progress in recruitment determined the Executive on a new approach to SIMA.[58] After two officers' meetings SIMA itself produced amalgamation proposals, and a sub-committee meeting on 14 October 1975 was marked by great cordiality. On 4 May 1976 both sides agreed final amendments to a document providing for SIMA to transfer engagements to the ISTC. This was considered in detail by the EC on 15 June and accepted.[59] Two months later it was agreed that the two national committees should be fused as soon as possible after the merger. Not all ISTC managers were content; the working party had to volunteer a briefing tour of MM branches to bring them on board. A commitment within the document, stipulating that for six years the new management section would vote only within its own section while previous ISTC members would not vote in the new management section, was among the topics of debate.

But it was internal SIMA developments which finally ended the merger. At its annual conference delegates carried an amendment fatal to the whole scheme. The SIMA National Council remained in discussions, and was to pledge a ballot of members on amalgamation, but a whole year now passed without visible sign of progress; indeed the disputed areas had widened to embrace the numerical strength of the combined EC, the method whereby SIMA representatives would be elected to it, and the status of SIMA funds. In the hope that it would allow the SIMA ballot to proceed, the ISTC accepted legal advice that its MM section should elect its own members for an initial period of six years; but, ominously, discussions were now under way between lawyers for both sides.[60]

It was therefore no surprise when in February 1978 SIMA's General Secretary, Bob Muir, wrote indicating that his association was no longer prepared to ballot its membership on the merger agreement.[61] On the ground it had become apparent that the ISTC's MM members were being pressed to defect by SIMA members and in some instances by senior management, suspected of acting on SIMA's behalf. Vigilance had to be exercised to prevent members being forced to resign on promotion or transfer.

That autumn even BSC became alarmed when press reports suggested that SIMA was now seeking a merger with other unions; the EC had already endorsed proposals for meetings on the matter with the Chief Executive, Bob Scholey, and Len Murray. At the meeting with Murray, Muir declared his willingness to keep talking under a TUC chairperson, but also indicated that his association was pressing for affiliation to the TUC in its own right.[62] But with the two organisations now drifting apart there was little to stop clashes developing. Recognition of MM membership at Scunthorpe and on the north-east coast was particularly elusive, leading Sirs to meet Muir in an attempt to defuse a fierce local conflict. In August 1979 he went further and suggested to the EC that the two executives should have a wide-ranging discussion;[63] but by then larger events were in the wings which were to destroy amalgamation hopes forever.

Frustration at the absence of progress towards middle management recognition boiled over that November. To impasses at Scunthorpe, Hartlepool Tube and Teesside Research Labs could be added problems at BSC Head Office, Corby and the Hoyle Street (Sheffield) Labs. In several cases recognition was being blocked for groups of members larger than those for whom it had been conceded under the agreement of June 1974. In a continuation of the mood which had led them to sanction industrial action to resist closures (see below), the Executive decided on selective strikes for recognition on a plant basis organised by the Divisional Officers, followed up by a demand that local managements should bring the existence of MM branches to the attention of new members of staff.[64]

Three weeks later the Executive agreed to a BSC suggestion of a national meeting to address middle management problems, and there was by then some success to report, with recognition having been achieved at Hoyle Street, followed on 5 December by success at Corby and, at last, at Scunthorpe. The Corporation had also forwarded to SIMA an ISTC suggestion of a tripartite meeting, but had received no reply. The Executive unavoidably concluded that SIMA was uninterested in a merger and that the matter was closed.[65]

Modernising the union

The Sirs era was associated with significant changes to the ISTC's constitution and to the structure so familiar to members. New offices were opened in

Nos. 2, 3, 4 and 7 Divisions, and refurbishment was undertaken at Central Office and elsewhere. Changes to legislation, notably the Health and Safety at Work Act 1974, offered new opportunities to promote safe working, with a special attraction for unions in the shape of safety committees and accredited safety representatives. Health and safety had previously been seen, with education, as the responsibility of the Assistant General Secretary; indeed, at the 1976 TUC Roy Evans had spoken powerfully for legislation to restrain noise levels in the steel industry.[66] But now, in order to co-ordinate the ISTC's approach, the Executive decided to bring on to the staff a specialist 'National Officer, Health and Safety' and at the end of the year appointed Ken Clarke,[67] who took up his post in January 1977. Clarke, who later added education and recruitment to his responsibilities, shortly joined the Joint Accident Prevention Advisory Committee (JAPAC) and ISITB, and that summer launched the first in a series of Health and Safety Bulletins, and began to campaign for a more sympathetic treatment of the vibration-induced ailment known as Raynaud's Phenomenon. During 1977 guidelines for safety representatives and safety committees were agreed at JAPAC along lines acceptable to the Steel Committee, and parallel arrangements were sought with ISEA during 1978.[68] However, the training of safety representatives proved contentious with both sets of employers – an unexpected setback in the year which saw the introduction of a statutory right to paid time off for training. Guidelines for Branch Safety Reps were issued in November 1978.

Staffing changes now brought a number of younger faces to the fore. No. 2 Divisional Officer Jim Drinkwater[69] died late in 1975 after a long illness, and was replaced by Peter Woods.[70] With the retirement of Jack Gavin imminent and Bill Homewood's[71] prospects strong in Corby, Roy Bishop[72] was blooded in No. 4 Division, the first staff organiser to achieve Divisional Officer status. Meanwhile the EC agreed to the secondment of Brian Connolly, No. 5 Senior Divisional Organiser, as an EEC consultant to help with the management of steel redundancies in South Wales steel communities. Stan Biddiscombe[73] had been appointed to run No. 6 Division in November 1969 and George Cooper[74] In No. 1 Division the long-established Arthur Bell was the 1977–8 President of the TUC,[75] and in No. 3 Division Alex Hogg had retired in 1973, to be replaced by Joe Pickles.[76] Meanwhile, veteran Executive member Jack Clark was awarded the TUC Gold Badge at the 1978 Congress.

The momentum gathered in 1974 by the demand for an annual conference was sustained in 1975 by Divisions Nos. 1, 3, 4 and the London Area, and by Divisions Nos. 5 and 7. The May 1975 Executive was the last to be attended by Davies, who was opposed, whereas Sirs was known to be in favour. The change in atmosphere proved significant when the EC upheld the No. 5 Division's resolution calling for 'an annual delegate conference representing all our members', but did not specify policy-making powers. The Executive had thus accommodated the demand for a national gathering but forestalled the emergence of a rival authoritative forum. The following month, after reviewing the costs of a one-, two-, and four-day conference, it opted to begin with a one-day event in 1976. That November it was determined that EC members would not vote at the conference, and that if they spoke they would be deemed to do so in a personal capacity – important stipulations if the event was to retain its advisory character.[77] When the votes were counted in the Rules Revision Ballot it was found that the members had voted overwhelmingly for change.[78]

When the ADC finally met at the TUC on 14 July 1976 it proved relatively uncontroversial. The EC accepted resolutions on the subjects of industrial democracy, unemployment, retirement age, hours of work, single status, the Steel Committee, the closed shop and Spain, in some instances with qualifications. In a practice that was to become more common, it amended or referred to other bodies' resolutions which had been remitted.[79] For 1977 the Executive deemed that BOCs would continue as before, but the Staff Conference would meet for the last time, after which there would be area staff conferences parallel to those held by the heavy steel trades.[80] The ADC would now be extended to three days to celebrate the Organisation's sixtieth anniversary, and attendance would be extended to include the chairmen of Area Committees and the vice-chairmen of the Sheet Trade Board and Midland Wages Board, as well as international visitors.[81] These were significant changes, but the appetite had been whetted. A last-ditch call to retain the Staff Conference failed that autumn, but the Executive was inclined to view more sympathetically requests for an extension of representation at the ADC.[82]

The 1977 (Scarborough) agenda was considerably broader,[83] suggesting that the membership was beginning to look to the ADC as the arena where concerns and policy could be aired. The 194 delegates and others attending were addressed by Eric Varley, the two top men at the IMF and Sir Charles Villiers (chairman of BSC since 1976), who faced a lively question-and-answer session. In 1978, the ADC – again in Scarborough – really came of age, for it witnessed the dramatic events associated with the bungled Bilston closure (see below); this necessitated reconvening the ADC in London in August for half a day. After this it adopted its modern form: for a two-year trial period the BOCs were brought within its framework, and delegates were allocated on the basis of three per 1000 members at each of the works;

all sections having membership within the works were entitled to direct representation.[84]

The 1979 (Bournemouth) ADC scaled a peak of prestige. Major debates were held by the 304 delegates on the future of bulk steelmaking, possible denationalisation, closures, unemployment and incomes policy; there was extensive political debate, since Labour had lost office just one month before; and publicity was guaranteed by the attendance of HRH the Prince of Wales, who was warmly received when he addressed his first union conference. His comment on the industry's problems – 'I do believe that co-operation is the key to all this, not confrontation' – reads sadly in retrospect. Other speakers included Eric Varley, an ex-Minister, and Sir Charles Villiers, each making a third appearance.

But perhaps the most central and sensitive area of internal organisation was the electoral system of the Executive Council itself. Critics ranged from root-and-branch reformers to those requiring a clearer system of accountability than the complicated sectional system allowed; the long-standing practice of branch secretaries counting the ballot papers and returning voting return forms, rather than having a central count, was also increasingly controversial. A February 1976 Executive review of the system had attracted only twenty-five branch responses and this, after some hesitation, had been interpreted as a lack of desire for change.[85] But administrative difficulties persisted, and reform of the electoral areas attracted growing interest. A 1977 ADC resolution referring to EC election procedures was ruled out of order,[86] but in May 1978 a new Executive sub-committee was appointed to consider 'Rule 3, Clause 3, Sections within the Confederation'; its eleven-strong membership suggested that this was a matter of unusually compelling interest. One month later, the ADC passed resolutions describing sectional arrangements as out of date and calling for a greater degree of divisional representation to make candidates more identifiable, and for the circulation of addresses with the official ballot paper. The EC kept its options open by noting the first and rejecting the second.[87] Change was clearly coming, but a reform group which found its pace too slow circulated a pamphlet, 'Steelworkers and Constitutional Change', ahead of the 1979 ADC.[88] These internal preoccupations were about to be brushed aside by a huge conflict in the industry.

Politics: changes in the Labour Party

In August 1975 the EC acceded to a proposal from Roy Grantham, APEX General Secretary, suggesting a meeting of General Secretaries at the TUC to consider the lack of control of political extremists within the Labour

Party.[89] The ISTC had always firmly supported the Party leadership, and responded to a request for suggestions for a working party on the increasingly disputed system of electing the Party Leader with a terse statement that it did not regard any change as necessary.[90] In support of its robust stance the ISTC continued to keep its affiliated strength, and therefore its influence in the party, high.[91] At Conferences it took a higher profile than ever before, tabling motions and using the opportunity to press national or international matters: the steelworkers' case never went by default.

But the May 1979 the downfall of Jim Callaghan's government precipitated an orgy of Labour introspection as different explanations for the Party's defeat were canvassed. In its resolution to the 1979 conference, the ISTC reacted to the Tory general election victory by calling for an intensification of the union effort on Labour's behalf, including more sponsored candidates and the establishment of factory branches – a controversial issue at the time.[92] On 14 August Callaghan addressed met a specially convened meeting of ISTC and NUB executives at which he called for an agreed inquiry to look at all the constitutional changes now being proposed by the NEC. This event attracted much media interest, not least for the ringing declarations of Sirs and Hector Smith that the time had come for those who believed in democratic socialism to stand up and be counted. The ISTC's view was that arguments about Labour's constitution were really about policy and principles.

But the unpalatable truth was that the Conservatives were now the government of the country, and every day they spent in office changed the atmosphere. In February 1977 Ian Gow MP, known to be close to Mrs Thatcher, had introduced a Private Member's Bill to denationalise the steel industry. This proposal – which had elicited a scorching reply from Sirs and an illuminating correspondence with the then little-known Norman Tebbit – was easily shrugged off. One year later it became apparent that the Conservatives were contemplating public sector strikes to bring things to a head in the nationalised industries, among them BSC.[93] Again Sirs had warned that steelworkers were not a soft touch. However, an early act of the new administration was to instruct a willing BSC to reach break-even point by March 1980: steelworkers were to discover that the Tories really meant it this time.

BSC again: the cataclysm approaches

The ISTC's 1976 TUC resolution had called successfully for expansion of output beyond BSC's target of 38 million tonnes by the 1980s. In the Ten-Year Strategy BSC had proposed building a new giant plate mill at Redcar. Sirs was opposed to this proposal, and received Executive backing in advocating the strong claims of the existing mills at Consett and Hartlepool for expansion. He also persuaded the Steel Committee to back the case and it was presented to BSC in July: here was an unusual case of the Organisation not wanting investment, and indeed the new mill did not proceed. But most pressure was to achieve investment. At the 1977 STUC, the ISTC called for acceleration of the planned developments at Ravenscraig and Clydebridge, and establishment of the spoken-of 'major steel complex' at Hunterston, where work on a direct-reduction plant was proceeding on schedule. The weakness of the union's case was evident, in that the only justification for upgrading the investment which was advanced in the text of a long resolution was the recent loss of 3000 steel jobs in Scotland.[94] In an increasingly market-oriented world, social arguments were soon to yield to business arguments.

Meanwhile the months passed inexorably towards the intended dates for closure under the Beswick Report. Sirs had met representatives of the East Moors Works in July 1976; as expounded in an amendment tabled at the Labour conference, the ISTC's position was to press for maintenance of steelmaking at their site as long as it was economically practicable.[95] In Scotland the 1977 BOC expressed 'concern and alarm' that the Beswick closure dates in its Division were now imminent with no provision for alternative employment made. In the late summer of 1977 the East Moors Mill Staff Branch protested about closure of departments at the works before the Beswick dates and alleged that the ISTC's 1973 Special Delegate Conference resolution was not being adhered to. In an important response the EC reiterated its policy, but the minutes of its deliberations tellingly record 'that a different situation existed at the present time than [that] which existed during the period when the resolution was passed in 1973 and this organisation would have extreme difficulty in implementing the terms of the resolution'.[96] Yet the Labour government still seemed supportive of steel, and in March 1977 announced authorisation of the Port Talbot expansion programme and the withdrawal of proposals to shut the heavy end of production at Shotton, a decision to which even Sir Keith Joseph, the Opposition's industry spokesman, gave his qualified blessing.

This decision was taken because BSC regarded market prospects as 'uncertain'; yet within months the ISTC was facing a grave crisis as BSC began to act rapidly on its gathering losses. On 30 September 1977 a Special Executive heard reports from all Divisions detailing redundancy and closure proposals ahead of the Beswick dates. Sirs was asked to request BSC's Chief Executive, Bob Scholey, to brief the EC. The Steel Committee met management on these matters twice in early November, and on the 14th Scholey and the Director of Industrial Relations, Dr David Grieves, duly attended the Executive. In his address Scholey outlined the gloomy BSC view: collapsing prices, rising costs, US exports lost to dumping duties and thus growing under-utilisation of capacity. Government help might be forthcoming, but BSC had to make its own efforts: he floated the possibility of buying out the GWA, improving separation payments, and ceasing investments when projects under way had been completed. EC members countered with their concerns: the restructuring taking place under the agreement of 23 January 1976 and the issue of whether WMIS lead-in payments should be self-financing.[97]

Time, once a friend to the threatened works, was now an enemy. Even the Beswick closure dates had arrived, and BSC was neglecting the doomed works where demoralisation was setting in, making many of the employees biddable. The policy vacuum at national level had to be filled. The November 1977 EC came up with a five-point plan:

1   a National Redundancy Compensation Scheme
2   imports: further information via a Research inquiry
3   BSC should continue with its investment commitments and the Beswick dates for plant lives should be honoured
4   no general commitment to load low-cost plants at the expense of high-cost plants, but a willingness to examine each BSC plant individually
5   restructuring to be accepted 'where applicable', but a new meeting would be sought with Scholey to gain further information on the steel crisis.[98]

For many there was no way of disguising that this represented a retreat. With a national redundancy compensation scheme in existence jobs could be bought out, while the commitment to restructuring was no longer an abstract one. The wish for more information was an attempt to gain some kind of independent foothold to contest the BSC view, but it was unlikely to succeed. Nor was there any mechanism for enforcing on BSC an obligation to honour the closure dates.

Clearly there would be some kind of resolution at local level. At Clyde Iron, soon after, an agreement was made which facilitated early closure, though national officials were not party to the talks.[99] Iron and steelmaking at Hartlepool was another matter: on 23 December 1977 the Steel Committee attended local talks there with national officers of the BSC. The end of steelmaking and primary rolling was that day agreed, operative from 2 January 1978. With this arranged, the dates for many other works loomed into view. Glengarnock staff affirmed their determination not to yield to early closure, and were still fighting in February 1978. The Bilston and Wolverhampton Works Action Committee fiercely resisted management's decision to mothball the Bilston blastfurnace, a stance endorsed by the EC.[100] At Shelton, a major action campaign was set in motion early in 1978 to ensure that the promised arc furnaces, intended to replace the plant's unique Kaldo furnaces, should be installed. A gloomy Jack Gavin noted the paradox that had taken his Division's membership back above 19,000 on the eve of major BSC cutbacks which must inexorably send it plummeting.

On 1 February 1978 BSC tabled further Beswick proposals, which it coupled with ideas intended to govern the commissioning of new plant. The EC acquiesced in the fact of early closures now conceded by the Steel Committee, but determined to extend access to severance payments to those losing jobs as a result of partial closures.[101] As the sheer scale of the crisis grew more and more evident, Sirs and the Steel Committee secretary, Denis Delay, met Scholey, to be informed that new proposals were being prepared by BSC and the government. In February 1978 Sirs had informed the EC that he anticipated a contraction greater than that envisaged in Beswick, in addition to which there would be cuts in the investment strategy.[102] His fears were soon borne out: Labour's Steel White Paper of 22 March 1978, 'The Road to Viability', virtually endorsed BSC's now maturing closure programme. What had happened, asked a bitter Sirs, to the 'new life and hope' promised in 'Labour's Programme 1973'?[103] The report of Sub-committee 'B' of the Select Committee on Nationalised Industries (SCNI) also caused great alarm. Labour and Conservative MPs alike – Neil Kinnock among them – appeared to agree that manning levels were the principal problem at BSC. There would be no rescue.[104] Severance payments for early closure were agreed that month for East Moors[105] and on 12 April for Ebbw Vale, which had already lost its coke ovens, blastfurnaces and the hot strip mill famously gained in 1938:[106] the last cast was tapped from 'A' furnace on 19 May. That month's Executive heard that the Shotton Works was to be visited by the Steel Committee to ascertain the wishes of members there for a similar agreement. Glengarnock's spirited fight had now ended. It looked like a rout, but this dismal sequence was now to be interrupted.

A suddenly posted letter of intent to close Bilston Works early provoked dramatic events at Scarborough, where the 1978 ADC was meeting. An emergency Executive authorised Sirs to make the only possible response to this attempt to dump the procedure: BSC was threatened with a national strike unless the letter was withdrawn.[107] This was perhaps the high point of resistance to the closures. Few who heard it will forget Sirs' electrifying speech to the conference: it eloquently captured the grim mood of determination of every delegate. Conference also passed an emergency motion requesting all unions to co-operate with the Bilston fight by refusing to handle materials or orders diverted from the Bilston Works, and to formulate contingency plans to protect members against further contraction of the industry.[108] This ISTC action gave BSC the jolt it needed, and the notice was withdrawn inside a day: there now followed a lengthy series of meetings which gave works representatives the opportunity to take their case to the wider movement.

It was a much-needed success, but the nightmare of mass unemployment now faced steelworkers. An effort had been made unilaterally to distribute the diminishing amount of work among the greatest number of plants – to 'spread the misery'. An Executive instruction to cut systematic weekly over-time above eight hours was imaginative, but hard to enforce in the face of a great diversity of responses from the branches. The Organisation's 1978 TUC motion suggested a complementary approach: a campaign for a phased reduction over three years to a thirty-five-hour week. But there were not three years left. BSC, confirming Sirs's fears, was now moving beyond Beswick. Not only Bilston, but also Cookley, Orb[109] and the Consett plate mill now found their future clouded, if not extinguished. Sirs had been sent 'Future Prospects', a BSC document which envisaged some of the horrors to come. A 1978 ADC resolution which called for a halt to non-Beswick clo-sures had been accepted by an uncertain EC, though with reservations 'bearing in mind that the ultimate decision rests with the Plant's work-force'.[110] It was an attack on all fronts.

And BSC would not be denied even at Bilston: on 15 March 1979 they gave the plant twelve months' notice of closure from 1 April. The next day, a special EC heard six works representatives plead for help in retaining iron and steelmaking; Sirs gave his view that he thought they had reached the end of existing procedures. The local membership had commissioned help from the University of Aston and sought a meeting with Vicomte D'Avignon, the EEC Industry Commissioner, in support of their plea for investment in bottom-blowing (Q-bop) steelmaking to replace the plant's open-hearth fur-naces. The issue was referred to a further special EC on 11 April, by which time it was apparent that all avenues had been blocked. An exhausted Spring Vale No. 1 Branch now suggested that negotiations be entered into for a sev-erance agreement, and the EC reluctantly concluded that 'frustration and confusion' would be ended by Sirs involving himself in discussions aimed at maintaining the Bilston mills at 'a level of operation satisfactory to this organisation'.[111] Closure of the heavy end followed soon after.

Long before Bilston closed the stage was set for even more devastating closures. Late in 1978 a meeting of the Economic (EY) Committee of the Labour Cabinet had before it proposals to shut both the Corby and the Shotton Works in 1979–80. Ministers on the left and right clashed over whether to support the unions in their resistance: the Cabinet finally felt it had to back the Corporation, but Varley was told to keep talking to Sirs.[112] By January 1979 rumours were being freely aired in the press concerning not only Shotton and Corby, but also the Consett works. Assurances had been received about Shotton, but BSC had requested discussions with the Steel Committee on Corby. Sirs himself had already been in local and national discussions over the sister electrical steelworks of Cookley and Orb. On 25 January the Executive accepted that it would in the near future have to examine 'the whole position of future closures and make decisions on their [*sic*] future policy'.[113]

In February BSC went public about Corby in a dramatic statement which doomed the 5500 steelmaking jobs on which the town's economy depended. The local membership began by preferring to make their own fight, with the EC maintaining a watching brief. A central dilemma for the union leadership lay, here as elsewhere, in the area of negotiations for severance pay. As experienced negotiators they naturally wished to reach the best possible terms for their membership. Yet the knowledge that enhanced severance pay was on offer tended to weaken resistance to closure proposals, and even to awaken an appetite where none previously existed. With membership already down to 112,075 in March 1979, it was hardly surprising that the EC would only 'note' a call from HST Area Conference No. 1 for enhanced redundancy payments to apply in all closure situations, 'and not only where a political closure programme is decided upon'.[114] In the late summer Sirs wrote to BSC calling for improvements to the redundancy payments agreement. The EC, concerned that redundancy pay seemed to have been referred to the Steel Committee, resolved to seek an extension of redundancy payments at local level.[115]

In their different ways the two ISTC resolutions to the 1979 TUC projected dismay at the gathering threat to jobs. 'Steelmaking at Corby' ranged more widely than its title suggested, advancing demands for an end to closures nationwide and calling for an urgent tripartite inquiry into imports; it also anticipated the arguments of the 1980 strike by pointing to the BSC predilection for saving only labour costs. The resolution on a '35-hour week' condemned a lack of vigour at the TUC in its campaigns for shorter working time.[116]

By late that summer local Corby officials had concluded that national union officers had to be called in to lift the campaign. The Steel Committee met BSC on 20 September, but the best it could achieve was a stay of execution to allow a case to be built. The Research Department, the TUC and sympathetic accountants from the University of Warwick[117] devised cases – not without internal strains – and these were presented on 1 November.

Scholey brusquely dismissed them at a tense encounter in the town, whilst a huge demonstration milled about outside. Shotton too had gone to immense trouble to produce a viable case, but suffered the same experience eight days later.

On 2 November Sirs reported on the impasse to his EC, commenting that BSC was determined to break even by the first quarter of 1980 and only ever blamed external factors for its difficulties. Each closure seemed only to bring others forward; there could be no job security when any plant was threatened immediately it made a loss. The EC was increasingly militant, prodded by telegrams urging action from Corby and Shotton. It resolved to instruct the Corby branches to stop all steel imports into the plant, to withdraw all public sector branches from joint consultation[118] and from manpower reduction negotiations, and to recommend that the Steel Committee impose an absolute overtime ban; organise a twenty-four-hour national stoppage and demonstration; end negotiations on severance pay; stage selective strikes; and act in parallel with the ISTC's other decisions.[119] It was a near-total breakdown: the ISTC had concluded that 'no plant is safe under this management'.

An angry Commons debate on 7 November revealed that the Conservative government was already dug in. The Steel Committee met the next day, but failed to offer the kind of enthusiastic support looked for by the ISTC. Its most concrete proposal was a commitment by various members to refer the ISTC's recommendations to their executives. A disappointed Sirs reported back. His own membership's attitude was now clarified. At Shotton a consensus had emerged that in the absence of alternative steelmaking investment closure had to be accepted: the branches wished to concentrate on retaining the hot mill. The EC empowered Divisional Officer George Cooper to seek an early meeting with local management.[120] This was a severe blow, but Corby remained in play.[121] Only after a demoralising December did spirits in the town collapse: a redundancy package was finally agreed on 27 December.[122]

Even these developments were only a prelude. On 29 November the BSC Board had authorised Scholey to take the ISTC into its confidence on future plans, and this he proceeded to do at a special meeting the next day. BSC, he told it, was unable to sell its products, and was thereby creating over-capacity. Base costs had to be reduced so as to maintain or increase orders, and all unions should be brought together to examine methods of making the industry more efficient. What this meant in detail was then spelled out by Sambrook. Five million tonnes of 'spare capacity' would be taken out; maximum use would be made of Lackenby and its new blastfurnace at Redcar; Ravenscraig would be held at two million tonnes a year; two million tonnes of poorly priced export orders would be withdrawn. BSC would effectively retrench manned capacity to 1.5 million tonnes annually, overwhelmingly for the home market. To meet the demands of competitiveness, manning should be reduced to approximately 100,000.[123] Scholey promised the Executive that the full briefing paper would go to the BSC Main Board on 10 December. Stunned and angry EC Members dispersed to consult their membership on this grim news.

They reconvened on 7 December to hear that Scholey had rescinded his offer of prior sight of the a board briefing paper in view of substantive leaks following his address of the previous week. Executive members lambasted senior BSC management, and alarm was expressed about the rumoured RDL-BSC (Chemicals) link and a proposed billet joint venture with GKN. Members agreed to await the BSC document (now promised for after the Board meeting). They agreed to oppose further closures and to place before the Corporation an alternative based on their traditional policy of sharing orders between the plants. They opened the door to the possibility of waiving the GWA at local level, while feeling that this should be discussed with their own CNC. For Shotton and Cleveland, however, the die was cast and it was agreed that severance payment negotiations should be begun at local level.[124]

After this Sirs briefed Len Murray at the TUC and led the Steel Committee to a meeting with the Industry Secretary, Sir Keith Joseph. Joseph had declined to change BSC policy or even to become involved, let alone extend new funding. At the General Council of the TUC and at its Economic Committee Sirs expounded the ISTC's policy of order-sharing in preference to complete closures. The EC met again on 19 December and now heard for themselves the grisly details prepared for the Main Board: Consett, currently profitable, was to close; there were 11,000 jobs at risk at Port Talbot and Llanwern; and mills across the country were to shut.[125] The biggest-ever contraction of steel was about to take place when Britain suddenly woke up to the fact that a national steel strike over pay was about to break out.

Notes

1 Bill Sirs (1920–), sometime crane driver and a former secretary of Greatham No. 3 Branch, became Divisional Organiser, No. 2 Division, in 1963 and moved to No. 7 Division as Divisional Officer in 1970. He was appointed Assistant General Secretary in 1973.

2 Henceforth the more familiar 'ISTC' will be used in place of 'BISAKTA', and 'confederation' in place of 'association'.

3 From about this time TUCSICC became more familiar under this name, and the pattern is followed in this book.

4 *Reports* (1975), 79–80.

5 This was qualified by BSC in certain particulars.

6 This entailed one blastfurnace operation at Clyde Iron, and one OH production at Clydebridge and Lanarkshire, with consequent operation of only one blastfurnace at Ravenscraig; heavy end operation at Shelton geared to the reduced level of mill demand but expedition of development plans on the electric-arc project; Ebbw Vale closures to be confined to one blastfurnace and one converter in line with Beswick's interim document of July 1975, but OH steelmaking to continue with consequent reduction at Shotton to 4/5 furnace operation; heavy end production at East Moors at a level to support the reduced order load on the billet mill. Outside these provisions the unions agreed that BSC should have 'a degree of flexibility' in the loading of other plants. *Reports* (1975), 100–1.

7 In a paradox of the records, steel-industry employment actually grew (by over 6000) between 1974 and 1975, and ISTC membership, which had been falling for some time before it stabilised at 119,000 in 1974, had risen to almost 122,000 by March 1975 (*Reports*, 1975, 109).

8 In fact the fall in home consumption only bottomed out in 1977–8 and at a level (measured in crude steel equivalent) similar to that of 1963. Few contemporaries grasped that this was not a mere cyclical dip.

9 Special meeting, 23 June 1975 (*Reports*, 150). It was the Confederation's view that this dispute was about more than the implementation of the WMIS agreement: it also concerned management's decision to eliminate completely weekend working at the plant. The local membership had stayed out for some weeks in defiance of Central Office. Though the strike was now official, no strike pay was paid.

10 *Reports* (1975), 153–4.

11 For details of the conflicting offers, see *Reports* (1976), 3–4.

12 *Reports* (1976), 5–6.

13 The complaint of Stan Biddiscombe, No. 6 Divisional Officer, was that Port Talbot management were keeping him out of local talks until the men returned on its terms. He had insisted on a return to the status quo to enable local talks to resume (*Reports*, 1976, 9).

14 Its full title is 'Joint Statement on Reductions in Employment Costs and Improvements in Labour Productivity'.

15 With the greatest impact being absorbed by production workers. The agreement extended coverage of WMIS to them, but no deals went live until 1978, hampered as they were by pay policy which prevented lead-in payments to match those already paid to craft grades.

16 *Reports* (1975), 124–5.

17 The White Paper was appraised by the Executive on 15 July and the views of each DO were heard on its likely impact on the WMIS agreement (*Reports*, 1975, 151).

18 *Reports* (1975), 181.

19 And took the best part of a week's continuous negotiations to achieve.

20 That year's Staff Conference did make the plea that annual fixed increments be applied in addition to any annual norm (*Reports*, 1976, 134), but rejected a return to free collective bargaining under the current economic circumstances.

21 Six branches wrote to complain about the 1977 award (*Reports*, 1977, 30).

22 *Reports* (1976), 252. In 1977 letters began to be received by the EC from branches calling for the restoration of free collective bargaining.

23 He was also looking for consolidation of the previous two years' pay awards into basic rates.

24 *Reports* (1977), 149.

25 *Reports* (1978), 3.

26 *Reports* (1978), 108.

27 *Reports* (1978), 225. His action was endorsed by the Executive on 15 November.

28 *Reports* (1979), 6.

29 *Reports* (1979), 7.

30 *Reports* (1979), 118.

31 *Reports* (1978), 254.

32 *Reports* (1979), 35.

33 *Reports* (1979), 228.

34 For the EC members and Divisional Officers who were on the various working parties see *Reports* (1975), 3.

35 *Reports* (1975), 147. The Hoogovens visit took place on 30–31 March 1976, and ISTC representatives returned with positive recommendations for single status on the model they had observed, provided it could be introduced without impairing efficiency (*Reports*, 1976, 94).

36 The Contract proposed active participation and involvement in the development of BSC at every level, discussions on all subjects continuously held, monitoring of the implementation of agreements, inclusion of all Steel Committee unions and achievement of an NJC or NJCC by 31 December 1977.

37 *Reports* (1976), 3.

38 *Reports* (1977), 219.

39 The purpose of the draft was for incorporation in a Steel Committee document to be submitted to the Industry Department, where the Lord Inquiry was working on public-sector proposals in parallel with Bullock (*Reports*, 1976, 149).

40 *Reports* (1977), 149.

41 White and MacLaren were designated for the first two seats which were already achieved, with Caddick for the third when granted.

42 They attended their first EC as Main Board members on 16 November, and their written report (written jointly with the other four union appointees) was appended to the Minutes. *Reports* (1979), 48–9.

43 *Reports* (1979), 161.

44 This move was anticipated in 'BSC: Future Prospects', a key document of the Steel Contract initiative.

45 *Reports* (1979), 10.

46 *Reports* (1979), 162. He was empowered to bring in outside assistance if necessary, but this turned out to be a momentous decision which eventually was to lead to the appearance of 'New Deal for Steel' from within the Organisation.

47 *Reports* (1979), 190.

48 *Reports* (1976), 121.

49 See for example the resolution from Area 1 HST in 1978 (*Reports*, 1978, 124).

50 *Reports* (1976), 87.

51 *Reports* (1977), 76.

52 *Reports* (1977), 150. Provision was made for a review in the event that the President or Vice-president should come from the private sector.

53 *Reports* (1975), 149.

54 On 10 June 1977.

55 The ISTC nominees were No. 4 Divisional Officer Jack Gavin and Frank Bradley of the EC (*Reports*, 1975, 173). During the year the EC was alarmed to read rumours in the press that the NUB was in amalgamation talks with the National Union of Mineworkers.

56 An example of the cold came in summer 1978, when Billy Booth of the South Wales NUB made serious allegations against Sirs and John Foley for which he later publicly apologised (*Man and Metal*, September 1978, 187).

57 *Reports* (1975), 185. In November the EC deferred a request for the establishment of a place on the EC for middle management, pending a general review of the system of EC elections.

58 *Reports* (1975), 148.

59 *Reports* (1976), 13, 149.

60 *Reports* (1977), 80.

61 Sirs replied inquiring if this meant the end of the courtship. Meanwhile the Research Department drew up a document detailing the history of the SIMA/ISTC discussions. The May EC received and endorsed the document.

62 *Reports* (1979), 11.

63 After Muir and Sirs had met the proposal was altered to one of holding a tripartite meeting so that BSC senior management could attend (*Reports*, 1979, 93).

64 *Reports* (1979), 228. These decisions were taken at a meeting on 2 November – the same special meeting which heard Sirs's dramatic Corby report.

65 *Reports* (1979), 238; (1980), 26.

66 The ISTC put on considerable pressure to achieve a revision of the 1974 regulations on industrial injury benefits, including a seventeen-page submission in 1977. The burden of its complaint was that some processes only counted as 'noisy' (and bring benefit entitlement) if operated in shipbuilding, and that there was *a twenty-year qualification period.*

67 Ken Clarke (1929–), former Secretary of Lackenby 5 Branch, was appointed Divisional Organiser, No. 1 Division, in 1968 and to the same post in No. 2 Division in 1970. He later became Senior Divisional Organiser, No. 2 Division.

68 Agreement in principle on guidelines for safety reps was reached that summer (*Reports*, 1978, 184).

69 Jim Drinkwater (1918–75), a former second hand melter at Appleby-Frodingham, was appointed Divisional Organiser, No. 5 Division, in 1947, moved to No. 2 Division, in 1963 and became Divisional Officer there in 1964. The year after his death, the EC established the Jim Drinkwater Memorial Scholarship in his memory (*Reports*, 1976, 54). Following the refusal of the most senior organiser to move to No. 2 Division the EC determined that from now on absolute flexibility would be required of applicants 'to any division or Central Office, as required' (*Reports*, 1975, 260).

70 Peter Woods (1922–89) had entered the industry in 1938 and returned after war service. He was Secretary of Clydebridge No. 2 branch and briefly an EC member in 1966 before being appointed Divisional Organiser, No. 1 Division, later that year. In 1975 he was appointed Divisional Officer, No. 2 Division.

71 Bill Homewood (1920–89), Senior Organiser in No. 4 Division, was sent to Ruskin on a two-year diploma by his branch (Corby 10) at the age of thirty-two. He had narrowly lost the race to stand as Labour candidate in the Kettering and Corby seat in 1963 and left the panel two years later on first being appointed an organiser. In 1978 he gained the Kettering and Corby nomination, and succeeded Sir Geoffrey de Freitas as Labour MP for the constituency the following year.

72 Roy Bishop (1932–) entered the steel industry in 1949 and was appointed staff organiser, No. 3 Division, twenty years later. In 1971 he moved to No. 2 Division and became senior organiser in 1978. The following year he transferred to No. 4 Division.

73 Stan Biddiscombe was appointed Divisional Organiser, No. 4 Division, in 1957 and transferred to No. 6 Division three years later.

74 George Cooper (1916–) had replaced Sirs in No. 7 Division. He was appointed Divisional Organiser, No. 2 Division, in 1964 and Divisional Organiser, No. 3 Division, in 1967.

75 Arthur Bell (1918–88) entered the steel industry in 1935 and rose to be Branch Secretary of Glengarnock No. 1. He was appointed Divisional Organiser, No. 1 Division, in 1957 and Divisional Officer in 1968. He was chairman of the Scottish Council of the Labour Party that same year.

76 Jo Pickles (1920–83) had been employed by Steel, Peech and Tozer before his appointment as Divisional Organiser, No. 3 Division, in 1961. He retired as Divisional Officer in 1982, sadly for a very short retirement.

77 For the report of the Conference Arrangements and Agenda Committee, see *Reports* (1975), 219–20.

78 *Man and Metal* calculated that there had been seventy-five BOC motions on the subject between 1941 and 1973. Only one-third had been carried, however.

79 *Reports* (1976), 187–9.

80 The last Staff Conference met on 13 May 1977; it had been held annually for the last thirty-one years (*Reports*, 1977, 181). Retiring Chairman John Donovan pre-

sented a tankard to his successor, John Whittingham, and pointedly remarked that this was meant to keep the spirit of the conference alive!

81 *Reports* (1976), 234.

82 *Reports* (1977), 196–7.

83 Resolutions were accepted by the EC on buying BSC products, steel investment, BSC Industry Ltd., steel privatisation, the Social Contract, the Employment and Income Security Agreement, early retirement, single status, the BSC superannuation scheme, travel to work subsidies, protective clothing and safety equipment, the fire, ambulance and rescue services, Dupuytren's Contracture, training of school leavers, human rights, Argentina and holidays with pay. (*Reports*, 1977, 179–80).

84 *Reports* (1978), 155. Provisions were made for small works and for the allocation of additional sectional delegates. A suggestion from the 1978 ADC that the procedure was tilted towards high-voting plants was dismissed. Later in the year the conference was extended to four days, with a free period on Wednesday afternoon. A Youth of the Year award was also inaugurated.

85 Two improvements were introduced: possible block voting was to be discouraged by spot checks of ballot papers undertaken annually by the Auditors; EC members were forbidden to issue circular letters urging support of certain candidates (*Reports*, 1976, 225).

86 *Reports* (1977), 80. Sirs advised that the 1976 EC decision precluded a vote.

87 *Reports* (1978), 255. The EC received its own sub-committee's report in February 1979.

88 *Reports* (1979), 91. A Special EC held during the ADC condemned the 'underhand and undemocratic methods' employed by the authors. The Organisation and Staffing Sub-committee later interviewed certain full-time organisers about their role in support of the pamphlet. All denied that any approaches had been made to them or that they had been involved in Reform Group activities (*Reports*, 1979, 245).

89 *Reports* (1975), 163.

90 *Reports* (1977), 4.

91 See *Reports* (1977), 159, and the Sirs correspondence with Labour Party Secretary Ron Hayward in December 1978 (*Man and Metal*, January 1979).

92 *Reports* (1979), 162.

93 'Appomattox or Civil War?', *The Economist* (27 May 1978); see also *Man and Metal* (June 1978).

94 *Reports* (1977), 7.

95 *Reports* (1976), 161. For a detailed account of the sequence of closures and the debate over productivity between BSC and the ISTC see M. Upham, 'The British Steel Corporation: Retrospect and Prospect', *Industrial Relations Journal* (July–August 1980), 5–21.

96 *Reports* (1977), 197.

97 *Reports* (1977), 222.

 98 *Reports* (1977), 283.
 99 The cessation of ironmaking at the end of the year ended 191 years of activity at this site.
100 *Reports* (1977), 270.
101 *Reports* (1978), 3.
102 *Reports* (1978), 7.
103 *Man and Metal* (April 1978).
104 An emergency motion tabled for Labour's Northern Region Conference damned the SCNI report as posing 'a direct threat to employment possibilities in the Teesside area'. The ISTC's motion to the 1978 Labour Conference coupled the White Paper with the SCNI report as representing 'a trend away from the commitments of Labour's programme 1973'; it called for reactivation of the modernisation plan, no 'hiving-off' from BSC and for government pressure on industry to maintain market shares (*Reports*, 1978, 83, 152).
105 In August 1985 some former East Moors members sued the ISTC (and the NUB), arguing that they had received inappropriate advice when taking voluntary redundancy in 1978 before the main closure. Mr Justice Knox struck out the claims on 10 November 1987, but the plaintiffs appealed and the costly legal proceedings were dragged out until 13 October 1988, when the appeals were dismissed by the Court of Appeal.
106 Brian Connolly and Keith Brookman were seconded from Divisional Office to East Moors and Ebbw Vale respectively to deal with the massive counselling task thrown up by these major redundancies.
107 See letter to all branches, 30 June 1978. An attempt by the local trades council to obtain support for a further local general strike was deemed unhelpful by the EC (*Reports*, 1978, 197).
108 In the cooler atmosphere of the November EC this call was 'noted' (*Reports*, 1978, 255).
109 In its original form the plan was to close Cookley and concentrate output of electrical steels at Orb; by August 1979 the Cookley membership had accepted the inevitability of closure at local meetings and Swinton House was arranging severance pay negotiations (*Reports*, 1979, 161).
110 *Reports* (1978), 254.
111 *Reports* (1979), 88.
112 Tony Benn, *Diaries, 1977–80* (1990), 414ff. Benn records that Denis Healy (who insisted that the decision could not be taken out of BSC's hands) thought Sirs was 'in a very difficult mood'.
113 *Reports* (1979), 4. Also see above.
114 *Reports* (1979), 135.
115 *Reports* (1979), 205.
116 *Reports* (1979), 162–3.
117 Many of their arguments are presented in R.A. Beyer, T.J. Brignall and A.R. Maunders, *Accounting for British Steel* (1982).

118 With the exception of safety matters. On 7 November three local officials crossed a picket line outside a JCC at Redcar.
119 *Reports* (1979), 227–8.
120 *Reports* (1979), 237.
121 The EC rejected any collaboration with BSC (Industry), which was now establishing itself in the town (*Reports*, 1979, 295).
122 Corby steel's fight to survive is told in detail in A. Maunders, *A Process of Struggle* (1987).
123 *Reports* (1979), 230.
124 *Reports* (1979), 231.
125 *Reports* (1979), 233.

7

Strike

Bill Sirs (1980)

'. . . that strike also challenged our economic strategy directly; and it
is unlikely, once the strike had begun, that our economic policies
would have survived if we had suffered defeat.'
(Margaret Thatcher)[1]

'They are trying to make us look small and we have no intention of
accepting it . . . It is important for us to cripple the industry as quickly
as we can and get it over as quickly as we can.'
(Bill Sirs)[2]

Soon after the general election victory which brought Mrs Thatcher's Conservatives to power, the 1979 ADC passed a resolution opposing the wages
policy of the new government on the grounds that it treated the public and
private sectors unequally. The ADC concluded presciently that such policies
would 'inevitably lead to industrial conflict with the whole trade union movement'.[3] The joint national negotiating teams met on 24–5 September to formulate a claim for a 'substantial' increase in the new year. They had good
reason to do so: inflation was accelerating fast, assisted by a huge rise in VAT
from the June budget; and though few steelworkers knew it at the time, their
hourly labour costs were less than half that of Belgian or German steelworkers, and two-thirds that of the French.[4] Worse still, the 1979 *New Earnings Survey* (long the basis of annual ISTC pay claims) showed iron and steel
workers on £66.10 basic weekly pay – below the average for production,
manufacturing, and even for all industries and services in the UK. However,
BSC was already seeking revision to the national bargaining procedure,[5] and
it now went further, intimating on the eve of pay talks that it would not be in
a position to make any offer at national level apart from the much-sought-
after consolidation of the 5 per cent supplement from 1976. Any future pay
progress would be based on improved performance with negotiations conducted at local level: local deals would, it was claimed, yield quarterly
bonuses of up to 10 per cent of earnings.[6] When the Joint Negotiating Committees met BSC on 3 December they rejected this offer, if offer it was. The
Executive which met on 7 December had received calls for strike action from

many joint committees and was not disposed to disagree: this was the same management which had just announced the biggest redundancy programme British industry had ever known. It voted rapidly for national strike action at BSC from 2 January, exempting the private sector, though the latter would be instructed not to take BSC orders: three weeks' notice was given on 10 December. Divisional Officers were to convene meetings of joint committees to discuss picketing, and a special strike committee of eight EC members was established.[7] BSC and the government had sown the wind and were now to reap the whirlwind.

The crisis atmosphere mounted. All steel unions had received the same offer, and on 19 December a meeting of their General Secretaries described it as 'completely unrealistic', promising their backing for a strike if it remained unaltered. Later that day, the EC met and took a number of operational decisions: there would be no strike pay except in cases of special hardship; full-time officers would not draw their pay during the strike; an attempt would be made to protect plants threatened with closure; five BSC branches unaffected by the negotiations would be exempt.[8] A pledge of support in blocking the movement of steel by rail was received from the National Union of Railwaymen (NUR), and Sirs was able to report that following a meeting of European steel unions backing had been received from the Germans, French, Belgians and Swedes.[9]

On 20 December the EC met Sir Charles Villiers, and soon afterwards the Joint Negotiating Committees. These convened the next day to hear an address by Scholey and Grieves. Later, on 21 December, a meeting of the ECs of both the ISTC and the NUB[10] was held at Hector Smith's request. That day the NUB, too, gave strike notice. BSC, in what it termed a final offer, reiterated the earlier bid, adding only a 3 per cent incentive to buy out the GWA, plus talks on a thirty-nine-hour week to be phased in during 1982. On 21 December the CNC rejected this, and on 28 December it also rejected additional refinements – another 'final' offer.[11] The time for talking, at least on pay, was over.

On 2 January work stopped completely at the British Steel Corporation. The ISTC's public sector membership walked out, giving 100 per cent backing to their Executive's call. TV pictures of picket lines projected to the nation an unmistakable image of absolute solidarity, but picketing of ISTC members was scarcely necessary after the first enthusiastic few days: it was to be the last of the big loyal strikes. The ability of the Organisation to shut down BSC plants had been doubted by few: the outcome of the strike would be determined by the movement, and not the production, of steel.

On 4 January 1980 BSC seemed willing to raise the 'with-strings'[12] element to 6 or even 8 per cent, to guarantee 3 per cent in exchange for local demanning agreements and to pay a lead-in 1 per cent for local deals: this found no takers. To the first Joint Executives of the strike, meeting in London on 7 January, Sirs could report full membership solidarity, the backing of the three rail unions and the IMF, and that day's decision of the TGWU to bring out their BSC members also. (They were joined on 8 January by the GMWU and the next day by the NCCC.) The TUC, Sirs reported to the Executive, 'were expressing grave concern at the situation which could develop into a General Strike'.[13] The pattern of new incremental BSC offers continued the next day, but these suggestions always declined in value once examined;[14] the unions countered with a claim for an 8 per cent general increase and guaranteed 5 per cent local bonuses. Neither side moved. Many Executive members disliked the prospect of joint local negotiations with the craft unions (which the original offer implied), and also reported that the membership wanted a settlement with no strings attached; the NUB wanted a rise at the current inflation rate. Calls were indeed being made for a 20 per cent general increase, which would have been a rise in real earnings during that high-inflation winter, but Sirs asserted himself to keep his negotiating hands free.

A taste of what was to come arose when some EC members reported a feeling that the fight was being jeopardised by keeping the private sector at work; supportive dockers and railwaymen could not distinguish between public and private steel. It was agreed to convene representatives of the ISEA, MWB and Sheffield Shift Committees before the next Executive. Activities in the Divisions were also facilitated by an agreement to supply officers with cash as required to pay pickets' expenses: they would be needed, as thousands of active members were crossing the country in search of movements of steel.

A small group of government ministers and officials, with the Prime Minister in the chair, had been monitoring the steel situation since the end of December. Its view of steel supplies makes a sharp contrast with reports to the Executive Council.[15] A 'new' BSC offer of 11 January still provided no new money, and yet required acceptance of streamlining (later to be known as slimlining) of ongoing plants in addition to the closures notified in December. Three days later Sirs told ACAS at an informal meeting that there was little point in further meetings with BSC unless more money was put on the table. The dispute, he thought, was becoming political with the government listening only to one side.[16] This point was highly relevant to the possible involvement of the ISTC's membership in the private sector, representatives of which were consulted on 14 January. An orthodox wage dispute lay between a specific group of employees and their employer; if this was a dispute about the union, and the government was ranged with its enemies, then the whole union was in it, a point made that day by at least one private sector representative. Earlier, the ISTC had signalled that it expected a 'short sharp strike': two weeks on, issues once on the margins had moved to centre stage. To call private sector members out when they were not in primary dispute with their own employers would test their loyalty, especially when their own national negotiating structures were in jeopardy apparently because of the vulnerability of a number of companies. But not to call them out might jeopardise the strike itself, because private firms were in production and because so many transport workers whose support was essential could not identify the point of origin of steel products in transit.

On 16 January, having heard private sector representations on both sides of the argument, the EC reached a fateful decision. If the BSC dispute was not settled by Sunday 27 January then the private sector of the steel industry would be called out; the membership would be instructed to institute a complete stoppage of the movement of steel throughout the country; to cement solidarity, the Organisation would seek a common settlement date for public and private sector wage reviews.[17] This was the nuclear option. Armed with it, Sirs and Smith on 19 January met Sir Keith Joseph and Jim Prior – the Employment Secretary and the one minister who had been heard to utter some public criticism of BSC. Two days later these ministers were present when the leaders of the ISTC and NUB met the Prime Minister herself. She reiterated the government's 'non-interventionist' position and insisted that the heart of the dispute was productivity;[18] this provoked a clash between her and Sirs, who by now was making considerable headway in undermining the assumptions behind the BSC figures.[19] After the meeting the two unions were themselves approached (at the employer's request) by ACAS, but they stayed aloof, fearing arbitration: the members were solid and the strike could still be won. On 24 January the Joint Executives convened to hear an impressive array of international speakers pledging solidarity with Britain's steelworkers. Support from transport workers in Britain remained solid: the internal movement of steel was being significantly slowed. But the plant-extraction juggernaut was still rolling: BSC had extended the closure shroud to cover the RDL Group's activities at the Britannia works, Glengarnock (where mills had survived the heavy-end closure), Consett and Normanby Park. This massive blow might yet strengthen the strikers' determination – and the whole union was about to come out as one.

On 25 January the Executive firmed up the private strike instruction – only to receive a letter from the BISPA chairman stating that sixteen member companies were taking out a High Court writ together with a restraining injunction to prevent private sector members becoming involved in the BSC dispute. The writ (on behalf of Duport Steels *et al.*) was served that day; the EC, under unwavering legal advice, decided it should be defended, and the decision was taken to brief Counsel.[20] At the High Court the BISPA writ was refused by Judge Kenneth Jones, but the action now entered the realms of extreme legal controversy. On 26 January, at remarkably short notice, the Court of Appeal agreed to sit, and there Lord Denning, Master of the Rolls, granted BISPA its injunction, essentially on the grounds that the ISTC argument was with the government not BSC. For a British judge accustomed to upholding Parliament's sovereign legislative powers it was a surprising decision. A copy of this injunction was handed to every member of the EC when they convened in London three days later.

Away from this rarefied legal world a substantial part of the private sector had struck – a remarkable, even chivalrous, action, since however bad their employer relations were, total breakdown had not been reached. But there were significant exceptions, and so for the first time the Executive had to consider its own authority as well as this controversial extension of the law. The nub of the issue was what had become known as secondary picketing. The Employment Bill 1980, then before the Commons, proposed to withdraw immunities in secondary action,[21] but it was not yet law. The legal services advised that the Denning judgement simply could not be allowed to stand. It represented an extension of the law to a ban on secondary picketing beyond what had yet been legislated by parliament, and thus had an impact on more than twelve million trade unionists. Moreover, Denning had argued that the private sector strike was a political and not a trade union dispute, since the private sector strikers were not acting in furtherance of a trade dispute. The lawyers had been promised an early hearing by the Law Lords and thought the chances of overturning Denning very strong – but to ensure this the EC had to comply with the injunction and call off the private sector strike.

This was a bitter pill. The original decision had been contested: Sirs, for one, had resisted extension of the strike. After the solicitors had spoken he was blunt with the Executive: he would keep members there until they came to the right decision.[22] They retained legal services in order to receive advice: the ISTC could not embarrass its lawyers before the Law Lords, but must persist with its traditional policy of obeying the law. If the injunction was unchallenged, private firms would be entitled to sue and the Organisation's structure would collapse. The meeting was deluged with messages from joint branches, public and private sector, across the country, as well as from local units of other unions. There were local and national voices advocating defiance. A long and agonised discussion culminated in a decision to follow the legal advice, and the instruction was lifted.[23]

In the short run, the legal advice was validated by events. Leave to appeal was quickly obtained on 31 January, and the next day the Law Lords unanimously overturned Denning.[24] But arguments at the highest court in the land, in the middle of a national dispute, can never purely be a legal matter, and some loss of momentum is traceable from this point. The Joint Executives reconvened on the afternoon of 1 February. They received a plea from Alec Mortimer, director general of BISPA, to allow the private sector to stay at work despite the Law Lords, but with the union's legal obligations discharged there was little prospect of his plea being heard. The strike instruction was reinstated with effect from 6 a.m. on Sunday 3 February, and the earlier decision to picket and prevent all movement of steel was reaffirmed.[25] But legal victories without an effective strike were pyrrhic, and private sector solidarity remained only partial. Some plants willing to obey the original instruction were now reluctant. Union and media attention now focused intensely on the continued activity of two plants: Hadfield in Sheffield and Sheerness, each of which was still producing though each also had ISTC members on strike.

On 18 February the Executive received a broad private sector delegation, all of whom accepted the concept of a common bargaining date. Their complaint was the continued failure of the Sheerness membership to strike – unsurprisingly in view of the massive publicity given to the clashes at the works and the way that strikers at other plants were being told that Sheerness was taking their orders. Sheerness members still at work were expelled that day, but there were other fears: some weakening of resolve was directly attributable to the threat of private sector redundancies and closures. Sheerness indeed was being held up by the Prime Minister as an example; as Sirs commented glumly to the EC, the Sheerness membership did not have the same traditions of trade union solidarity as did other works.[26]

Whatever its economic impact, the publicity impact of the strike on the public was immense. In later years Mrs Thatcher made no secret of her annoyance at BSC's failure to get its case across to the public.[27] In fact, as the dispute wore on the union grew more adept at projecting its view. This was partly the result of retaining professional assistance and partly the outcome of creating its own media. Every week of the strike the ISTC published *Steelworkers' Banner*, which popularised the union case and fed pickets with originally-researched arguments; a steady stream of handbills, lapel stickers, placards and pamphlets was put out by Central Office. The strike blew away some of the cobwebs which had obscured debates on steel policy. The Research Department was set free to challenge the assumptions underlying the management case for retrenchment, and seized its opportunity with devastating effect. For a number of years the parameters of the argument had been defined by BSC; now the chance had come to explode the case for retrenchment and the provocative '0 per cent' pay offer.[28]

The propaganda war reached its peak on 4 February, when Granada TV's *World in Action* produced its programme 'The Steel Papers', which purported to show that government intervention in the events leading up to the strike had been critical.[29] *Steelworkers' Banner* reproduced the transcript of the programme, which had been broadcast despite intense litigation by BSC. In many ways the propaganda argument had wider terms of reference than the strike, since many of those on the picket lines were also victims of the savage run-down of the industry, either that already achieved or that to come. One consequence of this would be to make the Lever proceedings (see below) quite uncomfortable for senior BSC figures, who found themselves challenged by union arguments.

By the time of the quarterly Executive meeting in February there was a depressing outlook in the private sector. Closure of Patent Shaft had been announced; at Round Oak, Manchester Steels and Hadfields the membership had returned to work, and officials who had stayed out on strike were in an exposed position; worried GKN strikers wanted a meeting with the General Secretary.

On 29 February the EC was addressed by seventeen private-sector delegates.[30] After they had withdrawn there was a protracted debate. Sirs drew the attention of those present to the approach of the annual review date with ISEA on 31 March and to a bargaining stalemate at the MWB which could not be resolved while the strike continued. Members commented that mass picketing and the coverage of it in the press was distracting attention from the actual wage dispute with BSC. The outcome was an uneasy compromise: policy was restated, but 'where private sector membership had returned to work . . . the General Secretary [should] instruct the branch officials to return to work with the membership so that they could exercise control and surveillance within the Works'.[31]

With the position slipping in the private sector there was all the more reason to firm up the public sector, but gaps were developing between the unions. On 8 February the Joint Executives had rejected a new BSC offer of 9 + 4 per cent – a more attractive version of which was accepted by NCCC leaders two days later. Yet within three days this too was rejected by NCCC

144

members, who shared the common mood of defiance. BSC now circulated details of the offer to all employees; but they had been given a lesson in the robustness of negotiations with a lay participating element. On 17 February the ISTC proposed a 15 per cent rise on basic rates from the settlement date, and a further (guaranteed) bonus payment of 5 per cent from April 1980. The settlement date would be shifted to the end of March 1981, and consolidation of the Phase 2 supplement would be deferred. This initiative was backed by the Joint Executives, but to the union's consternation the employers rejected it rapidly and started to talk of a ballot of BSC employees.

On 19 February, Sirs told the EC that the strike 'was beginning to take effect',[32] but not everyone agreed. The Rotherham Strike Committee, source of many flying pickets across the country, passed a highly publicised motion of no confidence in him.[33] Central Office, fearing a loss of control, reminded all strike committees that they should not leave their divisions without permission from the Divisional Officer: pickets outside their own division would come under the control of the Divisional Officer in whose division they were located. Measures were taken to improve the monitoring of collections and ensure that they were given to the division in which they were raised. But the policy of no strike pay was reaffirmed while hardship money continued to be available via the divisional offices.

It was one thing to achieve internal coherence, but inter-union solidarity was also vital. On 29 February the ISTC called a national delegate conference along with the NUB and the TGWU, and invited other nationally recognised unions to attend; a simultaneous decision was taken to meet Jim Callaghan, who had suggested mediation.[34] The conference met at Congress House on 5 March and was attended by delegates from each nationally recognised union. The previous evening Murray had convened two delegates from each of these organisations to agree a common policy for intensifying the strike: subsequently an Iron and Steel Co-ordinating Committee (I & SCC) was established.

With the errors and blunders of higher management being aired weekly by *Steelworkers' Banner*, the possibility of an inquiry into BSC policies and management was also discussed. The I & SCC now fashioned a common document from an ISTC/NUB paper and an NCCC document. This was put to BSC on 10 March, and provoked three days of negotiations, but the two sides could not agree on the value of the terms under discussion: with BSC reiterated its offer of 10 per cent plus 4 per cent on the value-added bonus, while the unions now sought 14 per cent on the basic plus 5 per cent on the bonus. The two sides were as far apart as ever. On 18 March the Joint Executives endorsed rejection of the BSC offer, but authorised Smith and Sirs to seek third-party intervention, preferably through a Committee of Inquiry, the route Sirs now believed most likely to provide opportunities to challenge BSC.

As expected, BSC had proceeded to ballot employees on its pay offer of 8 February. The ISTC had already received complaints about this breach of procedure, the cost of advertisements and maladministration.[35] When the results emerged on 10 March it was apparent that 56 per cent of those on strike had, by abstention or rejection, failed to back the BSC proposal. The public sector employer had still failed to get its case across.

But the sad denouement in the private sector occurred in March. By 14 March all private firms but one were back in production, and four days later the resumption of work was total. To a request from Sirs for discussions in the 1980 pay round, Ken Hale, ISEA General Secretary, had replied that the strike was unconstitutional and had precipitated such a serious situation that member companies were not prepared to negotiate nationally on an award. In fact many firms were withdrawing from ISEA and would conduct their own pay talks. Sirs had to warn the EC that this meant that procedures would lapse: a failure to agree would from now on have to be resolved within the individual firm.[36] These bleak developments were referred to the ISEA CNC.

Back in the public sector, the CNC too rejected the BSC offer and backed the proposal to seek a Committee of Inquiry. Here at least there was substantial agreement on terms of reference, except that the Corporation would not agree to any inquiry into its own management. The I & SCC sought government involvement, in the person of Jim Prior, on the morning of 24 March, but he insisted this would happen only through the auspices of ACAS.[37] If the unions did not wish to involve ACAS, he continued, then a jointly approved chairman should be appointed, the parties should set up their own committee, and they might employ ACAS in a secretarial capacity. This was the course of action adopted by both sides at BSC that afternoon: most arrangements were put in hand at once, though the nomination of a chairman was deferred. Finally the name of the businessman and former Labour minister Lord Lever emerged. He was joined by Richard (now Lord) Marsh, who as Minister for Power had nationalised BSC and led the British Iron and Steel Consumers' Council (BRISCC) but was now firmly of the political right, and Bill Keys, leader of the Society of Graphical and Allied Trades (SOGAT).

The Lever Committee met for the first time on 29 March. At 3 p.m. that afternoon the Joint Executives also met. The choices were stark. Before them were telegrams from the Scottish and Rotherham strike committees requesting that there be no return to work, since an (unrelated) dock strike which had now begun in Liverpool might spread nationally; from Tinsley Park, however, both joint committees urged a rapid settlement. There had been no movement on establishing an inquiry into BSC management, a step the top men at BSC were determined to resist. Only after a lengthy debate did the Executives resolve to accept a Committee of Inquiry on pay. They did not, however, pick up a BSC suggestion of returning to work while the inquiry got underway, despite the offer of a 10 per cent interim payment with the possibility of tax rebates if a settlement was reached before 30 March.

The Committee of Inquiry began its public deliberations on 30 March and the next day reported recommending an increase of 11 per cent on gross earnings; a 4.5 per cent minimum bonus guarantee; and concessions on the lump sum payment, holiday payments and pensions. The national negotiating committees met on 1 April, and after an anguished discussion voted 42:27 to accept the recommendation. At 4.30 on 1 April the Joint Executives reconvened. Sirs told them that the fight for jobs would have to continue, as would the drive to establish an inquiry into BSC management. His view was formalised in a resolution which was coupled with a vote of no confidence in the Board.[38] They then called for a return to work of the BSC membership on Thursday 3 April at 6.00 a.m.

On 2 April the ISTC Executive, meeting alone, had to consider a number of outstanding matters, including what action to take against lorry drivers who had crossed picket lines. Resolution of this problem, together with that of certain private sector branch officials who had broken the strike, was deferred. Management members who had crossed picket lines would be informed that they had been expelled. The strike committees were now disbanded, and it was resolved that all business should henceforth be carried out through the constituted joint committees and branches. Unused money held by officers was directed back to Swinton House. Independent funds held by the strike committees were directed towards hardship use. The SIMA issue had also arisen in new guise, since so many members of it had habitually crossed picket lines, and the Executive decided on total non-co-operation with that organisation.[39] Finally the leaders of the NUR, ASLEF and other organisations were thanked for their whole-hearted support.[40]

Two weeks later a further special Executive tidied up some of the outstanding business of the strike. A number of Corby members had worked from day one: they were reported to the Executive and expelled.[41] The officers were able to report that their various Divisional and Works Strike Committees had been wound down. Some full-time officers and some strike committee members were still communicating with the press: it was reaffirmed that the situation 'should now revert to normality and all constitutional procedures should be strictly observed'.[42] Sorting out finances took a great deal longer. On 16 September, the Executive received a report of the Finance Committee into the finances of No. 3 Division during the strike, which concluded that much expenditure could not be accounted for, and it authorised an in-depth inquiry.[43] In 1981, accountants identified £1,462,398 of expenses on the dispute which were disbursed from individual divisional headquarters without control; the accountants went further and entered a doubt as to whether this was the final net amount.[44] A year after this, the Stocksbridge Multi-union Joint Shop Stewards Committee agreed to return £4000 arising out of strike payments made during the strike.[45]

An August 1980 financial review made grim reading even before the cost of the strike was taken into account and without any allowance for future capital expenditure. Immediate action was taken to raise contributions to 60p weekly for AA grade members, with proportionate increases for the rest.[46] A Rule amendment, giving powers to raise a levy on the membership if funds did not grow annually at the rate of £1 per member, was rather unconvincingly approved by ballot. Savings were achieved by curtailing the plans for a normal conference, substituting a one-day event which was eventually held on 22 November at Congress House. There were no resolutions.

On 23 May 1980 the Executive had received appeals against its decision to expel the Sheerness membership, and extensive correspondence from Round Oak raising analogous issues. In the case of Sheerness provision was made for a Special Executive to hear the local officials; the Round Oak Joint Committee officials were suspended, but informed that they too would have the right of appeal to the Executive should they decide to appeal. On 22 July the Special Executive interviewed officials of the Sheerness 1, 2, 3 and Technical Staff branches, who explained that their decision to continue working had been taken because of threats from the employers and fears for the future of the works. Sheerness Steel had received an Aims for Industry award for staying in, a presentation which had appalled them because their decision had been based on fear of unemployment and not on admiration for the ideals of free enterprise: their views had been made clear to their employers who, under threat of industrial action, had returned the award. The EC had to weigh the need to demonstrate the consequences of defying the union against the need to build solidarity in the face of new public and private sector threats. It resolved to administer a stern reprimand, coupled with a warning about future transgressions.

After this the EC interviewed three officials of the Round Oak Joint Committee, Jack Bate, Tom Bate, and John Smith, all of whom had been suspended from office following the decision to return to work at their plant on 25 February. Their case was that keeping the workforce out on strike until that date was a major achievement in view of the parlous finances of the company. On similar grounds to their Sheerness decision the EC determined upon reinstatement coupled with a strong warning.[47] These wise decisions helped to preserve the fabric of the union when it could have been torn apart.

The winding down of operations only paralleled the sharp contraction of the industry. At the Hallside Works notice of closure at the end of March 1980 was issued during the stoppage. Local officials agreed to negotiate the terms, which would cost 600 jobs.[48] RDL shut their construction plants at Consett and Britannia, putting an end to 600 jobs in the ISTC alone. Severance pay had been agreed at Cleveland on the eve of the strike. The Redbourne blastfurnaces and coke ovens also shut about this time. The Warrington mills at Bewsey and Dallam closed in July. With the strike over, the spotlight switched to Consett as the biggest works under threat and still resisting: a mini-steel committee was established there to co-ordinate opposition to a closure which threatened 3700 jobs, and the Durham people fought a doughty campaign including marches in their own town, rallies in London, and serious proposals for development.

This works was making a profit, but nobody seemed to care: 'Consett in the Black – Faced with Sack' read one much-seen banner. Eventually BSC indifference to these pleas produced a crack in the resistance: Consett 1 branch staged its own ballot which duly produced a majority favouring negotiations for severance payments, an alarming development which left other branches stranded. In September 1980 the moving televised appeal of Consett Executive member Ken Sessford from the TUC rostrum – 'Lord, Lord, where art thou?' – fell on deaf ears and Consett closed on time. This bitter outcome left a legacy of complaints from the works' joint committee, and new difficulties emerged when those made redundant in the 1979 Hownsgill plate mill closure complained at the disparity between their treatment and that of those who had left in the general closure.[49]

In No. 3 Division 'normal' relations were resumed, but were blighted by the closure of the Osborn Hadfields foundry (with a loss of 850 jobs), Park View Forge and Habershons hot strip mill. Aurora began its melancholy rationalisation with the proposal to shut Low Moor Steel Works before the following year. In Corby the worst fears seemed to materialise when management tabled their intention to close three of the four CW mills: so much for saving the tube works by letting the steel plant go! The Patent Shaft closure, already announced, took place in stages between March and June 1980: local officials ruefully recalled how completely dependent the company had been on a declining plate market. At Round Oak, original redundancy expectations of 80 rose to 1000.

In South Wales enormous job losses loomed: BSC began by talking openly of shutting either Llanwern or Port Talbot, and then tabled 'slimline' proposals which would have left each of the two sites with half a steelworks. It was local union initiatives which found a solution: 'slimlining' which left each as an integrated plant. They still lost 12,000 jobs, but Llanwern and Port Talbot remain in production to this day. In the Tinplate Group unilateral action in defiance of the GWA had been taken by the management, resulting in each of its three plants closing in turn, a move which posed a serious threat to procedures.[50] Even in the London Area the non-ferrous trade, which was totally unaffected by the strike, experienced the separation of Enfield Rolling Mills (ERM) into two separate companies. This led directly to closure of the newly formed ERM Rolled Metals Ltd at a cost of 850 jobs: redundancies began in May 1980, and complete closure was achieved by the end of the year.

What survived of private-sector bargaining now began a bumpy ride. The private sector CNC met on 2 and 17 April 1980 to discuss ISEA's threat to withdraw from national negotiations. It drew up a common policy document, and circulated guidelines to heavy steel branches on the content of claims falling under the 1980 review.[51] But no one could hold out any realistic prospect of returning to central negotiations. In 1981 and 1982 the HST Central Negotiating Committee again met and drew up guidelines for a national claim, but the ISEA dissolved at the end of 1982, its disappearance being formally notified to the EC in February 1983.

This was bad (though expected), but worse was to come. On 9 April 1980 the MWB employers had made an offer valued at 17 per cent, a bid rejected by the Operatives' Standing Committee which wanted a strike, though the EC insisted on a further meeting. In fact a settlement was reached on 18 April involving a 17 per cent increase, an extra day's holiday, and double time for all work performed on the 10 p.m./6 a.m. Sunday shift. It proved a false dawn: soon after, Board chairman J.G. Standish resigned, and Sirs encountered employer resistance to convening an early meeting of the Board. By August he was warning of a possible break-up as employers sought individual company settlements. More disturbing still was the news that where redundancies were occurring they seemed to fall upon branch officials who had been active during the strike.[52] Finally in November 1980 Sirs had to report that all employer members had now resigned, effectively ending 114 years of joint negotiations. It was a miserable end, though postponed for a time while the operatives' side continued to meet alone.

Future policy and events within the union

At the February 1980 Executive, Main Board directors MacLaren and White had warned that BSC's new plan proposed to cut manned capacity to fifteen million tonnes and asked for clear policy guidance as to how they should react. This was a further stimulus to ideas already in gestation. The ISTC began to prepare alternative plans for submission to the BSC Main Board, but they blossomed into the full-blown strategy envisaged before the strike. That May *New Deal for Steel*, a 179-page paperback, was published and warmly received by members and the wider world. The ISTC had indeed moved a long way from its reluctance to be involved in planning in the previous decade.[53] Its three key themes – that BSC could cut prices, make savings, and yet grow by aggressive selling – broke new ground: for the first time an alternative could be advocated to the spiral of decline at BSC. It was a rare case of a union attempting to meet management on its own terms, with business arguments.

Over the next two years no organisation did more to canvass and persuade public opinion of the crisis which faced basic production. Concern about steel imports had surfaced in ADC resolutions from the mid-1970s. As a rule this concern took the form of a call for import controls, though *New Deal for Steel* had broadened the discussion to focus on the impact on domestic steel demand of deteriorating competitiveness in the steel-using industries. In order to develop a database on imports, Sirs mounted a prolonged correspondence with private re-rolling companies and Divisional Officers. The former had complained of a serious shortage of BSC steel, and of strip billets and blooms in particular. By 1981, due to devaluation, prices had moved in favour of domestically produced steel, but it was not available from the Corporation. In November 1981 Sirs urged that capacity be pushed to maximum use in order to avoid imports,[54] and reported that BSC expected higher output at Teesside to bring some alleviation.[55] There was of course a contradiction between reluctance to engage in local productivity arrangements and calls to drive plant harder; the argument was made more complex by demands heard at the EC and elsewhere that excessive overtime working should cease.

After a period there was a partial thaw in public-sector industrial relations. In August 1980 the ISTC relaxed its ban on consultative participation at BSC. Members at Normanby Park and Velindre, both of which were to suffer under the 1981 Plan, had urged a resumption of contacts; in the end the EC resolved to reissue its guidelines of 1978, which had been published after the 1978 Steel Contract report.[56] Effectively this act opened the way for joint union committees to be established at the various works. Another rapprochement came when the ISTC agreed to co-operate in BSC's use of the Temporary Short-time Working Compensation Scheme (TSWCS) in conjunction with the GWA, a move which facilitated certain savings. A circular was issued to branches and guidelines were laid down, though some anomalies later emerged. In Yorkshire the TSWCS proved especially effective in putting off major redundancies in the Special Steels sector.

Many leading local figures were now redundant as a result of closure of their works or department. Some of these, still in the prime of life, wished to maintain their activity in the labour movement, and there was some room for manoeuvre in the Rule Book to allow this.[57] Under Rule 33 it was possible to claim contribution credits under certain circumstances, but some abuse of this provision had arisen when it was used to extend membership for benefit purposes under Rules 35 and 37. This growing difficulty placed new burdens on the straitened finances. From November 1980 a member's title to benefit was assessed at the date of cessation of employment; members qualifying under Rule 37 would become 'holding members' until employment resumed, and might be formed into branches 'where desirable', such branches being excluded from ballots on administrative matters and established for advisory purposes only.[58] In May, after a review, Sirs was able to recommend continuation of these arrangements, stipulating also that members would not be allowed to extend their membership by means of credits in order to accumulate sufficient entitlements by the cut-off date of 1 September 1979. There was a new dimension, however, in that members who ceased employment before this date and maintained membership by claiming credits would be granted benefit provided that they could fulfil the requirements of Rule 35 before 31 December 1983; a member made redundant before the earlier date, and aged between sixty and sixty-three at the later date, would not be allowed to submit a medical certificate after redundancy in order to obtain benefit.[59]

A number of key personalities were now approaching retirement. Arthur Bell was discussing early retirement because of his own ill-health and that of his wife. Since the most senior organiser, Brian Connolly, was tied by European commitments, Bell was succeeded by Clive Lewis, another of the first generation of staff organisers and the next most senior man.[60] Roy Bishop became No. 3 Divisional Officer to replace Joe Pickles. No. 7 Divisional Officer George Cooper retired in November 1981, at the same time as Stan Biddiscombe in No. 6 Division. From now on Nos. 5 and 6 Divisions, while remaining electorally separate, were administratively combined under Divisional Officer John Foley; in February 1983 they were rehoused in Cardiff. When these and consequential changes at lower levels had been completed or determined upon, Central Office was instructed to draw up a document on the future shape of the Organisation.[61] Among other changes was an over-haul of publications. The strike had demonstrated the need for colourful communications, and this was tacitly acknowledged when *Man and Metal* effectively ceased publication at the end of 1979. In July 1980, a new and pro-fessionally produced monthly tabloid, *ISTC Banner*, appeared.

1980 had been a catastrophic year for the ISTC. At times it had seemed to monopolise the headlines with its industrial action, punchy arguments and colourful propaganda. The spectacle of steelworkers resisting without pay for three months had borne out every knowledgeable forecast.[62] Yet the price had been enormous. The most charitable interpretation of the settlement suggested those still employed would at best break even, given current infla-tion rates;[63] but so many would not be employed, and sheer exhaustion and depression at the prospects for steel demand after the strike made a haemor-rhage of jobs impossible to staunch. Those made redundant in the months following the strike lost virtually all their income, though of course some of the pain was eased by the severance package. The damage to the industry itself was enormous: even in 1996 UK steel output had not climbed back to that of 1979, the last complete year before the strike began.[64] And the pre-posterous break-even instruction to BSC, cause of all this trouble, was missed by a mile.

Such reflections are historical hindsight, however. In the concrete cir-cumstances of December 1979 the ISTC faced a challenge that no other union in modern history had faced. The extinction of one third of the industry, simultaneously with a refusal to grant any central improvement in pay, was the last straw for the Organisation. Its members had co-operated beyond the call of duty in trying to put right industrial problems not of their making. What other response could they possibly have made?

Notes

1 M. Thatcher, *The Downing Street Years* (1993), 108.

2 Quoted in *The Times*, 8 December 1979.

3 *Reports* (1979), 189. The resolution was accepted by the EC.

4 Eurostat, *Iron and Steel Yearbook* (1979).

5 Scholey had written to all unions at BSC, whether nationally recognised or not, to secure combined negotiations, a concept which found favour with the TGWU (*Reports*, 1979, 205).

6 *Reports* (1979), 229. This was estimated to be worth 2 per cent of 'new' money.

7 *Reports* (1979), 231–2.

8 Another dispensation was granted to Oswald staff and some members in Aldwarke, in order that the processing of pensions should not be hindered.

9 *Reports* (1979), 234.

10 Referred to henceforth as the Joint Executives.

11 Including a 4 per cent 'with-things' payment and no ceiling on the local productivity deals, soon to be known to all as lump-sum bonus schemes.

12 A term used to distinguish the kind of pay offers received from now on from the general increases negotiated in the past.

13 *Reports* (1980), 3.

14 Thus the 8 per cent was a self-financing offer, and 4 per cent on local deals would flow only if local deals were agreed by 31 March.

15 Thatcher, *op. cit.*, 108–14.

16 *Reports* (1980), 5. In fact the government harboured deep misgivings about management's handling of the strike and lacked confidence in its figures, but interpreted its fundamental duty as not 'to substitute our judgement as politicians for that of the industry' (Thatcher, *op. cit.*, 109).

17 *Reports* (1980), 6.

18 Thatcher, *op. cit.*, 112–13.

19 See below.

20 *Reports* (1980), 8.

21 Thatcher, *op. cit.*, 102.

22 Recollection of author.

23 Bizarrely there was an MWB meeting in the middle of all this.

24 The whole process famously entered the legal archives as Duport vs. Sirs.

25 *Reports* (1980), 12.

26 *Reports* (1980), 24.

27 Thatcher, *op. cit.*, 109–110.

28 A BSC briefing to senior managers of 17 January got particularly savage treatment: see the pamphlet 'Sense or Non-sense' (undated, but probably January 1980).

29 BSC was still pursuing the executives of Granada eleven months later (*Reports*, 1980, 267–8).

30 From Patent Shaft, Darlington & Simpson Rolling Mills, Meadowhall, Alpha Steel, GKN Cardiff, Firth Brown, British Rolling Mills, Duport, Templeborough Rolling Mills, Natural Gas Tubes, Spencer Clark, Brymbo, JR Steels, Manchester Steels, Parkgate, Derwenthaugh and the MWB. Delegates from other private works were present but did not speak (*Reports*, 1980, 15).

31 *Reports* (1980), 15.

32 In sharp contrast to Mrs Thatcher, who claims to have concluded as early as 18 January that 'the strike had so far had little effect on industrial production' (Thatcher, *op. cit.*, 111).

33 For the strike in Rotherham see J. Hartley *et al.*, *Steel Strike: a Case Study in Industrial Relations* (1983).

34 Sirs met Callaghan and Michael Foot early in March. They believed it was a question of the unions avoiding a defeat, but Sirs still declined mediation, arguing that
the strike must be prosecuted through strength to allow the resumption of negotiations, a view echoed by Hector Smith at the Joint Executives on 5 March (*Reports*,
1980, 17).

35 Monitoring disclosed ISTC members with two papers, papers sent to the
deceased, retired and those in another industry. BSC had established offices in the
Works for those who had claimed to have lost or mislaid theirs.

36 *Reports* (1980), 20.

37 The Prime Minister was determined to resist a Court of Inquiry, but was prepared
to acquiesce in the use of ACAS. When the Lever Inquiry was eventually established she felt the government was merely 'condemned to watch' (Thatcher, *op.
cit.*, 113).

38 'That the two Organisations should press for a public Committee of Inquiry into
the management and policies of BSC and that a vote of no confidence be passed on
the current Management of the BSC' (*Reports*, 1980, 79).

39 There would be voluntary redundancy only where non-union or non-TUC mem-
bers were employed; ISTC members would refuse to attend meetings where
SIMA members were present, and Works Councils would be considered defunct
(*Reports*, 1980, 81). The first decision was completely unrealistic. The May 1980
EC was informed that SIMA were to ballot on amalgamation with the EETPU.
Paradoxically, MM activity picked up after the strike, boosted by publication of
the Middle Management Bulletin which was followed up by meetings in most
areas.

40 In August gold statuettes were awarded to the NUR, ASLEF, the NUM, the NUS,
and the Dockers and Lorry Drivers sections of the TGWU in recognition of their
solidarity.

41 An appeal by members of the Corby BOS Foremen's Branch was referred to the
DO on 21 May; other expulsions were reaffirmed.

42 *Reports* (1980), 82.

43 *Reports* (1980), 155. As a result of the inquiry money was recovered from the
Rotherham and Stocksbridge Joint Committees, and the property acquired by
the multi-union joint shop stewards committee was put up for sale. The Confederation was prepared to meet the bill for legal representation for pickets by Yorkshire
solicitors, but only if they were ISTC members. Strike accounts were recovered
from the home of a full-time organiser who was subsequently interviewed by the
Organisation and Staffing Sub-committee (*Reports*, 1980, 233, 234).

44 'Report of the Auditors (Shipley Blackburn)', *Reports* (1981), 68–9.

45 *Reports* (1982), 82.

46 The increase generated a considerable branch correspondence (*Reports*, 1980,
233).

47 For details of the appeals see *Reports* (1980), 152.

48 *Reports* (1980), 48.

49 Some of the Hownsgill employees had received no severance pay at all, but union pressure on BSC proved unavailing (*Reports*, 1981, 45).

50 *Reports* (1980), 153.

51 *Reports* (1980), 106.

52 Three years later there was to be a welcome legal success with the award of almost £100,000 to members made redundant from Glynwed's Stourbridge Rolling Mills. In January 1981 the sixty-two members, nearly all of whom had been active in the strike and who included EC member Alan Farley, had successfully appealed to an industrial tribunal against unfair dismissal, but the company dragged its heels over compensation for a further thirty months.

53 A steel committee document was also presented; the NCCC convenor had objected to the presentation of a separate ISTC document (*Reports*, 1980, 159).

54 In 1982 the Executive discussed the possibility of establishing token pickets at Immingham and Newport, two busy access points for the UK steel market.

55 About this time the Iron and Steel Working Party of NEDO published a report apparently demonstrating the price disadvantage suffered by UK energy consumers.

56 *Reports* (1980), 159.

57 One example was Joe Atkinson (Hawarden 5) who retained his delegateship to the Trades Council by application of the authority contained in Rule 22.

58 The Finance Committee, which originated these steps after receiving a report on 22 October, also recommended that those reaching the age of sixty-two before the end of the year and ceasing employment on non-medical grounds would be allowed contribution credits to qualify for benefit under Rule 35 up to the age of sixty-five. Unlike the other proposals of the Committee this could not, in the view of the legal services, be presented as a clarification of the existing rules, and it was dropped (*Reports*, 1980, 234).

59 *Reports* (1981), 88.

60 This was arranged without prejudice to Connolly's seniority (*Reports*, 1980, 96). Clive Lewis (1938–) entered the steel industry in Ebbw Vale in 1959 and was appointed No. 4 Division Staff Organiser ten years later.

61 In November 1980, the concluded report was held over.

62 'You don't understand these people. They will never give in,' Aberavon MP John Morris had told an uncomprehending Sir Keith Joseph on the eve of the strike.

63 See S. Meredeen, *Managing Industrial Conflict: Seven Major Disputes* (1988), 169–205, for much the most balanced account of the dispute and a fair assessment of the settlement value.

64 Naturally not all of this can be attributed to the strike.

8

Rage against fate
Bill Sirs (1981–3)

'We have lost some members, but this union is still strong and powerful and a major name which commands high respect. People know when you fight, you fight as hard as you can and as hard as anyone ever did.'

After the climactic year 1980, the ISTC entered a new phase. It was marked by an increased willingness to work with other unions on industrial matters, but growing involvement in the political struggle for the soul of the Labour Party. With the Conservatives in office there were few allies in the battle to maintain union structures and procedures either at British Steel or in the private sector. At BSC Ian MacGregor had replaced Sir Charles Villiers: his arrival heralded an abrasive industrial relations policy stance which reflected MacGregor's American experience, and which was to take the ISTC's relations with BSC to their lowest point.

But MacGregor's arrival had one positive effect. In November 1980 the EC had considered a document reviewing the common interests of the rail, coal and steel unions and had sanctioned a meeting of the executives of the three biggest unions (ISTC, NUM and NUR, later expanded to include the smaller unions as well). This blossomed the following year into what the public quickly christened the Triple Alliance. The executives met in January 1981 amid great public interest. On 26 February the leaders of the participating unions met four cabinet ministers to air the common problems of their industries in the wake of an apparent U-turn by the government over coal-pit closures; soon, divisional meetings of the Alliance started to brief the public. In 1982 the EC agreed in principle to a new national meeting of executives, though it greeted with caution a conference call for a federation with the railwaymen and miners. Sirs stayed in informal contact with the NUM president and the NUR General Secretary, and did not exclude the possibility of a more formal arrangement some time in the future.

British Steel

Everything in steel was dominated by a recession which was the product of a downturn in the economic cycle and of Conservative economic policy, which served industry ill. Steel output, which had reached 21.4 million tonnes in 1979, slumped to 11.3 million tonnes in 1980, recovered only to 15.5 million tonnes in 1981 and then fell back again. By May 1981 employment in general iron and steelmaking and steel tubes had gone down from 226,500 to 170,400 in just twelve months. The contributing membership of the ISTC had fallen from 107,346 at the end of the first quarter to 73,492: in six months there had been a net loss of sixty-seven branches. If the number of recorded members was relatively stable, at around 103,000, this was because of the retention of large numbers of redundant members. A great deal of experience was flooding out of the Organisation, causing much anxiety. The establishment of unemployed branches had already been agreed, and early in 1981 No. 7 Division successfully requested permission to admit to these branches school-leavers who had left school without a job. Further provision was made for visitors from holding branches to attend conference,[1] but there was still dissatisfaction with the extent to which active members generally were debarred from union events. The 1981 ADC remitted a motion which virtually proposed to extend full rights to redundant members, but the EC found it impracticable. How could such generosity be funded?

In 1980 BSC had approached the unions suggesting 'working party' meetings involving all unions following the annual round, and calling for suggestions as to how its competitiveness could be improved: this of course was a subject BSC was always interested to discuss, provided the discussion centred on working practices. But it soon concluded that the financial position was so dire that it could not discuss pay until the end of November. To a request to review the structure of negotiations, the EC entered a refusal to consider change, at least for this year.[2] Recent experiences, still fresh, had reinforced its wish to bargain as a single unit. Then, in meetings to brief the Steel Committee on the 1981 Corporate Plan, MacGregor suggested to Sirs that the ISTC defer its wage claim and accept a 7 per cent award six months late, an idea he had already canvassed in two letters sent direct to British Steel employees. In the Plan itself there was more: huge closures were pending which would reduce manned capacity by more than a quarter. Templeborough would move to one-furnace operation and Velindre to a single shift; there were 2800 redundancies planned at Normanby Park through complete closure. Until late 1980 there had been some grounds for hoping that this tough Americanised businessman might be open to ideas: those hopes were dashed as he cut capacity and endorsed BSC management as one of the best he had known.

Led by the ISTC, the Steel Committee refused to endorse the Corporate Plan. Realising BSC might again ballot the membership, the union launched a pre-emptive strike and balloted instead on the deferment of the wage deal which was clearly integral to it. The ballot was intended purely to give guidance to the CNC, but the move alarmed a large number of joint branches.[3] There was even a question over whether – should there be a 'yes' vote – the national Organisation could endorse the Plan, in view of its implications for procedures.

The BSC ballot, published on 16 January, recorded 63,237 votes for the Plan, 17,900 against and no fewer than 43,225 abstentions.[4] The ISTC's results, published three days later, were mixed, and if anything likely to give some encouragement to BSC. Those voting cast their ballots 5:4 against the pay offer of 7 per cent from 1 July 1981, but this final outcome arose from 2:1 opposition among manual grades and 5:3 in favour among the staff. Likewise on the Corporate Plan (which, as the ballot paper reminded voters, would create at least 22,000 redundancies), the manual grades' rejection was 3.5:1 whereas the staff voted narrowly for acceptance. The net result was comfortably more than a 2:1 majority. But when it came to agreement on continuing with multi-union bargaining at local level on lump-sum bonus schemes, the 5:4 rejection among manual grades was narrow, while the staff voted more than 2:1 for acceptance. Staff and MM grades voted separately on deferment of their salary increments until July 1981, rejecting it by 5:3.[5] The salient feature of these results was the divergence between staff and manual grades, but even the net results gave little encouragement to a militant stance. The lack of confidence which had led to the decision to ballot had been fleshed out, a development which now left little room for manoeuvre.[6]

In three meetings the CNC could not persuade BSC to abandon the Corporate Plan, but the former still firmly rejected the 7 per cent pay offer. On 10 February a draft ISTC agreement was drawn up for the heavy steel trades, while parallel developments took place at the STB. Further contacts, culminating in a meeting of the CNCs with BSC on 18 May, failed to break the impasse, and so in the end the pay increase was imposed by the management on 1 July. To this day, 1981 remains a unique year, in that public sector pay moved centrally without a national agreement.

Things were just as dispiriting outside the pay talks. In April 1981 the Main Board refused to meet the ISTC Executive, offering only smaller-scale conversations to which information would be imparted only confidentially. The EC accepted Sirs's recommendation to allow a certain amount of leeway to explore BSC's willingness to talk,[7] but distrust of management ran deep, and HST Area 4, in a recommendation substantially endorsed by the EC, reiterated the call for monitoring of 'wasteful expenditure' across the Corporation and dismissal of those responsible for it. Then, in June 1981, Don Caddick and Terry Butterworth were nominated as trade union members of the Main Board, more in hope than in expectation that such appointments would survive the present incumbents. BSC was prepared only to reappoint the present group – an adverse development for the ISTC, since Alan White was retiring on grounds of ill-health, while Butterworth had been preferred to McLaren from the names submitted by branches. On being invited to serve McLaren had declined, since he lacked union backing.[8] In effect the ISTC lost its entire representation on the Main Board, a point Sirs lost no time in conveying to the press.[9]

Correspondence with Industry and Employment ministers elicited only a letter from Patrick Jenkin suggesting that the EC reconsider allowing McLaren to take his seat.[10] Only in February 1982 did a solution emerge when Terry Butterworth was elected to the Executive, membership of which had always been thought incompatible with membership of the Main Board.[11] Down at the worker director level few hopes were entertained of being able to replace Doug Farrell on his retirement in February 1983. The assumption of management prerogative had also reached the superannuation scheme: in October 1982 a BSC wish to restrict the number of union members on the Scheme's Committee of Management led to the barring of A.C. ('Tony') Cook, whom the ISTC wanted to appoint as a middle management representative. One by one every foothold of union influence was being loosened.

In summer 1982 it was discovered that the Opinion Research Centre (ORC) had circulated BSC employees, seeking their views on wage negotiations and future closures. This was clearly another example of MacGregor's preference for ignoring the unions as representative organisations. Many ORC questions seemed designed to elicit the extent to which members supported union policy; there was a strong suspicion that the questionnaires had been introduced by management, and Sirs circulated the branches, asking them to ignore them.[12] Other new employment practices were surfacing. At the Corby Works temporary employees had been engaged on a forty-eight-week contract: a dispute over this was the subject of a national ad hoc meeting on 3 September 1981, at which it speedily became apparent that there was a national trend. Roy Evans was empowered by the Executive to seek a resolution with BSC, and he eventually gained some reassurance at discussions held in April 1982. Unfortunately this still left outstanding the vital issue of temporary employees being regarded as permanent employees when placed in permanent jobs in promotion line structures.[13] The 1982 ADC called for a campaign 'to win back to the direct labour force [those] jobs which have been given up to private outside contractors', and showed a new sophistication in emphasising that this object should be pursued both in the public and the private sectors. Success in such endeavours would also boost membership in departments where the ISTC traditionally held the bargaining rights.

By the autumn of 1982 exasperation with BSC had again reached crisis point. The media were starting to show increasing understanding of the unions' wish at least to be told where the 'bottom line' of closures lay. The Steel Committee met Industry Secretary Patrick Jenkin on 4 October, and MacGregor the following day. The latter revealed that further capacity cutbacks now under consideration might entail the closure of either one or two major plants. When this was reported to a multi-union conference in Sheffield two days later, there were calls for strong action. At its conclusion the Steel Committee drew up a series of recommendations which included a twenty-four hour day of action (including a stoppage) in all BSC plants on Friday 22 October; ending all negotiations on local redundancies or closures; resignation by worker directors; and an end to co-operation in redundancy counselling. At the ISTC Executive on 12 October, Sirs strongly backed the recommendations, urging that it was necessary for the unions to demonstrate their unity. A proposal from Stocksbridge for a total overtime ban was not adopted, but the EC did endorse the Steel Committee programme, as well as a suggestion to lobby the imminent conference of the Conservative Party. EC members made it clear that they expected SIMA, now part of a TUC union, to follow instructions as well.[14] The membership was circulated with the instructions, and safety cover for the day's stoppage was agreed.

On this occasion the resort to action seems to have been more successful than hitherto, taking closure decisions out of MacGregor's hands and making them political. The hope was to maintain the general fabric of the industry, and in particular the five big plants. The day of action was fully supported by the membership, and favourable publicity was gained. The ISTC's arguments were couched to gather and widen political support, for example by pointing to the way European subsidies were weighted against BSC, and to the disadvantage steel companies suffered from paying high energy costs. Local councils across Britain rallied to the cause, and Conservative MPs were skilfully wooed. A national conference on steel was convened in Central Hall, Westminster, on 23 November 1982, with attendance by MPs of all parties and local authority leaders. Its purpose was to bring the massive crisis in the industry to the attention of the public and to stimulate action: the threat to major plants was a relatively simple message to convey. Sandy Feather believed that the argument over retaining the major sites had been won,[15] but that maximum pressure would be needed to stop BSC implementing wholesale closures of smaller plants.

That autumn's campaign by the ISTC and other BSC unions won admiration from many observers. At the end of an intensive ten weeks, new government instructions were issued to MacGregor to plan for 1983–6 on the assumption that the major plants would stay in production, and with the dispensation that break-even at BSC could wait until 1985. With this significant victory, the ISTC was prepared to lift the withdrawal of the worker directors and reopen negotiations on redundancies (under DO supervision),[16] but the commitment to the fabric of the industry fell short of guaranteeing the smaller plants: there the picture was grim. At Corby, 570 redundancies arose from centralisation of the finishing and despatch departments; Dowlais Foundry was reduced to one-furnace operation; above all, Ravenscraig was reduced to two-furnace operation at a cost of 400 redundancies, while workers remaining on site suffered 'production pauses', a practice which put them under the terms of the Guaranteed Working Week Agreement (GWWA). That was not all Scotland's bad news: the Hunterston membership was working one week on and one week off under the TSTWCS; Clydebridge was under notice of closure, the only jobs expected to survive being those in the heat-treatment department; and at Dalzell there was short-time working. In November 1982 the Clydebridge Joint Committee could no longer dissuade members from taking up a redundancy offer which would precipitate closure of the historic mills: the plate mill went out of business at the turn of the year with a loss of 575 jobs, soon followed by the Craigneuk bar mills with more than 400. In the Scottish Steel & Tube Group there were fifty redundancies at Clydesdale and 130 at Imperial, with further reductions anticipated as Clydesdale reduced to one-furnace operation. The only positive development in No. 1 Division was the official opening, early in 1983, of the Anchor chain plant at depressed Glengarnock. A desperate STUC delegation to the Prime Minister brought little satisfaction.[17]

Of these Scottish problems, the one facing Ravenscraig was much the most serious: it had always seemed the plant most at risk among the 'Big Five', but the 1982 steel campaign had been powerfully persuasive in bringing political and national support. But this flattered to deceive, because the commitment was to steelmaking alone, and BSC swiftly tabled its intention to reduce the works to the status of a slab provider with the loss of up to 2000 jobs. The unions immediately met this new threat by reviving their campaign. BSC then raised the stakes by canvassing a plan to feed United

Steels' Fairless works near Philadelphia with Ravenscraig slabs; but the ISTC, after contact with the USWA, was not enthusiastic. There would still be 2000 jobs at risk at Ravenscraig and they would be joined by 3000 redundancies at US Steel. The two unions forged an effective publicity alliance, which hit the national press and seems to have deepened ministers' anxieties about the extent to which their appointee, Ian MacGregor, was a loose cannon. Further meetings with George Younger, the Scottish Secretary, were held and the STUC-sponsored Steel Conference was reconvened, again with wide backing.

Private sector developments

The sale of former BSC plants to the private sector now began to raise tricky problems for negotiating structures. Allied Steel and Wire (ASW), the first public/private joint venture company or 'phoenix', which had fused BSC's Scunthorpe No. 2 rod mill with the Cardiff steel and rod plant of GKN, had proved difficult to deal with, and in May 1982 Temple No. 5 branch pressed the Executive to demand company-wide negotiations on pay and conditions. ASW management rejected the proposal, countering with a suggestion of department-based negotiations at Cardiff which the local branches found distasteful. The EC, meeting in August, had to advise the membership to insist on works-level negotiations at least, but remained resolved to seek national meetings annually on a consultative basis, distinct from bargaining for wages and conditions.[18]

The EC had accepted a resolution of the 1979 ADC urging it to take 'whatever steps are necessary' to oppose denationalisation of BSC, 'including if appropriate, concerted industrial action'.[19] But in practice private ownership in steel was a piecemeal experience before 1988, and was not on the scale of general rationalisation in the industry as a whole. Protests against the rapidity of the sale of Redpath Dorman Long (RDL) to Trafalgar House, and against the share price asked, were unavailing.[20] In what was to become a depressing pattern, the ISTC was left to deal with the impact of privatisation on the membership rather than being in the happy position of being able to prevent it. Two meetings at York allowed full-time officials to press the case for protecting the terms and conditions of employment of the people at RDL; but a major concern, future pension arrangements, remained unresolved as 1982 drew to a close.

The ISTC made a real effort to give the highest profile to the travails of the private sector membership, old and new. A Private Sector Action Committee was formed to defend the many works now threatened by recession and high interest rates, and it gained a meeting with Sir Keith Joseph in February

1981. Extensive publicity in the ISTC media lifted morale in private sector works, which were, in the words of Round Oak's Jack Bate, 'bleeding quietly to death'. Against the gloomy background of reduction of the TSTWCS from 75 to 50 per cent, the ISTC refused an ISEA request for suspension of the Guaranteed Week Agreement, leaving this to local negotiations. Matters were worse at the MWB, where the employers had resigned *en masse* the previous 24 November: the 1981 award had to be approached on a local works-by-works basis, not without difficulty. To compound the problem, some former member firms were refusing to collect MWB and even general union contributions; legal advice was taken on whether it would be constitutional to keep just the employees' side in being.[21]

But there was not merely an industrial relations crisis. A side-effect of the recession was paradoxically to *increase* the dominance of BSC within the industry. Many smaller private firms could not withstand the impact of the measures taken by the Corporation to restore its profitability, above all heavy discounting of steel prices. A Private Sector Steel Scheme (PSSS), underwritten by the government, facilitated exits from the industry by private firms, and in February 1981 Duport Steel left the sector by this route. This galling loss deprived steel of modern plant and no less than 1200 jobs in Llanelli, only three years after a move from Bridgend had entailed the abandonment of obsolete plant. To rub salt in the wounds, an agreement at the heart of the deal forbade the sale of the new arc furnaces at Llanelli to another UK company.[22]

In October 1982 it was learned that BSC, ASW and Sheerness were authors of a plan to buy and shut the Manchester Steel and Bidston plants of Elkem Springvert with a view to acquiring their order books. Alarm at this prospect led to early meetings at Central Office with management and union delegations from the works concerned. There was relief when the parent company rejected the offer;[23] but it then introduced a new plan, including redundancy announcements in all departments and at all levels plus reduced shifts in the steel plant and the rod mill. For a time, this seemed to have secured the company's position in the market – but survival clearly did not mean security.

'Phoenix III', a much-bruited scheme to bring together the UK's forging businesses, finally materialised at the end of 1982 in the shape of a scheme to unite the River Don works of BSC with Firth Browns under the name Sheffield Forgemasters. Here the ISTC's strategy was to argue for two-furnace operation rather than a concentration of output at one site. This approach, which would have maximised employment, did not carry the day,[24] and management pursued its original plan, which concentrated output on the Atlas melting shop, involving closure of the Norfolk plant with huge redundancies.[25] Glasgow's historic Parkhead Forge closed, with the loss of 370 jobs, upon the launch of Sheffield Forgemasters.

At GKN's Brymbo Works orders fell throughout 1982, causing management to introduce production pauses. Its plan was to cut capacity from 335,000 tonnes to 250,000, a step which would certainly entail new redundancies over and above the 300 already announced. In the opinion of the ISTC the principal problem was imports of special steels, at costs which Brymbo found it difficult to match due to the lack of a continuous caster. The following year all departments were suffering from diminished activity, though there was some consolation in the thought that one-furnace operation potentially offered 350,000 tonnes of liquid steel annually – 250,000 tonnes of actual output in depressed current conditions.

To complete a dismal 1982, Sirs received a letter from the management of the BSC/Tube Investments company Round Oak, long outside the ISEA, informing him that the works had suffered mounting losses due to lack of orders and that production would cease in December.[26] This plant had continued with national-level meetings, and its annual review had yielded an improved Extended Working Week Agreement. Management gave the workforce just five weeks' notice of closure, so the EC, notified of the wish of the branch to resist, gave Sirs authority to take whatever actions were necessary. A campaign was rapidly organised and representations were made to BSC to help retain a viable works unit. Finally, in the face of a refusal to reconsider, the membership agreed to redundancy negotiations, and severance terms were finalised at a meeting on 12 January 1983.

Frustration grew as the union was compelled to watch a firm of consultants (Deloitts, Haskins & Sells) study BSC's narrow-strip business without any input from the membership. Eventually the consultants agreed to meet Sirs and a Divisional Office team. In South Wales John Foley and Divisional Office staff campaigned to maintain support among customers for the Whiteheads and Godins Works, but were finally forced to accept reduction to one-crew manning at Whiteheads.

Meanwhile there were also difficulties at the Sheet Trade Board Works of Cookley and Orb. Already in 1982 management had canvassed the transfer of orders from the Midlands to the South Wales Works. At MWB works things were just as bad: London Works Steel Co was closed in the autumn of 1982 after BSC refused to consider buying it out; there was no doubt that this was the mere prelude to a major rationalisation of engineering steels: the much-anticipated but as yet little-seen 'Phoenix II'. BSC Wolverhampton gained some short-term benefit when it received some former London Works orders. The whole of the Midlands was sorely afflicted. In November 1982 came the closure of Lilleshall: as was often the case, the chimera of a rescue operation had appeared, but only briefly. The Bright Bar sector – full of small mills – was another location of plans to concentrate production: in 1982 the Department of Industry itself introduced consultants whom the union struggled vainly to influence. No. 4 Divisional Office was also dealing with the backwash of the take-over of Ductile Steels by Glynwed, which had begun, unusually, with redundancies at a very senior level. The arrival of 1983 brought little relief, since the year opened with the closure of Flather Bright at Haybridge, though there was some small – and rare – compensation when staffing was increased at Brymill, Tipton.[27]

At Railway and Ring Rolled Products matters were further advanced. The 1982 publication of the Serpell Report on rail supplies provided few grounds for optimism about future demand for rail products. The future of either the Trafford Park Works or the Ickles Works was at stake: a tricky problem in prospect for a union with members on both sites. Early in 1983 the competition was resolved in favour of Trafford Park. But when a new company, United plc, was established early in 1984, it proved short-lived. After a sudden collapse it was replaced by the former Railway & Ring Rolled Products group under the name of Precis 217, a free-standing plc. This rapid shift of structure brought with it redundancy notices for no less than half the workforce.

The north-west offered little relief. In one single quarter (the first of 1983) Fred Brooks,[28] who had succeeded George Cooper, reported that Aurora Steels of Manchester had cut its workforce from 350 to 200, admittedly with relatively minor impact on the ISTC membership. Not long before, this works had shifted output away from South Yorkshire in search of competitive advantage. Bidston Works enjoyed a brief moment of hope among many shifts of ownership, but the clouds were soon to gather again. Thomas Walmsley reduced its operation from re-rolling and became merely a stockist. British Steel's Barrow Works, historically the first concast plant in Britain, was under serious threat[29] due to loss of orders, though Monks Hall was still managing to operate two mills. The Bredbury plant of Exors of James Mills was phased out; its order book was ceded to the newly formed British Bright Bar.[30]

And so rationalisation rolled on. 1983 brought the acquisition of Hadfields, the 1980 flashpoint, by a joint company (Hadfield Holding) formed by BSC, GKN and Lonrho. The Tinsley No. 2 branch initially opposed the closure. The EC resolved to pursue a strategy of maximum job and capacity retention, and determined to build up the case for the plant to stay in business; there would be an approach to the Monopolies and Mergers Commission, and relevant branches were circulated with an instruction not to accept Hadfield's order book. Prospects for a successful campaign of resistance rapidly waned, however: lack of investment, and the realisation of the extent to which the negotiating parties had reached agreement, sapped the will of the workforce to resist closure, and Hadfields was to close in the spring of 1984. Phoenix II was in fact to take another three years to appear, but the union put a heavy commitment of time into preparing against it, including a pamphlet – 'Phoenix Two and You' – and the most detailed scheme ever developed for sharing orders between participating works as an alternative to outright closure of any one or more of them.

'Phoenix Two and You', with its plans for control of order switching, was adopted by the EC in November 1983 and then circulated among the relevant plants. Representations against privatisation had already been laid before EEC Industry Commissioner D'Avignon and Cecil Parkinson, who had succeeded Patrick Jenkin as UK Industry Secretary. The committee designed to resist the closures met regularly late in 1983 and in early 1984 and prepared proposals for action in the event of further closures being threatened. The February 1984 EC endorsed the plan for production quotas presented to it by Roy Bishop on behalf of the committee, and he was given full power to implement them.

The signs were auspicious, since the committee had members not only from No. 3 Division, the heart of special steels, but also from Nos. 4 and 7 Divisions, raising hopes that parochialism would not prevent a united fight. On 18 February 1984 a major Labour movement conference was convened in Sheffield Town Hall to formulate a clear programme of action. Widely attended by unions, local authorities and the media, this event was judged a success and was followed up by a programme of shop-floor education in South Yorkshire. The advent of the 1984–5 miners' strike now shifted the public gaze away from the privatisation of special steels,[31] and made it more difficult for the ISTC to gain a favourable hearing in some quarters where sympathy might have been expected. For a time, indeed, the prospect itself seemed to recede, assisted by the withdrawal of so much capacity.

Once again the thirty-nine-hour week and pay

The thirty-nine-hour week had been discussed at a May 1981 meeting, at which the ISTC refused a BSC invitation to countenance a self-funding exercise, or an approach which entailed adding time to meal breaks. There was a consensus that the basis of aggregation should be time off outside the plant, whether by accumulation or rota; if the latter, the extra time should to be taken in periods of not less than one shift. Subject to these details, BSC committed itself to introducing the shorter week on 1 January 1982. Membership briefings followed in the autumn – but then, on 15 September, stunned Steel Committee members were informed by BSC that introduction of the shorter week was to be deferred. The ISTC challenged BSC to take the matter to arbitration, which was available only under a joint reference. But the employers refused, leaving the union with the rather feebler option of approaching Lord Lever, author of the original 1980 award.

Soon after this came a statement from MacGregor to the effect that BSC had no money to pay for an award for 1982: any movement in pay could occur only on the basis of local bargaining. At a Special Executive Meeting of 6 October, this threat to the traditional pattern of bargaining was addressed. Sirs was empowered to instruct all branches to abstain from productivity negotiations in connection with the Annual Review. On 23 October BSC reaffirmed its position, and it now emerged that localising of pay settlements was part of a move to reduce manning levels by some 20,000 Corporation-wide.

November brought a severe setback to the ISTC's plans to resist, when it was learned that the NUB and the NCCC had both made agreements with BSC which incorporated local productivity bargaining. A BSC delegation to the Executive, led by Industrial Relations Director Peter Broxham, painted a grim picture of a cost-strapped Corporation and appealed for branches to be allowed to participate in local discussions. The Executive did not immediately lift the ban, but did adopt Broxham's suggestion that a sub-committee meet BSC to gain details of the proposed local schemes. BSC staff had already felt the need to pursue locally their claims for restoration of differentials with MM and manual grades; in December the EC reluctantly accepted that local bargaining might have to be accepted, though within national guidelines that had been agreed with BSC.[32]

The CNC, presented with this unpalatable option, drew up a series of amendments in an attempt, *inter alia*, to shift a proportion of local savings onto the basic rate. BSC refused any changes, though further pressed by Sirs in December. This further frustrated the CNC, which called for sanctions. The Executive met in special session on 8 January 1982 and determined a programme of action, to be initiated on 7 February, which included a complete overtime ban, the withdrawal of all flexibility and interchangeability, and cancellation of the Extended Working Week Agreement. Armed with these proposals Sirs was given permission to convene the pay review working party as necessary. A working party of EC members and full-time officers met BSC on 26 January and learned that consolidation would also be deferred until January 1983; nor would there be any consolidation of bonus earnings into basic rates. On 2 February the Executive issued revised guidelines to shape the impact of the proposed overtime ban, and gave plenary powers to the working party. The next day the working party met BSC again, and at last obtained a concession. This took the form of allowing national meetings in August 1982 – by which time an assessment of two quarters of local lump-sum bonuses would have been made – at which there would be some consolidation of the bonuses. In return, the working party agreed to talks for 1982 – though only on local bonus schemes – and lifted the programme of industrial action. On 1 September representatives of all nationally recognised unions met BSC and agreed on consolidation of 2.5 per cent onto basic rates, effective from 1 July, affecting all employees covered by a lump-sum bonus agreement which had been agreed during the year.[33]

The referral to Lord Lever was not a success. He had passed on the ISTC complaint to ACAS, which was certainly willing to approach BSC; but BSC was implacable, leaving the ISTC with little alternative to steering branches towards meeting their local managements with a view to agreeing on methods of application on the new introduction date, 1 January 1983. Meetings took place during the closing weeks of 1982 to finalise the arrangements, and implementation was generally smooth. Thus the principle of nationwide bargaining had been upheld, though its monetary value had been small; but these severe structural upheavals at BSC, as well as parallel private sector developments, boded ill for central bargaining. Local negotiations were of course traditional in the steel industry, and a jealously guarded branch prerogative, but central bargaining had become a unifying force and had helped to consolidate newer sectors of the organised membership such as white-collar employees and ancillary (often female) staff. No more ground could be yielded without drastic consequences, and any groups seeking to go it alone would have to be curbed.

Early in 1983, some members of the Port Talbot HST had signed a local multi-union agreement which effectively replaced the Annual Review, clearly a national responsibility. As a result of this action, taken in defiance of a warning from Divisional Office, the individuals concerned were deposed, and management was notified that the agreement was invalid. Some attempt was made to defend the officials' actions by references to the negotiations which had taken place at Port Talbot in the 1960s, outside the framework of ISTEA;[34] but the EC wished to uphold the Divisional Officer's actions, reaffirm its policy, and issue new guidelines. Sirs managed to fend off this resolution, arguing that the EC should first wait to hear the views of other unions which were similarly challenged. In the end decisions were deferred pending the outcome of a forthcoming conference at Sheffield which was due to discuss multi-union negotiations. Further concern arose when it was learned that the whole of the Ravenscraig Works had signed another such agreement.[35] This development, which dwarfed that in Port Talbot, was another symptom of desperation at a works which no longer seemed to look to national solutions.

At the opening of the annual round on 1 December 1982, an appointed EC sub-committee tabled a claim for a general increase of 9.5 per cent. BSC offered only to initiate local negotiations on diverse bonus schemes; by this means alone would any new money flow in 1983. The full CNCs met BSC on 22 December without success – indeed, their despondency increased when management confided some of the detail of the new schemes it had in mind. After a third abortive meeting on 11 January 1983, the CNCs authorised the EC sub-committee to approach other nationally recognised unions, seeking a common front. Two weeks later these unions met and agreed to reject the BSC proposals and refuse to participate in local negotiations.

A new meeting with BSC broke up acrimoniously. One by one the options were exhausted. An attempt to invoke arbitration clauses was again blocked by management: ACAS was brought in by the union but only as a conciliator. All unions deliberated on the next steps. Should they resort to some form of industrial action, should they reopen negotiations under the auspices of ACAS, or should they side-step a national agreement and sanction whatever action members might wish to take locally? Again an attempt to draw up guidelines for local negotiations was deferred, pending the outcome of the delegate conference at Sheffield.

The Executive met on 12 April 1983 knowing that BSC had again refused arbitration; that SIMA had now made an agreement; and that the NUB were seeking legal advice on the arbitration issue.[36] Sirs wanted to protect national bargaining, a step which implied disciplining both the Port Talbot and the Ravenscraig officials. In the lengthy debate which followed, the accuracy of the minutes recording earlier relevant decisions of the EC was questioned and the issue of the local officials was broached in the mildest possible way, by asking them only for assurances that they would follow EC instructions in future.[37] The mood of gloomy resignation continued with a decision that the union should again meet BSC while employing ACAS in its conciliatory capacity. Confronted once more with a draft agreement which still entailed a loss of jobs, the unions all refused finally to make an agreement, and the EC backed them.

In a separate move (though one which illustrated the nadir to which employment relations had fallen), BSC Special Steels branches at Aldwarke and Templeborough had struck on 4 April against the unilateral imposition of new shift patterns. They received official ISTC backing and the solidarity of a twenty-four-hour strike at Scunthorpe Works, though there was some slippage of support among certain staff grades. An agreed formula, reported to the EC of 12 April, allowed a return to work the next day, though recovery at the works was bedevilled by a separate craftsmen's dispute at the Rotherham Works. It was spring 1983, three years after the great steel strike had ended, and relations were as bad as ever.

Notes

1 The branches themselves had to cover the costs, after a token contribution from Divisional Office (*Reports*, 1981, 150). However, a decision of the February 1981 EC allowed branch officers of the Hawarden Central branch to attend the ADC as observers at their own expense.

2 The ISTC was prepared to participate along with the TGWU and the NUB, but had been given to understand that the NCCC had withdrawn from joint negotiations (*Reports*, 1980, 197, 267). A meeting was later held with the NCCC to discuss a NJIC.

3 The EC was bombarded with letters objecting to a ballot, but also to the Plan itself (*Reports*, 1981, 3).

4 This meant that about half the workforce had endorsed the Plan, but some 35,000 employees not in iron and steel had been included. The ISTC bitterly complained that many managers had campaigned for a 'yes' vote, arguing that without it works would shut.

5 The actual voting figures were as follows: (1) to accept the 7 per cent increase from 1 July – 11,558 for and 15,525 against; to endorse the Corporate Plan – 8442 for and 18,392 against; to continue local multi-union bargaining on lump-sum bonus schemes – 13,863 for and 13,163 against; and to defer salary increments – 3070 for and 592 against (*Reports*, 1981, 4).

6 One route which was probed was to question the figures underlying the BSC proposals, and research officers met BSC representatives in the spring to clarify them.

7 A report of the talks was circulated to EC members in August 1981.

8 In August the EC passed a vote of confidence in McLaren for his 'service and loyalty to the Confederation whilst a Main Board member' (*Reports*, 1981, 182). For his part McLaren kept the union informed about the invitations he continued to receive from BSC.

9 No one's temper was improved by the news that Sir John Boyd of the AUEW had been invited to join BSC as a part-time Board member. The ISTC remained opposed to full-time officers on the Board, as BSC was well aware.

10 In November the EC received its first protest against his exclusion, from Clydebridge No. 2 branch.

11 This opinion was challenged, provoking a dramatic adjournment to look for a

minuted decision. When none could be found, the EC resolved there and then that membership of the two bodies was mutually exclusive and, to remove any possibility, added that no member of either body could sit on the other body (*Reports*, 1982, 9). The significance of this decision was signalled when in November 1982 the EC nominated Jim McLaren and Don Caddick to the Main Board when the terms of the present members should expire.

12 Frustration with the increasingly cavalier approach of BSC was to lead the following year to tabling of an identical motion at the TUC and Labour conferences, calling for an examination of policy 'for restoring and increasing the democratic control of Nationalised Industries'.

13 *Reports* (1982), 145.

14 These expectations were not fulfilled: SIMA members ignored the day of action in all steel areas.

15 *Reports* (1983), 19.

16 The union had to pay lock-out benefit in some cases; written warnings were issued to all members who had breached discipline on the day of action.

17 Clive Lewis, one of its members, was not impressed to hear Mrs Thatcher's response to his complaint about redundancies: too many steelworkers, he was told, drove foreign cars. Total 'recessionary redundancies' arising from the Scottish Steel & Tube Group reached no fewer than 721.

18 *Reports* (1982), 134.

19 *Reports* (1979), 188.

20 *Reports* (1982), 108.

21 *Reports* (1981), 26.

22 *Reports* (1981), 76–7. The corollary of the demise of the old private sector was the emergence of a new one, with BSC the centre of a general rationalisation plan. The same EC which heard the final report on Duport also had early notice of the formation of Allied Steel & Wire, the first of the 'phoenix' projects.

23 *Reports* (1982), 190.

24 Meetings towards the end of the campaign proved the last battle of Harry Parnham, recently appointed Senior Divisional Organiser, No. 3 Division, who was found dead in his car on 23 March 1983 after a sudden heart attack.

25 On the eve of implementation, a serious fire broke out at the Atlas shop during the first week of trading and production had to be switched to the discarded Norfolk shop. When full manning up was being completed at the River Don site, a significant dispute over seniority arose which had implications for rationalisation elsewhere. By a decision of the November 1983 EC, it was ruled that members transferring from one site to another would take bottom positions on the new site. The fire delayed the introduction of one-site melting until June 1984.

26 *Reports* (1982), 218.

27 The ISTC had sole negotiating rights for all grades at Brymill.

28 G.F. (Fred) Brooks (1921–) had entered the industry in 1937, undertaking many occupations at Stocksbridge until his appointment as No. 7 Divisional Organiser in 1970. He was made Senior Organiser in 1975 and Divisional Officer in 1981.

29 Despite the introduction of flexible operations in the Hoop Works, Barrow was closed in the autumn.

30 There was some consolation in that the agreements allowed for transfers to the Midlands by Cheshire workers.

31 Ironically the strike led to an increase in output at the relevant plants, as orders were reallocated to BSC Special Steels from elsewhere in the Corporation. This effect did not cease until near the end of the year, when the miners' strike was in decline. Special Steels' arc furnaces melted scrap and so did not suffer from feedstock shortages. Quite independently of this, Brymbo was operating full-time on only one furnace, and in the summer of 1984 reached a record output of 8000 tonnes a week.

32 *Reports* (1981), 214.

33 Even with this settlement the problems had not all been resolved; disputes in the Strip Mills division over how to consolidate the bonus had to be put through procedure later in the year (*Reports*, 1982, 202). A national meeting on 24 January 1983 made some progress towards resolving outstanding disagreements. Union officers were careful to specify that this payment came out of the 1982 award and not from the 1983 agreement, which was already proving vexatious.

34 See Chapter 3.

35 *Reports* (1983), 2–3.

36 *Reports* (1983), 59.

37 The assurances were received and all concerned were reinstated in office.

9

Progress amid the ruins
Bill Sirs (1983–5)

'We have been fighting rearguard actions, but at the same time
constructively trying to help to create an industry capable of meeting
the opposition and capable of standing on its own feet.'

Trading conditions and the membership

By the middle of 1983 the industrial recovery from the recession of 1979–81
was palpable. In South Wales the Port Talbot hot-strip mill produced 36,800
tonnes of coil in a week – a slimline record. The works greeted with confidence clearance of the proposal to build a new mill, a major £171m development. At Llanwern, the other leg of slimline, plant loadings were at their best
since 1979 thanks to new car models and rising exports. Shotton, a recipient
of much of this strip, recorded record lump-sum bonus earnings for ISTC
members in the second quarter of the year. At Ravenscraig the order book
was full. Nor was the recovery confined to strip. The Lackenby BOS plant
reached its highest ever weekly average output of 61,627 tonnes in May 1983,
leading in turn to record outputs in excess of 30,000 tonnes at the coil plate
mill. Extra rolling shifts were introduced at Aldwarke, Tinsley Park and
Stocksbridge. It was all a stark contrast to the fate awaiting smaller and older
works away from the integrated centres and South Yorkshire.[1]

For the shrinkage of rolling capacity continued. In November 1984 BSC
announced its intention to close Glengarnock mill, lone survivor of the 1978
closure, in March 1985. Stocksbridge Spring Works was scheduled to shut
the same month, making way for a one-site operation at Tinsley Park, a move
designed to establish a new business for privatisation. At the turn of the year
the Hartlepool plate mill was marked down for closure at the same date. Even
where plants stayed in production there was a steady outflow of jobs: the collapse of steel employment is apparent from the figures for contributing
ISTC membership. They record a decline from 58,181 to 46,580 during the

four quarters from September 1982 to June 1983. The drop was steepest in No. 4 Division, where membership fell from 7612 to 4437, but all major Divisions suffered a loss well in excess of 1000. These numbers posed a structural as well as a financial challenge: the number of branches fell to a much smaller extent (from 641 to 617) during the six months to June 1983 while recorded members declined by little more than 2000 in the first half of the year. The consequent financial rationalisation included the shedding of staff at Central Office, where the amalgamation of departments had released floors available for rent, and a number of steps were taken in the Divisions. Necessary changes now fused with constitutional change.

A number of difficulties had accumulated over the method of electing Executive members. An EC sub-committee reported to the full Executive on 30 April 1981 about three principal areas. The concept of 'pithead' balloting had grown in popularity within the Organisation. The ISTC was constrained by its own decision (in line with TUC policy) not to apply for funds for the holding ballots as provided for by the Employment Act 1980, and so any extra electoral costs would have to be met. Nevertheless this new method was agreed to, and it was determined that Central Office guidelines would be issued and the proposal put out to ballot in a rule-change amendment after discussion at that year's ADC.

Complaints had been received about Executive members retaining their places after leaving their employment or even the industry. This precipitated a long discussion, which culminated in a decision to permit such individuals to attend one meeting after termination of employment.[2] The key change concerned the historic system of electing executive members from sections. Here the sub-committee had recommended a system of four sections, but following a prolonged debate it was agreed to establish a system with no sections at all, based purely on divisional representation. This too was subject to ADC discussion, but there was no minimising the significance of the shift. The historic sectional system had as its objective the representation of all trades and departments on the ruling body, a very necessary aim for a new organisation which needed to give all its component parts a say in the future. But the membership was now reduced to less than half its peak, and accountability might benefit from clearly understood lines of responsibility: divisional representation seemed to offer this. In the interests of open discussion, and to underline the non-policy-making status of the ADC, no resolutions on the subject were tabled (though a discussion took place), and afterwards a new sub-committee was established to make progress.[3]

This sub-committee reported in November. From its findings, proposals to establish just three sections – public sector (manual), public sector (staff), and private sector – were, after lengthy discussion, adopted subject to membership endorsement. The November 1981 EC put flesh on the bones by agreeing that each Division would be represented proportionally according to a membership divisor, with an overall limit of four seats per division.[4] A mode of transition had now to be devised by the legal services, which in February 1982 recommended that all Executive members should resign in December 1982 to allow a new method of election from January 1983. This elicited three further schemes, each implementing the reform in a different way. Initially, that proposed by EC member John Linighan was selected, but the legal services later advised against it and it was withdrawn.[5] Amended proposals were then put out to ballot with a view to meeting the originally intended date for change, and in 1983 they duly took effect.

Further constitutional change arose from the fall in membership. By February 1982 the EC had concluded that each CNC had excessive representation. It adopted a new constitution for each as follows: one per Division plus seven Executive members (including the President and Vice-president) on the Manual Grades CNC; one per Division and four Executive members for the Staff CNC; and one per Division and one EC member for the Middle Management CNC.[6]

Thus matters remained for nearly two years until the end of 1983, when Danny Foley, a private-sector Executive member from Allied Steel and Wire, called for CNC meetings at national level for the private sector. Though the Foley proposals only made the case for consultative status, Pandora's box had been opened and doubts were frankly expressed by Executive members about the value of HST area meetings *per se*. The outcome was a resolution to end area committees and to accept CNC nominations for the public sector on the same basis as for the National Staff Negotiating Committee. The demand for greater representation in the private sector would be met by reserving a private session for both private and public sectors to discuss wages and conditions at the ADC.[7] In effect the conference, despite its lack of policy-making status, was becoming the arena for many key decisions and exchanges.

Yet the relationship between the Executive itself and the Conference remained largely undefined. The 1982 ADC declared its wish to become a policy-making body, 'thereby extending democracy within the union', and called upon the EC to pursue those objects approved by a majority conference vote. This decision provoked an extended debate at the EC, which was effectively being asked to give up some of its power. It nevertheless resolved to accept the resolution.[8] At its inception the ADC had clearly not been a policy-making body, but its importance had grown, and some members of the Executive were increasingly uncomfortable about rejecting conference decisions. This discomfiture was sometimes increased when the EC picked out parts of conference motions it was prepared to accept. There had also been controversy over the role of Executive members at the ADC: they were enjoined to support EC decisions at the conference. After the 1984 ADC the Rules Revision Committee produced proposals as to how the conference could make policy. Its solution, which was endorsed by the EC, was that the ADC could not have powers 'which are covered by the Rules and Constitution'[9]. It would not therefore be policy-making, but at the discretion of the EC items under the headings 'political, environmental, EEC, nuclear armaments, and defence' might be referred to it for a policy decision. Two years later, another dimension of the relationship was tidied up when it was ruled that Executive members of the Agenda Committee could not participate in ADC debates, and that Executive members could vote and speak only as individuals in situations where the ADC had the right to make policy. On matters which would ultimately be referred to the EC for a policy decision, Executive members were now debarred from any form of participation other than attendance.[10]

Political developments

With the tide in the Labour Party flowing strongly against the EEC, The ISTC unsuccessfully tabled a motion to the 1981 conference calling for a referendum on continuing membership, a move intended to forestall calls for withdrawal.[11] Earlier in the year the EC had agreed to make a donation to Labour Solidarity, the Party faction with strongest allegiance to the EEC now that so many Labour MPs had left to form the SDP.[12] Yet there was an ambivalence here. For that year's TUC the union had tabled a full-blooded socialist resolution calling for iron and steel 'socialisation' to extend BSC's industrial coverage and social responsibilities; the restoration of privatised parts of the Corporation without compensation; and the introduction of new forms of industrial democracy.[13] This was very much in the mainstream of current Labour thinking. Perhaps even more remarkably, the EC upheld the 1981 and 1982 ADC motions calling for support for CND and for unilateral nuclear disarmament (the ADC urged 'active support').[14]

At the 1981 Party conference, Roy Evans was triumphantly elected to the NEC, ending a six-year ISTC absence and opening a three-year spell on that body for the Assistant General Secretary. In that position he took a strongly loyalist stance, and the ISTC reliably backed the existing leadership of the Party. A new focus for affiliated unions, Trade Unions for a Labour Victory (TULV), began to make its mark the following year with a special effort to co-ordinate union help for the Party in the by-election at Glasgow Hillhead. The ISTC was a founder member of the body and agreed in principle to the establishment of a special TULV fund raised by a levy of 10p per member.[15] The amount was raised to 15p the following year.

When the 1982 ADC called for the ISTC vote at future electoral colleges to be determined by a national ballot of the affiliated membership, the EC rejected this, but relations between Party and union at grassroots level continued to be the subject of debate: a 1982 ADC resolution proposed the amalgamation of small branches to fund the affiliation fee to the Party, a move intended to promote Party activity and maximise ISTC influence at the local level.[16]

In the 1983 general election the Conservatives romped home, with 397 seats in the Commons to Labour's 209. This was especially bitter for the ISTC which had, as usual, virtually emptied its political fund in support of the Party, making a straight donation of £10,000 and much else besides. Bill Homewood had gained the Kettering and Corby seat for Labour in 1979 (also an adverse year for the Party), but now, following boundary changes, he became candidate for a new Corby seat and went down to defeat. Though Donald Coleman easily held Neath, this was little consolation.[17] Yet in a period when there was no shortage of factious advice, the ISTC did not join in. An emergency resolution of the 1983 ADC hovered between Sirs's personal unease at programmatic trends and the more defensive attitude of the active membership. It reaffirmed the union's support for Labour and backed the Party's industrial policies. Loss of electoral support was attributed to 'internal strife and a mainly hostile press', though the need for 'a programme and policy that is more attractive to the public in general' was identified; ISTC leaders were called upon to work for changes in Labour 'where necessary'.[18]

After the Tory landslide Michael Foot's resignation ushered in a four-way leadership contest, with Roy Hattersley, Eric Heffer, Neil Kinnock and Peter Shore declaring their candidatures. The union responded to the appetite of members for a wide participation in the selection of its nominee by circulating branches for their views and then inviting candidates to address the Executive. Shore – who had addressed the ADC – was closely associated with Labour Solidarity, which the ISTC had backed, but although he and Hattersley attended the EC meeting and Kinnock and Heffer did not, it nominated Kinnock as Leader and Hattersley as Deputy Leader.[19]

Pay and pensions

Ian MacGregor switched chairs from BSC to the National Coal Board in 1983, but his legacy was great and lasting. From the 1950s, and especially since 1967, central negotiations had taken an extremely high profile. Now, the raison d'être of national organisation was plainly under attack. Lump-sum bonus schemes, the absence of central awards, and the challenge of multi-union negotiations all threatened the status quo. Traditional attitudes were reasserted, sometimes even more strongly than before, yet they were becoming harder to implement.[20] In August 1984 the EC acceded to a BSC request for a review of bargaining structures and procedures.[21] The BSC tabled its proposals on 18 September 1984, and these were circulated. The response from the branches was overwhelmingly hostile: of fifty-five replies processed by November, hardly any were prepared to countenance the BSC proposals.

The 1984 BSC annual round was mercifully brief. Two meetings sufficed to clinch a deal under which local lump-sum bonus schemes applied in 1984, and 3 per cent from the 1983 schemes, would be consolidated onto basic rates. At long last the 5 per cent incomes-policy supplement, separate in pay elements since the 1970s, was also consolidated, while the minimum earnings level (MEL) rose to £80 weekly. But the following year matters progressed less smoothly. To a claim of 13 November 1984 BSC responded only with a final offer of 2.5 per cent on all elements of pay plus 2 per cent consolidation of lump-sum bonus schemes. In return for this bounty a fifteen-month agreement was expected. It was little surprise that a meeting of 8 January registered a failure to agree. Evans, now leading the main negotiations with BSC for the first time, summoned a Special Executive prior to a resumption on 15 January, when an agreement could be achieved only after protracted negotiations. The fifteen-month demand of BSC was conceded, but the addition on all elements of pay was raised to 3.25 per cent for 1985, with a further 1 per cent in the first quarter of 1986. Where local lump-sum bonus negotiations were concluded by 28 February 1985, 2 per cent could be consolidated. The MEL rose from £80 to £90 (the weekly rate for plant labourers) and £391.11 (the monthly rate for staff grades). This settlement also marked the introduction of bereavement leave.

Back in May 1979 the Executive had considered proposals for harmonising the pension schemes at BSC, a major focus of the desire for single status.[22] Until late in 1981 BSC had been reluctant to move towards a common pension scheme except in the context of discussions about the 1982 annual review. At the end of the year, however, it opened negotiations on a free-standing proposal, and harmonisation reached the Executive for endorsement at their meeting of 8 January 1982. The new scheme came into operation on 1 April and based pensionable earnings on the best single year of earnings, a considerable advance over the previously obtaining average of three years. A tax-free payment of three years' average pension was also to be paid at retirement. The twenty-five-year service requirement would be waived for those over sixty who took early retirement, and lump-sum death benefit rose to two years' earnings. There were other improvements, but staff members currently entitled to better benefits still continued to receive them. To fund the scheme in the future there was a new unified superannuation rate of 7 per cent, and the feared loss of benefits for staff grades would be avoided provided they maintained their current level of contributions.[23]

This was a real achievement, and now horizons broadened. The 1982 ADC called for 'a new common status for all members in employment', elements of which (it proposed) should feature in the formulation of the 1983 claim. This was significant in that it embraced the entire membership. Great vigilance was needed at BSC, however: some local deals negotiated under the 1982 agreement appeared to include a change from manual to staff grades with very little change in job content. Sandy Feather reflected a widely held view when he dubbed such alterations 'purely cosmetic', intended to demonstrate a spurious fall in the ratio of staff to manual grades.[24] But an agreement was finally reached to allow for the phased introduction of a harmonised BSC sick-pay scheme in autumn 1983 thus meeting another long-cherished target of the ISTC. The first phase, introduced in 1984, was expected to be smoothly followed by others provided there was no explosion of absenteeism.

The miners and other unions

The ISTC was not the only union facing a significant loss of members in the mid-1980s, and the overall drop left its mark on the Trades Union Congress. When the TUC leadership responded by initiating a debate on the reform of the structure of the General Council, Sirs was quick to communicate his concern. The ISTC had long since ceased to be one of the largest unions, yet by common consent it represented a vital national manufacturing interest. What would happen to the representation of the smaller unions if, as was being proposed, only those with more than 100,000 members were guaranteed a General Council place? In February 1983 he reported that he had received assurances from TUC General Secretary Len Murray about the number of seats available collectively to the smaller unions, and so it proved. But it was still necessary to organise, and when the new system was implemented at that year's Congress, Sirs received the second-highest vote among smaller union leaders and easily kept his place on the General Council.

In common with other TUC unions, the ISTC had committed itself against the Employment Act 1982, the second in the great series of anti-union statutes legislated by the Conservatives during their long term of office. A critique of this statute was part of the Organisation's education programme from the beginning of the year, and in the summer all members of industrial tribunals were instructed not to participate in cases arising from the application of union membership agreements.[25] The 1982 ADC called for full mobilisation of the ISTC's strength behind the TUC campaign of resistance. It was a sharp contrast to the events of ten years earlier; two years later, however, the ISTC had to fight events that threatened to isolate it again.

Winter 1983 had seen the imposition of an overtime ban by the NUM – merely an overture to what was to be a year-long miners' strike from March 1984. This dispute, unlike the *pay* strike of the steelworkers in 1980, was intended to prevent closures of pits, but the mineworkers were to prove far less able to preserve unity than the ISTC. While the overtime ban was under way the 'Triple Alliance' – now seven unions strong – had experienced a revival, including a nationwide programme of rallies. They had even agreed a nine-point plan to maximise the common concerns of the three industries, but this unity was now to be put to the ultimate test.

As a traditionally loyal union, wishing to adhere to the views of the TUC and respond to the general sympathy which miners in dispute always attracted, the ISTC was also uncomfortably aware of the divisions within the NUM membership and determined to keep steel plants in production. The outlook of many miners was that the road to a successful conclusion of the strike lay in shutting down coal-burning steel plants; this objective could hardly be endorsed by members of a union which had spent the last six years trying to keep them open and whose memories of the aftermath of strike action on employment were all too fresh.

The Organisation faced an anguished dilemma. In many communities steelworkers and miners were neighbours – even families could be divided between the two industries. Yet every success for one could seem to be a setback for the other. The regional committees of the Triple Alliance met, but increasingly witnessed failures to agree as miners' pickets pressed on steelworks more and more: the mass picketing was having an effect. All divisions raised money for the striking miners, but there could be no disguising the fact that the major steelworks were existing only on a drip-feed of coal supplies. In early April Ravenscraig, already fighting for survival and needing two trains of coal a day to stay in production, was down to four or five days' stocks. More vulnerable still was Scunthorpe, which needed 15,000 tonnes of coal a week. Roy Bishop, as No. 3 Divisional Officer, had sought local dispensation from

Jack Taylor of the Yorkshire NUM, to be told that this could be obtained only at the national level of his union. In early April this meant that one coke oven and one blastfurnace was already in difficulties and sufficient coal remained for only ten days' production. Up to the strike Scunthorpe had been supplied from five or six Yorkshire pits; ominously, small amounts of supplies were now being imported through Flixborough wharf.

Teesside and Port Talbot depended on imported coal,[26] but Llanwern traditionally used domestic supplies. While Llanwern stocks were reported adequate in early April (the level of 90,000 tonnes represented nearly four weeks' supply), requests for coal from the NUM had been refused. The discussions of the EC were dominated by a fear that idle steel plants would lose orders to foreign competitors, but there was a deep reluctance to act in any way that would weaken the NUM's case: the miners were, after all, facing the same Ian MacGregor who had savaged the steel industry between 1980 and 1983.[27] An ISTC statement of 5 April recalled how steel had suffered so recently from the same closure-driven approach now being applied to coal, and called for the withdrawal of the NCB proposals and a return to negotiations. Nevertheless the EC upheld instructions already issued by Sirs for members to work normally, and declared its intention to stay in dialogue with the other unions. It would, additionally, press for the maximum use of British coal by BSC.

By May Bishop was reporting that production levels at Scunthorpe were below 30 per cent of normal. With the involvement of other unions, agreement had finally been reached with the Yorkshire NUM, but only to ensure coal supplies sufficient to keep the coke ovens in working order and provide enough coke to maintain the minimal sustainable blastfurnace output – a grand total of 15,700 tonnes. But there was a price to pay: BSC observed GWA provisions for ISTC members short of work, but a number of contractors had had their contracts terminated, with dire consequences for the most disadvantaged members of the Organisation.

At the same date the situation at Llanwern had deteriorated considerably: it was leading a 'hand-to-mouth' existence, receiving 6000 tonnes of coal and 10,000 tonnes of coke weekly, and its stocks were gone. Port Talbot remained untroubled, and in fact supplied a number of local foundries with coke – to the consternation of the local NUM. The Quarterly Executive, having heard these reports, and stung by jeering press comment, instructed Sirs to write to the miners nationally and express the ISTC's solidarity with them. It was not just words. In April and May the union donated £10,000 to the miners' hardship fund,[28] and local agreements with the NUM ensured adequate supplies to Ravenscraig, Scunthorpe and Llanwern until the middle of June. A new crisis then arose when the Scunthorpe Works required supplies of metallur-gical coal from Orgreave in Yorkshire, and approaches from Bishop and Evans to the NUM to facilitate them were rebuffed. Members of the NUR and ASLEF refused to carry the coal, precipitating BSC's decision to supply Scunthorpe from Orgreave by lorry, an act which provoked the bitterest picket-line clashes of the entire dispute. On 7 June Evans and Feather had to endure a tough Triple Alliance meeting at which the transport unions effect-ively endorsed the NUM demand that steel production cease.

It was a miserable situation for both unions, not improved when a new approach from Sirs provoked an embittered reply from miners' leader Arthur Scargill. This did not improve the mood of delegates when read out on 21 June to a Special Executive at the ADC, then meeting in Scarborough. The EC nonetheless decided to respond to a letter from Peter Heathfield, the NUM General Secretary, suggesting that the two unions reach a national agreement on BSC coal supplies. A motion was tabled for a private session of the conference which reiterated the ISTC backing for the NUM cause, but for the first time referred to the impact of the dispute on community relations in Yorkshire, South Wales and Scotland;[29] it went on to call on the NUM to recognise the 'precarious state' of the steel industry and the effect *on mining communities* (author's emphasis) if any works should suffer irreparable damage due to an insufficiency of supplies. Steel was, after the Central Elec-tricity Generating Board, the country's second biggest market for coal. The ADC had a head, but it also had a heart, and delegates gave a warm and sym-pathetic reception to miners' pickets who were invited to address them.

The meeting with the NUM took place on at 11.00 a.m. on 29 June. By that date the steel industry was more embattled still: the transport and rail unions had now blacked supplies of coal and iron ore to all works, with severe impact on Llanwern;[30] Ravenscraig was surviving by bringing in both raw materials by road.[31] Scunthorpe returned to 80 per cent of pre-strike output by dint of its road supplies, only to find output again curtailed when a blockade of iron ore imports was imposed at Immingham docks.

The NUM argued that they had supported the steelworkers during their strike and were entitled to reciprocal backing; the ISTC countered that no pits had closed in 1980 and that coal output had actually risen during the steel strike. During the meeting it became quite clear that Scargill was seeking the cessation of all steel production: coal and ore were to come in only in suf-ficient quantities to ensure safety at the coke ovens and blastfurnaces. The EC, reconvened that afternoon, could not accept the NUM proposal but floated the possibility of an output ceiling of 80 per cent, a policy it proposed to canvass at joint committees and at the Steel Committee.

The Steel Committee met in the morning of 2 July, and it was apparent that there was unanimous resistance to the NUM's call to stop steel production. On the production limit there were divided views, with some unions opposed to any concession whatever. The gap was bridged by a statement which rejected the NUM call as impracticable, 'damaging to the industry and completely unacceptable to their [i.e. the steel unions'] members', but sugared the pill somewhat by signalling continued willingness to reach an agreement.[32]

In August a dispute broke out at Hunterston, where TGWU dockers, supported by tugmen and boatmen, agreed to black all coal cargoes while protesting that ISTC members at the port were doing normal unloading work. BSC and the Clyde Port Authority responded by bringing in a cargo ship, the *Ostia*, without TGWU assistance, and a national dock strike ensued. The view of the ISTC was that action in support of the miners, rather than an industrial dispute *sui generis*, was underway. It was finally resolved by a local agreement between the TGWU and the Glasgow office to bring in 18,000 tonnes of coal a week, rising to 22,000 tonnes. The agreement was later repudiated by the NUM nationally, and also by the rail unions, but supplies continued to come into the plant by road.

Early in September the TUC in Congress adopted a policy which seemed in some respects to increase general union support for the miners but in reality, fell short of giving the NUM the concrete backing it sought. However, a statement put to Congress with General Council support contained a commitment not to move coal or coke across official NUM picket lines, nor to use any such materials which had been taken across official NUM picket lines. Faced with this, the ISTC delegation decided to abstain when the motion was put to the vote, and brought back to the EC a recommendation to ballot the membership on TUC policy.

The NUM sought a meeting with the Steel Committee immediately after Congress had upheld this statement, but the encounter did not take place until 9 October in the form of a meeting of all unions in steel under the chairmanship of Norman Willis, who had succeeded Len Murray as General Secretary of the TUC. The consensus of those present was that there was no possibility of a nil-production policy. Knowing this, the ISTC's EC reaffirmed its own policy the next day and resolved meanwhile to assist with food parcels to alleviate hardship in the mining areas. A further £10,000 was to be donated in February 1985, and the ISTC's General Secretary (by now Evans had taken over from Sirs) was given authority to use his discretion over future funds.

By the middle of October Scunthorpe was producing 50,000 tonnes of

22 No vacancies: Bilston, March 1979

23 Fighting closure: Corby, 20 September 1979

24   The strike: Port Talbot at a standstill, 2 January 1980

25   The strike: pickets outside Corby works, 8 January 1980

26 The strike: Ravenscraig, 21 March 1980

27 The strike: outside Pressed Steel Fisher, 7 February 1980

28 Harry Douglass

29 Dai Davies

30   Lincoln Evans

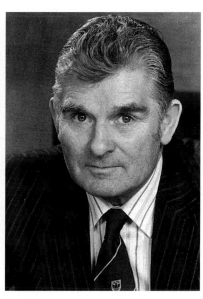

31   Roy Evans

32   Bill Sirs

33 Triple Alliance Mark I: Sid Weighell, Joe Gormley, Bill Sirs

34 Triple Alliance Mark II: Bill Sirs, Arthur Scargill, Jimmy Knapp

35 The Triple Alliance backs Clydebridge's fight, 23 October 1982

36 Keith Brookman,
ISTC General
Secretary from
1993

37 ISTC Executive Council, summer 1997

1 Rob Middlemas, 2 Tony Poynter, 3 Mick Mannion (EC members); 4 Tony Myhill,
5 Kevin Pass (Research Officers), 6 Mick Barnett (Head of General Secretary's Department);
7 Roger Stone, 8 Terry Butterworth, 9 Pat Boyle, 10 Mick Simpson, 11 John Lenaghan,
12 Ray Hill, 13 Ray Ardron (EC members); 14 Mel Williams, 15 Eric Caudwell,
16 Terry Butcher, 17 Stephen Gale, 18 Tommy Fellows, 19 Colin Griffiths (EC members);
20 John Brierley (Head of Finance and Membership Department), 21 Michael Leahy (Assistant
General Secretary), 22 Keith Brookman (General Secretary), 23 Austin Senior (President),
24 Tony McCarthy (Vice-President); 25 Harry Cooper (EC member), 26 Peter Lightfoot,
27 John Clarke, 28 Mick Adams, 29 Brian Connolly (Divisional Officers), 30 Lyn James (EC
member), 31 Eddie Lynch (National Secretary/Divisional Officer)

Not present: Pat Donnolly (EC member) and Gareth Howells (Head of Research Department) liquid steel a week, levels facilitated by imports of raw materials from a large number of wharves. Such actions, though necessary, were not cheap, and production costs were significantly increased by lorry-intensive transport. Port Talbot and Llanwern were each producing in excess of 40,000 tonnes weekly by this date, a performance made possible at Llanwern by supplies from Port Talbot and the Orb Works wharf. Higher transport costs for transferring ore caused a deterioration in lump-sum bonus earnings in the materials processing department: for the third quarter of 1984 they were 7.02 per cent, one percentage point below Port Talbot's and far adrift of mill bonuses in the Division. Yet one paradoxical development was that plant tonnage had actually risen, due to the use of low-sulphur coal which allowed a higher utilisation of blastfurnace capacity.

The first quarter of 1985 proved the last quarter of the miners' strike. Coal and ore continued to travel by road from Hunterston to Ravenscraig. The Colliery Arch plant in Cleveland continued to operate mainly under the GWA. At Scunthorpe production continued at 70/80 per cent, and Llanwern sustained full production with raw materials from Port Talbot and elsewhere. While the suffering inflicted on steelworkers during this troubled year did not compare to that of the miners, it had been bad enough: earnings had tumbled, plants been brought to the brink of extinction, and traditional warm relationships brought to – and sometimes beyond – breaking point. A positive development in the ISTC's relations with other unions was badly needed.

In this difficult period came at last the long-sought and troubled merger with the National Union of Blastfurnacemen. After their close co-operation during the 1980 strike, the NUB and the ISTC had had informal talks to meet the challenge of contracting memberships.[33] The correspondence had become more concrete, and on 16 September 1980 the EC had established a sub-committee to take the process further, with a special interest in the future status of full-time NUB officers. Then in 1981 the NUB executive suddenly voted to suspend further discussions on amalgamation: things slumbered until June, but after that progress accelerated. The NUB now presented minimum conditions for merger, and by January 1982 the EC had substantially narrowed down the range of its concerns about this. A joint working party had actually drafted a common document when there came an announcement that Hector Smith intended to retire. Nick Leadley, his successor as NUB General Secretary, rapidly made his mark by indicating that the NUB wished to have discussions with other unions prior to consummating its relationship with the ISTC. And now it was one step forward two steps back, for a special NUB conference on 26 May opposed merger or amalgamation with the ISTC. After that discussions not surprisingly lapsed until 12 October, when the ISTC agreed to a request to reopen negotiations.

One month later representatives of the two sides met to discuss eighteen contentious points which had been identified during earlier meetings. The NUB team was now prepared to recommend a merger to its executive, but its goal had become a merger rather than a transfer of engagements – a shift of emphasis on which the ISTC felt it must take legal advice. The smaller union had, it transpired, been having parallel discussions with the AUEW, but this did not hinder the ISTC talks. By February 1983 only one question remained unresolved: whether the putative 'National Secretary of the Coke and Iron Section' (CIS) – the intended title of the former NUB General Secretary – would be replaced if he retired after the amalgamation.

Then events again intervened. The NUB decided to upgrade its talks with the AUEW to negotiations. An exasperated ISTC went public on the terms offered to the NUB.[34] But the smaller union continued in its courtship with the engineers, and only after this had irretrievably broken down at the end of 1983 did it again turn to the ISTC, rapidly moving towards the formulation of documents which could be submitted to the two executives.[35] The August 1984 EC heard that the final Transfer of Engagements document had been approved by the certification officer and that the NUB was to recommend it to the membership. The NUB ballot was held in December and its positive result was published in the New Year.[36]

In May 1981 the ISTC had been informally approached by the Amalgamated Society of Wire Drawers & Kindred Workers,[37] but owing to lack of interest on the smaller union's executive there was no immediate outcome.[38] In 1981 and 1982 conversations were also held with the British Roll Turners Society, but with no concrete result.[39] The traditional industrial stance of the Organisation was reaffirmed by the 1984 conference, which called on a willing Executive Council to amalgamate only with unions within the industry.[40]

In 1980 the ISTC had reviewed the history of its relationship with SIMA and of that body's subsequent evolution towards a merger with the EEPTU, to the consternation of the electricians.[41] Little of note followed until the summer of 1982, when Len Murray chaired a meeting of the ISTC and SIMA/EEPTU. The two protagonists, Sirs and EEPTU General Secretary Frank Chapple, agreed to hold national meetings with a view to arriving at an agreement over spheres of influence in middle management. But the meeting was far from decisive, and concern was sufficient to cause renewed dialogue under TUC chairmanship the following year. At Scunthorpe ISTC middle management members were still denied recognition and negotiating rights, as they had been for years. The August 1984 EC received a large number of protests from MM branches backing a proposal that no agreement be concluded with SIMA over spheres of influence unless this long-denied MM demand was conceded wherever the ISTC had significant membership. It took a bilateral meeting under the auspices of the TUC before a resolution could be found,[42] and Sirs achieved a spheres-of-influence agreement on the eve of his retirement.

But the ISTC itself was eyed during the 1980s by larger organisations. On 23 August 1981 the *Sunday Times* bizarrely suggested that the ISTC might be taken over by the NUM and that meetings of members had already taken place. Sirs circulated the offices to discover if there was any substance in these rumours, but on the basis of the replies received it was concluded that they were unfounded.[43] Nor were the miners the only beasts in the jungle. A February 1981 initiative to meet the NCCC to discuss a national joint committee foundered: there was little scope for agreement in view of the constitutional diversity of the participating organisations. Eighteen months later a merger approach by Sir John Boyd of the AUEW was merely 'noted'. Finally, in 1983, the ISTC was wooed by no less than three unions: the NUM now offered a federation, the AUEW (Engineering Section) an umbrella group covering the metal trades,[44] and GMBATU outright amalgamation. All were informed that the ISTC was uninterested in entering such discussions.

New leaders

A new post of Senior Divisional Organiser had been established to reflect the extra responsibilities taken on by the most senior man when the Divisional Officer was absent; at the same time considerable movement also took place among the newly promoted holders of this rank. At the start of 1983 Peter Lightfoot,[45] another of the first generation of staff organisers, moved to No. 3 Division to replace Joe Pickles, who had sought, and been granted, early retirement. Almost at once the plan was superseded and Lightfoot switched places with Roy Bishop, the Yorkshire-born staff organiser who had become Divisional Officer in the Midlands.[46] The staff of No. 7 Division was cut back, causing some murmurings among the membership. The retirement of Les Bambury, long-standing Senior Organiser in the London area, had been announced in August 1982, shortly after he was awarded his shield.[47] He was replaced, for a tragically brief period, by Bert Smith.[48]

At the end of 1981 the Executive reluctantly addressed the future of its convalescent home: it was a melancholy financial footnote to the severe deterioration in income. The Executive notified 2000 businesses that the ISTC planned to sell Larkhill, which had in fact been closed to entrants since the beginning of December. Central Office was given plenary power to proceed with the sale, and redundancy arrangements were satisfactorily concluded with the staff to take effect in April 1982.[49] That summer it was sold to the TGWU for £300,000. The need to provide for convalescence was acknowledged in February 1982, from which date qualifying members went to homes in Llandudno, Dawlish, Margate or on the Isle of Bute. The August EC decided not to bring forward a change to Rule (2), Clause 31, thus deferring any decision to buy a new home.

With Bill Sirs due to reach retirement age in January 1985, the November 1983 Executive invited nominations for General Secretary and Assistant General Secretary, to be submitted by 9 January 1984. In February 1984 it agreed after a ballot to uphold the recommendation of the Organisation and Staffing Sub-committee that Sirs be succeeded by Roy Evans, who had faced competition from Senior Organiser Keith Jones and an Executive member, John Cowling. The May EC reduced ten applicants for the post of AGS in Evans's place to five: Jimmy Brandon, Keith Brookman, John Clarke, Sandy Feather and Ted Hardaker. These were examined and interviewed by the Staffing Sub-committee and then by the full Executive, after which Keith Brookman[50] was appointed AGS Designate.

Bill Sirs retired on 5 January 1985. At his last ADC he bade an emotional farewell to the ISTC, declaring that he went out 'with his head held high'. His ten years at the top had bridged huge changes. His arrival had expressed the wish of the membership for a more militant defence of their interests, and he had championed innovation right across the Organisation. But the combined power of industry and government had proved too much for the ISTC, and indeed for all the unions, as the miners – still on strike at the date of his retirement – were bitterly discovering. As a strike leader he had been demonised; yet simultaneously he was reviled for his politically flamboyant views. Modest in his personal bearing, he could appear dictatorial on a platform. He may have had the most difficult hand to play of any ISTC leader; any assessment of his career must acknowledge the way he kept the union in the public eye long after its national industrial strength had gone.[51]

Notes

1 Some among the membership continued to anticipate a threat to the major plants; a resolution for occupying them and maintaining production if they were threatened with closure was tabled at the 1984 ADC.

2 There was less certainty about another recommendation to the effect that the seat of a member leaving the EC with less than twelve months to go should be 'left in abeyance'.

3 *Reports* (1981), 143. The status of the ADC was enhanced, however, when the EC agreed in August to drop BOCs in its favour forthwith. However, a resolution of the 1981 ADC to make it a policy-making body was rejected by the EC, as was a proposal to establish a quinquennial conference on rule revision. In February 1982 the EC determined that replies to resolutions at the ADC would be given by national officials, and that its own members would not vote on, propose or second resolutions; they would, however, have a right to speak at the chairman's discretion.

4 The possibility of reserved women's seats was discussed on request from the Manchester Steels Staff branch, but the EC concluded that divisional representation would increase the chances of a female member being elected. *Reports* (1981), 252. The branch returned to the subject in 1983 without success; but a request from the Irlam, Warrington and Manchester Joint Committee for women's representation at the ADC was met with an allocation of three seats (*Reports*, 1983, 33).

5 *Reports* (1982), 77.

6 The new formula was hastily devised in an adjournment (*Reports*, 1982, 9–10). When the Area Committees met, two of them (1 and 3) opposed the change; conference voted to 'recognise the need for proportional representation at national negotiating level', but the resolution was only 'noted' by the EC.

7 *Reports* (1983), 173.

8 *Reports* (1982), 148. The same EC merely noted another call from the ADC calling for the allocation of additional seats to give additional representation for women in line with the TUC Charter of Equality for Women within Trade Unions. One year later it was apparent that there was a shortage of women prepared to come forward as delegates, and No. 7 unsuccessfully raised the possibility of other divisions being circulated in the event that Nos. 2, 3, 4, and 6 Divisions were unable to find women delegates (*Reports*, 1983, 161).

9 *Reports* (1984), 169.

10 *Reports* (1986), 5.

11 The 1981 ADC resolved that EEC membership was 'detrimental to the interest of the British people' and called for an active campaign of withdrawal. This was not a policy-making decision, and the referendum call made a bridge between the hostility of active members and the caution of the leadership on this contentious issue.

12 A pointed ADC resolution urged that there be no shift of allegiance away from Labour and that the union should not cause 'any more aggravation within'. This was probably aimed at the outspoken support Sirs had given to the right of the Party, and was so interpreted by the EC which noted these words. There was nonetheless no question of disaffiliation, and at the same moment the EC resolved that 'this organisation would remain committed to the Labour Party' (*Reports*, 1981, 167).

13 *Reports* (1981), 121. A similar resolution was tabled for the 1982 Labour Conference. The 1982 ADC called for 'any action necessary' to resist privatisation, recommending that it be concerted with the Triple Alliance; the EC accepted this too.

14 After some delay the EC resolved in February 1983 to affiliate 'in the sum of £25 when the Finance Committee decide that this can be met from the appropriate fund'.

15 At this point (February 1982) severe cash shortage prevented contributions which had to come from the political fund, but the ISTC later became a mainstay of TULV. Political expenses were strictly curtailed during 1982 in view of the parlous state of the fund; the standard function held by the ISTC at the annual conference was also not held. Although the outcome had been less severe than anticipated, the Executive nonetheless raised the weekly levy by 1p later in 1982. That year's ADC requested more money to be diverted to the political fund, a suggestion with which the EC concurred.

16 The EC somewhat surprisingly accepted this suggestion, though it was arguable that it would lead to a diminution in influence. The Party constitution allowed all affiliated branches to nominate candidates, permitting the ISTC (which tended to have a large number of branches in a given plant) to delay the impact of a falling membership during the selection process and in elections for local Labour positions.

17 Homewood, who was eighteen months short of retirement age, was re-engaged as an organiser, a move taken in response to membership feelings. He died in January 1989, tragically soon after his retirement. The previous year Paul Flynn of Spencer Technical Staff, had resigned from the ISTC Parliamentary Panel; in 1987 he was elected MP for Newport West.

18 The EC accepted this resolution. One practical instance of firmer support was the reintroduction of sponsorship in local elections. A conference resolution calling for nuclear disarmament did not include the word 'unilateral', and the EC rejected the claim in another that EEC membership had 'done nothing' for the people.

19 At the 1983 ADC, which staged a lengthy inquest into Labour's crushing defeat, Gwyneth Dunwoody – who had been invited to speak on Health matters – stunned delegates by announcing her own candidacy for Deputy Leader.

20 The 1983 ADC called for officials seeking redundancy to be removed from office, and for BSC to be informed that further cuts in the workforce were not acceptable.

21 There was a slight hiccup when BSC declined to meet the entire ISTC executive, arguing that this was a BSC matter only. Three-quarters of Executive members were employed by BSC.

22 *Reports* (1979), 135.

23 In a perverse application of single-status thinking, the 1982 ADC called for reinstatement of weekly pay for staff members!

24 *Reports* (1983), 19.

25 All obeyed the directive, though there was a delay in the case of Scunthorpe's Harry Skinner (*Reports*, 1982, 133, 190).

26 Indeed, the Lackenby BOS plant and its feeder blastfurnace at Redcar broke production records that spring.

27 MacGregor was still a member of the BSC board at this date. He was replaced as chairman by Sir Robert Haslam, who in 1986 made way for Bob Scholey to step up from the position of chief executive.

28 A further £10,000 was given in August.

29 This was a reference to relations not between steelworkers and miners but between miners and miners.

30 While the regional agreements held, Llanwern's production had touched 70 per cent, but when the local NUM began to apply national union policy it dipped to 50 per cent. The rupture of the national agreement led to Llanwern seeking supplies wherever it could, and by August John Foley was reporting that the works was operating at 'normal' levels.

31 The greatest fear at Ravenscraig was for No. 2 furnace, but this was saved: production figures were sustained at between 60 and 80 per cent that summer. Lump-sum bonus earnings fell only 10 per cent.

32 That is, an agreement which would protect mining and steel jobs in the longer term. The ISTC's EC endorsed the statement later that day.

33 The date of these was June 1980, by which time the ISTC's contributing membership had fallen in nine months from 107,695 to 98,163 with much more to come. The first six months of the year saw the closure of thirty-two branches.

34 See *ISTC Banner* (May 1983), 4–5.

35 *Reports* (1984), 6.

36 See Chapter 10 for the sequel.

37 *Reports* (1981), 117.

38 In 1984 the ISTC kept communications open by advising on computerisation of the Wire-Drawers' head office.

39 *Reports* (1982), 76. No action was taken on an invitation from the EETPU to discuss a merger. In June 1981 the EC reaffirmed its attitude to SIMA, which had now entered the TUC as a section of the EEPTU.

40 In fact this call was not as clear-cut as at first appeared, since No. 8 Division contained non-ferrous workers almost exclusively.

41 *Reports* (1980), 160.

42 *Reports* (1984), 181.

43 In 1982 the ADC itself suggested that if the ISTC was forced to amalgamate owing to loss of membership, the NUM should be its partner; the EC 'noted' the point.

44 They had already approached the NUB with the same proposal (see above).

45 Peter Lightfoot (1924–) worked at John Summers, Shotton, before being appointed Staff Organiser, No. 3 Division, in 1970. He was made Senior Organiser in 1975.

46 Tensions among the staff at No. 3 office culminated when an EC sub-committee probed the formula employed to secure a return to work after a local strike in April 1983. Its report ranged widely over relations and behavioural patterns in the No. 3 Divisional Office and recommended support for Roy Bishop in his efforts 'to

alleviate some of the tensions and past practices that seem to have been the previous standards in No. 3 Divisional Office' (*Reports*, 1983, 112).

47 Les Bambury (1918–96) was a former member of the Executive who, when elected to it in 1964, had been the first ever from the London Area. He had joined BISAKTA in 1946 and been secretary of the Enfield 2 branch for ten years. He served continuously on the Executive until appointed London Area organiser following the retirement of Bert Dismore in 1972.

48 A. ('Bert') Smith (1927–84) had been appointed Divisional Organiser, London Area, in September 1975. He died in service after less than two years as Senior London Organiser.

49 Mr and Mrs Charles Jones, respectively sister-in-charge and gardener at Larkhill, were feted at the Royal Scot Hotel in London on 17 August 1982. The Executive took the unprecedented step of awarding them Confederation shields for their services over so many years.

50 D.K. (Keith) Brookman (1937–), a former crane driver from the Ebbw Vale Works, was appointed Divisional Organiser, No. 5 Division, in 1973. He was a member of the Parliamentary Panel.

51 After his retirement Sirs published his memoirs, the only ISTC General Secretary to do so: see *Hard Labour* (1987).

10

Last years at BSC
Roy Evans (1985–8)

'The truth is we are going to need steel in this country for years
to come.'

New leadership

Roy Evans[1] succeeded Sirs in January 1985 and replaced his predecessor as
Chairman of the Steel Committee. He became President of the IMF Iron and
Steel Department in June 1985. Evans's hope was that the industry would
now enter 'a period of stability and expansion'; he believed that the painful
period of contraction was coming to an end. To the 1985 ADC he declared 'we
now have a substantial membership in the non-ferrous industry, and we have a
changing membership – a bigger private sector and members working with
many metals, not just iron and steel'. His early call to consider a new union
name which would reflect the kindred trades membership did not succeed,
but with Delta Metals' Paddy Belton President of the Executive in Evans's
first year, this section of the membership had a higher profile than usual.

Evans's term of office brought a major change in style, though initially
disguised when the new General Secretary had to convene a Special Executive because pay talks with BSC were – as ever – in crisis. Prolonged negotiations were needed when BSC advanced an offer which satisfied the NCCC
but failed to meet the requirements either of the Executive or the ISTC's
central negotiating committees. This toughness brought its reward in the
shape of the first centrally negotiated pay increase for three years and a 3.25
per cent increase on all pay elements with 1 per cent in the first quarter of
1986, a 2 per cent lump sum bonus consolidation, a higher minimum wage
and improved sick pay. The general rise was 1 per cent higher than that
accepted by the NCCC, and the MEL was higher too, cause for considerable

satisfaction. This outcome was not calculated to whet the ISTC's appetite for co-ordinated collective bargaining, when this was again canvassed by the secretary of the National Joint Committee (NJC) some months later. (The NJC was a new co-ordinating body for BSC unions.)

The ISTC and the wider movement

Evans brought to the chair of the TUC Steel Committee a less tense relationship with other unions than before. The February 1987 Executive decided that Officers could circulate Steel Committee minutes to their EC members and that Steel Committee business would be tabled as an agenda item at future EC meetings. The General Secretary was personally better disposed to co-operation with other unions in the industry, and during 1985, a trial period of multi-union joint consultation was introduced at Scunthorpe on a BSC initiative, and in 1987 the ADC reflected some relaxation when it urged greater inter-union co-operation and the establishment of consultative apparatus ahead of annual pay bargaining. In autumn 1985 Evans came joint top of the poll in the election of leaders from smaller unions to the TUC General Council, a significant achievement since it was the first time he had stood.

When Evans took up the reins the union's position in the steel industry had just been secured with the resolution of two outstanding problems; shortly afterwards the miners' strike, which had caused such anxiety, was resolved. Early in 1985, the NUB membership voted to merge with the ISTC on a solid 71.9 per cent 'yes' vote.[2] The February 1985 EC approved proposals for rule changes entailing the establishment of a Coke and Iron Section (CIS). Representation at the ADC would be on the same basis as for ISTC members together with the three Section District Chairmen, District Secretaries, and National Secretary. The District Chairmen were also appointed to membership of the EC for the rest of the current term (1983–5) and the next term (1985–8). The amalgamation came into effect on 15 April 1985, and from 22 April the NUB began to meet as the ISTC (Coke and Iron Section – CIS). The first Quarterly Meeting of the Sectional Executive was held on 14 May, and the next day, the new Executive members, led by the CIS National Secretary Nick Leadley[3] attended their first EC. One month later CIS delegates were welcomed to the Annual Delegate Conference with a huge ovation.

The new CIS brought in 4861 members, of whom 1306 were retired.[4] There were still some outstanding matters to resolve, notably whether or not it would continue the NUB practice of distributing 10 per cent of contributions in salaries among Lodge officials on the pattern of four-ninths each for the Delegate and the Secretary and one-ninth for the Chairman. CIS leaders were reluctant to sanction the transfer of remaining assets to the ISTC before a final audit and wanted reassurances about lay representation on the Steel Committee. The resolution of these and other matters occupied the rest of the year.

In 1986 integration of the two organisations proceeded extensively – as with the amalgamation of offices – but sometimes controversially, as over the composition of the unified organisation's Steel Committee representation. There was some discontent in South Wales over the non-replacement of John Perring, its district secretary,[5] and this was voiced at a Special Meeting of the Welsh District Committee and the CIS Executive. Finally, under continued pressure from the CIS, Central Office early in 1987 took legal advice about its action in leaving the post vacant; this proved supportive and the matter was allowed to rest.[6] Later in the year the General Secretary was authorised to begin discussions with Nick Leadley on his possible early retirement. He finally retired in August 1987 to be replaced by the CIS North Midlands district secretary Brian Fisher.[7]

Under Fisher, the marriage was to enter a more tranquil era. When in May 1988 the Executive came, as the Transfer of Engagements required it, to review the continuation of the Section, it responded positively, subject to an annual review. Evidence of closer integration came when CIS representatives attended the meetings of the CNCs for the first time that spring;[8] soon after the ISTC's Roger Stone became the first EC member to act on behalf of the CIS at a Neutral Committee. In May 1988 it was determined that the CIS would finally be wound up at the end of 1990, to coincide with the conclusion of the extended term of office[9] of the present Executive. Two years later, the Executive heard that Fisher himself wished to retire and concluded that, 'in accordance with the Transfer of Engagements document', he should not be replaced.[10] The final meeting of the CIS Executive Committee was held on Tuesday 20 November, and after this all former blastfurnace union members were in the ISTC alone.

The second long-standing problem was SIMA: two unsuccessful attempts to merge with the management outfit had absorbed huge amounts of time and energy, and after the second it had gained entry to the TUC by joining the staff section of the EEPTU. While SIMA certainly had much the larger management membership, ISTC MM members were fiercely loyal to their own union and insisted on their rights to representation: it was a situation which could only bring benefits to the employer. The TUC-led talks begun in 1982[11] had during three years explored management relationships at BSC. This now bore fruit in a future recruitment accord – the TUC Spheres of Influence Agreement – the gist of which was that the unions would move towards joint national negotiating arrangements and generally improve relationships. Meanwhile all locations and functions were specified in a schedule of spheres of influence, and above all, the right of a member to remain in the union of his choice was recognised.

The agreement did not end conflict forever: six years on at Scunthorpe Works, ISTC foremen (i.e. staff members) were being transferred to MM grades as operation managers. They did not wish to be switched to SIMA, but were confronted with this fate under the TUC Spheres of Influence Agreement. Not until May did local management seem to edge their way toward conceding local recognition to the ISTC, a concession which allowed the members to retain their membership in a middle management branch. The exceptions were ISTC middle managers with responsibilities for coke ovens; they were willing to transfer to SIMA and SIMA to take them, but the organisation felt confident that this breach could be staunched.[12]

The miners' strike had ended in March 1985. After this rail deliveries of coal to Ravenscraig from Hunterston were resumed, though the principal source – Polkemmet Colliery – had flooded during the dispute and some coal still came in by road as a result. In addition to direct donations the ISTC distributed some £450,000 on behalf of the IMF. This money had been raised from American and European unions and was distributed to NUM branches across the country. The Organisation itself had given the NUM £65,000 nationally and almost the same amount at local level. In addition it had mounted a considerable relief effort to obtain children's toys, food parcels and clothes. At the 1985 ADC Evans reflected on the painful dispute. The ISTC, he told delegates, had nothing to be ashamed of over its conduct. It had been the only union to offer and to make its own arrangements to limit production, and these cuts had been severe: almost by two-thirds in Scunthorpe, and almost one-third in Llanwern and Ravenscraig with smaller proportions elsewhere. If local deals with the NUM had stuck there would have been co-operation, but the national miners' leadership had wanted a complete stoppage.

Pleasure and pain in steel

In many respects Evans's industrial inheritance from Sirs could be described under the heading 'as you were'. Ravenscraig performed well in the first part of 1985, though there were worries about the future due to the continued delay of any investment announcements. The team defending the complex was weakened by the death of John McTaggart at the ADC that June.[13] The Gartcosh announcement of 6 August (see below) was to throw the future of the whole complex into doubt. By the late summer the whole of Scotland was again on alert to save the 'Craig'. Meanwhile, the stream of mill closures continued. The BSC intention to close Glengarnock has already been noted; early closure was negotiated and it shut at the end of March after a strenuous campaign which drew in support from Nos. 2 and 4 Divisions.

A grim year for Scotland concluded under a new shadow: substantial redundancy announcements at the Scottish Steel and Tube Works following a bad business year. Plans were made for the Steel Committee to visit the works.[14] Early in 1986 the workforce at Clydesdale, Imperial and Calder were confronted with the full impact of BSC's 'Survival Plan' which brought to them consequences far harsher than those experienced by threatened works elsewhere. Management proposed to implement these without an agreement and at once found themselves faced with a walk-out. The EC had solidly supported disputes in recent times, but was now in a straitjacket imposed by new government legislation, the Trade Union Act 1984, which prescribed statutorily determined pre-strike ballots. A holding resolution of the February Quarterly Meeting recognised that the dispute was outside the law and ordered an immediate ballot. This returned a fairly substantial majority but a rather narrow vote affirming the principal lines on which an agreement could be made, signed on 10 April 1986, took the workforce back four days later. They had been out for eight weeks and seemed to have obtained assurances that there would be no compulsory redundancies and that wage levels, for the most part, would be maintained.

These hopes proved short-lived. By August BSC had announced that 308 redundancies were to be sought through cutting manned capacity; a further sixty-two jobs were to be lost with the closure of Calder Works. What remained of the business relations between management and unions were poor, a decline BSC acknowledged when it agreed to a national level meeting on 3 October. On this occasion it for once acknowledged some responsibility, recognising that the absence of a Business Committee had allowed problems in the Survival Plan to accumulate.

In No. 2 Division the closure of Jarrow section mill evoked memories of the fight of an earlier generation, though Divisional Office launched a vigorous campaign of defiance with local authority and Central Office help. Hope flickered for a time when tripartite meetings (drawing in Caparo Industries, owners of the UMB as third party) were held, but negotiations to achieve severance terms opened on 20 May and the works finally closed on 5 August. Nearby the Hartlepool Plate Mill, idle for lack of orders to the Wide Pipe Mill since October 1984 was also shutting. On 8 February 1985 an early closure agreement was negotiated, and some cross-matching was achieved; another agreement was reached for the Ayrton Sheet works. Naturally enough there were fears for the 44" Pipe Mill itself, now to be sourced from Scunthorpe. In May the place was reported as having only one order; tempers were not improved when the EC learned that slabs to feed the Pipe Mill were being sent to Mannesman's 44" Plate Mill for rolling. Consett, Jarrow and Newfield all shared an announcement of 300 redundancies with the privatisation of BSC Refractories. More positively, however, output from the Lackenby BOS Plant rose still further, and the nearby Skinningrove 18" Mill put on another shift. The 20" Hartlepool Pipe Mill was operating at 100 per cent capacity utilisation. Quite the reverse too were the fortunes of those centrally employed nearby at the Redcar/Lackenby complex, fed by the giant furnace commissioned in 1979. 1985 marked the first year since 1980 when the number of people employed there did not fall and output was high.[15]

Parts of Light Products, a successful business in No. 3 Division, were converted into an independent profit centre within BSC Holdings as of 1 April and traded henceforth as Precision Strip. Other parts, such as Tinsley Bridge plc (the former Tinsley Park Spring Works) were fully privatised. At Scunthorpe production rose again, with record tonnages in excess of 80,000 tonnes coming out of the BOS Plant. Still higher production was envisaged for 1985–6 with the Redcar Blast Furnace nearing the end of its first campaign. Some indication of the diverse fortunes among the different product businesses may be derived from the way Sheffield Forgemasters was reduced from twenty to fifteen shifts at this time.[16] By the end of the year officials were confronted with an amazing BSC plan to convert Forgemasters into no less than seven separate businesses.

By November Roy Bishop had to report to the EC that Railway and Ring Rolled Products plc proposed to close No. 1 Tyre Mill along with all its associated areas and the mill rebuilt at Trafford Park. The management case was that the Rotherham cost base was too high, a claim they linked to the earnings of the Yorkshire workforce, allegedly higher than those in Manchester. Under extreme pressure, the members found themselves confronted by demands on terms and conditions of employment, pension schemes, a wages freeze, and modification of payment systems. Ickles 5 Branch put strong demands on the EC for a refusal to accept the transfer of orders or machinery to Trafford Park and their pressure resulted in a National Ad-hoc Meeting of 13 January 1986. This proved unavailing, however.[17]

No. 3 melting shop in Stocksbridge was also shut at the end of the year after a lengthy period on the GWA. The membership there had resisted, worried about the impact on No. 4 melting shop. There was extra disappointment when subsequent negotiations failed to achieve a level of severance pay commensurate with that obtained at Tinsley Park. On the positive side in No. 3

Division a landmark agreement was reached for the Stainless Plate development in Sheffield, and after protracted negotiations recognition was achieved at the new UMB works in Scunthorpe.

In the Midlands BSC's electrical steels activity at Cookley closed with the loss of sixty-seven jobs though the terne line continued in production. In South Wales orders were strong at the two big BSC plants. The giant Port Talbot works, with a capacity of 2.2 million tonnes annually, still employing 5570 people (800 of them indirectly), was well advanced in the switch from the slabbing route to continuous cast sourcing. The major refurbishment of the hot mill promised heavier coil weight for the near future, energy economies, and a product range which would embrace cross-sections. If output faltered at Llanwern it was only because of a partial reline at one of its blast furnaces. Elsewhere in Division 5, Orb Works had completed the integration of the Cookley plant equipment, while Whiteheads, the narrow strip producer once threatened with closure, had beaten off all threats and consolidated work once done at Ayrton, Landore and Godins.

However, redundancies were under discussion at ASW's Tremorfa and Castle works where pressures to achieve 'European' manning levels were every bit as intense in the public sector. The union pressed for those to be made redundant to receive ISERBS, a claim rebuffed by the management. To facilitate future negotiations the ISTC began to press for a national framework to encompass its bargaining with ASW. Still frustrated in August the EC resolved that if a new local approach was rebuffed it would take legal advice.[18] After a works visit of 15 October 1985, union leaders made an interim agreement covering pay since June of the previous year, but major changes were expected in November.

More positively, pressure from the union led to new bonus arrangements being installed to cope with the impact of developments which had raised expected throughput from its original 8500 tonnes a week to 20,200 tonnes a week. And a breakthrough was achieved with pensions on 6 June when enhancements were agreed for pensioners employed by GKN prior to 1974 as well as early payment of deferred pensions (themselves to be raised) where there was redundancy, and additional temporary pension to retirement age in the event of early retirement.

In the north-west, a new blow had fallen, this time on Monks Hall. BSC at the turn of the year announced a closure to make way for a new company in which it would take a 25 per cent stake; the order book would of course be transferred. But in a small works resistance was relatively easy to organise and an Action Committee sprang into being in support of the development of alternative plans centred on the No. 5 Mill. In its efforts the Committee had the declared backing of the Wolverhampton and Ductile Glynwed Joint Committees. Finally when all efforts proved unavailing severance terms were asked for and achieved. A closure agreement was signed on 5 August but normal severance terms were not offered by BSC in any kind of recognition of the way the workforce was safeguarding the order book for the new firm.[19]

Meanwhile, Brymbo's melting shop in the spring of 1985 was breaking all records for one-furnace operation, output which exposed bottlenecks further down the production process. Exports were up by 62 per cent in a year. Manchester Steel – also smashing production records – was at the centre of rumours linking it with Bidston in a merger with a third company, which many on the EC believed might be Allied Steel and Wire. While the May EC was meeting, the news was confirmed, tellingly with an announcement from ASW that it had acquired both plants and that all of Bidston and the Manchester Steels rod mill would shut. The official closing date turned out to be 24 August. This was quota stealing with a vengeance.[20] Bidston and the Manchester rod mill members received identical terms, but a meeting to press ASW management on outstanding issues such as ISERBS was held on 5 November 1985. Hopes that the Manchester melting shop would escape closure were dashed in November when all activity on the site was ended.[21] But all was not gloom in No. 7 Division, the jewel in whose crown was Shotton, which had led BSC Coatings into profit. By 1985 Shotton was diversifying its range for the motor industry and a new development – the Sceptre Line – had been commissioned. Fred Brooks reported to the Executive in August that 'records were being broken in every department'.

In No. 8 Division, taken over by Eddie Marsh[22] during this period, the only steelmaker was Sheerness, the arc-process producer with its own disembarkation facilities at Ridham Dock. In the recession of the early 1980s Sheerness had benefited from some of the lost business of other works, a development which had not increased the popularity of its membership with that elsewhere. But it was also in an economic bind due to the imposition of quotas and its operating in the depressed rebar market, dependent on fluctuations in the construction industry. By the late summer of 1986 Marsh was reporting that steelmaking was at reduced levels due to lost non-quota markets and the curtailing of major construction projects in the Middle East.[23] Spirits lifted at the end of the year with the announcement of a progressive capital investment programme to begin at once in the bar mill and melting shop.

Apart from stockists the rest of the Division consisted of non-ferrous works. Here the news was mixed. Output rose steadily at Delta Enfield (Cables) with the Brimsdown plant working at full capacity, but the opening weeks of 1987 brought a threat of a major strike over the annual staff salary review before a settlement was made on the eve of a ballot. The 1987 pay award was in fact imposed by the company, though it did give assurances about proper negotiations in the future. However, the platinum refinery of Johnson Matthey at Royston, built only three years earlier at a cost of £3m, shut in the summer of 1986 with the loss of eighty-six jobs, fifty-two of them ISTC, in a move intended to benefit a new plant being constructed by the company at Rustenberg, South Africa.

In steel the persistence of closures was only one side of the coin. The industry was being modernised. The 1986 ADC called for a review of future strategy at BSC; in fact the future was being shaped by corporate investment decisions. That year brought the reline of the Teesside blast furnace after a seven-year campaign, far longer than originally envisaged. The thirty-month refurbishment of Port Talbot's hot-strip mill was also completed, the show-piece of a renovation that embraced virtually every facility from the harbour to the finishing process at a cost of some £620m.[24] A new bloom caster was begun for Rotherham Engineering Steels at Aldwarke early in 1987. 1987 also saw Scunthorpe breaking records regularly, with liquid steel output reaching a record level of 100,000 tonnes one week in April. Nor was this kind of success confined to the integrated works: average weekly output from Shotton's cold mill likewise reached a record 17,000 tonnes in March. Down in Sheerness, summer 1987 brought record output both in the rod mill (17,350 tonnes) and in the bar mill (29,003 tonnes). Since 1986 the economy had been expanding and inflation – for the moment – was low: sadly so many fewer ISTC members were still employed to benefit from this upturn in fortunes.

The European background was increasingly influential on the fortunes of the British steel industry. As 1987 opened, a new threat to UK plants appeared in the form of an initiative from Eurofer (the producers' association for European Community Member States) for a phased reduction of 12.5 million tonnes in hot-rolled capacity. This, coming as it did from the producers, was at least preferable to an earlier scheme of Community Industry Commissioner Narjes for an immediate cut of 20 million tonnes. For this relative blessing, at least, it had the backing of the trade union section of the ECSC, of whose Consultative Committee Evans had become chairman the previous year.[25] Across the table, he shortly faced none other than BSC Chairman Bob Scholey, who had become Eurofer chairman. The view of British ministers was that Britain was in a relatively strong position since it had taken greater strides in the direction of viability, but nervousness persisted[26] and Evans was instructed by his Executive to pursue national-level meetings to communicate the union's concerns. In the event, however, it was to be national rather than international developments which brought the return of major closures to Britain.

Industrial relations in the private and public sectors

In 1986, the transfer of a Gartcosh member under cross-matching arrangements to the Llanwern Cold Mill raised the important issue of whether or not the two-year seniority rule under Clause 12 of the March 1969 National Agreement should be invoked. In fact Central Office had addressed this matter in a series of meetings leading up to a circular of 5 March 1981 to BSC branches. This had defined clause 12 as being intended to facilitate modernisation and not the massive closure programme of that era, and the EC upheld current arrangements in Llanwern accordingly.[27]

The following year, the Executive three times discussed disciplinary procedures, finally attempting to secure a formal agreement from BSC to plug the gap wherever they were absent in the HST structure. The most management would concede, however, was agreement on a procedure to be used 'where appropriate'. This was hopelessly inadequate, and in 1988 left the Organisation little alternative but to fall back on insistence that – locally at least – agreements must be honoured.

Scunthorpe – which always seemed to figure in BSC experiments on introducing greater management control – also witnessed attempts to introduce temporary labour on a significant scale. At the end of 1986 Roy Bishop reported to the EC his fears about the use of contractors by BSC outside guidelines jointly agreed between the two sides.[28] Management rapidly moved to an announcement that it intended to introduce contractors into a number of areas within the ISTC sphere of influence from 29 March 1987, and despite pressure at a national meeting of 13 January showed no willingness to relent. A Special EC the next day gave permission for a ballot to be held by the threatened branch (Scunthorpe Anchor No. 1). This branch was, however, faced with eighty-six redundancy notices and *in extremis* made an agreement in February. Even this degree of accommodation did not mollify a management which was determined to exercise entire control over the redundancy selection procedure.

This dispute had drawn the attention of all to a growing practice of introducing contractors where there had once been 'permanent' employees. The Abbey 9 Branch was confronted by just such a proposal at Port Talbot and was refusing to negotiate with management on the issue. A Research Department survey had found that there was a national trend and the leadership was instructed to meet BSC to insist that there be no incursions into those areas where the ISTC had recognition rights.

To strengthen the position of the threatened branches it was agreed in February 1987 that BSC intransigence should be met with a ballot of the membership they employed. In March the union met BSC in quest of an agreement which would define those areas where direct labour alone would be employed. This BSC declined to give. At first the EC considered issuing guidelines to the branches about the employment of contractors, but then reconsidered, opting instead for a declaration that it would back industrial action by branches whose members were faced with displacement at the hands of contractors. In fact the position of the union was less clear-cut than it seemed. At least one EC member had a significant number of contract workers in his branch, and there was an alternative approach: to organise this under-privileged group of workers. Such a course was implicitly urged on the union by a resolution of the 1987 ADC which called for the 'forming and execution of policies designed to protect and enhance the living standards of our members employed by . . . sub contractors'.

Every point of union influence registered the imprint of management aggression. Main Board Trade Union Directors' representation had collapsed earlier in the decade. Back in February 1985, at BSC's request, the union had met it to discuss the employee-director scheme; consultations were later held at divisional level. At the Steel Committee, the surviving employee-directors left union leaders in no doubt that they wished to carry on. Evans thought management remained committed to the scheme but were unlikely to rebuild it to its size before recent reductions. Worst fears were confirmed in April 1986 when the BSC Scottish Steel and Tubes director summarily dismissed John Allan from his post as employee director in the teeth of stiff union protests. A resolution of the 1986 ADC called, unsurprisingly, for review of the whole scheme. The following year, however, BSC indicated that they were prepared to persist with the scheme (though they redefined 'parishes' and numbers).[29] It died soon after privatisation.[30]

The separate elements in public sector pay negotiations were drawn together as the Collective Negotiating Committees (a move made easier by the convergence of conditions). Union leaders met BSC on 11 November 1985 against a background of papers proposing new bargaining structures. It became apparent that while the Corporation was prepared to bargain centrally over pay for 1986 it intended to exclude some of its Companies Act companies (freestanding enterprises of which it retained 100 per cent ownership). 1987, however, brought more radical change: a BSC paper reaffirmed that the aim of the Corporation was to achieve financial self-sufficiency and eventually profitability, and to this end Rail and Ring Rolled Products and

Stocksbridge Precision Strip would be excluded from the ambit of central negotiations.[31]

The 1986 public-sector pay round was settled on 2 April, when all elements of pay were raised by 5 per cent (a 2 per cent general increase and a 3 per cent lump sum bonus consolidation); pension contributions were cut by 1 per cent without loss of benefit;[32] the MEL rose to £94.50, qualifying conditions in the manual workers' holiday scheme were eased; and the 3 per cent headroom in local lump-sum bonus schemes was restored to take account of consolidation under the previous agreement. Meanwhile there had been a long-standing problem of pay anomalies affecting staff grades at BSC which rumbled through meetings in 1985 and 1986. These had caused the accumulation of disadvantages against manual grades and middle management. The pay grievance was pursued by the National Staff Negotiating Committee. Concurrently the Steel Committee was pursuing change in a number of conditions of staff employment, notably over job evaluation where a number of out-of-date schemes were extant. Job evaluation had of course been a source of considerable advances for the staff membership in the 1960s and 1970s, but the introduction of local lump-sum bonus schemes had altered the situation radically, while many top-graded staff had been redesignated as middle management. By the mid-1980s most staff regarded the basic scheme and its appeal structure as obsolete. Imprecision in the 1974 Agreement in respect of hours of shift-working staff had allowed disputes to arise about levels of shift allowance, but as late as February 1987 no progress had been made in persuading management of the need to improve it.

The 1987 BSC settlement was made on time and brought further real progress in pay, but what caught the eye was the provision for extra holidays after three and fifteen years, and the breakthrough in winning early retirement on a voluntary basis at sixty, on pretty generous terms. But LSB negotiations were becoming increasingly conditional. At Clydesdale, management attempted to make an agreement dependent on branch officials accepting contractors into the core workforce, and across the country negotiators were being faced with demands to accept routine medical examinations. The ISTC had been in the forefront of the fight to establish decent standards, but could management be trusted not to turn this into a new element of increased control? The call, turned down by the EC previously, was considered enough of a challenge to justify a Special EC in April 1987; but this reaffirmed the earlier stance. When a national agreement was finally made in June, it only covered certain grades.[33] By February 1988 it was already apparent that very few local agreements were being concluded, and even these were bedevilled by problems of interpretation.[34]

In the private sector ASW settled for 5 per cent retrospective to 1985, in stark contrast to Brymbo, now part of United Engineering Steels (UES – see below), where a six-month wage freeze was agreed in acknowledgement of the uncertainties ahead of it.[35] At the Midland Wages Board the Operatives' side still continued to meet on its own, and a portfolio of agreements was kept in place at every plant. Indeed in 1985 most works achieved annual pay awards matching inflation, though emphasis was shifting towards improved sick-pay schemes and holidays, with most works thought to be giving thirty days off annually. To celebrate the the Board's 110th anniversary its vice-chairman presented the EC with a commemorative plaque. The Operatives' one-sided arrangement could not continue indefinitely, however, and at a meeting on 18 July 1987 their representatives finally accepted that the Board's affairs be wound up. Their final meeting took place in West Bromwich on 5 March 1988. Seven years later No. 4 Divisional Officer Peter Lightfoot could truthfully reflect that the network of agreements still in place at many Midlands plants was inspired by the Midland Wages Board.

Employment relations were little better elsewhere in the private sector: Edgar Allen management unilaterally imposed a new wages structure effective from 11 November 1985. This news outraged the workforce and dismayed the EC, which authorised a ballot for industrial action in protest, and the threat provided the extra stimulus needed to achieve an informal solution. It became apparent in 1985 that no Sheffield Shift employers were willing to conduct an annual review. The response of the membership at Firth Brown was to make a local agreement, and other branches covered by Sheffield Shift determined to do likewise. Only in spring 1985 was a new procedural agreement made: the union then approached each employer with a view to concluding an agreement based on a new Sheffield Shift model agreement. But by February 1987 coverage had shrunk to only six companies with some 300 employees. Here was a rare instance where not the management but the union itself questioned whether continuance was worthwhile. These doubts were confirmed at Unbrako Sheffield which had withdrawn from the Sheffield Shift and concluded company agreements, including one for a new guaranteed week. This, however, was rapidly followed by an announcement that the company intended to introduce national Engineering Conditions[36] for its process workers, over which the ISTC could have no influence. Developments such as these could only heighten a sense of insecurity and lead to stronger attachment to the existing framework of agreements.

Political success

Early in 1984, the legal services had briefed the Executive on proposals in the Green Paper on Trade Unions, later the Trade Union Act 1984. The statute required unions to ballot every ten years to review the existence of their political funds: it was a fundamental attack on the right of unions to be in politics, which the ISTC was determined to repel. That year's ADC passed a Central Office-drafted framework resolution in favour of 'independent representation of working people in Parliament'. In August the EC resolved on an early ballot after the legislative requirement went live in March 1985. Following soundings among the full-time officers an eight-strong supervisory EC sub-committee was established in November, and its report was endorsed after a probing discussion at the February 1985 Executive.

The theme of the union's campaign was that unions were entitled to a voice in parliament. This argument was eventually to be mounted by all unions, but the ISTC case was especially significant for two reasons. The Steel Smelters had been the first union to vote expenses to fund an MP's activity back in 1899, and significantly had insisted that John Hodge (their General Secretary and candidate) should stand not as a Liberal but as an independent trade union candidate – the very philosophy which shortly was to lead to the formation of the Labour Representation Committee. To the significance of history was added urgency from the present: the ISTC and the printworkers' union SOGAT were clearly going to be the first two unions to ballot their members under this vindictive new legislation.

The ISTC devised an elaborate campaign built around the responsibility of individual volunteer political organisers to deliver the vote. The full-time officers briefed them, and they in turn were armed with the arguments to convince those they worked with. There was provision for postal and workplace balloting, with the latter taking place from 7 to 16 May. The ballot count, triumphantly reported on 22 May 1985, recorded 28,633 'yes' votes, 4404 'no' votes and 93 rejected. It was a spectacular result in only the second such ballot ever held: the 'yes' vote at SOGAT, declared two weeks earlier, was only half this size. From this point on, fears that unions would be driven out of politics began to diminish.

With a recovery taking place in the political fund, all payments in existence prior to February 1982 were reinstated as from the start of 1986. A motion from the 1985 ADC called for contributions to be raised to a realistic level by an increase greater than that in general contributions. The Political Levy was finally raised in January 1987 by 1p, though this was done simultaneously with a contributions hike. An act of great generosity by the Executive at this time was to donate the shares the ISTC had acquired in Labour's Property Development Fund to the Party: they were worth £33,501.[37] On the eve of the 1987 election, the ISTC donated £25,000 to Trade Unions for a Labour Victory (TULV). The 1986 ADC proposed development of the campaigning work on behalf of the Party, suggesting more localised campaigning, political meetings in factories, and affiliating to CLPs where possible.

With battles over policy and its constitution raging throughout the decade, the 1980s were not a happy time for Labour, despite the result of the political fund ballots. For most of the decade the ISTC too, despite its traditions was – at least formally – unilateralist.[38] The 1986 ADC voted for the repeal of anti-union legislation and called for the re-nationalisation of privatised industries. On internal matters, conference voted in 1985 for one-member, one-vote to be the principle underlying parliamentary selections, and the following year for its delegates to back moves to expel Militant Tendency members from the Party. When the Party established its National Constitutional Committee (NCC) in 1986 to process disciplinary procedures, Keith Brookman was one of five trade unionists elected; it was his first national political contest.

From 1983 Donald Coleman single-handedly represented the ISTC in parliament until he was joined after merger with the NUB, by that organisation's sponsored member, the Redcar MP Jim Tinn. Their partnership lasted for two years, until Tinn's retirement on the eve of the 1987 election. The previous year National Staff Officer Sandy Feather and Research Officer Martin Upham were adopted as PPCs in the constituencies of Corby and Enfield North, the former still with substantial steel membership, the latter the only concentration of the ISTC in London. But the general election gave the Conservatives a comfortable margin of 147 seats over Labour and neither man was elected.

The Parliamentary Panel was reduced to six in August 1988. Donald Coleman meanwhile continued to represent Neath, and the ISTC marked his twenty-five years as its sponsored MP in 1989. The only ISTC member who bid to join him during this parliament was Sandy Feather, who was again adopted at Corby with ISTC backing. This was relatively thin representation, and the EC accepted a 1989 ADC motion which proposed rules revisions which would allow maximum affiliation to Labour Parties and Trades Councils in order to obtain 'a stronger voice in Parliament'. But there were other political causes too, and now for the first time the ISTC made donations to Euro-constituencies in which it had an interest ahead of the 1989 European elections. That year the union also collaborated in an intensive

207

Party recruitment campaign: by November it could identify that 332 members had joined up with Labour.

Labour policy, of course, was changing. In 1989 a series of papers, 'Meet the Challenge, Make the Change', presented the union with a series of policy shifts. There was an extensive discussion at the August 1989 EC, with anxieties expressed over the Party's new views on nuclear disarmament and water privatisation. The ISTC itself took a new departure by deciding to conduct a ballot of the ADC delegates to determine their views.[39] Like the Party it was confronted by developments which were distasteful but which it seemed powerless to prevent, and like the Party it drew the same painful conclusions.

Privatisation

United Merchant Bar plc (UMB) – a BSC/Caparo Industries partnership – was formally launched on 15 January 1985 but it took the whole of that year to formalise union recognition. Even after this had been achieved (on 5 December) the ISTC was not free of the interference of other unions and there were difficulties over recruitment. The ISTC agreement was for single membership, a provision which upset some former members of the AUEW and EEPTU, especially since pay rates were so low. There was sufficient concern to seek a national meeting with the AUEW, one of the predators.

The June 1985 ADC again passed a motion calling for an all-embracing campaign against privatisation. More concretely, another motion called for an agreement to be made with the Corporation to sustain agreements following transfers out of the public sector. Pensions seemed everywhere at risk, to the detriment not only of those still in employment but to pensioners as well.[40] At Cold Drawn Tubes, established in 1985, members were hustled into the Tube Investments Scheme, a switch which entailed a considerable loss of benefits. At Fox Wire plc, the Stocksbridge-based Light Products business, staff were informed that the BSC procedure was no longer considered appropriate. A new agreement was reached in April 1986 on a local basis and the EC felt powerless to resist.[41]

The most dramatic privatisation of all now burst upon the ISTC. In the winter of 1984–5 the prospects for Phoenix II had faded sufficiently for the Committee not to meet, but by February there was considerable pressure to reconvene the Committee on a more formal basis of having the No. 3 Divisional Officer as secretary and No. 7 Divisional Officer as chairman. For the first time, other unions participated.

The first challenge was soon upon them with the announcement by BSC on 27 March of possible closure of the Tinsley Park Works itself. This predated the formation of the new firm and threatened 800 jobs. The workforce, drawing on the union's experience of so many closures, immediately organised an Action Committee, assisted by an Ad Hoc Multi-union Special Steels Committee which met once a week. In accordance with EC policy an instruction was issued not to transfer orders nor to increase shifts to facilitate the closure: this applied to Aldwarke, Templeborough and Stocksbridge. To make this concrete a full list of customers, sizes, qualities and tonnages of the Works' order book was circulated to all No. 3 Division branches. It was soon discovered that other intended destinations were BSC Clydesdale and GKN Brymbo; information was passed to Central Office to allow those works to be drawn into the instruction. This industrial stance was reinforced with political action. Labour's Industry spokesman John Smith had recently visited the plant: he and members of the Commons Trade and Industry Select Committee received copies of the alternative plan for the works drawn up by the ISTC and other unions. The plan reiterated the ISTC's charge: that BSC was once again aiming at the bottom of the market, closing a plant whose performance was rapidly improving, that it was assuming the plant's orders could be switched to other works in command fashion, and that extraneous factors such as scrap and energy costs were being ignored.

The May EC extended the instruction to Clydesdale, which had been outside the 1983 decisions. It committed the Research Department to assistance, and also issued a statement of national policy following adverse press coverage.[42] The Steel Committee met the Action Committee on 24 May, and from then on assumed control over negotiations. On 21 June, however, BSC refused to rescind the Tinsley Park closure notice pending a government reappraisal of the Corporate Plan the following month. Six days later an outraged Executive reaffirmed its non-transfer policy, began to explore the possibility of an injunction, decided to prepare for ballots throughout Special Steels and Scunthorpe, and to seek an urgent meeting of the Steel Committee and the minister responsible. The ADC, then meeting in Jersey, passed an emergency motion calling on the EC and the Steel Committee 'to formulate and authorise' a programme of industrial action in support of the Tinsley Park workforce. ISTC, said Tinsley Park delegate Geoff Stronach, should stand for 'I Stand Totally Committed' (to keeping the place open). All Division 3 branches adhered to the instruction; the toughest pressure on many Tinsley Park employees, however, was to fill in 'cross-match' forms before any closure had been agreed.

But eventually the resistance at Tinsley Park crumbled. BSC's corporate announcement of 7 August (see below) included affirmation of government support for the new 'phoenix' company that was supposed to get the benefit of the closure. In August the Executive was presented with a *fait accompli*.

Redundancies were staggered through the Autumn and the final end to melting and rolling occurred in November. The Phoenix II committee was kept in being with a new remit as a negotiating body. The non-transfer policy was kept in place.[43] In November it was learned that Brinsworth Strip Mill was to be established as a separate profit centre outside the project.

With the plant configuration thus altered, United Engineering Steels (UES) was launched on 1 April 1986, uniting the BSC special steels plants at Rotherham and Stocksbridge (plus the Tinsley Park bar mill), Brymbo and GKN's forging activities. These units were intended to be autonomous and to compete on quality and service, though not on price. Union worries about the structure centred on how GKN, with 42 per cent of the equity to BSC's 58 per cent could have equal voting rights and a majority of board directors. Attention soon turned to negotiating structures, and it was encouraging that management were prepared to meet the union to discuss these matters before vesting date. As a holding position the EC adopted a plan devised by Divisional Office containing a proposed consultative committee. Meanwhile BSC branches affected by the announcement received EC backing for their demand to be included at least in the 1986 BSC pay negotiations, due for the same date. Balked of success for its proposals the Phoenix II Committee approached other unions for support.

The pill was not sweetened by an announcement of 650 redundancies at Rotherham Works to be achieved by the end of March. In November it was learned that the 14" Mill at Wolverhampton would follow by July 1987. In February 1987 the axe fell on Stocksbridge Engineering Steels with the announcement that management were to seek 600 redundancies. This target was part of an intended job reduction across the firm, with 400 to be lost in the Midlands and a further 600 to go at Rotherham Engineering Steels. Just as expected, UES management gave notification of their intention to terminate six agreements on Employment and Income Security, though they were prepared to negotiate a new agreement. A procedural agreement was ready for signature by November 1986 but a new Agreement on the Improvement and Harmonisation of Conditions of Employment proved more intractable.

Meanwhile Brymbo Works had survived the launch of UES, but the risks inherent in its location at a distance of 150 miles from the new venture's heart in South Yorkshire had escaped no one. A Campaign Committee to retain the works had been set up in 1986, and had held meetings with MPs, the local authorities and balloted the workforce on their views. The issuing of ninety-six redundancy notices in January 1987 suggested that fears for the future were well-founded. The melting shop, so recently breaking records, had reported a reduction in capacity to the ECSC; ironically, though there had been reduced shifts in all departments, overtime working had been required to ensure that orders were met.

In January 1987, UES began to flex its muscles with the acquisition of Midland arc steelmaker F.H. Lloyd. The Midlands had already witnessed a very broad rationalisation under the umbrella of Glynwed, which by 1989 owned the Stourbridge Rolling Mills, Firth Cleveland Steel Strip, J.B. & S. Lees, Ductile Cold and Hot Mills, William Wesson, Dudley Port Rolling Mills, George Gadd and Monmore Tubes – all with ISTC representation. In 1988 BSC bought out Tube Investments' stake of 24.5 per cent in Seamless Tubes Ltd and the same company's 75 per cent share in Cold Drawn Tubes Ltd. Both these Corby companies stayed in the private sector as wholly-owned BSC subsidiaries. Early in 1989, British Steel (by now itself a private company) and GKN transferred their British Bright Bar holdings to UES. Later in the year an agreement with BS allowed Johnson & Firth Brown to obtain 100 per cent ownership of Ring Rolled Products Ltd. Yet while shedding businesses it considered peripheral, BS was strengthening its position in the market interface. The 1989 acquisition of C. Walker & Sons Holdings for £330m brought the UK's biggest stockist (and its largest single customer) under its control; though operated at arm's length with British Steel Distribution, the BS stockholder division, the Walker Group did bring in 3400 employees and recruitment opportunities. Early in 1990, British Rolling Mills of Tipton were acquired by Firsteel, part of the Lonrho Group.

Meanwhile in the non-ferrous sector, Delta Enfield Cables and Crompton Parkinson merged their electrical cable interests in a new firm Delta Crompton Cables. High hopes that the new company would expedite the resolution of long-standing relationship problems were speedily dashed when large-scale redundancies were announced at its main Brimsdown location together with the total closure of the Charlton site. The membership opted for a severance package, and No. 8 Divisional Officer Ian Scobbie[44] expected cross-matching to reduce some of the pain. Each lost job which arose from these developments was an individual and personal tragedy, but before many of them came to pass there had occurred a catastrophe on a national, Scottish, scale.

The new Corporate Plan

On 7 August 1985 the new BSC Corporate Plan had been launched by Chairman Sir Robert Haslam who had taken over from MacGregor in 1983. It was predicated on five integrated plants being in action for the next three years, albeit subject to product performance and demand; the withdrawal of Alphasteel from production as of January 1986,[45] its business acquired by

BSC and its concasters transferred to Llanwern; closure of Gartcosh (where downstream treatment of Ravenscraig's strip output took place); no new investment in coke ovens – a real blow for Ravenscraig; refurbishment of the Port Talbot hot mill with a second re-heating furnace installed; and government financial support for the establishment of the Phoenix II business. Few were taken in: a paper commitment to retaining the Ravenscraig complex was invalid if it was not to be given the chance to remain competitive, and that meant capital spending: the coke ovens in particular urgently needed attention. New investment in the South Wales plants could only be welcome, but AGS Keith Brookman expressed the whole membership's opinion of the Scottish dimension of the Plan when he declared 'there can be no room in anyone's heart at this moment to express any feelings other than disgust, anger and betrayal'.

The seriousness of this announcement provoked a Steel Committee meeting on 19 August. Closure of the Gartcosh mill must inevitably bring forward the threat to Ravenscraig,[46] especially since there was a moratorium on coke-oven improvement. Scottish full-time officers foresaw the demise of Ravenscraig within three years. Evans committed himself to attend a conference at the main works on 29 August, and to see the managing director of the Strip Mills Division on 12 September. The STUC and Wales TUC co-ordinated their opposition to the closures at a meeting on 14 August, and urgent attempts to convene meetings with the Parliamentary Labour Party, BSC, and the European Industry Commissioner were mounted.

Meeting one day ahead of schedule on 20 August the Executive prioritised the Gartcosh announcement as its biggest headache, giving the General Secretary plenary powers, to spend money, to issue instructions not to accommodate order transfers or extra shifts which would undermine the works, and to involve the Ravenscraig membership in any ballots of Gartcosh. An emergency resolution was tabled for the TUC and moved there by Keith Brookman. All party conferences were lobbied, and extensive propaganda was put out in the ISTC's own media. The same Executive meeting directed local discussions to take place over Alpha Steel where the membership called for a campaign to resist cannibalisation of the plant.[47]

By November the Organisation had pressed the Gartcosh case on ministers, the PLP Steel Group, senior executives of BSC and the Commons Committee for Scottish Affairs. The Committee published a very supportive report near the end of the year, stimulating the EC to consider national newspaper publicity, new approaches to MPs and a Steel Conference to focus the resistance. On the initiative of Strathclyde Regional Council, the Committee for the Retention of the Scottish Steel Industry was formed, uniting all the political parties and churches, the STUC, Chambers of Commerce and the Scottish Council. This Committee organised a march from Motherwell to London which attracted a lot of favourable media coverage.[48] More welcome news came with the backing of the Scottish Home Affairs Committee.

Labour tested out the chances of a Tory revolt in parliament, but in a fateful Commons vote of 23 January 1986 on an Opposition motion to retain Gartcosh until the next BSC Corporate Review, the government triumphed by sixty-one. This seemed to remove a last hope from Gartcosh which came to terms shortly afterwards. Following the agreement of terms a high percentage of the workforce opted for cross-matching, a reflection of their dismay at the persistently high unemployment which afflicted Lanarkshire and their attachment to the steel industry.

Within the union

Personnel changes abounded when the new General Secretary entered office. Fred Brooks, Divisional Officer No. 7 Division, was due to retire, and there was a feeling that he should not be replaced 'in view of the uncertainties surrounding the membership in that division'. This view was not shared by Executive members Neville Lea and Eric Caudwell. Thwarted in May, they returned to the attack during the summer and Ron Wilson[49] returned to replace Brooks as Divisional Officer on his retirement in March 1986. Senior Organiser Keith Jones left at this time and was not replaced, and arrangements were made to cover the Division from No. 4 Office during Wilson's absence. In No. 2 Division Peter Woods retired early in June 1986, to be succeeded by Tom Davey,[50] who himself took early retirement in March 1988 when he was replaced by No. 3 Divisional Officer Roy Bishop. Bishop's place went to the newly-promoted Dick Knox.[51] Divisional Officer status was also extended to Ian Scobbie, who for some years had been stationed at Swinton House, heading the General Secretary's department. On the retirement of Eddie Marsh in January 1988, Scobbie replaced him, transferring his duties at Central Office to Sandy Feather. During Marsh's term of office the London Area was upgraded to Division No. 8.

The Finance Committee on 19 December 1984 had recommended the expenditure of an additional £15,000 on 'further improving' the computer system. By the end of the year Swinton House was in a position to envisage membership cards being produced by computer. Out in the field the Young Workers Scheme (YWS) was in operation. The ISTC adjusted to this by offering membership at £1 in the first year and £2 in the second to YWS trainees. Full contributions were finally raised in January 1987 by 10p a week, the first increase for three years.

The membership also directly experienced changes. May 1985 brought a new procedure for awarding Confederation shields. It was agreed that members who completed forty years' membership would receive a silver badge, 'suitably designed'. EC members who had served a term and been re-elected would receive a shield, as would those who had been 'specially active and rendered meritorious service', if recommended by their branch. The minimum requirement was fifteen active years as an official and twenty years' membership. Ten cumulative years as a principal branch or joint committee officer would cause the shield to be inscribed 'branch officer'. No one would be entitled to two shields but re-elected EC members might have an extra inscription.

Things were less happy with the education programme, interest in which had outstripped the means to fund it. The August 1986 Education Sub-committee noted with concern that the Education Fund had fallen by more than half between January 1984 and June 1986 and enjoined strict economies. The programme was nevertheless expanding: the 1986 ADC had called for a specialist Health and Safety course and National Officer Ken Clarke was actively discussing its introduction with the TUC and other advisors.

Naturally the need for an emphasis on the maintenance of safe working never diminished. On the whole the industry tended to become slowly safer all the time. But progress was not even, and two years illustrated how bad things could get: 1982 saw one division alone suffering eight fatalities in just nine months, with an overall rise both in fatal and non-fatal accidents; 1984 also brought death at work to no less than eight ISTC members and a rising trend of non-fatal accidents. This was alarming, but the ISTC's own figures also reflected increased activism in taking up compensation cases, notably for industrial deafness, for which the numbers eligible had increased sharply. Having scored some success in extension of the ambit of deafness compensation, the ISTC sought to prevent the membership being disadvantaged in another area – that of respiratory diseases. In 1985 Clarke urgently collected evidence of the incidence of emphysema and chronic bronchitis, fearing that they were about to be prescribed industrial diseases (bringing entitlement to compensation) in trades other than steel. There had been success outside the steel trades when in February 1981, Platinum Asthma joined the list of recognised industrial diseases, a triumph for the combined efforts of management, Central Office and the local branches of Johnson Matthey, which had campaigned tirelessly.

In 1989 BS management returned to an earlier idea – safety incentive schemes – which it wanted to introduce in pilot form in Skinningrove. But though it had changed, the ISTC had not, and reiterated its view of 1986 that such schemes were not welcome. Yet BSC, laggard as it could be, did at least communicate regularly with the union, even if the news was not always welcome. Few other employers felt under compulsion to do so, as Clarke lamented in his report to the Executive of August 1989. The ISTC tried to remain pro-active. The (tripartite) Sheffield Occupational Health Project had long been union-supported, and received grants of £1500 in 1989 and 1990. Yet this too was a casualty of the deteriorating industrial relations climate: when BS gained no satisfaction from a tripartite meeting on a respiratory diseases study it processed an application for European funding for such a study unilaterally. The ISTC gave a final grant of £1000 but coupled it with a warning to the project that it could not continue to bear the burden of funding alone.

Internally important behavioural shifts were taking place. To forestall the impact of the Trade Union Act 1984 the Executive had advanced the 1985 EC elections to the last two weeks of August. This cautious step was part of a new concern for the proprieties. Evans was anxious to define what he felt was a proper understanding of the relationship between the Executive and full-time officers. From the outset he insisted that the President of the Executive Council was just that, and not President of the ISTC as he was sometimes termed. But this approach was even-handed, and he drew the attention of the Organisation and Staffing Sub-committee to the increasing practice of National and Divisional Officers intervening in Executive discussions and making recommendations. He secured the Committee's agreement to pointing out to Officers that their presence at Executive meetings was to give reports and factual information. Recommendations or advice to Executive members should be channeled via the General Secretary.

Change loomed additionally in the Central Negotiating Committees, stimulated by falling membership, a factor which argued for reduced numbers of delegates, and by spiralling decentralisation at BSC which posed a threat to co-ordinated bargaining itself. To a certain extent this was disguised when the negotiating committees began to be drawn together. In 1987 the ADC passed a resolution, which the Executive accepted, that conference representation be raised from three per thousand to four.

The approach of privatisation at BSC

Even before the 1983 general election, Industry Minister Norman Lamont had declared steel's future to lie in the private sector, 'economic rubbish' according to former General Secretary Bill Sirs. The 1984 ADC was one of many which had reaffirmed the Organisation's traditional oppositionist stance, but there was little immediate prospect of the core industry being sold

off. By contrast in 1987 the Steel Committee had become sufficiently concerned to meet Industry Minister Giles Shaw in the hope of discovering government intentions towards BSC. It had good reason to worry: the
bloodletting of a decade was finally paying off in financial terms and the Corporation returned net profits in 1985–6 for the first time in eleven years. With
its mandate refreshed by another huge electoral victory in June 1987 the Conservative government rapidly moved towards the mainstream privatisation,
uninhibited by the absence of any commitment in its manifesto. On 20 October the Steel Committee met Scholey and his Finance Director, and later Ian
Blakey, BISPA General Secretary, who offered his paper 'A Private Sector
View of the Future' to the Executive the following month. It also considered a
draft from Ricky Clayton, Head of Research, entitled 'A Policy for the 1990s'.

The half-year results of BSC, announced on 3 December, suggested that
its profitability would grow. £190m after all charges was a sharp contrast to
the £60m earned in the corresponding period of the previous year. To little
surprise they were accompanied by announcement of the government's
intention to privatise the Corporation. Evans told the Executive in December
that there had finally been no agreement on the European Commission's proposals to reduce steel capacity. It was likely therefore that the quota regime for
hot-rolled strip would end six months hence, though for plate and sections
the outlook was less certain: British Steel would soon be in a free market for
the first time in recent memory. Scholey had intimated to Evans that he
foresaw no major configuration changes when BSC's present strategy
expired in August 1988, a heartening assurance which was taken to mean that
the Corporation continued to be committed to steelmaking and concasting at
the five integrated plants, though with a much more attenuated pledge in
terms of mills.[52]

But the sky was coloured by the prospect of much greater influence of
market forces. The ISTC membership would soon be at work for a privatised
steelmaker which itself would be producing in a Europe where there would
be a free internal market for the first time in a decade. The Organisation was
committed to public ownership but felt it had to safeguard its members'
employment interests in an adverse political climate. Evans was commissioned to clarify government intentions with ministers, to keep a high profile
on the ownership and European issues, and to draw up a policy document
which would reflect the Executive view and which could define the ISTC's
stance to the Steel Committee.

In response to these instructions, the statement *British Steel and Privatisation* was issued, but things were moving fast.[53] The government rapidly
produced the British Steel Bill intended to set up the Corporation

as a company with equity which could be bought on the capital markets, and it received its First Reading in December 1987. Central Office officials met Industry spokesman Austin Mitchell who, under the leadership of Bryan Gould, had been deputised to handle the resistance to the Bill. Correspondence received from Labour figures was broadly supportive, and the 'Original Seven' of the Steel Committee had met the Parliamentary Steel Group. During Standing Committee a researcher was loaned to the Labour Party full-time to fight the Bill. Evans was prepared to go this far, but he made no secret of his belief that the Organisation simply did not have the resources to match the propaganda effort of BSC and the government. He also came to believe, however, that this assistance had led the government to protect the future company from foreign ownership by means of a 'golden share'.

It had been hoped to co-ordinate all meetings on privatisation through the Steel Committee, but the ISTC was inevitably the centre of all resistance because of its unique industrial position, so a group from the Executive met Robert Atkins, the Junior Industry Minister in March 1988. The Executive's objectives were being clarified. If privatisation could not be stopped then the bottom line would be drawn elsewhere. The ISTC was at least determined to safeguard its agreements and if possible to gain a new one for local dispute resolution. It also hoped to prevent the dismemberment of the Corporation. This disclosed a disagreement between Central Office and No. 1 Division, where saving Ravenscraig was quite naturally uppermost in all minds. The STUC had commissioned the firm of Arthur Young to produce a feasibility study of a Scottish business which then might be saved, an objective which did not fit within the overall view: in May the EC reaffirmed its objective of maintaining BSC as a single entity. In June 1988 the ADC seemed to signal a change of direction when it called for a campaign of anti-privatisation information to counter that of the government, but by then the die was cast.

The British Steel Bill had reached the Statute Book in May and so the question of having an attitude to its shares now arose anew. The Executive preferred not to negotiate a collective share deal for the membership, though Evans commended his personal view to the ADC in June: 'if the shares are on offer, then you should take them'. But the main focus was the highly practical anxiety about the future for pensions, harmonisation and the manual sick-pay scheme. At the TUC that September Roy Evans gained unanimous backing for a motion noting the proposal to privatise 'with concern' and calling on the government to maintain the degree of control necessary to influence its economic, strategic and social performance. But the juggernaut of privatisation rumbled on, crushing the views of unions in its path. In October an advertising campaign to push the shares to the public was launched and dealing opened on 5 December 1988. British Steel plc – henceforth BS – was now a private company.[54]

Notes

1 Roy Evans (1932–) joined BISAKTA in 1951 and was employed at Trostre Works. As an Organiser in No. 7 Division from 1964, Evans had come to wider notice with his occasional contributions to *Man and Metal*. He transferred to No. 6 Division in 1969 and was appointed Assistant General Secretary in 1973. As AGS he had served on the ISITB, been operatives secretary of the Joint Industrial Council of the Slag Industry, and chairman of JAPAC. In 1986, Evans was elected President of the Industrial Orthopaedic Society, parent organisation of the Manor House hospital scheme.

2 Of the 3858 votes cast, 2774 were for the merger and 1084 against.

3 Nick Leadley (1924–97) was District Secretary of the NUB Northern area and last general secretary of the blastfurnacemen's union.

4 Figures relate to the end of 1984 (*Reports*, 1985).

5 Perring had left office abruptly under controversial circumstances, *Reports* (1986), 123.

6 *Reports* (1987), 14.

7 Brian Fisher (1930–) was District Secretary of the NUB South Midlands Mines District from 1971 and later stationed in the NUB Scunthorpe office.

8 Each District was represented by its Chairman, with the Staff member from Scunthorpe representing staff.

9 Due to the impact of legislation; see below.

10 *Reports* (1990), 82.

11 See previous chapter.

12 See *Staff Officer's report* (1991), 88.

13 The popular McTaggart, Secretary of Ravenscraig No. 1 Branch, died on the Wednesday night of Conference. Thursday morning's session was cancelled as a mark of respect and on the resumption Roy Evans's proposal that future ADCs would be called to order with a bell named in his honour was carried with roars of approval.

14 The temper of the Clydesdale membership had not been improved by being put on the GWA when imported materials were brought into the plant to offset losses. The Corporation rebuffed a claim for compensatory payments. This matter was the subject of a National Joint Ad Hoc Committee of 12 November 1985.

15 Though it was about to drop with the reline of the blast furnace in 1986, see below.

16 A serious dispute broke out at Forgemasters in Autumn 1985. Failure to agree over the annual review and termination of the position of the day convenor and of the GWA opened up hostilities on a broad front. After a ballot the workforce downed tools on 16 October and stayed out for a month with official backing. A joint approach by the leaders of all unions involved was made to management in November, and the EC endorsed the terms of a further initiative canvassed by

Evans at the Quarterly Meeting. This initiative did not find favour with the membership who continued in dispute with a highly belligerent management and a return to work did not take place until the new tear. Developments were then overtaken when the resolution of GWA problems at River Don was neutralised by a dispute on the Atlas site which led pickets there to turn up on the gates. The dispute was only finally resolved in the early summer.

17 The Tyre Mill and most associated activities at Ickles finally closed on 26 September 1986 with the loss of 120 jobs. In an ironic development, management subsequently obtained an entirely new mill at a lower price. Much of Trafford Park itself closed in autumn 1986: of the consequent 146 redundancies, 91 were ISTC members. What remained transferred to the employment of Wheelset Manufacturers Ltd in March of the following year.

18 At the Scunthorpe rod mill of ASW, the EC gave support to the wish of the members to hold a ballot authorising industrial action. This did not materialise and a settlement was made on 18 November.

19 *Reports* (1985), 140.

20 The output of most steel products was at this time controlled by a Community-wide quota system.

21 In 1986 the Bidston workforce opted to seek its own legal advice in pursuing ISERBS benefits and, unusually, received retrospective support from the EC.

22 Eddie Marsh (1925–) was employed at the Anchor Works in the 1950s and appointed Divisional Organiser, No. 2 Division in 1975, moving shortly afterwards to No. 1 Division. In 1983 he was appointed Senior Organiser, London Area and made Divisional Officer when the No. 8 division was created. The appointment of the Yorkshire-born Marsh marked a new departure for London since he brought in steel expertise: previous appointments – Dismore, Bambury, Smith, had all been made from the ranks of the non-ferrous membership.

23 In the autumn the twin-strand concast plant produced a concast slab equivalent to five miles long, during one 100-ladle sequence.

24 Markets for steel products not specified by the Treaty of Paris, which established the ECSC, were not subject to quota restrictions.

25 Evans was the fourth British president and the second (after Sir Dai Davies) from the ISTC. Evans was not deflected from attending meetings by the withdrawal of the NUM and NACODS following the appointment of the (non-TUC affiliated) UDM general secretary to the Committee.

26 Not surprisingly: in March 1987 Eurofer gave the job of identifying redundant capacity to consultants.

27 *Reports* (1986), 158.

28 One instance he gave was of a contractor who gave his staff no holidays and worked them on 12-hour shifts.

29 Subsequent Steel Committee discussions governed allocation of places between the unions.

30 The BS plc intention to phase out the employee-director scheme was notified in 1989. It was done, as planned, 'on an appropriate timescale' by senior management at each relevant works.

31 The unacceptability of this was signalled to BSC, but it proved intransigent; in February the EC's response was to seek the value of the pay offer to be made at the two excluded businesses. As late as February 1988 the ISTC was pressing for Stocksbridge Precision Strip – now part of BSC Stainless – to be returned to HST negotiations. Only in April, as a by-product of the annual BSC negotiations, did management yield any ground, and even this was only a pledge to review the matter at the end of the year. When the review occurred it was half-way through a two-year pay deal at what was now British Steel plc: management shattered everyone's hopes by insisting that the plant's parlous financial situation meant any settlement had to be self-financing. In November 1989 some kind of settlement was reached, with manual grades returned to heavy steel conditions, but staff and middle management still excluded.

32 This was a considerable lift for the employers whose contributions fell by 2 per cent.

33 The Steel Committee unions adhered to a similar agreement two months later.

34 Especially over Clause 5 (*Reports*, 1988, 7). After a meeting of 3 May the Corporation relaxed the provisions at Scunthorpe and Stainless.

35 One incentive for the workforce to agree to this proposal was as a possible encouragement of investment. In fact output roared ahead until the early Summer, melting shop and mill records were broken, and the works had commissioned the world's first DC ladle furnace in March 1986.

36 As negotiated by the Confederation of Shipbuilding Engineering Unions (CSEU) and the Engineering Employers' Federation, EEF.

37 The shares had been bought originally to allow Labour to buy its own headquarters: 150 Walworth Road (later John Smith House) was acquired by it in 1985.

38 By making defence a policy-making sector for the ADC, the EC had for the time being surrendered any possibility of reversing this.

39 They supported the NEC position, but much more narrowly over water privatisation (34:28) than over nuclear disarmament (46:12).

40 The exception was UES where the new company introduced a new scheme which effectively moved all former BSC employees onto GKN terms. They were, however, offered the opportunity to improve their benefits with a 1 per cent extra on contributions, an offer not available to the former GKN people either at UES or – five years earlier – at Allied Steel and Wire. Five ISTC members later became trustees of the Scheme at UES.

41 *Reports* (1985), 3. TWIL acquired the whole of Fox Wire the following year.

42 There had been press comment on the ISTC's donation of £300 to the Tinsley Park campaign. *Reports* (1985), 86.

43 *Reports* (1985), 110.

44 Ian Scobbie (1932–), formerly Senior Divisional Organiser, No. 1 Division, has moved to Central Office in 1983.

45 A redundancy agreement was reached between BSC and Alpha on 7 August 1985,

but problems over non receipt of readaptation payments rumbled on for more than a year, leading, *inter alia*, to a presentation to the DTI on 10 November 1986. The nub of the problem lay in whether or not the Alpha closure represented a permanent withdrawal of capacity and a solution was found when the company finally agreed to submit an application for the benefits. Negotiations led by AGS Keith Brookman led to 137 former employees receiving re-adaptation payments. The final Alpha employees left the plant in the weeks following January 1987.

46 A bizarre feature of the management case was the insistence that Gartcosh was not part of the Ravenscraig complex.

47 Alpha closed but was recommissioned in 1988 on one-furnace operation with 124 employees to produce slab, a scarce commodity in the boom conditions of the later 1980s.

48 Community leader Mary McKenna was commended by the EC in February 1986 for her organisation of this most successful event.

49 R.J. Wilson (1937–) was a former member of the Central Office Statistical Department who served in No. 7 Division as a Staff Organiser from 1970 and as Senior Organiser from 1971 to 1983. Before his appointment as Divisional Officer, he had spent three years in No. 3 Division. He was appointed Divisional Officer, No. 8 Division in 1993 and retired in 1995.

50 Tom Davey (1925–), once Secretary of Eston Grange 1 Branch was appointed No. 4 Divisional Organiser in 1971 and moved to No. 2 Division four years later. The following year and without precedent Ted Hardaker switched from No. 3 Division to become Senior Organiser in his place releasing John Clarke to return to his native Yorkshire (*Reports*, 1986, 13). For the CIS, Nick Leadley had requested integration of CIS district secretaries within the wider promotional structure but this was refused until such time as the section was a fully integral part of the ISTC.

51 Dick Knox (1933–), once Secretary of Ravenscraig 6 Branch, served on the Executive as a Section (a) representative from 1972 to 1974 when he was appointed Organiser No. 4 Division. He was made Senior Organiser in 1980.

52 These were guaranteed only until 1989. Ravenscraig, fighting for neighbouring outlets, was much exercised over this problem.

53 Unfortunately the Central Office statement reached the media before it reached EC members. This contributed to the controversy about passages of the statement which seemed to countenance the possibility of buying shares in the new plc and which, in the eyes of the critics, was insufficiently robust in its opposition the idea in principle, (*Reports*, 1988, 6). These were countered by a supplementary statement. One side-effect was to lead the EC to show a distinct lack of interest in a share options scheme canvassed by ASW Holdings, the guise in which Allied Steel & Wire was about to go to market. In fact 82 per cent of employees took up the share options: the equity they bought together with the free share issue meant they owned 12 per cent at privatisation.

54 The full story of how British Steel was privatised is told in M. Upham 'Passages on the Path to Privatisation: the case of British Steel', *Industrial Relations Journal*, vol. 21, no. 2, (Summer 1990).

11

Privatisation and recession
Roy Evans (1989–92)

'I hope for Peace rather than Armageddon.'

The steel trade and industrial relations

Steel thrived in the boom conditions of the late 1980s. The Divisional Offi-cers' uplifting reports record high outputs, broken production records and a requirement for high shift levels. At Scunthorpe output passed 4.3 million tonnes in 1988–9, a UK record for a single plant. Llanwern reached its best-ever steel output of 2,230,067 tonnes and established a new European record of 339 ladles sequence castings; the new (ex-Alpha) continuous caster was a quarter of a million tonnes ahead of its intended output in the plant's annual operating plan. The productivity gains of the decade tended to attenuate perceptions of the social impact of the high unemployment figures which continued side by side with this rosy performance in the steel areas.[1] At Brymbo, so recently threatened, investment in eccentric bottom furnace tap-ping raised productivity to a startling degree: average output from the melting shop hit 8000 tonnes a week late in 1988. Even in No. 8 Division, so often the exception to the steel cycle, there was a 'dramatic' movement into profit at Johnson Matthey (Brimsdown), while Sheerness crashed through the half million tonnes annual liquid output barrier.[2]

Closures continued in a minor key, though they were pregnant with sym-bolism as in the case of the Dowlais foundry which, at the date of its 1987 clo-sure, had been in action since 1759. Soon after flotation, however, BS rationalised its Tinplate Division, taking out Velindre Works at a cost of 719 jobs with another 218 to go at Ebbw Vale, Trostre and the Divisional HQ. The promise of 236 future jobs seemed small beer by comparison.[3] This should have been the end of job losses in Tinplate, but the spectre of redundancy returned to Nos. 5 and 6 Divisions in February 1990, lopping off no fewer than 524 further jobs at Trostre, Ebbw Vale and headquarters. There was gloom also at Clydesdale, where orders had slumped; management responded with production pauses that would bring employees under Guaranteed Week terms.

Of course, BS was investing as well as disinvesting, but the pay-off in jobs was increasingly small, and those who were working faced tough challenges as management drove its human as well as its capital resources to breaking point. An £80m investment programme at the Teesside Works was intended to inaugurate 'group working' at Nos. 1 and 10 beam mills. This posed a challenge to traditional methods of work control and in particular the century-old system of promotions, which had grown with every passing year. At Lackenby, and later at nearby Skinningrove, a long-running dispute erupted which could not easily be accommodated within traditional procedures. It was a sign of things to come.

The nature of annual awards was changing, with more and more emphasis on performance-related pay, tightened employment conditions, and shifts in the timing of settlements. Two-year agreements had appeared at BSC in 1988 and at UMB in 1988 and 1990: to management this offered the security of financial planning, but for the union the benefits, at a time of high inflation, were less certain. Year Two of the two-year BS agreement turned out to be a year of high inflation, forcing BS to concede a 1 per cent addition to the planned 4.5 per cent award. At UMB and Brymbo profit-related schemes[4] were in operation, and in autumn 1988 BS itself approached the ISTC on the matter. At this point the Organisation was not ready to decide and took professional and political advice: enthusiasm was dampened when BS itself warned that its profit-related schemes would not qualify for tax relief. Not wishing to deprive the membership of an opportunity, the ISTC authorised local discussions. LSBs, that controversial product of the 1980s, were now an integral part of the pay packet, pursued energetically by a 'flying squad' of Central Office officers who had developed expertise in making them work for the members. With outputs high in the late 1980s, many schemes were paying at maximum levels – in the region of 17 or 18 per cent. Pressure was also being felt in areas outside the pay element. Steel Committee meetings with BS during the winter of 1988–9 on manual and staff sick pay rang with management complaints about absenteeism and with suggestions that sickness payments might be triggered as absence targets were met. Evans, as chairman, rejected this out of hand, and a failure to agree was later recorded. The Original Seven met BS again in July 1989, but the two sides had quite opposite philosophies: an ADC motion calling for entitlements to sick pay from day one of employment was endorsed by the Executive the following month. All these incremental changes were now to be overshadowed by changes to the structure of bargaining itself.

The BS two-year review meeting on 28 February 1989 was used by management to announce the end of central pay reviews on expiry of the current agreement and their intention to cease negotiations with the Steel Committee.[5] This was not totally unexpected. The previous year, Steel Committee secretary Denis Delay had produced a valedictory view of its prospects. His paper 'Post-Privatisation: Trade Union Liaison' had envisaged co-ordinated negotiations on wages and employment conditions, which had been the principal sticking point for the ISTC ever since the Steel Committee had been created to handle central negotiations on employment conditions. BS wanted business-level deals and multi-union bargaining – centralisation for the unions and disaggregation for itself: this was therefore a double challenge. How was the ISTC to handle disaggregated bargaining for the first time in more than a generation?

That the BS move heralded major changes was beyond doubt: almost the first act of UES after withdrawing from national bargaining had been to re-introduce of the forty-hour week. To management the structure of bargaining was an obstacle to meeting its business objectives. The National Joint Council (NJC), which represented other nationally recognised unions in the company, proposed that the ISTC should collaborate in setting up multi-union machinery to match the intended structure of BS: in effect this meant conceding both points. But the ISTC's initial reaction was to oppose both ending the central review and scrapping the Steel Committee, and to seek the NJC's support for this.[6] The position was refined on 24 October when it was decided to keep in close touch with the NJC rather than adopt a joint approach.

The first requirement for a successful resistance was the backing of the membership. This was achieved when the 1989 ADC endorsed any action the Executive might take to retain central bargaining; soon afterwards branches were instructed to avoid local discussions on the matter until more information about management intentions had been obtained. After a national meeting on 13 September all BS branches were notified in detail about the company's plans, and within a month the Executive had correspondence from four joint committees and twenty-five branches opposed to the loss of national bargaining.[7] It resolved to conduct a 'high powered' campaign to brief the membership, after which there should be a ballot on a programme of positive action to force withdrawal of the proposals. BS was immediately informed of the ISTC's fears of a future attack on employment conditions and the arrival of plant bargaining; clarification was also sought from the company on its attitude to lay representation at business-level negotiations, to plants unspecified in the proposals, and to the new Steel Co-ordinating Committee (see below).

Some officers thought BS had shown some willingness to compromise and to address areas of union concern, and these views prevailed when in November the Executive halted its campaign in the light of assurances offered by BS's Industrial Relations Director. In the hope of avoiding a double setback, the Organisation agreed to attend multi-union negotiations on matters including pay.

Following a Steel Committee meeting with BS, on 22 November the ISTC joined the other nationally recognised members of the NJC at a meeting with the company to request the continuation of national multi-union bargaining. This represented a considerable shift by the Organisation, but it was not enough. Management flexibility on secondary matters, while real, did not extend to the principle; on the union side there was not even a united front, for the AEU had publicly indicated that it was prepared to enter into business bargaining. So it was that on 28 November the Organisation reluctantly agreed to negotiate on the BS plans. A Steel Co-ordinating Committee was established soon after to synchronise a union overview.

Central Office now had to lead teams to meet the businesses separately. In strip it took two months before an agreement was concluded on 27 February 1990. The Sheet Trade Board, an automatic casualty of the new strip negotiations, was wound up on 15–16 March.

The General Steels timetable was similar, spiced up with a tussle over continued MM representation. In addition to the two main groups there were others covering the laboratories and computer centre, Stainless (Sheffield and Panteg), Clydesdale, Brinsworth and Whiteheads, each of which was allowed its own arrangements. The wholly owned companies of BS were already going their own way.

For staff and middle management the prospects were, if anything, even more dire than they were for heavy steel. The collective bargaining machinery and grievance procedure agreement of 10 September 1969 had guaranteed equal treatment for all members in negotiations. It was now abrogated. Henceforth these categories of membership would be handled in the businesses and also represented in multi-union negotiations; no one could look with confidence to the future of ISTC management representation. Finally, on 28 March, a Memorandum of Agreement was concluded with General Steels which provided for a standing committee to resolve difficulties, with a business joint council (BJC) for negotiating pay and conditions. The strip agreement established a multi-union procedure for reviewing pay and conditions, which was preceded by a grievance procedure agreement.

The ISTC now had to gear up its own organisation to match the new bargaining units. The General Steels Standing Committee met on 4 April to elect representatives to the BJC which would meet management on the pay round one week later. That same day the Operatives side of the STB elected representatives to the Strip Products Management/Unions Joint Committee for a wages meeting on 12 April. A Special Executive of 10 April ratified these revolutionary changes and expressed the hope that any agreements made could be referred back to the General Steels Standing Committee and the STB Operatives; representatives of the Diversified Products Group[8] would attend. By the end of the month agreements had been concluded at the two main businesses: ironically, these agreements were – in their principal aspects – identical.[9]

The 1989 ADC had been firm in defence of the traditional arrangements, so naturally when it reconvened in June 1990 in Aberdeen, the loss of central bargaining was the paramount issue, and there was severe criticism of the leadership. Evans sought to defend the changes, arguing that 45 per cent of the members were already under decentralised bargaining and insisting that the final decision, though a narrow one, had been taken by lay Executive members who did represent the members' views. His defence did not prevent two critical motions being carried: one deplored the Executive's decision 'to decentralise' bargaining on pay and conditions without going to a national ballot, and the other demanded a fight to maintain common conditions. A third (composite) motion sought a 'central review body' to formulate policies for the new business units on an annual basis.[10] The subject was not a policy-making issue, and so the first motion was noted and the third remitted; only the second was accepted by the EC. The establishment of more equal bargaining units could also have a positive effect, however, as when the Executive, after reviewing continuing manual/staff differences, decided to identify common aims of employment with a view to using these to direct the negotiating bodies in future.

With BS dissolving as a bargaining unit, the time was ripe for reviewing bargaining arrangements elsewhere in the private sector. Some West Midland branches felt they should be affiliated to the Confederation of Shipbuilding and Engineering Unions (CSEU), since they were governed by that body's national agreement with the Engineering Employers' Federation (EEF) and yet had no input into its decision-making process. After correspondence between the ISTC and the CSEU, affiliation was agreed at a minimum level for eighteen sites.[11] Keith Brookman was nominated to the CSEU Executive Council in February 1990. From this point on the ISTC was represented at the CSEU annual conference, and to good effect when, in June 1990, it passed a resolution in solidarity with Ravenscraig. Units passing from one part of the private sector to another were less fortunate: in 1991 Steel Stockholders (Birmingham), on being acquired by BSSC, immediately sought to push the settlement date back six months from April to October.

The ISTC was now involved in multi-union negotiations across a broad front. What did the membership want from these bargaining arrangements? The 1988 ADC agenda had a variety of demands: withdrawal of the moratorium clauses on lump-sum bonuses; a minimum earnings level for sub-contract employees equal to the MEL at BS; correction of the long-neglected staff anomalies; common terms of employment at BSC; shift premiums for working over (as specified by the 1919 Newcastle Agreement); placing of temporary workers in key production posts on permanent contracts; improvement of the provisions on voluntary retirement at sixty to make them equal to standard pension provision; and alteration of the BSC YTS scheme to bring its quality of training and levels of earnings in line with TUC guidelines. In 1989 they sought enhanced shift premium payments for 2–10 and 10–6 and the introduction of a shift premium for day/bulk shift; greater choice over when to take holidays; more security in the provisions of the Guaranteed Week Agreement; and action to address 'the growing crisis of morale' in staff and MM grades. Low pay at BS – which had left members on or near the MEL on family income supplement and in receipt of rebates – was dubbed 'immoral'.

The problem was not lack of awareness among the membership, but how a concerned and frustrated union was to maintain decent standards in an industrial world where the odds were being tilted ever more in favour of the employer. Thus the ADC in 1990 demanded an end to jobs going out to contract firms; workplace crèches; a shorter working week; and the cessation of production pauses (which with the end of the Lawson boom had returned to haunt the plants). But how were these policies to be made to stick on an increasingly powerful and unconstrained management? Even if the members' aspirations could be negotiated during a period of prosperity, a downturn in the trade would threaten gains. Across the industry, managements were using their power as a licence to base pay on performance alone. What would happen when the next downturn in the steel cycle nullified workers' efforts with low-volume sales?

At Teesside the lump-sum bonus for the second quarter of 1990 dipped below the maximum: it was the first time in three years that this had happened.

At the 1991 General Steels annual review, management sought a short-term agreement on a figure of 5.5 per cent, pleading depressed trade conditions, but when this did not find favour they refused to agree to arbitration after exhausting the procedure. The Executive authorised a ballot on industrial action, and the General Steels membership voted 2:1 to reject the offer: this must have concentrated the minds of management, for a settlement was reached on 30 July. In Strip Products a 5.5 per cent addition to basic rates was agreed, to which was added a 1.5 per cent consolidation and a lump-sum payment of £100.

But the new bargaining units also began to use their autonomy to reshape the substance of collective arrangements. In 1991 both General Steels and Strip Products gave notice of their intention to terminate the Employment and Income Security Agreement (EISA) and the Severance Agreement as of 31 March 1992 and introduce new arrangements. The union reaction was now handled by the Steel Co-ordinating Committee, the objective of which was a common agreement across all BS sections. But top management simply refused to meet the unions on behalf of all businesses, and pursued its objectives business by business. That was what finally happened in the first months of 1992: the Strip Mills management was prepared to put forward an agreement, but at General Steels the employers had a preference for discussion via a sub-committee. Only in March were new agreements made for the two divisions.

The curtain now fell on a bargaining unit overtaken by time. For many years the National Joint Industrial Council (JIC) for the Slag Industry had regulated relations, with the ISTC leading a union side which also included the GMB and TGWU. But the closure of Ravenscraig in 1992 (see below) had sounded the death knell of Colville Clugston Shanks Ltd, and decisions taken by the Appleby Group had resulted in East Coast Slag Products Ltd being the only company left in the Slag Employers' Association. Clearly there was no alternative to winding up the JIC, and the Executive concurred when abolition was suggested in February 1993 by the employers' secretary.

Internal affairs

The ISTC's weekly contributions were raised by 5p in April 1989, and the political levy itself was raised to 5p. A steady increase of this order was the only way the Organisation could hope to sustain a high level of services at a time of shrinking membership. By the late 1980s this seemed to have stabilised at 41/42,000: closures loomed, but they were partially offset by recruitment. For some years all Divisional Officers had been required to feature recruitment efforts in their quarterly reports, and this was a major responsibility of National Officer Ken Clarke. Awareness of the need to recruit was paying small but substantial dividends. Thus during the first half of 1989 full-time officers had campaigned for recognition at Steel Stock-holders (Birmingham), where more than 50 per cent had joined up; and at a national meeting on 25 July their efforts were crowned with a formal recognition and procedure agreement.

Of course the nature of the potential membership was changing. Steel was becoming a world of smaller and smaller workplaces, and those workplaces might be the location of several different employers, perhaps with diverse employment policies. Nowhere were the problems this posed to a union better illustrated than at Llanwern. In February 1990 the Spencer (Manual) Joint Committee complained to the Executive of progressive incursions by contractors into areas of traditional permanent employment; Central Office was sufficiently concerned to trigger a survey of BS contractors only three years after the previous one. But the ISTC also sought to organise contractors, and once membership was extended to them they were likely to put forward demands for representation. Thus the same Executive also faced a request from the Spencer Heckett branch for a contractors' joint committee, which claimed its interests were not being regarded by the Joint Committee. After the Divisional Officer had made his own inquiries as to whether proper consultations had been carried out, the branch withdrew its request, but the potential for conflict was evident.[12] The survey, when completed,[13] revealed a clear growth in the number of companies contracting on BS plants, and the dramatic extent to which they had established themselves within production itself. The 1991 ADC proposed a variety of suggestions to make the union's approach more effective. They included supporting contractors who had good employment practices; declaring a policy on contractors' wages and conditions of service; and seeking a contractors' federation to negotiate and oversee them at British Steel. In the medium term delegates looked to a Labour government to create the employment conditions that would allow contractors to achieve permanent employee status.

A further structural issue was how to represent this changing membership within a rational structure. Here the problem was to reflect important changes to the ownership of companies employing ISTC members, and to stay within the ambit of ever-changing employment law. Section (z) – the public sector – was one of the three constituencies represented on the EC. To be eligible for election a prospective member had to be 'employed by the British Steel Corporation or in any other like public body'. 1988 was an election year for the EC, and it was also known that by autumn (the usual time for elections) BSC was likely to be a plc. Until such time as it was floated on the stock exchange, however, it would be a public sector company. In May the Executive resolved to advance the elections and to review the position at the Rules Revision, due in 1989, if BSC had been privatised by then.

Recent legal changes now required these elections to be conducted via a full postal ballot, and after some discussion over the allocation of seats,[14] the Executive held to the view that it should proceed to elections following the August meeting. But when the calculations indicating seat allocations were presented in August 1988, they pointed towards reduced representation in Nos. 1 and 4 Divisions. This naturally stimulated protests, and the Executive looked to another approach to accommodate these varied issues: they balloted the membership on proposals to extend the current term of office for two years, fill any vacancies at by-elections, and move to a Rules Revision on the impact of privatisation early in 1989. The results of the ballot (which effectively introduced temporary suspension of Rule 3, Clause 11) showed a majority of almost 2:1 in favour, and by-elections followed in Nos. 4, 5, and 6 Divisions. In 1990 the deferred Executive elections took place under the new dispensation: election addresses were circulated on behalf of nominees, and for the first time an outside body, the Electoral Reform Society, oversaw the ballot.

But legislative requirements continued to bear down on unions' constitutions. Legal advice directed that elections would also now be needed for the General Secretary and perhaps for others. It was decided to refer these too to the 1989 Rules Revision. The Rules Revision Committee and the Organisation and Staffing Sub-committee, operating under legal advice, made recommendations which were endorsed by the February 1989 EC.[15] They entailed providing for the General Secretary to be elected by a simple majority of ISTC members voting. Fifteen branches would have to nominate an individual before his nomination would be valid, and he would have to have ten years' membership and five years in office behind him. Moreover, no nominations would be accepted of an individual who had violated any of the ISTC's principles or deliberately acted against its interests.[16] In making these changes the ISTC followed other precedents and moved rapidly to comply with the law, however distasteful. The incumbents, Roy Evans and Keith Brookman, were returned to office in the absence of rival nominations,[17] reflecting the dominant mood of solidarity against what was seen as Conservative interference in the union's internal affairs.

Contributions had risen to sustain the services the ISTC offered its members. Throughout the period of restructuring in the steel industry, the legal services had been at work. Throughout the period vast sums – £4 million in one year (1986) alone – were recovered on behalf of members through the use of legal representation in compensation cases which the individual unaided might never have been able to afford.[18] For example, a claim for compensation for industrial deafness on behalf of an ex-member was taken right through the legal system, though he was required to pay only a flat-rate contribution of £15. By the early 1990s the fifty lawyers engaged at one time or another by Russell Jones and Walker to work on the ISTC deafness scheme, compensation for asbestos exposure, chemical and metal burns, fume inhalation, lifting and strain injuries, and slipping and tripping injuries were recovering even greater amounts: £16m between 1990 and 1992, and £27m between 1988 and 1992.

The range of publications with which the ISTC had begun the decade came under review in the middle of it. *ISTC Banner* had been well received, but its popular full-colour tabloid format was expensive. From July 1986 a new quarterly journal, *ISTC Phoenix*, appeared, and was supplemented (for lay officers) by the *Branch Officers' Bulletin* (*BOB*) whenever there was an urgent need to communicate bargaining information: the first *BOB* appeared in June 1986. The *Branch Officers' Manual* had featured in the education programme since the 1970s. A new edition was distributed early in 1992, and soon afterwards the first ISTC video appeared.

New employment law and industrial change also shaped the ISTC's relations with other unions. The 1988 Trades Union Congress witnessed the expulsion of the electricians' union, its second in thirty-seven years, confirming the suspension of 8 July. In special session five days later the ISTC, while making it clear that it had no poaching intentions, did indicate that it would be prepared to represent ex-EEPTU members on a temporary basis, if they wished to keep their TUC links pending the latter union's return to affiliation. The ISTC's points of contact with the disaffiliates in steel were with craftsmen and managers. However, EEPTU's affiliate EESA (which included the formerly contentious SIMA), had informed the Organisation that it intended to honour all agreements, and the ISTC endorsed the TUC's approach in its recently issued guidelines on relations with the EEPTU and its sections.

The combined impact of privatisation and the loss of central bargaining was certain to be substantial. After BS had formalised its intentions towards the Steel Committee, the ISTC decided to propose to other member unions the formation of a TUC Industry Committee to review steel's strategic and economic position once a quarter; they should, in the ISTC's view, also attempt to set up an ad hoc committee which might meet with BS management, and this eventually appeared in the guise of the National Co-ordinating Committee (NCC). A strategic view was certainly needed. Fears about pension entitlements were central to almost every privatisation in the 1980s, and with good reason. The take-over of Stanton & Staveley by Pont-a-Mousin led directly to the loss of inflation-linking both for pensions in payment and for those deferred; provision for early retirement was also eroded.[19] Steel was afflicted by the 1980s practice of companies pocketing pension-fund surpluses, which had had been denounced by two resolutions to the 1987 ADC. A further trend of the times arose from changes to the Social Security Act and the enactment of the Financial Services Act 1986. Among smaller companies there were many instances of individuals being encouraged to leave their company schemes and take out private pensions.[20]

From 5 April 1989 it was no longer possible to gain two years' refund of pension contributions from SERPS if this irrevocable step was taken, and there was no shortage of salesmen hurrying inadequately briefed Scheme members into an unwise decision. ISTC staff had been encouraging members to resist, but much depended on the willingness of employers to launch their own schemes. By May 1989 Feather was reporting that 'the vast majority' of ISTC members were covered by company schemes, and that there was a trend towards improved provision under pressure of competition from the private market. Less positive was the unwillingness of employers to permit union representation among the trustees. While BS, UES, ASW, ABB and Delta Metals set a good example, it was not followed that widely.

A 1989 ADC motion set out a wish list for the BS scheme, now of course a private-sector operation. It included credits for manual workers aged between fifty and sixty with twenty years' service, normal payment of sixtieths, higher widows' pensions and an improved ill-health minimum to 20/60ths. Denis Delay prepared a Steel Committee claim based on possible improvements to the scheme, and when BS began to publicise its new company pension proposals in summer 1990, Sandy Feather was able to report, with some satisfaction, that most of ADC's suggestions had been incorporated.[21] The new BS scheme was introduced at the start of 1991, and all members transferred, leaving only deferred pensioners and superannuated members connected to the previous scheme.

The announcement of a substantial surplus in the fund stimulated great union interest in negotiating further improvements for deferred and retired pensioners, and a new demand that benefit provisions should be widened to include common-law wives. On the structure of the scheme, however, the ISTC acquiesced in a BS proposal to let the number of union trustees fall from twelve to eight by natural wastage. At a national-level meeting on 10 June management signalled that it could live with employees of wholly owned BS subsidiaries joining the scheme, subject to a close examination of the circumstances of each company. The two Corby firms of Seamless and Cold Drawn had in fact already announced their intention to join.

Amid the retrenchment one very positive inter-union development stood out. Exploratory meetings with officers of the Amalgamated Society of Wire Workers had been held at the end of the 1980s,[22] and they culminated in a formal encounter on 10/11 May 1990 at which Executive members and national officers from both sides conferred on their common interests. Sufficient progress was made to justify considering a set of proposals for a transfer of engagements. Events moved rapidly, with Brookman addressing the Wire Workers' Annual Conference in Blackpool on 14/15 June: there he followed the smaller union's President, Tom Littlemore, in recommending a merger, and watched as the overwhelming majority of delegates voted to ballot the membership, with a strong recommendation to transfer engagements to the ISTC. The legal services were commissioned to draw up the necessary documents, the principles of which were endorsed by the August Quarterly Executive.

After some delay in discussions with the Certification Officer, the proposal went out to ballot, and the Wire Workers' membership returned a 91.7 per cent vote in favour of a transfer of engagements. On a turnout in excess of 60 per cent, 2852 voted in favour and 252 against. The transfer was formally accepted by the ISTC Executive on 22 February 1991, and Wire Workers representatives (of the newly established Wire Workers Section – WWS) attended their first meeting on 23 April. From now on Matt Ardron, the former General Secretary, functioned as National Secretary, and the Wire Workers' executive became the ISTC Industrial Committee. Eddie Lynch and Jack Claughton continued to steer the section in the regions. Its annual industrial conference was timed and set to run into the main ADC.

The wire industry had its own Joint Industrial Council (JIC), though by 1991 it was a very lean organisation indeed and was about to lose its responsibilities for training and health and safety. It continued, however, to set basic terms and conditions for the industry and a national disputes procedure. The wire, wire rope and wire goods industries were not exempt from the processes at work throughout the metal goods sector, and in his first report as National Secretary Matt Ardron had to record the loss of seventy jobs at Rylands Whitecross of Warrington and the closure of Steadfast Tools of Sheffield. It was not the last time he would have to do this.

To help in the process of integration a member of the Wire Workers' Section was co-opted onto the Education Sub-committee early in 1992. When the two-year guarantee of sickness benefit expired on 9 April 1993, wire workers were moved to convalescent home benefit in common with the rest of the ISTC membership. On 11 October the Executive met the section's Industrial Committee and agreed that the wire workers' industrial conference would cease after 1994 and be integrated with the ISTC Conference, places being allocated according to rule. The Industrial Committee and the post of National Secretary were reaffirmed, but it was agreed that the 'supernumerary' EC membership would be discontinued after 1996.[23]

Recession arrives

In the last quarter of 1989, an incipient economic slowdown was discernible. Patchy at first, it began to affect all works as the winter wore on. Though no one then suspected it, the UK was entering the longest recession since World War II. Soon after the New Year the storm broke. Clive Lewis reported that there had been a slump in output of 3000 tonnes at the Ravenscraig hot mill, and an extended production pause at Christmas. There was a clear threat to one of the blastfurnaces, and four hot-mill enhancement projects, to the value of £10m, had been discarded. Questioned by an anxious Evans, Scholey – now Sir Robert – and Brian Moffat, his chief executive, had replied that overall orders were down 5 per cent, leading management to deploy its usual preference for loading 'low-cost' plants. On top of this there were worrying rumours, specifically about plate. BS had in fact been privately considering whether to remain in the plate business; it anticipated a significant home market and profitable export opportunities, but would existing plant be used? Soon it was discovered that kit for a new mill had been brought in from overseas and stored in parts at Teesside. Management parried anxious inquiries with assurances that no strategic decisions had yet been taken.

This was as nothing compared to Scottish anxieties, which were at a peak. Speaking at the launch of BS's Annual Report and Accounts on 6 July, Scholey referred to 'the probable closure in 1989' of the Ravenscraig hot strip mill. This caused consternation at the ISTC. It reiterated its resistance to closure in special session and directed Evans to attend a conference on steel, speedily organised by the STUC for 20 September. In November the EC donated £1000 to the multi-trade-union delegations at the works to help them sustain its campaign. No one was in any doubt that this would be a fight to the death. The notion of using shareholdings in a more positive way had been canvassed at the 1990 ADC, and ISTC representatives attended BS's Annual Meeting on 27 July. The occasion was used as a platform to state the case for Ravenscraig, and Sir Kenneth Alexander, nominee of the Scottish workforce, was nominated by Dr Jeremy Bray, MP and seconded by Brookman in his unsuccessful bid for election to the board.

Ravenscraig had been battling to survive throughout the 1980s. What of the rest of Scotland? Its tube industry (the Clydesdale and Imperial Works) had not been pulling in what it considered its share of investment even during the good years: what were the prospects in the lean ones now arriving? Meetings of local authority members and union officers with Scottish Office ministers failed to yield tangible results, while rumours of joint ventures abounded. And then there was Dalzell, where prospects had been clouded for some time, and which was understandably destabilised by the new plate mill rumours. The Executive affirmed its commitment to five integrated plants, but approached meetings with management with foreboding. Clive Lewis, now STUC President, prepared to renew the defence of the whole Scottish industry. There was an unproductive Steel Committee meeting with Moffat on 19 January to discuss the half-year results. Little the wiser, Evans agreed to confer with the STUC and representatives of Scottish works on 8 March – but the crisis was not to begin in Scotland.

Like vultures circling in a clouding sky, the closure announcements began again. Orgreave coke works (not an ISTC plant) was scheduled to shut in July 1990. Whitehead Pickle line was also shut, though its employees were found alternative employment (its narrow strip business was returned to the BS parent body). Much worse was UES's announcement that F. H. Lloyd Engineering Steels was to go: only four years earlier, it had been seen as a hopeful sign of skill-rescuing in a bleak West Midlands environment. There was brief resistance and willing support from politicians and the local authority, but melting, casting and rolling ceased on 29 April. This closure extinguished the connection of the Black Country with commercial steelmaking.

May 1990 was the cruellest month. At Derwenthaugh, the management announced the total closure of Raine & Co., where production had fallen by 30 per cent in three months due to the loss of coal-industry orders. Thus was pronounced the doom of perhaps the most loyal trade unionists in the ISTC, who in 1980 had struck without complaint in a cause not their own. Their mill shut on 27 July, and the rest of the works two weeks later. Unsurprisingly, the last days at the works were very unhappy ones, and the discussion of severance terms was abruptly curtailed by management. Then on 14 May the complete closure of Brymbo was declared by UES, dooming no less than 1125 jobs. The Executive at once donated £1000 to the Brymbo fighting fund and committed itself to defence of steelmaking there, calling on the branches to convene urgently to co-ordinate their fight. National-level meetings were held on 5 and 21 June and on 2 July, but at the last of these management were told that the multi-union committee had decided to negotiate a closure agreement while still pressing for employment at Brymbo. The agreement itself was made on 24 July. The usual depressing sequence followed: counsellors arrived and the search for new investment began. The hope of a new buyer – almost invariably a chimera – had faded by August. The melting shop shut on 26 September, and the gates closed forever on 23 November.

One week after the original Brymbo announcement, the thunderbolt struck as BS announced its intention to shut the Ravenscraig hot strip mill, at a cost of 770 jobs, during the first half of 1991. The coupling of the announcement with one of a new concaster at Llanwern, to be operative by 1993, was little consolation. The Executive's position was clear: it was ready for 'any action' to save the mill, in line with the five-plants policy to which it had adhered for eight years. On 29 May Evans led national officers of interested unions at a meeting with the multi-union campaign committee at which plans were laid for a publicity drive. The 'Rolling Mill Record', published by the ISTC as a focus for resistance, was an early fruit of this. Plans were soon laid for a Steel Conference on 19 September, and this gathering unanimously[24] endorsed a composite defensive resolution: the Ravenscraig case was laid before the chief executive nine days later. The PLP and the Trade and Industry Select Committee were contacted, the latter with a request for a public inquiry since it was believed there was no economic case for shutting Ravenscraig. On 20 October 1990 a rally was convened in Motherwell, but that month management declared its intention to achieve the closure by 5 April 1991.

On 6 November the Executive met BS's Chief Executive, its Director of Social Policy and Ravenscraig management, together with the Ravenscraig Joint Branches, at the neutral venue of British Steel Stainless. For the local membership Tommy Brennan, the works convenor, emphasised the extra difficulties imposed by pause weeks, as well as the weakness of the closure case. Afterwards, Evans informed union representatives that BS was operating a preferential loading policy in breach of past understandings. He would demand a fair loading of the plants, and if this was not arranged by agreement then the entire Strip Division would be balloted for appropriate action. Management countered that the May 1990 lump-sum bonus agreement had provided for preferential loading and pause periods, and indeed that the agreement contained a clause of unique advantage to Ravenscraig. Little redress was to be expected from this quarter, but politically events were more encouraging: the Department of Trade and Industry agreed to a Select Committee inquiry, and the ISTC would give evidence on 28 November. Because of this rather than because of the management letter, the threatened Strip Division ballot was not held. Meanwhile, all Ravenscraig branches were circulated for their views on how to proceed.

The ISTC briefed Labour's Parliamentary Steel Committee on 14 January 1991; three days earlier BS had published its intention to cease rolling at Ravenscraig on 15 February and begin banking down the blast-furnaces on 9 February. Management would not be deflected from its purpose of preferential loading in favour of the 'low-cost' plants. To the local membership the closure juggernaut seemed, as it was meant to seem, unstoppable, and on 15 January a closure agreement for the mills was signed. The endgame was inescapable. Formal notice soon arrived of management's intention to cut back to one- furnace operation at Ravenscraig, abolishing a further 1100 jobs, 770 of them those of direct employees). From August, Dalzell plate mill would be supplied by the General Steels division, so degassing and ingot casting would cease in July. Local officials had been unable to draw BS into any kind of serious discussion about Ravenscraig. Reflecting the frustrations of all Scots, one newspaper reported Sir Robert Scholey's popularity in the country as somewhere between that of the Pox and the Poll Tax. The Scottish Development Agency had commissioned a review of the prospects for the steel industry in Scotland. Its author, Arthur D. Little, concluded in the bleakest possible terms for Ravenscraig, and with good reason.

On 8 January 1992 the plant's works director announced British Steel's intention to cease its Ravenscraig operations entirely, pleading the influence of market forces. Eight days later, the EC published a wide-ranging policy statement stimulated by the Ravenscraig tragedy. It pinpointed under-investment over a period of eight years as opening the way to closure, lamented the utter failure of the company to explain its actions to the work-force or the House of Commons, and then bit the bullet: 'Faced with these facts the Executive Council affirmed the decision of the membership to reluctantly accept an orderly decommissioning of the plant by September 1992.'[25]

The statement reminded all concerned of the assurances given by BS that full production would continue until 1994; it called on the government to assist any prospective purchaser and to maintain the plant as a viable concern, or to commit resources to make it a research centre, since this would be permitted under the ECSC regime. But the closure of Ravenscraig proceeded, spreading its dismal impact to the terminal at Hunterston and all contractors at either site. The agreement on severance was almost identical to that under which the hot mill had shut. It was some consolation that ISERBS benefits had been obtained for most contractor members.[26]

At a consultative meeting earlier in the year there had been an exchange of views about the Scottish Tube industry between national officers and Martin

Llowarch, who had succeeded Moffat as chief executive when the latter took Scholey's place as BS chairman. Nothing tangible emerged, however, and news soon broke that local representatives were to be briefed on an 'austerity plan' precipitated by the economic crisis. Some inflammatory remarks uttered by the managing director of Diversified Products, did not raise anybody's hopes. In November, the year's final dismal announcement was made: closure of the steel and tube works at Clydesdale with a loss of 1200 jobs, leaving in Scotland only the Imperial finishing works, which would receive imported feedstock after it had been quenched and tempered at Clydesdale. Evans met local union representatives on 15 November and immediately took to the chief executive the news that the plan was completely unacceptable.

The closure proposals were the subject of a meeting with Llowarch in Corby on 18 January. As was often the case, local officials had received alternative plans, and as was always the case BS, while polite, evinced little interest. It was another mirage. Local negotiations on 25 January resulted in a failure to agree, and management instantly put out redundancy notices to all Clydesdale employees for the last week of the month. The sense of powerlessness was palpable, and at a national-level meeting on 15 February a closure agreement was signed. In the course of just one year British Steel had obliterated No. 1 Division. At its quarterly meeting in February a shell-shocked EC insisted on a Special Executive to discuss the grave crisis into which they had been plunged. In May they drew up a list of recommendations which reflected the irritation of the Scottish membership at BS's indifference to their views.[27]

Right across the industry management was cutting back. Where there were not closures there were interruptions to production and recourse to the Guaranteed Week.[28] Ongoing works suffered shake-outs of labour, with sixty redundancies at UES's Aldwarke site and 200 at Stocksbridge (though these had been signalled as far back as 1988). March 1992 brought yet another closure in the tube sector with the shutting of Seamless Tube in Corby at a cost of 175 jobs, nearly all of them ISTC, though there were slight consequent employment gains at Imperial (Airdrie) and Wednesfield. This closure was not even negotiated, and occasioned a CSEU-led meeting on 21 February at which there was harsh criticism of management.[29] All of this was a response to the downturn in trade, but the ISTC also faced provocative new attempts by management to increase its control over the workforce.

New tough management

There were many local disputes over working practices. At Brinsworth the ISTC branch, faced with stonewalling over a local claim, had balloted for industrial action, but stayed at work in the hope of finding a peaceful solution through talks. Unilateral action by management then provoked a stoppage on 28 February 1990, followed by a complete refusal to negotiate, and on 1 April all employees were given notice of termination unless they returned within eight days. The branch felt it had to return to work, but the dispute had disclosed the absence of a procedural agreement, and one positive result was national talks to establish one. Several BS plants experienced the opposite problem when a 'memorandum of agreement' was tabled by management, its gloss causing consternation in South Yorkshire and South Wales. At Ebbw Vale management tabled proposals to contract out the cleaning, maintenance and oil cellar/Titzel plant operations. It was a bitter shock to discover that this was not up for any kind of negotiation and that the proposals would be introduced in April 1991 regardless of union views. Central Office representatives met higher management of BS Diversified Products at the works on 28 June 1990 and, surprisingly, persuaded them to acknowledge that plant relationships were at a low ebb.

Outside BS the trend was, if anything, worse. At Rotherham Engineering Steels manpower reductions were declared in June 1992 on a redundancy selection procedure of management's own devising. The dispute was partly resolved by branch-by-branch talks, but only after the Thrybergh 1 and Aldwarke 3 branches had put ten cases through industrial tribunals. Ironically, the Aldwarke melting shop had broken production records during this quarter, so the motive for management's action had been low realised prices rather than adverse working practices.

At Forgemasters Engineering Ltd, management dragged negotiations on a pay claim lodged in October 1989 through the entire national engineering procedure; in frustration, ISTC members (in a minority at the plant) withdrew their labour on 30 March. Perhaps the most iniquitous steps of all were taken at Firsteel Ltd, where the branch had put up tough resistance to a plan to reduce their shifts from ten to five. Management retaliated by selectively imposing redundancy on twenty-six individuals, virtually reversing the 'last-in, first-out' principle, and cashiered the three branch officials, including EC member John Marston.[30] Long-established practices were not safe. BISAKTA had first gained the principle of eight-hour rotas through the 1919 Newcastle Agreement, but in the recession of the early 1990s employers were pressing for twelve-hour patterns. In a February 1993 decision the EC reaffirmed its wish to retain the agreement; but if branches or units of plant wished to work longer it would be on their own responsibility: the Organisation would not 'condone or interfere'.[31]

Events at Sheerness Steel were on a dramatic scale. The Kent coast plant had steadily expanded, and had received full backing from the union in its quest to gain greater efficiencies and drive down electricity costs. In March 1990 the Sheerness personnel director, Hugh Billot, stated that he had no intention of derecognising non-supervisory grades. But in April 1992 the management announced that collective bargaining would cease, that employees would be put on individual contracts, and that unions would be derecognised. At branch meetings the membership solidly resisted these appalling changes, but each individual employee was put under extreme pressure to sign a contract, with a warning that his employment would cease if he did not. Divisional Officer Ian Scobbie had regretfully to conclude that in the face of this relentless hostility there was not sufficient support to conduct a ballot on industrial action.

Failing collective action, measures were taken to retain as much of the union structure as possible. Contributions were now made by bank transfer, and the branch continued to meet, though not at the workplace. Once again, changes in bargaining arrangements were only a prelude to a deterioration in working conditions: the new contract confirmed everyone's worst fears, bringing longer hours under new practices and lower pay. Legal advice was sought, and officers met the members whenever they could to beef up morale. An approach to the Commission of the European Communities proved fruitless, but contact with the USWA (whose Canadian membership was employed at Co-Steel's parent plant) and IG Metall was more encouraging.

Finally there was Spartan Redheugh, a Gateshead plant which encountered trading difficulties in 1992 and tried to resolve them with wage cuts and arbitrary changes to working practices. In a ballot 96 per cent of the membership voted for strike action. The union attempted to use this vote as a stimulus for intensive talks, but when management began to move semi-finished material to a sister company, in an obvious defensive move, the employees (AEEU as well as ISTC) withdrew their labour on 6 July. Nine days later management issued dismissal notices to ISTC members, including the sick and those on holiday; staff grades received letters demanding that they dissociate themselves from the dispute, and three who refused were dismissed. All ISTC members received strike and lock-out benefit. On 22 July, strike-breakers were introduced into the plant.

The dispute proved long and bitter, a real anachronism. On 16/17 November 1992 the unions, through the auspices of ACAS, finalised a set of proposals to put to management, but in the meantime every effort was made to sustain the workforce by means of food parcels from No. 2 and neighbouring Divisions. Management were in fact offered a wide-ranging set of commitments, to be governed by an agreement before the workforce went back to work. In return they were asked to reinstate those who wished to come back, with redundancy payments in lieu of entitlements for the rest. Only a grudging response was forthcoming. The dispute was not resolved until the end of the year, when the works reopened with provision for voluntary redundancies and acceptable rates and conditions for those continuing to be employed there.

The 1990–2 recession was patchier than its predecessors. Side by side with the grim news of plant closures from Scotland, North Wales and the north-east were cheerier developments in South Wales and the south-east. At Llanwern most departments were still operating at annual operating plan standards in the third quarter of 1990, and tonnages at Port Talbot were high. British Steel Electrical reported both high quality and high volume, as it had been doing for some time. By the autumn of 1990 ASW Cardiff had a record output of 1.3 million tonnes annually, though it was under pressure due to weak rebar prices. At Sheerness, even before its assault on the union, management claimed that it was turning out the lowest-cost steel in Europe and that the plant was being driven in the direction of a 1 million tonne target for 1992, with expectations that 1.2 million tonnes would be reached soon after; unsurprisingly, both rod and bar mills were breaking records. All works without exception reported intense competition.

And in this capital-intensive industry, labour was a diminishing cost. True to its nature, the ISTC was always vigilant in protecting steel's interests. Thus, with arc production taking an increasing share of output, electricity prices were a sensitive issue. The ISTC campaigned consistently over this, in just the same way as it had shown solidarity with the employers in the 1960s. During the recession all arc producers, whether in South Yorkshire or at Sheerness, were at risk. The ISTC helped devise a 1991 motion to the House of Commons which deplored the additional cost burden of £65 per tonne to output from Rotherham Engineering Steels. In November 1991 Evans wrote to the Office of Fair Trading director-general about this unpleasant consequence of electricity privatisation. Correspondence and pressure continued, and in 1992 the ISTC affiliated to the Coalition for Fair Electricity Regulation (COFFER), a union and community pressure group.

A further feature of the new decade was increasing internationalisation. BS acquired the Mannstaedt division of the German firm Klockner, which made sections, as well as two smaller subsidiaries, one of which produced colliery arches. The Skinningrove Works became a profit centre within a new Special Products Business as part of the Mannstaedt venture. And in February 1991 BS and Bethlehem Steel Corporation agreed to launch a feasibility study into a joint venture to make and market structural and rail products.

May brought more developments, with BS in discussions with the Swedish producer SSAB to found a joint electrical steels venture embracing the Orb Works. Meanwhile Templeborough Rolling Mills reverted to 100 per cent ownership when BS bought out Bridon Wire. In November 1992 Avesta Sheffield Ltd, a joint stainless venture, was launched, the biggest in Europe. This internationalisation worried the 1991 ADC, which called on the government to use its golden share 'to prevent denationalised companies investing abroad to the detriment of the industry in Britain.' A further proposal from the ADC suggested something which the union had a better chance of implementing, for it called on closer international union co-operation wherever BS had a financial involvement abroad.

The ISTC in the 1990s

A horrid 1990 had seemed to pose point-blank the question of the future financial viability of the Organisation: talk of stabilisation had been blown apart by recession and the management offensive. Early in 1991 reviews were inaugurated of several major problems facing the Organisation. Merger, a theoretical possibility, was attractive to very few, and a Special Executive of 23 April rejected an approach, the latest of many, from Bill Jordan of the AEU.[32] But action had to be taken on finances if independence was to be sustained. Since income would still have to be raised, contributions were increased by 5p weekly from January 1992, with an additional 1p for the political fund. The following year the pressure of the continued loss of membership was evident in a further increase – of 7p – in weekly contributions, with the political levy raised to 8p.

The membership could not be expected simply to pay more for an unamended ISTC: there would have to be savings too. It was therefore agreed to reduce national and divisional full-time staff from seventeen to thirteen by voluntary redundancy. Three of the reductions were achieved by combining Nos. 1 and 2 Divisions with three staff; giving the same treatment to Divisions Nos. 4 and 7, and 5 and 6; reducing No. 3 to three staff; and having only a Divisional Officer in No. 8. In a sharp break with tradition it was agreed that in future all Divisional Officer posts would be filled by selection. Evans himself suggested that moving Central Office from London might allow much-needed cash to be realised,[33] but low expectations on property prices, and developments pending in the Kings Cross area which might improve the situation, led to deferral of this decision for five years. Quarterly Executive meetings were reduced to two days with effect from August 1991, with Divisional Officers attending only on Thursday. The size of the EC itself (aside from the impact of amalgamations) was referred to the next Rules Revision, scheduled for 1995. At the 1991 ADC a motion was passed calling for a very wide consultation on future structure: the membership wanted to be part of any radical change. A further reflection of the pressure for information was a successful motion which called for a summary of EC business to be carried in each issue of *Phoenix*.

Turning to the wider organisation, it was agreed to continue to encourage branch amalgamations in view of the high cost of administering small branches. The ADC would continue, but representation would be reduced to three delegates per thousand members.[34] From 1987 it had been the practice to rotate ADC venues between England, Scotland and Wales, but some of the old ambition survived: the 1992 ADC was held at Sparrenduin, De Haan, Belgium, making the ISTC one of the first British unions to hold its annual event outside the country. Finally, in a landmark decision of August 1991, the Executive ruled that Rule 2, Clause 1 foreclosed the possibility that retired members could hold office in the Confederation.[35] The continued activity of such members was a reminder that the days of seriously long service in the industry were gone, and a wise decision of November 1992 reduced the period of membership required to qualify for a long service award from forty to thirty years.

The staff implications of the savings measures became more concrete in the summer, when retirement plans were announced for Ken Clarke, John Foley and Roy Bishop. Foley was replaced by Brian Connolly,[36] and the opportunity was taken to run Nos. 1 and 2 Divisions under J.C. (Clive) Lewis while still maintaining an office in Scotland. John Clarke, Divisional Organiser in No. 3 Division, was appointed to replace his namesake.[37] The fourth reduction turned out to be Evans himself, who volunteered for early retirement in January 1992, though he was not to leave his post until the following year.

In the 1993 New Year's Honours List Roy Evans was awarded an OBE, and he retired on 28 February. His unopposed re-election in 1990 had postponed the ISTC's first experience of the election of the General Secretary and Assistant General Secretary as legislation now required. In the knowledge that his retirement date was now approaching, preparations to elect a successor to Evans had to be made. In February 1992 the EC agreed to begin the procedure after 15 June.[38] This time there was a contest, with Assistant General Secretary Keith Brookman challenged by Senior Divisional Organiser Ted Hardaker. The campaign proved rumbustious, with several Divisional Officers and the National Wire Workers' Secretary complaining of Hardaker's conduct. This was investigated after the result was declared, and led to the Organisation and Staffing Committee expressing deep concern at the conduct of branches supporting Hardaker. The outcome of the ballot was a 31.4 per cent turnout and a convincing vote of 6797 (65.7 per cent) for Brookman against 3549 (34.3 per cent) for Hardaker. The election for Assistant General Secretary followed immediately afterwards and resulted in a victory for Mick Leahy,[39] who polled 4868 votes (46.3 per cent) against 2904 votes (27.6 per cent) for Hardaker and 2742 votes (26.1 per cent) for Roy Knight, Divisional Organiser, Nos. 5/6 Divisions. Both victors were to take up their positions on 1 March 1993.

Evans led the ISTC for eight years which were divided by the watershed of privatisation. He was a natural conciliator who would only reluctantly take radical action. Controversially, he saw little point in spending precious resources on a futile attempt to resist the launch of BS on the capital markets, but he was taken to the brink over what he saw as an issue more fundamental than ownership: central bargaining procedures. Yet under his leadership the ISTC was faced by the most ferocious assault on established industrial practices any General Secretary had faced since the days of Arthur Pugh. Moreover, Evans was at the helm during the worst recession since Pugh's day, and the combination of the two destroyed his hopes – expressed when he took office – that the period of major closures had ended and sunnier days lay ahead. When his period of office drew to a close the Organisation had retrenched in order to remain financially viable. The question asked by the active membership was whether the ISTC, under new leadership, could do more than manage its own decline.

Notes

1 There were exceptions, as at the Thrybergh bar mill where forty extra men were taken on in April 1989.

2 As Britain's only southern steelworks, Sheerness was ideally placed to supply structural products to major public projects such as the Channel Tunnel, Docklands and the Thames Barrier. This works offered a rare example of rising output leading to higher staffing, with forty extra men being taken on during 1988 and an extra shift in the rod mill. Investment was attracted and management claimed that the new bar mill, inaugurated in January 1990, was the most advanced in the world. The place boomed until the first quarter of 1991, when stocks began to rise.

3 Disillusionment with the possibility of stopping closures was widespread, and the Velindre membership sought severance terms almost at once. The works closed in September 1989.

4 The payments could be substantial: the assumption for 1989 at UMB was that employees would receive £2700 for the year. At this company another indication of the new style was that the workforce took up an offer of no-cost private medical

care which full-time officers, led by the General Secretary, had not even been prepared to discuss in negotiations.

5　BS reminded union representatives that all its statements of wage and employment conditions since 1989 had said that it would, at an appropriate time, decentralise the bargaining and procedure agreements.

6　*Reports* (1989), 96.

7　This was one of the biggest responses ever to a circular. It was noticeable, however, that while the BS branches in Nos. 1, 2 and 3 Divisions were well represented, there were no South Wales branches at all.

8　Another BS business, with miscellaneous interests.

9　There was a 7.5 per cent general increase on gross earnings, 2 per cent consolidation of previous LSB earnings, and an across-the-board payment of £225 to be triggered locally if schemes went live within six weeks; there was a new MEL of £130. *Reports* (1990), 84. Middle managers were treated the same under each agreement.

10　An interesting dimension of this motion was its call for these reviews to take account of European trends.

11　These were Barton Abrasives, Tipton, Ralph Martindale, Wednesfield, Morris Derby Forgings of Dudley, Monmore Tube (which had brought the issue to the attention of the EC), Cold Drawn Tubes and Seamless Tubes, Church Bramhall, Griffin Woodhouse, Woodhouse Bros, British Bright Bar, British Rolling Mills, Coated Strip, Firsteel, F.H. Lloyd, Hayes Tubes, G.T. Bell, and Parker Hannifin.

12　John Foley's report was considered and approved by the August 1990 EC.

13　The Research Department estimated that 3320 (8.3 per cent of a 40,000-strong membership) were working for contractors, but this was disputed at the Executive in May 1991.

14　The legal services were asked independently to assess the Research Department's recommendations for the allocation of seats. This had traditionally been an entirely in-house operation.

15　When put out to ballot they received the endorsement of the membership by 14,068 to 3539, a majority of 10,529.

16　At that date consideration of the position of the AGS was deferred, though it was soon obvious that this position, unlike that of National and Divisional Officers, did fall within the terms of the 1988 legislation, since the incumbent advised the Executive. From this time, too, the ISTC followed altered TUC policy and accepted government financial assistance with balloting costs.

17　*Reports* (1989), 80.

18　Yet a generous union courts risks: in 1987, for example, a member who had claimed to be virtually unable to walk after an accident was secretly filmed walking by the defendants (BSC). Some £10,000 in damages, together with costs of between £5000 and £10,000, were incurred when the deception was discovered (*Reports*, 1988, 80).

19　*Reports* (1985), 187.

20 *Reports* (1987), 139.

21 The changes were stimulated by over-funding and changes relating to the law on pension age. The union's view of BS proposals was publicised in issues of *BOB* at this time.

22 The Wire Workers had their own list of objectives. Several unions were courting them at this time, but the ISTC alone was prepared to discuss these in detail (A. Bullen, *Drawn Together: One Hundred and Fifty Years of Wire Workers' Trade Unionism*, 1992, 126).

23 *Reports* (1993), 215.

24 There was some dissension in Scotland over the nature of the campaign, which at times seemed almost to take the form of rivalry between Ravenscraig and Dalzell for the attention of the unions. In November the Executive warned Tommy Brennan of Ravenscraig and Frank Shannon of Dalzell of its 1988 ruling that comments to the press should relate only to members' own works. Brennan came to embody the spirit of the plan and was honoured by the Queen after its final closure. The efforts of the two Motherwell MPs, Dr Jeremy Bray and Dr John Reid, were also unstinting.

25 *Reports* (1992), 4.

26 The works, commissioned in 1957 (see Chapter 3) and once one of three giant strip mills in the UK, was finally demolished in 1996–7.

27 Among new suggestions were the storing of the hot strip mill in such wise as to make it capable of rebuilding as long as the heavy end was operating; a new look at the competitive possibilities for the mill; and an early parliamentary debate (*Reports*, 1991, 71).

28 For example at Bryngwyn and Tafarnaubach, which were afflicted in June 1991.

29 This encounter brought no improvement in the severance terms, and the workforce acquiesced in closure on 23 February.

30 The case went to an industrial tribunal, and satisfactory settlements were achieved for the branch officials in the summer. At British Rolling Mills Ltd, part of the same group, thirteen redundancies were achieved at the same time by conventional means.

31 *Reports* (1993), 43.

32 Subsequent events were to suggest that the merger option, though it would have introduced the membership to a much larger group, would not necessarily have been a financial solution.

33 Such a suggestion had been unsuccessfully put at the 1986 ADC.

34 *Reports* (1991), 68–9. Ironically, the 1991 ADC was to call for four full days of business to reflect the recent increase from three delegates to four per thousand!

35 This had a disappointing impact for two veteran officials, Ted Thorne and Gil Stroud, each of whom had continued to administer branches after losing their jobs through redundancy.

36 Brian Connolly (1939–), whose EEC consultancy had lasted three years, had been appointed Staff Organiser, No. 5 Division, in 1969, and Senior Organiser in 1975

(later for Nos. 5 and 6 Divisions). He was a long-standing member of the Wales Labour Party.

37 John Clarke (1941–), former Secretary of Thrybergh 1 Branch, was appointed Divisional Organiser, No. 2 Division, in 1979, transferring to No. 3 Division seven years later. He took up his post in February 1992, five months before Ken Clarke's retirement.

38 There were other innovations, such as funding for candidates who were invited to branches, branch committees, or joint committees.

39 M.J. Leahy (1949–), sometime of Panteg No. 2 branch, was the youngest ever member of the Sheet Trade Board and its President. He was appointed Divisional Organiser, No. 3 division, in 1977, was transferred to No. 4 Division in 1980, and was made Senior Organiser in 1986.

12

Tempered – not quenched
Keith Brookman (1993–7)

'Restore the pride in the union.'

A Fresh Start

As Assistant General Secretary since 1985, Keith Brookman had handled political affairs and taken on increasing responsibilities under Roy Evans.[1] He was now the first General Secretary of the ISTC ever to have been elected by a ballot of the membership. It was expected that his leadership would release the pent-up appetite for dynamic activity among the active members, and so it proved. Where previous General Secretaries and Assistant General Secretaries had sometimes been rivals, Brookman and Leahy had run as a team on a common programme to transform the Organisation in style and substance over the next three years.

Recent manning reductions had been significant. A loss of 9800 metal-manufacturing jobs during 1992 had brought the total remaining to 116,000. Contributing membership at the ISTC (including wire worker members) at the end of that year was 34,743. The implications of a continued decline in membership had not been lost on active members,[2] and the new leadership wasted no time[3] in laying before the Executive a 'Short to Medium Term Strategic Manpower Plan' (soon known by all as the 'Fresh Start' after the title of a popular version laid before the 1993 ADC), which was taken out to consultation. Their concern was that the steady reduction in the complement of full-time officers was a financially driven approach which did not include any plan for halting the decline. Most aspects of the document elicited a positive response, and at the 1993 ADC delegates heard the plans in detail. Brookman's theme was that the ISTC should become 'a modern, forward-looking, forward-thinking professional union'. It would reach this goal by team working, with the ISTC's full-time team, in particular, having clear responsibilities and accounting for itself in a clear fashion. The principal elements of the Fresh Start would be:

- better internal communications, including a new direct-mailed journal, *ISTC Today*, and a revamped *BOB*;[4] there would also be substantial investment in electronic systems within the Organisation, and a membership survey to discover what was expected of the Organisation
- better external communications in order to raise the union's profile: the ISTC's views would be projected more effectively in the TUC, the Labour Party and to the public, and a 'Buy British' campaign was envisaged.[5] The leadership pledged itself to take ISTC policy seriously and make sure it was implemented
- an education and training programme which benefited all the membership. Members would gain the opportunity to acquire National Vocational Qualifications (NVQs) within an expanded education service. Special courses would be designed for those wishing to become union officials, and an integrated hierarchy of schools would allow those members who had attended divisional schools to be guaranteed a place on a national or specialist school; the number of national schools would be raised to four. Full-time officers would themselves be expected to upgrade their qualifications
- a substantial improvement in benefits, including wider legal benefits: the cutting edge of the latter was access to accident-compensation representation for members and their dependants for all accidents which occurred outside the working environment. There would also be advice on employment law for branch secretaries and full-time officers at an early stage in the development of disputes[6]
- trading benefits would be extended and made more attractive, and the range of financial services offered via Unity Trust Bank would become more ambitious.

Funding for these initiatives would arise from two sources. A long-term and sustained recruitment campaign would proceed from a systematic survey of membership opportunities across the country; the new benefits and communication improvements would make also it easier to retain members. But the decisive contribution would have to come from the existing membership. In June 1993 income from contributions had covered less than half of current expenditure: in effect the contributions of past members (converted into assets over time) were subsidising current activity through investment income. Eventually, such practices must compromise the ISTC's independence. No responsible leadership could allow this to continue on such a scale, and so it was proposed to raise the contributions of Grade AA members from £1 to £1.23 from 1 October. Nor was this the whole proposal, for Central Office was even then working on a new contributions structure for the medium term. It had planned ahead for further major initiatives in 1995.

These changes, which were acclaimed at the 1993 ADC, speedily took effect. Two new organisers and a research officer were taken on, and new rules were drawn up on membership grades. The programme of training for full-time officers had already been upgraded with a seminar in May on the Transfer of Undertakings (Protection of Employment) Regulations (TUPE) and the Acquired Rights Directive. A further innovation was the introduction of courses for Executive Council members. 1994 also became the first year of mandatory full-time officer training for existing staff: from now on all new appointees would take three courses during their first twelve months. That year's ADC called for a doubling of divisional-school provision. The Executive was not prepared to go so far, but it did launch a new teaching pack for the 1995 schools.

The Executive also resolved that there would be no recruitment of full-time officers until late in 1995 following decisions scheduled for that August. A paper, 'Officer Development in ISTC: a TUC Proposal', envisaged an ambitious scheme for training members aspiring to join the staff. TUC tutors were appointed, and at the end of October 1994 an inaugural seminar was conducted with twenty-seven potential appointees attending. From these a panel of sixteen was selected (known thereafter as the 'Fast Track'), whose advancement was reviewed at a seminar on training needs two months later. During the following year a series of residential modules was held for panel members, and they were invited to 'shadow' existing staff.

And by 1995 the staffing picture had indeed been clarified. The previous April Sandy Feather, National Staff Officer for a quarter of a century, had taken early retirement. Others who left office early were Gordon Roberts and Frank Lyons, together with Matt Ardron[7] and Jack Claughton of the Wire Workers. Dick Knox was to follow them at the end of 1996. E.B. ('Eddie') Lynch took over leadership of the Wire Workers' Section as National Secretary. With a number of senior staff considering early retirement, the time was ripe to take a new crop of potential full-time officers, some of whom were emerging from the Fast Track: Roger Marsh, Bernard Rooney and Steve Stacey were appointed in August 1995 to Nos. 3, 4, and 5/6 Divisions respectively. Since one of those about to retire was No. 8 Divisional Officer Ron Wilson, responsibility for the Division was handed to the Assistant General

Secretary. In August 1993 the establishment of brand-new premises in Bramley to serve the No.3 Division membership was authorised; new offices were soon found in Cardiff for Divisions 5 and 6.[8]

With the Fresh Start about to mature, the Staffing Committee met on 7 November 1995 to consider the next steps. They had before them a new Central Office paper, entitled 'Securing our Future – A Manpower Strategy', which canvassed a number of ideas, including proposals to group Divisions into regions under a new category of official (Strategic Development Officers); but at this point the majority feeling on the Executive was for proceeding with replacement of those Divisional Officers whose retirement was now due. Nevertheless, important steps were still taken, including the transfer of National Officer John Clarke to head the No. 3 Divisional Office. His former portfolio was now to be divided; health and safety policy was to be pursued by a new specialist research officer answering to the Assistant General Secretary, who already had oversight of education and training.

The reconception of education and training would now have to be undertaken without state assistance: in February 1993 the ISTC was officially notified that Disbursement Grant Aid for trade union education purposes would be reduced, and phased out by 1996. In the early 1990s interest in the national education programme had seemed in decline, but the changes reawakened it and there were encouraging applications for the autumn 1993 Specialist School on Health and Safety.[9] A JAPAC initiative proposed to rebase the training of Health and Safety reps, but the ISTC grew increasingly dissatisfied with the slowness of progress, and Central Office questioned the absence of training applicants from Nos. 1 and 4 Divisions. Clearly training, like education, could no longer be left on a take-it-or-leave-it basis.

The central feature of the new training programme would be the provision of access to NVQs at future divisional schools on a voluntary basis; accreditation would be sought through the TUC, and the possibility of the ISTC's training its own assessors was explored. From January 1994 the outmoded distinction between national and specialist schools was discontinued: in the place of both would be national courses, at least four per year, one of which would have a multi-subject syllabus. Restrictions on the number of attendances would be dropped, and to eradicate any possible disadvantages to wire workers the number allowed to enrol would be raised from twenty-four to twenty-seven.[10] A new facility opened up to ISTC members following affiliation to the GFTU (see below), which ran an extensive programme of residential schools.

The 1993 ADC had called for a new programme of training in negotiating techniques, but this and any other ideas had to be considered against the background of rapidly diminishing state support for union education, already down by a quarter. The February 1994 EC decided to award bursaries of £50 per student to those attending day-release courses. The union had always supported members seeking to advance their education through full-time studies, but the value of the bursary had fallen steadily in the 1970s and 1980s: it was raised to £200 a year in January 1995.[11]

The communications initiative was clearly signalled in November 1993 when the new colour tabloid, *ISTC Today*, was launched, and from 1994 all members received a diary. *ISTC Today* carried news of two draws for the prize of a car, and displayed a new union logo. It was the most colourful ISTC publication since the days of *ISTC Banner* almost a decade before, and was innovative in that it turned up in members' post. The recruitment literature, also launched that autumn, had a new look, reflecting the altered profile of the membership which hitherto had not always been expressed: the ISTC had a significant membership among women and ethnic minorities, and all members were susceptible to the appeal of family-based benefits. This membership had rights – but it was also a database.

The 1993 TUC saw the launch of the 'Buy British Steel Products' campaign which had been envisaged in the Fresh Start, because 'we're fed up with seeing our markets disappear'. This campaign acknowledged how far demand for steel products was derived from the performance of metal-intensive British manufacturing industry. Unlike the import-control campaigns of previous decades, 'Buy British' was intended rather to raise awareness, and in particular to alert purchasers to the potential consequences of their decisions. A consumer guide was planned to alert buyers to which products in their shops were British-made, and a campaign action sheet was circulated to foster local activity. One key area for pressure was local authorities, some of which had been surprisingly lax.[12] This was not a broad-brush approach, for, as Brookman explained, 'we're not going to tell councils to buy British regardless of cost or quality but where they are equal they should buy British'.

In 1994 'Buy British' was energetically promoted at labour movement rallies across the country. The unions and councils were certainly not operating in a political vacuum, and the House of Commons Industry and Trade Committee, in a 1994–5 report, echoed anxieties that even BS, now clearly a world market leader, could be undermined by the continuation of illicit state subsidies elsewhere. Subsidies, supposedly outlawed in the European Union, clearly still continued, though no organisation had done more than the ISTC to rip aside the veil which often cloaked their continuation. But British steelworkers were now working for employers who had no subsidy whatsoever, as they knew to their social cost, and they demanded an even break. The union's pressure seemed to pay off with the establishment in 1995 of a Ministry-sponsored Steel Subsidies Monitoring Committee, intended by the British government to check the extent to which the European Commission actively discouraged such subsidies.

On 24 November 1993 Rotherham hosted seventy delegates from a number of local authorities who had gathered to discuss the protection of steel jobs. This project, soon named Steel Action, was the initiative of leading ISTC Executive members and was intended to raise public awareness of the effects on the British steel industry of unfair competition in Europe. Steel Action soon had twenty-four local authorities affiliated.[13] A meeting in Corby followed, and then others in steel areas, all under the chairmanship of Roger Stone and with wide union support. In the forefront of this was the ISTC, which helped financially with the building up of Steel Action staff. Steel Action arrived on the national scene when it mounted an impressive parliamentary lobby on 24 March 1994. In the years to come its staff were to show singular skill in obtaining disbursements of European Union money for the steel areas.

What could be done on a national scale could be done on an international scale, and on 25/26 April the ISTC, Rotherham Council and the IMF jointly sponsored a World Steel Conference in Rotherham. This kind of initiative would probably not have been undertaken by any other union in Britain; its focus was not industrial relations but the future of the industry itself, and significant media attention was attracted. With representation from forty-two countries, impressive presentations affirmed confidence in steel's future as a key material which was even strengthening its grip on demand. One clear conclusion was that there was still significant over-capacity, but Brookman used this platform to insist that there must be no more steel-plant closures in Britain. In 1996 Steel Action, which had continued to meet locally in the interim, moved into action once again, this time over the European Commission's cumbersome anti-dumping procedures.

The rule changes required to put Fresh Start into action were balloted on in autumn 1993. Writing to the members, the General Secretary called for a yes vote, insisting that his and Leahy's mandate was 'to restore the pride in ISTC'. The rule revision, if approved, would raise contributions to £1.30 a week – still a relatively low rate among manufacturing unions – but an amendment to the contribution scale, in line with the wishes of conference,[14] shielded many lower-paid employees from the increase. For the first time a proposal to raise contributions was coupled with a strong explanation of the reasons behind it, in particular the new educational opportunities made possible by expanded provision. Rule 4, which explicitly attached contributions to earnings, was approved by 8503 votes to 4437; Rule 39, which confined burial benefit once again to members with service from 31 December 1973, was upheld rather more convincingly, by 9486 to 3099.[15]

The 1993 ADC had called for flat-rate increases in contributions, and the following year the Executive used its new powers to raise them again within a revised contributions grade structure. Effective from 4 June 1994, members earning more than £300 a week (new Grade A) would pay £1.70 including the political levy; those on £200–300 (new Grade B) and £100–200 (new Grade C) would pay £1.50 and £1.30 respectively. Those earning less than £100 (new Grade D) would pay fifty pence. The rise left even Grade A members paying less than members of significant industrial organisations like the National Communications Union.

There was no enthusiasm for raising contributions again so soon, but as they increased so too did benefits. In 1994 an investigation was put underway into providing will-making facilities, and that autumn marriage benefit was placed on a flat-rate basis regardless of grade or length of membership. Meanwhile, accident (permanent incapacity) claimants under Rule 34 now had access to a £3000 maximum benefit regardless of grade or membership, a figure three times as high as previously; a new burial benefit of £200 was to be paid to the next of kin of members who died when in compliance; and termination-of-employment benefit, available on a length-of-service basis, was paid at a rate regardless of membership grade.

Changes in legal service provision were also tangible by the middle of 1995. With the initial advice system in place, Russell Jones and Walker published an approved panel of local solicitors to take cases further should the complainant wish; the ISTC's aim was to gain the best legal advice at known and reasonable prices. This service to members continued to apply in their retirement. Meanwhile those still working needed more legal representation than ever. The process of gaining compensation for employer negligence never ceased to bring tragic cases to public attention. And there was a positive side, as in 1995 when a five-year legal battle triumphantly concluded for forty-nine part-time women cleaners employed by OCS at the Port Talbot Works. The women, who had complained that free life assurance extended by their employers to full-time men cleaners was withheld from them, had their complaint of sex discrimination unanimously upheld at an industrial tribunal.

The lifeblood of the ISTC's presence in the workplace was membership, and this – in a last outburst of government spite – was about to be challenged. The Trade Union Reform and Employment Rights Act 1993 had heavy implications for the 'check-off' system on which the Organisation had relied for a generation. Some 90 per cent of the membership made its contributions directly at source. The Act required current members to assent triennially to deductions at source, a procedure triggered by an initial written author-isation which a union had to obtain before 30 August 1994. There had been no demand for such legislative intervention from the employers, most of whom preferred to structure their relationships with those they employed. There was, of course, a minority which did not come under this heading, but these were already demonstrating that they were all too capable of taking uni-lateral action without government help. The legislation stimulated the estab-lishment of a working party with BS to install new machinery to maintain trade union membership. Elsewhere, the Organisation simply rolled up its sleeves, just as it had during the political fund campaign, and set about securing its membership base.

Leahy had given each Division a membership recruitment target, and all responsible officers now had a 'welcome' package to consolidate those mem-bers who had newly joined. The union had also recognised that the easiest first step towards increasing the membership base was to absorb every potential recruit wherever recognition existed. Clive Lewis, Divisional Officer for Nos. 1/2 Divisions, led a day-to-day campaign to review progress branch by branch, and by July 1994 he was able to report that for the first time in years net membership had risen – by a figure of 104. While the pat-tern of net gains was not consistently maintained thereafter, the union could thenceforth rely on a steady positive flow to offset the continued and inevitable decline in the size of the workforce. To consolidate a new culture of growth a members' handbook had been distributed, and branch secre-taries able to report 100 per cent membership in their areas were awarded a new '100 per cent' badge.

But this achievement was not alone in contributing to an uplift in the total numbers in membership. In No. 4 Division the Shotton Security Ser-vices were drawn in, and the virgin territory of the UES Wednesbury Works turned into a 100 per cent site. The Wire Workers' Section scored a parallel success with the recruitment of fifty new members at Lander's, in the same region, and entered 1995 hopeful that they would soon surge past the 4000-member figure. This was a particularly remarkable achievement in view of the way the precipitate run-down of the coal-mining industry had damaged demand for winding equipment and wire rope, and after significant redun-dancies had been caused by the merger of Castle Wire and Somerset Wire. This enthusiastic participation in the new project was typical of the way these new ISTC members had transferred their loyalties to the larger organ-isation. The Wire Workers' Section had been fully represented by delegates for the first time at the 1994 ADC, and that September it held its last sectional conference in Blackpool. From New Year's Day 1996 it was to be fully integrated within the ISTC.

The inheritance

The crisis in European steelmaking had not gone away. Though Brookman had received assurances from British steel producers that they would not be agreeing to further capacity capacity cuts, experience suggested that such commitments could sometimes be less than total. In summer 1993 he spelled out to the Executive the union's determination to maintain current crude capacity of 21.5 million tonnes a year; but as the weeks passed it was apparent that capacity cutbacks in EU Member States were on nothing like the scale which the British industry had now suffered for a decade and a half. By the time the August 1993 Executive met, expectations of new capacity reductions had dissipated. The Executive decided to renew its opposition to any reductions in Britain whatsoever.

British Steel – still the employer of a large majority of ISTC members – was assailed on two fronts. At the end of 1993 it was fined by the European Commission for alleged price-fixing activities, yet also found itself challenged by subsidised competitors. To the Executive Council at the start of 1994, BS chairman Brian Moffat declared his determination to maintain capacity: there, at least, was common cause with the ISTC.[16] That autumn he asserted, at a second meeting with the Executive, that BS had now joined South Korea as the lowest-cost steel producer in the world: the pay-off was 95 per cent capacity working at a time when UK domestic demand for steel products was 25 per cent below its peak. Yet that same season the Commission's restructuring plans finally collapsed in the absence of co-operation by producers. The British concern was that higher prices, continued subsidies and the survival of controversial producer plants meant that over-capacity would continue. The impact of this would be felt during the *next* recession, in two to three years' time.

At the time of Moffat's speech the prospects for the British industry were looking increasingly bright. UK steel climbed out of recession from 1993 onward. With domestic consumption down at thirteen million tonnes of steel the home market was clearly not going to lead the way to higher growth.[17] By 1995, in contrast, home demand had risen to fifteen million tonnes, giving rise to some hope. Significant ownership changes had also occurred, the effect of which was to leave the Organisation facing a British Steel which was more relatively powerful than before.[18] To the employers the mid-1990s were dominated by cash problems instigated by low price levels, and also by the high value of the pound, which could price even competitive goods out of home and foreign markets. Thus within a relatively brief period the industry had somersaulted from experiencing weak domestic demand (and thus poor prices) to losing export markets because its product seemed over-priced! The same paradox could be noted at almost any point in the half-century covered by this book, though successive ISTC leaders had had occasion to remind employers' representatives that an over-valued currency also cheapened raw material costs.

Before returning to BS UES, which had recently commissioned an extra arc furnace at Aldwarke, announced the closure of the Templeborough steel plant in October 1993. Management seemed to be arguing that closure was necessary because of the impossibility of competing with subsidised steel-makers elsewhere. The prospect of this closure drew together the ISTC's recent experiences and its concerns about the failure of European firms to observe the provisions of the Treaty of Paris. Assurances from government ministers to requests by the ISTC for greater vigilance over capacity cuts and subsidies in Europe proved elusive, and a feeble EU agreement signed early in 1994 by Industry Minister Tim Sainsbury did little to improve matters. When terms for the Templeborough closure were discussed, UES management countered claims for additional severance payments with a statement that their already-existing provision exceeded that at British Steel. In November a further European meeting on over-capacity brought little relief: indeed Tim Eggar, who had replaced Sainsbury as Industry Minister, concurred in the dropping of import controls despite hearing representations from the ISTC and from Steel Action chairman Roger Stone. The ISTC could only ruefully reflect that it had taken this kind of ministerial bone-headedness to forge the closest alliance yet between BS, BISPA, Steel Action and the ISTC: there was now absolute unanimity that the British industry was getting a raw deal. Characteristically it was the vigilance of Steel Action, and not of the government, which ensured maximum British benefit from the EU 'Resider' programme of aid for depressed areas at the end of the year.

While 1994 brought improved prosperity to the four major plants still in production, it also saw the continued rationalisation of British Steel. The Newton Aycliffe profiling plant in County Durham was now marked down for closure by natural wastage, at an overall manpower cost of fifty-six jobs, while Cold Drawn Tubes in Corby was to shut bringing 164 job losses. Else-where the merger of Castle Wire and Somerset Wire brought major difficulties to the wire workers in South Wales, and in 1995 their organisation also had to cope with the consequences of closure at the Ambergate Works of Bridon International. But BS remained much the biggest of Britain's steel firms, and was able to sustain investment on a large scale – as at Llanwern, where a new slab caster was authorised early in 1995 along with relining of the No. 2 blastfurnace. When brought on stream, these developments represented the first increase in the steel giant's capacity for over a decade.

Collective bargaining: pay and pensions

Negotiations at BS General Steels had revealed that the employers wanted to progress radically in the direction of single status by a number of means, including replacement of the quarterly lump-sum bonus by a departmental bonus paid monthly. The attractions of this (for one part of the workforce) were of course balanced by the suspension of the national agreement in respect of career provisions. And a new challenge had appeared in the form of teamworking, which was now endemic at British Steel: disturbing reports had been received from Corby, Rotherham and Shotton. Teamworking implied the blurring of job boundaries and multi-union negotiations. The 1996 Biennial Delegate Conference canvassed various options for shaping the ISTC's response to teamworking, including the preparation of central negotiating guidelines and in-depth research: that spring, Central Office commissioned a consultant's report on the implications of teamworking for bargainers. Finally, in November 1996, it was agreed to establish a working group which would produce a guide for negotiators, drawing on the experience to date. In particular the guide would address relations with other unions; the education and training requirements of those involved; and the establishment of a monitoring mechanism.

British Steel Service Centres – the stockholding arm of Britain's major firm – had moved to *lengthen* the working week of some employees to 37.5 hours in 1993. While officials had stood firm on the working-hours agreement at national level, management had proved able to subvert this by local approaches: clearly there was a danger that, once again, a principled position might be undermined. More worrying still was the resistance of General Steels management to settling the annual review for 1993/4: only in late September was an agreement concluded. An agreement for the Strip Mills business of British Steel had been signed a month earlier, and the Strip Trade Board was also successful in achieving revision of the sick-pay agreement for manual grades.

Though separate, these two major bargaining units shadowed each others' progress: there was a common MEL of £165, for example, and both were moving in the direction of departmental bonuses. But whereas in General Steels there was a 1.25 per cent increase with 1.75 per cent consolidated from the lump-sum bonus, Strip Mills employees attracted 1 per cent under either heading. For most staff there was some consolation when the arbitrary blockage of incremental increases was lifted.[19]

The 1994/5 review in General Steels was sticky. It took five meetings – in six weeks – before a settlement was finally made, after protracted negotiations, on 13 April. But the outcome was a 3 per cent rise and a new departmental bonus scheme, to be paid monthly at an average level across the works. The MEL benefited from another hike to £173, and there was an enhancement to sick-pay benefits for long-serving manual grades. Overall prospects for pay improved at all major plants in 1994 as surging bonuses reflected higher-capacity working.

Negotiations in the 1995/6 annual review of BS's Strip Products Division were concluded on 10 November 1995. This agreement provided for a 2.5 per cent increase on all pay elements; a 2 per cent consolidation from the previous year's bonus schemes; the introduction of a new business bonus up to 3 per cent, paid on a quarterly basis; and provision to consolidate the stabilised weekly bonus within seven months. Two joint working groups were also established, to oversee the introduction of paternity leave and to ensure fair administration of bereavement leave. One year later an increase of 4.5 per cent was achieved, though half of this was accounted for by consolidation of local bonuses. The MEL was raised above the Long Products rate to £195 – an 18 per cent rise in three years for the lowest-paid – and there were improvements to bereavement leave, holidays for new employees and the sick-pay scheme.

At Avesta Sheffield Ltd, the stainless producer under joint BS and Swedish ownership, there had still been no agreement on the 1996/7 wage review as late as January 1996. Central Office had to engage in prolonged negotiations before coming out with a recommendation of a fifteen-month agreement, a 3.25 per cent general increase with 1.75 per cent consolidated from local bonus schemes, an ex-gratia payment of £175 and three days' paternity leave. Other unions at Avesta subsequently signed enabling agreements along those lines: it was a respectable award when measured against the (currently low) inflation rate. The corresponding agreement at BS Long Products brought a 4.7 per cent increase, though this included 2 per cent from consolidation of bonus schemes. The MEL rose to £191.10, and a new, much-improved sick-pay scheme was introduced. But what really caught the eye at Long Products was the achievement, at last, of a new job-evaluation scheme for staff employees, the product of extensive toil in the bargaining group's working party. It had taken no less than fifteen years to bring about this change.

1996 also brought an important development in the wire industry, where the first national settlement since 1990 was concluded. A 3 per cent general increase was a considerable advance on the local settlements reached in the intervening years, though every effort had been made to reach targets set by the Joint Industrial Council, which had continued to meet. But more important than the pay itself was the principle that wages should be centrally determined after years of local bargaining. The wire workers themselves were put into new heart by the agreement and immediately set about pressing their long-standing claim for a thirty-seven-hour week.

Interest in pension arrangements was, if anything, rising, attracting no less than five successful resolutions to the 1992 ADC and great interest the following year. Delegates were disenchanted with the once-standard basis for calculating superannuation – an average of the last three years' earnings – in view of the impact of inflation. At British Steel delegates sought to introduce a right to transfer to a private scheme at fifty rather than having a deferred pension at sixty-five. As to the pension-scheme funds themselves, the ADC reaffirmed its view that these were the members' property and called for continuing vigilance to prevent employers appropriating the surpluses unilaterally. Union trustees had already made their views clear on the issue to an unhappy British Steel, and the Association of British Steel Pensioners now took matters further, obtaining counsel's opinion on the circumstances surrounding the introduction of the British Steel (1990) Scheme.

This decision caused some embarrassment to the union trustees in view of their legal responsibilities to the funds; both the ISTC and the National Steel Co-ordinating Committee (NSCC) abstained from lending any support to the legal steps the Association was taking, and the possibility of a damaging conflict between natural allies loomed.[20] Detailed comments submitted by the union side were not taken into account by the Association as it proceeded with its legal action; in the opinion of Central Office legal success for the Association would place the scheme in jeopardy, and the ISTC, unlike two other unions in the industry, accordingly withheld its support for legal action. A meeting between the NSCC and the Association on 25 November 1993 did not resolve their differences of approach; indeed, starkly contrasting views of the launch of the new BS (1990) Scheme were evident in correspondence exchanged during the spring of 1994. There was some consolation, however, in an agreement that the two bodies should work together on the 'safeguard' clauses of the trust deed for the BS scheme. The eventual outcome of the Association's action was an agreement reached without court proceedings.

The rationalisation of the industry, and in particular its regrouping around British Steel, also had important implications for pensions. BS's response was to create an Acquisitions Pension Scheme rather than seek to integrate the employees of acquired companies into the British Steel (1990) Scheme, a step it took completely without consultation with the unions on the Steel Co-ordinating Committee, which were faced with a *fait accompli*.

Relations with employers

On 25 April 1993 Johnson Matthey broke the grim news that it intended to withdraw negotiating rights from the ISTC for terms and conditions at both its Brimsdown and its Royston sites.[21] It was little consolation to learn that the right to individual representation would be allowed to continue, leaving the Confederation marginally more fortunate than the AEEU which had been derecognised in its entirety. Pressure on senior management for a change of heart proved fruitless, and officials turned to the membership to learn their view. In fact ISTC members at Johnson Matthey remained remarkably constant, even resisting the offer of limited free legal services if they would only surrender their union membership.[22] But it was not a static situation, and 1995 brought news that as each new Royston business was established derecognition was introduced. Ominously, unpaid overtime, that bane of the Sheerness experience, had also begun to appear. The Johnson Matthey pattern was replicated at Albion Pressed Metals of Cannock, where management was in denial: it simply refused to acknowledge that the ISTC had substantial plant membership.

At Sheerness, which had pioneered the anti-union approach in steel, a 'general state of discontent' was said to exist. Branch meetings were still held, along with regular surgery sessions, and access to the legal services continued. But the contagion was spreading, and an associated company, Heckett Multiserv, had also derecognised the union. To broaden its attack, the union opened contacts with the United Steelworkers of America (USWA) and a Co-Steel Task force was established. In summer 1995 a delegation led by Mick Leahy visited USWA (Canada) to plan the campaign for restoration of union rights. Six solidarity meetings were held with local and regional officials; sympathy action at the sister plant of CoSteel Lasco in Whitby was promised, and nationwide publicity was gained across Canada. International solidarity is not a one-way street, and Leahy also met USWA representatives in the United States to discuss the proposed LTV-Sumitomo-BS Trico, Alabama development in which the British firm had a 25 per cent stake: the new company had stated its intention to set up a non-union operation.[23]

On 1 September the first fruits of Canadian co-operation were felt when a solidarity march and rally were held on the Isle of Sheppey, with prominent national and international union leaders in support. Torrential rain did not dampen the spirits of the marchers who had come from all over the country. With the issue of trade unionism itself at stake, it was depressing to learn that the Psychology Department of the University of Sheffield – with which the ISTC had enjoyed friendly relations over many years – was working with Sheerness management on an employee attitude survey. In these circumstances the survey could only be intended to demonstrate that companies were better off without unions. After its appeals to Sheffield for annulment of the survey had been rebuffed, the union exerted itself to persuade the Sheerness membership not to co-operate with it. In fact, when the survey appeared the following year it confirmed the burden of the ISTC's complaints, especially over unwanted or involuntary overtime. Job satisfaction, the researchers had concluded, was much lower at Sheerness than it was at comparable British companies. A further blow to the company's standing was landed in June 1996, when the ISTC secured the withdrawal of a British Safety Council award by informing the donor organisation of unsound health and safety practices at the plant.[24] Regrettably, the Royal Society for the Prevention of Accidents (ROSPA) was less sensitive.[25] The safety theme was to be pursued the following year, when the ISTC forwarded a dossier of complaints from Sheerness employees about unsafe working to the Health and Safety Executive.

But the real triumph for the union came when Sheerness Steel was roundly condemned by the International Labour Organisation (ILO). The TUC had taken the case to ILO on the ISTC's behalf, and a committee of the prestigious body had heard presentations from both sides and from the British government. Late in the summer of 1996 a tripartite committee concluded that the government evidence was flawed, and that it should ensure that employee organisations had adequate protection from employers and should begin an inquiry into events at Sheerness. This gave added ammunition to Leahy in his speech to that autumn's TUC. In November the ISTC and its partner in this conflict, AEEU, unveiled a hoarding poster condemning the parent company Co-Steel as an outfit with 'no heart' – believed to be the first occasion this kind of publicity had been used in a campaign against management.[26] These developments – the originality of which caught the attention of the national press[27] – did not stop an impenitent company from manufacturing the dismissal of Joe Davey, the Sheerness 1 branch secretary who had bravely been spearheading the drive to restore unions, early in 1997.

That month also saw the renewal of union activity at Johnson Matthey, where leaflets were handed out to employees as they arrived at work. Meanwhile the ISTC had been pursuing three separate sets of legal proceedings on behalf of Teesside members. BOS slag bay and scrap bay employees at Lackenby were faced with reduction to contractor status, a transition which would fill any union member with foreboding. They were casualties of the termination of security, cleaning and catering contracts previously held by SERCO, Clean Care and Gardner Merchant. No. 2 Division's full-time officers were armed with a long-standing Executive decision to back any members who wished to resist the change. The new feature in the situation was TUPE. The ISTC had a legal opinion that TUPE – which had first been applied in the public services – might well apply in industrial cases of this kind. It took the cases of 150 members to an industrial tribunal, where the proceedings rapidly revealed that earlier European Court of Justice rulings on the relevance of TUPE did apply: ultimately all three contractors which had wrongly dismissed employees were forced to pay compensation.

The backsliding of Sheerness and Johnson Matthey did not represent the dominant attitude of employers towards the unions. The 1994 chairman of BISPA was none other than Swarj Paul, who had joined with the ISTC in many past campaigns and always retained an optimistic outlook on the industry's future.[28] When he and BISPA secretary Ian Blakey attended the Executive in August 1994 there was a great deal of common ground, especially over the need to achieve competition on equal terms with rival European firms. And indeed, after years when employers had seemed to turn only to shedding labour in order to resolve their problems, this convergence of interest was welcome. It paid off handsomely in 1996, when Allied Steel and Wire became the host company of the first Steel Works Council in Britain, a forum for representatives from six countries where the company had locations. This broke the ice, and soon afterwards a works council agreement was also signed at British Steel to cover the company's 53,000 European employees.[29] The ISTC had eight seats at its disposal at British Steel, and distributed three to Long Products (two for four years and one for two years), three to Strip Products (two for two years and one for four years), and two to BSES and Avesta (one for two years and one for four). Even where there was a risk, as when BS resolved to outsource its IT activities and contracted them to the notoriously anti-union IBM, the ISTC was able to enter discussions with the new employers. The union rights of 100 members were at stake. One positive aspect of the experience was that the Organisation was able to work amicably to gain recognition along with SIMA, which represented the largest group of middle managers affected.

Employers might vary in their attitudes, but the government remained consistently hostile, as it was about to demonstrate. ISERBS had proved hard to get for those made redundant at Cleveland Iron Works early in 1993, and this, it turned out, was a omen. On 29 October a general blow fell when the Industry Minister, Tim Sainsbury, announced that ISERBS was to be terminated in its entirety.[30] His case for termination was that ISERBS had not assisted steelworkers to return to the market and had not been good value. Moreover, no further large-scale restructuring of the UK steel industry was contemplated and so its employees now stood in the same case as other redundant workers; the persistence of unemployment in steel areas from the huge job losses of the 1980s did not seem to enter into this assessment. In fact European restructuring was underway at the time of the announcement, and Brookman led an NSCC delegation demanding at the very least postponement until this was complete. The union approached all interested parties for support and gained it from the leaders of both BSC and BISPA, but the government juggernaut moved on, the only concession being extension of the transitional period to the end of January. There was a fear that once the incentive for early retirement was removed from older workers, employers seeking to cut costs would turn to the young, whose jobs were relatively easy to shed.

Government inflexibility was re-encountered the following year. After the announcement of substantial job losses at Ebbw Vale and Trostre, the NSCC persuaded the personnel department of Strip Products to mount a joint approach to the DTI in support of readaptation benefits. On 4 May 1994, an official – not even the minister – flatly rejected the claim.[31] More hope was entertained of a submission on behalf of employees at Clyde Shaw Ltd, which had ceased production on 25 January 1994 and thus fell within the transitional period. Great care – including legal advice – was taken over the claim to the DTI.

Political affairs

The 1992 general election, last in Labour's sequence of four national defeats, was in many ways the hardest to bear, for expectations of victory had been high. More specifically, it had proved yet another disappointment for the ISTC. Sandy Feather was again defeated in Corby, while Parliamentary Panel member Denis MacShane had been runner-up to Jimmy Boyce in the selection process for a Rotherham Labour candidate. After Neil Kinnock's resignation as Party Leader, the ISTC recommended John Smith (well known as a former Trade and Industry spokesman for the Party and the MP of many Ravenscraig members) and Margaret Beckett as Leader and Deputy Leader. These two were successful, with the backing of the ISTC delegation, at the Special Party Conference of July 1992, but one month earlier the 1992

ADC had agreed to call for all future leadership elections to move away from block voting and incorporate instead the principle of one member, one vote.

Some rebuilding of the political fund was now needed, and having emptied the coffers, the Organisation could not also bankroll Trade Unionists for Labour for the period 1991–3.[32] After this, a new Trade Union Co-ordinating Committee was established with a complement of three. The ISTC affiliated, and also backed the new Institute for Public Policy Research, which had informal links with Labour. In May a new, small Parliamentary Panel of four was adopted in the hope that targeting would yield greater rewards of candidates; in the current absence of representation at Westminster it was agreed to invite Denis Turner, a former steelworker, branch secretary and now MP for Bilston, to attend the EC to assist on relevant political issues. When in July Labour MPs formed a Steel Areas Sub-committee, Turner became secretary under the chairmanship of Jimmy Boyce. Boyce's early death in December 1993 gave MacShane a second chance to become Rotherham's Labour candidate, and this time there was no mistake. His success in the by-election of 5 May 1994 restored the ISTC's parliamentary representation.[33] Efforts continued to extend it, and in November 1995 the name of Ian Cawsey, already PPC for the new and highly winnable constituency of Brigg and Goole, was added. When the election of 1997 was finally fought the ISTC's list of key seats had seven entries which reflected the concentration of membership: Stirling, Stockton South, Middlesborough South, Brigg and Goole, Corby, Edmonton, Monmouth and Cardiff North.

The drive to use unions as a vehicle to recruit individual Labour Party members had become more sophisticated with time. Union members could now join the Party for a £3 fee, with significant membership rights. At times a lack of strength on the ground had weakened the Organisation's bid to achieve the selection of parliamentary candidates, but the August 1994 Executive heard the good news that 105 members had already been recruited to the Labour Party through their ISTC branches.

The year 1994–5 was highly significant for the ISTC's political activity, for it contained three vital votes which sustained the Organisation's political profile and set its policy course for years to come. Nine years had passed since the triumphant political fund ballot of 1985. The legislation governing political fund retention ballots had now been further refined, so a timetable was adopted which would allow the union to put draft rules before the Certification Officer and the Executive early in 1994 and before the ADC that summer, with a view to balloting later in the year. As in the previous decade, the ISTC intended to be quick off the mark.

The timetable proceeded smoothly: by February 1994, with the required approvals achieved, the union confidently set its course towards a September ballot.[34] A briefing pack was launched at ballot seminars for full-time officers that June and July; a briefing handbook was distributed to those entrusted with the vital task of getting a big turn-out; and on 4 October 1994 the result was declared. On a turnout of 34 per cent the vote was 8840 for retaining the fund and 1650 against it. This 84 per cent majority was the highest recorded by any union in the 1994–5 sequence of ballots. Reflecting on the increase in the 'yes' vote (which had been 82 per cent in 1985), Brookman could with justice conclude that the membership felt even more strongly that before about its right to be in politics. That autumn Leahy successfully moved at the Labour conference that companies should be enjoined to ballot shareholders and employees before they made political donations, with a considerable degree of satisfaction, since the ISTC had led from the front.

By then the Labour Party had a new leader. The tragic death of John Smith, only a week after Labour's local election triumph of May 1994, had stunned the Labour movement and in particular the ISTC, which held him in great affection. The election of Tony Blair as his successor was to open a new era in Labour politics. The ISTC was the only union affiliated to the Party to nominate both Blair as Leader and John Prescott as Deputy Leader, and so had special cause for satisfaction at the eventual election of each man. When balloted on 19 July the membership reflected this preference, with Blair gaining 57 per cent of votes cast for Leader, Prescott 24.1 per cent, and Margaret Beckett 18.9 per cent; in the Deputy Leadership contest Prescott's 56.5 per cent compared with Beckett's 43.5 per cent. The turnout in the ISTC ballot was 26 per cent, which was the highest of any union in the country.

At the 1994 ADC delegates had voted to retain Clause 4 of the Party constitution as an instrument of social justice, with specific reference to the need to keep the utilities and services in the public sector. This call had anticipated by four months Blair's declaration at the October 1994 Labour Conference that he wished to drop the Clause. However, Blair's proposed new clause was compatible with this approach, and when it was circulated to branches a majority of those replying endorsed it, and the union's backing for a new Clause Four was assured.[35] Over the next two years the Labour leader rapidly altered the Party's traditional positions on a number of key policy issues. These changes were incorporated in *The Road to the Manifesto*, which was put out to a ballot of Party members in autumn 1996; Brookman was prominent among those successfully calling for a resounding 'yes' vote.

The balance sheet

There had been one very controversial proposal in the Fresh Start: the plan to convert the ADC into a Biennial Delegate Conference (BDC) with regional meetings in alternate years. The 1994 ADC had (in a non-policy-making motion) voted to retain the annual gathering, but after inquiry by a sub-committee the full Executive voted to make the change in February 1995. The proposal was more positive than it seemed, in that its backers expected the prestige of the national event to rise, while it was hoped that the regional gatherings would enhance participation.

Though some unhappiness persisted at the loss of the annual event, there was general satisfaction with the new combined divisional conferences, each of which was presented with a professionalism and flair utterly different from the branch officers' conferences of yesteryear. The gatherings, held in June 1995 at Cardiff, Birmingham, Doncaster and Darlington, had a common format which included an overview of the industry, health and safety, political affairs, and internal matters. Backdrops of key points in speeches, and video contributions from BS chairman Brian Moffat, Tony Blair, Swarj Paul and John Marks, clearly signalled that a new era in steel union activity had arrived.

The first BDC, convened in Blackpool in June 1996, attracted 140 delegates, along with Labour's Foreign Affairs spokesman, Robin Cook, and Brendan Barber of the TUC. It was used, as the former ADC had been used, to air the problems the delegates faced in the industry as well as wider political and social concerns. If there had been fears that the shift to a biennial event was intended to defuse criticism of the leadership, they were surely dispelled when delegates forthrightly took officers to task over statements about the Shelton Works. Delegates defeated a call for an ISTC campaign to promote a single European currency, preferring to follow advice to wait and see. A bid to reduce the size of the Executive was, however, rejected as premature.

A fresh outlet for the new ISTC was the General Federation of Trade Unions (GFTU), to which the Organisation had affiliated in 1995, rapidly gaining a place on the Executive. GFTU's own ambitions – it had a two-year development plan to offer enhanced services and gain a higher profile for smaller unions – perfectly dovetailed with the ISTC's own objectives. And the new initiatives were bringing a return: in 1996 the ISTC membership reached the level of three years earlier and then passed it – an impressive achievement, since there had been closures in the meantime. Their effect on the membership had been neutralised by significant recruitment: Nos. 1 and 2 Divisions had raised their membership by 10 per cent in the year 1995–6 alone. That autumn membership grew fastest in the contracting sector, a natural development in view of the insecurity experienced by those so employed; but it was also a notoriously difficult area to organise. This success was partly an outgrowth of the new recruitment resources, but also an acknowledgement that TUPE offered opportunities which it would take a professional union to enforce.

By 1997 the Fresh Start could have run out of steam, but the initiatives continued. A Distance Learning programme was unveiled in February, offering the prospect of two years' home study in representational skills. Nominations for the two top posts had been invited at the start of the New Year, with both incumbents seeking re-election. But no election was necessary, as each received a nomination from no less than 219 of the 464 ISTC branches, and there were no other nominations. The EC declared each man re-appointed from 1 March 1998: with some justification Brookman could interpret the result as 'an endorsement of our work so far but also support for our continuing efforts to make progress'.

The union they led was changing. At the end of 1996 it had 34,610 members,[36] an increase of 1136 over the previous year. The bulk of these (21,483) were Grade AA members earning £300 or more a week, with only 503 in the lowest-paid (C) category. Over 6000 members – one in five – were under thirty years of age. There was a significant proportion of women members in the steel industry – and no longer just in ancillary, catering and clerical grades – and this too was reflected in the total. All these members worked in the private sector, but stupendous efforts had protected, and often enhanced, their package of employment conditions, and pay had significantly advanced.

The geographical distribution of the membership reflected the travails it had suffered since the start of the 1950s. No. 1 Division had fewer than 1000 members and No. 7 Division few more: each had been battered by large-scale redundancies, though the Coatings complex at Shotton was a source of pride to all employed there. The biggest Division (No. 3) held over 11,000 members because it served the country's engineering industry and a large integrated works at Scunthorpe, where a new caster had been installed the previous year. The 6536 members in No. 5 Division were principally the remarkable outcome of the battle to keep steelmaking at Llanwern against all the odds; the 3640 of No. 4 and the 3412 of No. 6, equally remarkable in their way, showed that steel trade unionism could survive whether dispersed in a large number of small plants or focused on one large centre. Teesside's No. 2 Division membership of 5070 was organised around one of the most modern steel complexes in the world; management hostility had reduced the numbers of steelworkers in No. 8 Division, but some 1000 remained in the non-ferrous trades.

Since 1994 the approach of the ISTC to new technology had been revolutionised. It was not merely a matter of buying new equipment, but also of rethinking the way the Organisation did its work. The aim was to build a document-handling system on which all reference papers would be stored and retrievable, and which would supply Central and Divisional offices; to give easy access to information for bargaining purposes held on the Web; and to develop efficient communications systems. But continued modernisation did not come cheap, and a further contributions review in the summer of 1996 looked to a medium-term solution. This involved raising the contributions level for A and AA members from June 1997, as well as for those who would fall into a new grade because they earned £401 or more: this last group would pay £2.15 weekly.[37] Looking ahead it was agreed by the Executive that there should be annual increases each June every year up to and including the year 2000.

Notes

1 Brookman was of course the first ISTC leader of modern times to have been a member of the Parliamentary Panel, and had been a member of Labour's NCC since its inception. After becoming General Secretary he relinquished some of his previous responsibilities such as the Executive of the CSEU to the new AGS. He joined the General Council of the TUC in September 1993.

2 1993 ADC resolutions included one calling for the decline to be reversed and another (noted by the EC) wishing to see the retired membership reintegrated into the ISTC.

3 This was done at a Special Executive of 5 April.

4 *Phoenix* was retained to report conferences and special events.

5 To shape this publicity drive the PR firm Union Communications, which had worked on the ISTC's behalf in the 1980s, was re-engaged.

6 Other existing legal services continued in place, including free initial legal advice for members on domestic matters.

7 Matt Ardron retired in June 1996. He had been appointed an Organiser with the Wire Workers' Union in 1970 and became its General Secretary in 1983. Since the transfer of engagements he had served as National Secretary of the WWS.

8 The new premises in Cathedral Road were occupied from November 1996.

9 So much so that John Clarke was authorised to organise a second school forthwith.

10 Further changes included putting back the starting time of schools in order to reduce the number of twenty-four-hour charges in order to reduce some of the extra costs now being incurred.

11 Precise criteria for the bursary were now established. If a member met them he might be able to obtain £800 for four separate periods of full-time study –

a substantial incentive during a period of increasingly expensive educational opportunities.

12 The town gates at Corby, erected late in 1993, were made of foreign steel simply out of inadvertence.

13 The roll-call of local authorities perfectly reflected the dense involvement of the ISTC's Labour Party members in local-authority politics: Barnsley, Cleveland, Clwyd, Corby, Cumbria, Doncaster, Glanford, Gwent, Humberside, Langbaurgh, Middlesborough, Motherwell, Newport, Northamptonshire, Port Talbot, Rotherham, Scunthorpe, Sheffield, South Glamorgan, Strathclyde, Swale, Swansea, Torfaen and West Glamorgan.

14 The 1993 ADC wished to see the lowest earners protected from increased costs (see below).

15 The Wire Workers' Section seems to have been an exception to these majorities, its members seemingly resentful at the early withdrawal of benefits to which they had been recently introduced (National Secretary, *Reports*, 1993, 221).

16 *Reports* (1994), 267.

17 In 1996 50 per cent of BS output went to export.

18 Among these changes was the purchase by BS of GKN's 34 per cent share in UES (subsequently renamed British Steel Engineering Steels – BSES) and its outright acquisition of ASW's Scunthorpe rod mill, both the outcome of 'Phoenix' initiatives in the 1980s. By the middle of 1995 BS accounted for 84 per cent of unfinished steel made in Britain.

19 *Reports* (1993), 222.

20 *Reports* (1993), 220.

21 The company had fallen under American control, a shift which, in the view of Divisional Officer Ian Scobbie, explained the deterioration in relationships.

22 *Reports* (1994), 332.

23 On 18 September 1995 the ISTC's objections were pressed with Mr. J. Bryant, the responsible BS Main Board member.

24 Absent employees at Sheerness were automatically disciplined even if they were away from work on a doctor's certificate; others were approached to return on 'light' duties!

25 ROSPA gave Sheerness its gold award for safety in autumn 1996.

26 A second hoarding poster was launched in February, after which the town of Sheerness was leafleted on the company's anti-union policies. The winter also brought an Early Day Motion (in the name of Dale Campbell Savours) which attracted the signatures of the Labour and Liberal Democrat Employment spokesmen.

27 'Steel unions in US-style drive for recognition', said *The Times* of 4 November 1996.

28 In 1997 Paul became a Labour peer.

29 The agreement provided for twice-yearly meetings, to be headed by national union officers and the BS chief executive.

30 This announcement, which radically affected severance arrangements that had

been in place for a generation, came on a Parliamentary Friday in written answer to a question from Bernard Jenkin MP. It had immediate effect, so much so that transitional arrangements subsequently had to be introduced to ease its impact.

31 Unsurprisingly the loss of ISERBS provoked anger at the 1994 ADC, which called for improved readaptation terms to be restored by the next Labour government.

32 *Reports* (1993), 13.

33 Denis MacShane, a journalist and author, and a former NUJ president, had worked for the IMF for many years. He received 14,912 votes, a majority of 6964 over the runner-up, a Liberal Democrat. His book, *Britain's Steel Industry in the 21st Century*, was published in 1996.

34 This determination did not deflect the ISTC from its deep resentment at the inequity of the legislation: the 1994 ADC called for corporate contributions to be put to a postal ballot of all shareholders. But the Organisation was also forced to acknowledge that politics did not come cheap, and had to put the political levy up to 10p from the start of 1995.

35 Labour's constitution was finally amended at a Special Party Conference of 29 April 1995. When Shadow Chancellor Gordon Brown attended the Executive on 17 May he thanked it for its backing of the leadership in this critical vote. A succession of leading Labour figures beat their path to the ISTC over the next months: in November the Executive hosted Labour's Employment front bencher, Harriet Harman; Robin Cook visited the BDC in June 1996; David Blunkett addressed the Executive that November.

36 Membership figures in the 1990s were much more accurate than formerly, without the large discrepancy between recorded and contributing figures which had occurred in the era of big redundancies.

37 The contributions of lowest-paid groups remained unchanged.

Conclusion
Lessons from history

An eightieth anniversary is an arbitrary date, but any birthday has an air of artificiality about it. As this book appears, in 1997, many developments referred to in the last chapter continue to unfold. It is too soon to draw any final conclusions about the Fresh Start and whether it will meet the longer-term targets it set for itself. Plans currently before the Executive Council include major constitutional changes which would radically restructure the ISTC in ways the 1950s membership could not have dreamed of. Meanwhile British Steel, still the steel industry's largest company in Britain, has unveiled a Five-Year Strategy with enormous implications for future employment and the way the industry is organised.

Looking ahead is a risky business. This book offers plenty of examples of forecasts which went wildly wrong, though almost everyone agreed with them at the time. But all forecasts proceed from an analysis of the past, and reflection on the story told in this book suggests some fairly safe bets as the ISTC prepares itself to meet these new challenges. They are the author's personal expectations.

Firstly, it needs to be recognised that the ISTC and the principal industry it organises have survived. This is no small boast in an era when hostility to the country's production industries has at times been displayed at the very highest levels, and when eight major statutes have been passed by parliament to emasculate trade unionism. The success of steel and that of its union are not unconnected, for the ISTC always advocated that only modernisation could afford competitive success, and stuck to its view in spite of employer neglect in the 1950s and political indifference in the 1980s. The caricature of 'luddite' trade unionism could never be less accurate than when applied to the ISTC. And because steelworkers have been through the worst, they can expect a better future.

Secondly, and something that is often overlooked, there needs to be recognition of the enormous social price paid when a neglected industry embarks on the wrong modernisation plan at breakneck speed. Steelworkers lost their jobs in their tens of thousands in the 1970s and 1980s, and thousands more went out of the non-ferrous metal industries. Whole towns were simply taken out of organised economic activity. When this happened the union was, with the churches and other community organisations, sometimes the only network holding people together. Partly in response to these issues the ISTC Executive is considering new constitutional proposals, which include one to relaunch as a family-based trade union. Thus, a second conclusion must be that the ISTC's community base will continue to be one of its greatest strengths.

A third inference from the history of the ISTC since 1950 must be that the Organisation will stay independent. There is too much that is distinct about it for it to be swallowed up by general or craft trade unionism. In the current wave of mergers sweeping Britain's unions it is becoming apparent that size is not everything. A union has to be financially viable, it has to have a reason to exist, and it must enjoy the support of a loyal membership: the ISTC meets all of these requirements. Those who doubt it are referred to almost any chapter of this book.

A fourth conclusion might be that a union which is really alive will do what is necessary to stay that way. The pages of this book show little evidence of ducking tough decisions. In the past there have been times when not enough was done to extend the membership when opportunities existed. The first priority for the ISTC today, however, is recruitment, and the Organisation intends to take the initiative in seeking out members.

While this book was being prepared for publication, the return of a Labour government to office after an absence of eighteen years cast a dramatic new light across Britain and rekindled hope in the country's industrial areas. Britain's steelworkers, and their union the ISTC, played a major part in achieving this elusive victory. Here is a fifth conclusion: the ISTC is part of the underlying granite from which the labour and trade union movement has been hewn. It is inconceivable that there could be a Labour Party or a Trades Union Congress without an ISTC; it is unimaginable that the ISTC would ever cease to play its role in either.

Appendix 1
Full-time officers 1950–March 1997

Adams, M.A. Divisional Organiser at 8 December 1986. Appointed Senior Organiser 1 September 1993. *Pro tem.* Divisional Officer, No. 2 Division, 1 January 1997. Appointed Divisional Officer, No. 2 Division, 10 March 1997.

Ardron, A.M. Appointed National Secretary, Wire Workers Section. Retired 30 June 1996.

Bambury, L.H. Divisional Organiser, London Area, at 6 November 1972. Appointed Senior Organiser 8 September 1975. Retired 20 August 1982.

Bell, A. Divisional Organiser, No. 1 Division, at August 1957. Divisional Officer, No. 1 Division, 30 September 1968. Retired 1 September 1980.

Biddiscombe, S.E. Divisional Organiser, No. 4 Division, at May 1957. Transferred to No. 6 Division, 19 September 1960. Divisional Officer, No. 6 Division, 22 November 1969. Retired 7 July 1981.

Bishop, R. Appointed Staff Organiser 10 March 1969. No. 2 Division. Appointed Senior Organiser 1978. Transferred to No. 4 Division, 19 March 1979. Appointed Divisional Officer 7 January 1980. Divisional Officer, No. 3 Division, 1 January 1983. Transferred to No. 2 Division, 14 March 1988. Retired 18 April 1992.

Brandon, J. Divisional Organiser, No. 5 Division, at 13 June 1977. Appointed Senior Organiser 4 May 1992. Transferred to No. 1 Division, 3 August 1995.

Brookman, D.K. Divisional Organiser, No. 5 Division, at 31 December 1973.

Appointed Assistant General Secretary Designate May 1984. Appointed Assistant General Secretary 7 January 1985. Appointed General Secretary Designate November 1992. Appointed General Secretary 1 March 1993.

Brooks, G.F. Divisional Organiser, No. 7 Division, at 6 July 1970. Appointed Senior Organiser August 1975. Appointed Divisional Officer, No. 7 Division, 15 July 1981. Retired 31 March 1986.

Carberry, W.T.J. Divisional Organiser, No. 5 Divisional Office, at 15 December 1969. Transferred to No. 6 Division, 24 December 1973. Senior Organiser 5 August 1975. February EC 1983. Instructed to move to No. 3 Division. Resigned 1983.

Clarke, J.B. Divisional Organiser, No. 2 Division, at 25 June 1979. Transferred to No. 3 Division, 1 April 1986. Appointed National Officer 1 August 1992. Divisional Officer, No. 3 Division, 1 July 1996.

Clarke, K. Divisional Organiser, No. 1 Division, at November 1968. Transferred to No. 2 Division, 23 June 1970. Senior Organiser 5 February 1975. National Officer January 1981. Retired 31 July 1992.

Clarke, R.W. Divisional Officer, No. 4 Division. Retired 27 December 1952.

Claughton, J. Appointed Divisional Organiser, Wire Workers Section. Retired 27 September 1996.

Connolly, A.B. Appointed Staff Organiser 10 March 1969, Nos. 5/6 Divisions. Transferred to No. 2 Division, 7 July 1975. Transferred to No. 5 Division, 18 August 1975. Appointed Senior Organiser 5 August 1975. Appointed Divisional Officer, Nos. 5/6 Division, 4 May 1992.

Cooper, G. Divisional Organiser, No. 2 Division, at 14 September 1964. Transferred to No. 3 Division, 5 June 1967. Divisional Officer, No. 7 Division, 20 August 1973. Retired 15 July 1981.

Davey, T. Divisional Organiser, No. 4 Division, 20 September 1971. Transferred to No. 2 Division, 6 January 1975. Divisional Officer, No. 2 Division, 1 July 1986. Retired 26 March 1988.

Davy, L.G.T. Appointed Staff Organiser No. 6 Division, 12 February 1975. Transferred to No. 2 Division, 6 January 1975. Transferred to No. 6 Division, 5 May 1975. Seconded to No. 4 Division, 1980. Resigned 5 November 1980.

Davies, D.H. Divisional Organiser, No. 2 Division. Assistant General Secretary 24 August 1953. General Secretary 1 January 1967. Retired 1 December 1974.

Diamond, J. Divisional Organiser, No. 1 Division, at 5 December 1960. Assistant General Secretary February 1966. Retired 10 August 1973.

Dismore, H.C. Divisional Organiser, London Area. Retired 17 November 1972.

Douglass, H. Assistant General Secretary. Appointed General Secretary 24 August 1953. Retired 31 December 1966.

Drinkwater, J. Divisional Organiser, No. 5 Division. Transferred to No. 2 Division, 27 April 1963. Divisional Officer, No. 2 Division, 24 February 1964. Died in service 17 October 1975.

Evans, L. General Secretary. Retired 23 August 1953.

Evans, R.L. Divisional Organiser, No. 7 Division, at 15 June 1964. Transferred to No. 6 Division, 22 November 1969. Appointed Assistant General Secretary 10 September 1973. Appointed General Secretary Designate February EC 1984. Appointed General Secretary 7 January 1985. Retired 28 February 1993.

Feather, H.A. Appointed National Staff Officer 10 March 1969. Resigned 15 April 1994.

Fisher, B.T. Appointed District Secretary Coke and Iron Section No. 3 Divisional Office. Appointed National Secretary 6 August 1987. Retired 6 September 1990.

Foley, J. Divisional Organiser, No. 7 Division, at 8 September 1965. Transferred to No. 5 Division, 23 August 1966. Appointed Divisional Officer, No. 5 Division, 28 September 1974. Appointed Divisional Officer, Nos. 5/6 Divisions, 6 December 1982. Retired 3 May 1992.

Gavin, J.A. Divisional Organiser, No. 4 Division, at 15 June 191964. Divisional Officer, No. 4 Division, 7 December 1970. *Pro tem.* Assistant General Secretary March Quarter 1976. Retired 6 January 1980.

Griffiths, A. Divisional Officer, No. 7 Division. Retired 18 September 1964.

Hardaker, E.M. Divisional Organiser, No. 2 Division, at 14 March 1977. Transferred to No. 3 Division, 1979. Transferred to No. 2 Division, 1 April 1986. Senior Organiser 30 June 1986. Dismissed 18 November 1993.

Hickery, E.H. Divisional Officer, No. 5 Division. National Officer 8 July 1968. Retired 22 November 1969.

Hogg, A.R. Appointed Divisional Organiser, No. 3 Division, May 1955. Divisional Officer, No. 3 Division, 6 March 1967. Retired 24 December 1973.

Homewood, W.D. Divisional Organiser, No. 4 Division, at 23 September 1965. Senior Organiser, No. 4 Division, 5 August 1975. Resigned 3 May 1979. Appointed Parliamentary Representative 3 May 1979.

Horn, W.E. Divisional Organiser, No. 4 Division, May 1952. Retired June 1961.

Irvine, J. Divisional Organiser, No. 1 Division, at January 1951. Divisional Officer February 1961. Retired 27 September 1968.

James, D.B.F. Appointed Staff Organiser, No. 1 Division, 30 June 1969. Resigned 13 September 1974.

Jenkins, I. Divisional Organiser, No. 2 Division, at 29 September 1969. Transferred to No. 5 Division, 6 January 1975. Retired 8 April 1977.

Jones, A.J. Divisional Organiser, No. 3 Division, at 1 September 1993. Senior Organiser 31 September 1995.

Jones, K.L. Divisional Organiser, No. 3 Division, at 16 April 1974. Transferred to No. 7 Division, 1984. Senior Organiser. Resigned 4 April 1986.

Knight, R. Divisional Organiser, Nos. 5/6 Divisions, at 1 June 1988. Appointed Senior Organiser 31 September 1995.

Knox, R. Divisional Organiser, No. 4 Division, at 9 December 1974. Senior Organiser 1 September 1980. Appointed Divisional Officer, No. 3 Division, 26 February 1988. Retired 20 December 1996.

Lang, J. Divisional Officer, No. 1 Division, at January 1951. Retired 4 March 1961.

Leadley, N. Appointed National Secretary, Coke and Iron Section, No. 2 Divisional Office. Retired 6 August 1987.

Leahy, M.J. Divisional Organiser, No. 3 Division, at 21 March 1977. Transferred to No. 4 Division, 1980. Senior Organiser 2 June 1986. Assistant General Secretary Designate, November 1992. Appointed Assistant General Secretary 1 March 1993.

Lewis, J.C. Appointed Staff Organiser, No. 4 Division, 22 June 1996. Appointed Divisional Officer, No. 1 Division, 1 September 1980. Appointed Divisional Officer, Nos. 1/2 Divisions, 19 April 1992. Seconded to Special Duties (Recruitment) 1 January 1997.

Lightfoot, P. Appointed Staff Organiser, No 3 Division, 4 March 1971. Appointed Senior Organiser 5 August 1975. Appointed Divisional Officer, No. 4 Division, 1 January 1983. Divisional Officer, Nos. 4/7 Divisions, 1 October 1993 – 8 May 1995. Divisional Officer, No. 4 Division, 8 May 1995.

Lynch, E.B. Appointed Divisional Officer, Wire Workers Section. Appointed National Secretary, Wire Workers Section, 30 June 1996. Additionally to undertake duties of Divisional Officer, No. 7 Division, 8 May 1995.

Lyons, F. Divisional Organiser, No. 1 Division, at 6 January 1975. Senior Organiser 5 January 1981. Retired 31 August 1995.

Mainwarring, W.T. Divisional Organiser, No. 6 Division. Retired 18 February 1961.

Marsh, C.R.J. Divisional Organiser, No. 3 Division, at 20 August 1995.

Marsh, E. Divisional Organiser, No. 2 Division, at 5 September 1975. Transferred to No. 1 Division, 1 December 1975. Senior Organiser.

Appointed Divisional Officer and transferred to No. 8 Division, 16 July 1984. Retired 18 December 1988.

Meehan, T. Divisional Officer, No. 2 Division. Retired 10 February 1951.

O'Dowd, J. Divisional Organiser, No. 3 Division. Retired February 1955.

Parker, R.W. Divisional Organiser, No. 4 Division, at 19 September 1960. Resigned 23 May 1964.

Parnham, H. Divisional Organiser, No. 3 Division, at 3 December 1973. Died in service 22 March 1983.

Paterson, W.J. Divisional Organiser, No. 4 Division, at 1 June 1988. Transferred to No. 3 Division, 15 June 1992. Senior Organiser and transferred to No. 4 Division, 6 June 1993.

Perring, J. Appointed District Secretary, Coke and Iron Section, Nos. 5/6 Divisional Office. Dismissed 10 September 1986.

Pickles, J.E. Divisional Organiser, No. 3 Division, at 4 September 1961. Divisional Officer, No. 3 Division, 31 December 1973. Retired 31 December 1982.

Pike, B. Divisional Organiser, No. 2 Division, at 6 December 1993. Appointed Senior Divisional Organiser 20 January 1997.

Potter, A.J. Divisional Organiser, No. 2 Division, at June 1953. Transferred to No. 6 Division, 1963. Transferred to No. 4 Division, 23 September 1963. Divisional Officer 23 May 1964. Resigned 7 December 1970.

Profitt, J.E. Divisional Organiser, No. 4 Division. Divisional Officer, No. 4 Division, 27 December 1952. Retired 23 May 1964.

Rickhuss, R. Divisional Organiser, Nos. 5/6 Divisions, at 1 September 1993.

Roberts, C.G. Divisional Organiser, No. 4 Division, at 15 March 1976. Transferred to No. 3 Division, 1 April 1985; Senior Organiser 1 April 1985. Retired 20 June 1995.

Roberts, E. Divisional Organiser, No. 3 Division. Divisional Officer, No. 3 Division, 28 November 1961. Retired 1 April 1967.

Rooney, B. Divisional Organiser, No. 8 Division, at 4 September 1995.

Scobbie, I. Divisional Organiser, No. 1 Division, at 6 September 1971. Senior Organiser 11 December 1975. Commenced duties at Central Office 5 January 1981. Appointed Head of General Secretary's Department 5 October 1981. Divisional Officer status 20 August 1986. Appointed Divisional Officer, No. 8 Division, 18 December 1988. Retired 30 September 1993.

Seed, A. Divisional Organiser, No. 7 Division, at September 1969. Resigned December 1969.

Senior, J. Divisional Organiser, No. 2 Division. Divisional Officer 10 February 1951. Retired 16 March 1964.

Sirs, W. Divisional Organiser, No. 2 Division, at 23 September 1963. Transferred to No. 7 Division, 22 June 1970. Divisional Officer, No. 7 Division, 30 September 1970. Assistant General Secretary 10 September 1973. General Secretary May 1975. Retired 6 January 1985.

Smith, A.P. Divisional Organiser, No. 8 Division, at 8 September 1975. Appointed Senior Organiser 23 August 1982. Died in service 15 July 1984.

Stacey, S. Divisional Organiser, Nos. 5/6 Divisions, at 18 September 1995.

Stead, W.E. Divisional Officer, No. 3 Division. Retired 20 November 1961.

Sykes, E. Divisional Organiser, No. 2 Division. Senior Organiser, No. 2 Division, 1 October 1966. Transferred to No. 5 Division, 23 September 1963. Senior Organiser 1 October 1966 Transferred to No. 5 Division, 6 October 1969. Divisional Officer, No. 5 Division, 22 November 1969. Retired 28 September 1974.

Vincent, A.E. Divisional Officer, No. 6 Division. Retired 18 May 1963.

Watson, T. Divisional Organiser, No. 7 Division. Appointed Divisional Officer 18 September 1964. Retired 30 August 1970.

Williams, J. Divisional Officer, No. 6 Division, at 29 April 1963. Retired 22 November 1969.

Wilson, R. Appointed Staff Organiser, No. 7 Division, 4 January 1971. Appointed Senior Organiser, No. 7 Division, 15 July 1981. Appointed Senior Organiser, No. 3 Division, 1984. Appointed Divisional Officer, No. 7 Division, 1 April 1986. Retired 29 September 1995.

Woods, P. Divisional Organiser, No. 1 Division, at 5 December 1966. Divisional Officer, No. 2 Division, 11 December 1975. Retired 30 June 1986.

Yates, O. Divisional Organiser, No. 5 Division, at August 1959. Acting Divisional Officer, No. 5 Division, 8 July 1968. Retired 10 September 1969.

NUB Transfer of Engagement into the ISTC 15 April 1985 to become the Coke and Iron Section of the union.

WWU Transfer of Engagement into the ISTC 15 April 1991 to become the Wire Workers Section of the union.

Appendix 2

Presidents of the Executive Council 1917–97

Year	Name	Branch	Division
1997	A.J. (Austin) Senior (65)	Aldwarke 1	3
1996	M. ('Mick') Mannion	Lackenby 5	2
1995	P.A. ('Tony') Poynter	Teesside Staff 5	2
1994	M.T. ('Mel') Williams	Ebbw Vale FB	5
1993	R. (Ray) Hill	Scunthorpe BF1	3
1992	J.M. (John) Thomas	Port Talbot 1	6
1991	C.H. ('Charlie') Hall	Corby TW Super	4
1990	R. (Roger) Stone	Shepcote 1	3
1989	T. ('Terry') Butterworth	Brinsworth Mills	3
1988	E. (Eric) Caudwell	Hawarden SM3	7
1987	J. ('Joe') McGuinness	Clydesdale 2	1
1986	J. ('Jim') Coyle	Clydesdale Tube 1	1
1985	H. (Hugh) Belton	Enfield 2	8
1984	W. ('Bill') Irvine	Ravenscraig Tech	1
1983	J. (John) Linighan	Greatham 4	2
1982	M. (Malcolm) Bourton (50)	Ebbw Vale 7	5
1981	P.J. (Peter) McKim	Llanwern 3	5
1980	E. ('Eddie') Makepeace	Enfield 1	8
1979	L.R. ('Les') Bramley	Scunthorpe F&S	3
1978	J.H. ('Joe') Lewis	Abbey 3	6

1977	A. ('Sandy') Stevenson	Clydesdale 2	1
1976	K. ('Ken') Clarke	Stocksbridge 4	3
1975	J.G. ('Jeff') Evans	Spencer LD	5
1974	D.H. (Hanbury) Williams	Abbey Mills Staff	6
1973	R.K. ('Bob') Codlin	Redcar 4	2
1972	R.C. ('Reg') Richards	Cardiff Nail	5
1971	J. (John) Clark	Aldwarke 1	3
1970	L.H. ('Les') Bambury	Enfield 2	8
1969	J.W. Jones	Cardiff 1	5
1968	M.F. Somerville	Parkhead F&S	1
1967[1]	J. McKay	Irlam 1	7
	M.F. Somerville	Parkhead F&S	1
1966	J.C. Leonard	Hawarden Armco 2	7
1965[2]	A.H. (Alfred) Braddock	Cargo Fleet 4	2
1964	W.B. Elias	Ebbw Vale BP	5
1963	N. Douglas	Corby Packers	4
1962	C.H. Bromley	Workington 3	2
1961	D.P. Draffan	Consett 3	2
1960	J. Donnelly	Consett 2	2
1959	W.E. Nutting	Round Oak 5	4
1958	H.H. Patrick	Temple 1	3
1957	G.E. (George) Lovelock	Cardiff Nail	5
1956	S. Harris	Temple 2	3
1955	J. Shea	Alloy 1	6
1954	H. Redgate	Tinsley 7	3
1953	G. Hotchkiss	Hawarden SM1	7
1952	D.G. Thomas	Pontardawe 2	6
1951	T. (Thomas) Donnachie	Cambuslang	1
1950	W. Evans	Gowerton	6
1949[3]	G.B. Lynch	Scotia 1	1
	W. Evans	Gowerton	6
1948	A.H. (Alfred) Braddock	Cargo Fleet 4	2
1947	D. (Dennis) O'Sullivan	Margam Coke	6
1946	J. Poole	Dallam 2	7
1945	J. ('Jake') Williams	Trostre 1	6
1944	R. O'Dowd	Appleby 2	3
1943	D.J. Thomas	Margam 2	6
1942	E. Roberts	Hawarden 10	7
1941	S. Garvey	Newport 3	5

1940	B. (Bertram) Ramsey	North Eastern 2	2
1939	R. (Rees) Richards	Landore Tube 3	6
1938	W. (William) Mawer	Motherwell 2	1
1937	T.J. Jeffreys	Albion 1	6
1936	E.C. Garrison	Temple 1	3
1935[2]	F.E. (Fred) Howells	Dyffryn 2	6
1934	F.E. (Fred) Howells	Dyffryn 2	6
1933	T.B. (Tom) Pugh JP	South Malleable	2
1932[4]	L. (Lincoln) Evans	Kings Dock 1	6
	T.B. (Tom) Pugh JP	South Malleable	2
1931[5]	J. (John) Hodge	–	–
	L. (Lincoln) Evans	Kings Dock 1	6
1930	J. (John) Hodge	–	–
1929	J. (John) Hodge	–	–
1928	J. (John) Hodge	–	–
1927	J. (John) Hodge	–	–
1926	J. (John) Hodge	–	–
1925	J. (John) Hodge	–	–
1924	J. (John) Hodge	–	–
1923	J. (John) Hodge	–	–
1922	J. (John) Hodge	–	–
1921	J. (John) Hodge	–	–
1920	J. (John) Hodge	–	–
1919	J. (John) Hodge	–	–
1918	J. (John) Hodge	–	–
1917	J. (John) Hodge	–	–

From 1917 to 1931 the President was a full-time officer.

[1] Bro McKay resigned 22 August 1967, died 4 September 1967
[2] Second term as President
[3] G.B. Lynch retired part way through the year
[4] Resigned part way through the year due to appointment as a full-time officer
[5] Retired part way through the year

Appendix 3
BISAKTA and ISTC members of parliament
1950–March 1997

Coleman, D.H. MP.
Griffiths, E. MP.
Homewood, W.D. MP.
Jones, J.H. JP, MP.
MacShane, D. MP.
Mort, D.L. MP.
Tinn, J. MP. (Coke and Iron Section)

Appendix 4
Heads of Central Office departments
1950–March 1997

Allen, B.F. Appointed Head General Secretary's Department November 1975. Retired 5 October 1981.

Barnett, M. Appointed Head of General Secretary's Department 6 May 1995.

Bernard, A.T.E. Appointed Head of Audit Department 30 May 1980. Retired 5 November 1984.

Brierley, J.J. Appointed Head of Accounts Department 1 March 1980.

Clayton, R.H. Appointed Head Statistical/Research Department 14 September 1973. Retired 8 September 1989.

Cobbett, S. Head of Accounts Department. Retired 24 February 1956.

Dickens, C. Appointed Head of Despatch Department November 1953 Appointed Head of Audit Department 7 June 1961. Retired 30 May 1980.

Dunne, W. Head of Statistical/Research Department . Retired 14 September 1973.

Gillingham, H. Head of Despatch Department. Died in service November 1953.

Howells, D.G. Appointed Head of Research Department 14 October 1994.

Mason, E.J. Appointed Head of Accounts Department 24 April 1972. Retired 29 February 1980.

Oates, M. Head of Audit Department. Retired 7 June 1961.

Powell, L.G. Appointed Head of Research Department 8 September 1989. Resigned 14 October 1994.

Stafford, F. Appointed Head of Accounts Department 24 February 1956. Retired 24 April 1972.

Wood, S.J. Head of Despatch Department 7 June 1961–November 1975. Retired 5 June 1983.

Despatch Department amalgamated into General Secretary's Department November 1975.

Accounts and Audit Departments amalgamated to form Finance and Membership Department 1985.

Index